Fi
Derivatives: M
and Appli

Financial Derivatives: Markets and Applications

Edited by
Ivy James

Willford Press
www.willfordpress.com

Published by Willford Press,
118-35 Queens Blvd., Suite 400,
Forest Hills, NY 11375, USA

ISBN: 978-1-64728-515-9

Cataloging-in-publication Data

Financial derivatives : markets and applications / edited by Ivy James.
p. cm.
Includes bibliographical references and index.
ISBN 978-1-64728-515-9
1. Derivative securities. 2. Futures. 3. Investments. 4. Finance.
5. Capital market. I. James, Ivy.

HG6024.A3 D47 2023
332.645--dc23

For information on all Willford Press publications
visit our website at www.willfordpress.com

Willford Press

Contents

Preface

Financial derivatives are financial instruments that derive their value from underlying assets such as stocks, bonds, commodities and currencies. Financial market for trading derivatives is known as derivatives market. There are four major types of financial derivatives including futures, options, forwards and swaps. Hedgers and speculators use derivative products to take advantage of the market fluctuations. Derivatives are used primarily for one of two purposes, namely, mitigating risk (hedging) or assuming risk in expectation of commensurate reward (speculation). Investors choose financial derivatives to deal with market volatility, take advantage of arbitrage opportunities, and to access different markets and assets. The type of derivative contract wherein the buyer and seller enter into an agreement to fix the quantity and price of an asset is called a future contract. The objective of this book is to give a general view of the different areas of financial derivatives including markets and their applications. Those in search of information to further their knowledge will be greatly assisted by this book.

The researches compiled throughout the book are authentic and of high quality, combining several disciplines and from very diverse regions from around the world. Drawing on the contributions of many researchers from diverse countries, the book's objective is to provide the readers with the latest achievements in the area of research. This book will surely be a source of knowledge to all interested and researching the field.

In the end, I would like to express my deep sense of gratitude to all the authors for meeting the set deadlines in completing and submitting their research chapters. I would also like to thank the publisher for the support offered to us throughout the course of the book. Finally, I extend my sincere thanks to my family for being a constant source of inspiration and encouragement.

Editor

1

Derivative Pricing for a Multi-Curve Extension of the Gaussian, Exponentially Quadratic Short Rate Model

Zorana Grbac, Laura Meneghello and Wolfgang J. Runggaldier

Abstract The recent financial crisis has led to so-called multi-curve models for the term structure. Here we study a multi-curve extension of short rate models where, in addition to the short rate itself, we introduce short rate spreads. In particular, we consider a Gaussian factor model where the short rate and the spreads are second order polynomials of Gaussian factor processes. This leads to an exponentially quadratic model class that is less well known than the exponentially affine class. In the latter class the factors enter linearly and for positivity one considers square root factor processes. While the square root factors in the affine class have more involved distributions, in the quadratic class the factors remain Gaussian and this leads to various advantages, in particular for derivative pricing. After some preliminaries on martingale modeling in the multi-curve setup, we concentrate on pricing of linear and optional derivatives. For linear derivatives, we exhibit an adjustment factor that allows one to pass from pre-crisis single curve values to the corresponding post-crisis multi-curve values.

Keywords Multi-curve models · Short rate models · Short rate spreads · Gaussian exponentially quadratic models · Pricing of linear and optional interest rate derivatives · Riccati equations · Adjustment factors

---

L. Meneghello Present affiliation: Gruppo Banco Popolare *Disclaimer: The views, thoughts and opinions expressed in this paper are those of the authors in their individual capacity and should not be attributed to Gruppo Banco Popolare or to the authors as representatives or employees of Gruppo Banco Popolare.*

Z. Grbac (✉)
Laboratoire de Probabilités et Modèles Aléatoires, Université Paris Diderot - Paris 7, Case 7012, 75205 Paris Cedex 13, France
e-mail: grbac@math.univ-paris-diderot.fr

L. Meneghello · W.J. Runggaldier
Dipartimento di Matematica Pura ed Applicata, Università di Padova, Via Trieste 63, 35121 Padova, Italy
e-mail: meneghello.laura@yahoo.com

W.J. Runggaldier
e-mail: runggal@math.unipd.it

1 Introduction

The recent financial crisis has heavily impacted the financial market and the fixed income markets in particular. Key features put forward by the crisis are counterparty and liquidity/funding risk. In interest rate derivatives the underlying rates are typically Libor/Euribor. These are determined by a panel of banks and thus reflect various risks in the interbank market, in particular counterparty and liquidity risk. The standard no-arbitrage relations between Libor rates of different maturities have broken down and significant spreads have been observed between Libor rates of different tenors, as well as between Libor and OIS swap rates, where OIS stands for Overnight Indexed Swap. For more details on this issue see Eqs. (5)–(7) and the paragraph following them, as well as the paper by Bormetti et al. [1] and a corresponding version in this volume. This has led practitioners and academics alike to construct multi-curve models where future cash flows are generated through curves associated to the underlying rates (typically the Libor, one for each tenor structure), but are discounted by another curve.

For the pre-crisis single-curve setup various interest rate models have been proposed. Some of the standard model classes are: the short rate models; the instantaneous forward rate models in an Heath–Jarrow–Morton (HJM) setup; the market forward rate models (Libor market models). In this paper we consider a possible multi-curve extension of the short rate model class that, with respect to the other model classes, has in particular the advantage of leading more easily to a Markovian structure. Other multi-curve extensions of short rate models have appeared in the literature such as Kijima et al. [22], Kenyon [20], Filipović and Trolle [14], Morino and Runggaldier [27]. The present paper considers an exponentially quadratic model, whereas the models in the mentioned papers concern mainly the exponentially affine framework, except for [22] in which the exponentially quadratic models are mentioned. More details on the difference between the exponentially affine and exponentially quadratic short rate models will be provided below.

Inspired by a credit risk analogy, but also by a common practice of deriving multi-curve quantities by adding a spread over the corresponding single-curve risk-free quantities, we shall consider, next to the short rate itself, a short rate spread to be added to the short rate, one for each possible tenor structure. Notice that these spreads are added from the outset.

To discuss the basic ideas in an as simple as possible way, we consider just a two-curve model, namely with one curve for discounting and one for generating future cash flows; in other words, we shall consider a single tenor structure. We shall thus concentrate on the short rate r_t and a single short rate spread s_t and, for their dynamics, introduce a factor model. In the pre-crisis single-curve setting there are two basic factor model classes for the short rate: the exponentially affine and the exponentially quadratic model classes. Here we shall concentrate on the less common quadratic class with Gaussian factors. In the exponentially affine class where, to guarantee positivity of rates and spreads, one considers generally square root models for the factors, the distribution of the factors is χ^2. In the exponentially quadratic class the factors have a more convenient Gaussian distribution.

The paper is structured as follows. In the preliminary Sect. 2 we mainly discuss issues related to martingale modeling. In Sect. 3 we introduce the multi-curve Gaussian, exponentially quadratic model class. In Sect. 4 we deal with pricing of linear interest rate derivatives and, finally, in Sect. 5 with nonlinear/optional interest rate derivatives.

2 Preliminaries

2.1 Discount Curve and Collateralization

In the presence of multiple curves, the choice of the curve for discounting the future cash flows, and a related choice of the numeraire for the standard martingale measure used for pricing, in other words, the question of absence of arbitrage, becomes nontrivial (see e.g. the discussion in Kijima and Muromachi [21]). To avoid issues of arbitrage, one should possibly have a common discount curve to be applied to all future cash flows independently of the tenor. A choice, which has been widely accepted and became practically standard, is given by the OIS-curve $T \mapsto p(t, T) = p^{OIS}(t, T)$ that can be stripped from OIS rates, namely the fair rates in an OIS. The arguments justifying this choice and which are typically evoked in practice, are the fact that the majority of the traded interest rate derivatives are nowadays being collateralized and the rate used for remuneration of the collateral is exactly the overnight rate, which is the rate the OIS are based on. Moreover, the overnight rate bears very little risk due to its short maturity and therefore can be considered relatively risk-free. In this context we also point out that prices, corresponding to fully collateralized transactions, are considered as clean prices (this terminology was first introduced by Crépey [6] and Crépey et al. [9]). Since collateralization is by now applied in the majority of cases, one may thus ignore counterparty and liquidity risk between individual parties when pricing interest rate derivatives, but cannot ignore the counterparty and liquidity risk in the interbank market as a whole. These risks are often jointly referred to as interbank risk and they are main drivers of the multi-curve phenomenon, as documented in the literature (see e.g. Crépey and Douady [7], Filipović and Trolle [14], and Gallitschke et al. [15]). We shall thus consider only *clean valuation* formulas, which take into account the multi-curve issue. Possible ways to account for counterparty risk and funding issues between individual counterparties in a contract are, among others, to follow a global valuation approach that leads to nonlinear derivative valuation (see Brigo et al. [3, 4] and other references therein, and in particular Pallavicini and Brigo [28] for a global valuation approach applied specifically to interest rate modeling), or to consider various valuation adjustments that are generally computed on top of the clean prices (see Crépey [6]). A fully nonlinear valuation is preferable, but is more difficult to achieve. On the other hand, valuation adjustments are more consolidated and also used in practice and this gives a further justification to still look for clean prices. Concerning the explicit role of collateral in the pricing of interest rate derivatives, we refer to the above-mentioned paper by Pallavicini and Brigo [28].

2.2 Martingale Measures

The fundamental theorem of asset pricing links the economic principle of absence of arbitrage with the notion of a martingale measure. As it is well known, this is a measure, under which the traded asset prices, expressed in units of a same numeraire, are local martingales. Models for interest rate markets are typically incomplete so that absence of arbitrage admits many martingale measures. A common approach in interest rate modeling is to perform martingale modeling, namely to model the quantities of interest directly under a generic martingale measure; one has then to perform a calibration in order to single out the specific martingale measure of interest. The modeling under a martingale measure now imposes some conditions on the model and, in interest rate theory, a typical such condition is the Heath–Jarrow–Morton (HJM) drift condition.

Starting from the OIS bonds, we shall first derive a suitable numeraire and then consider as martingale measure a measure Q under which not only the OIS bonds, but also the FRA contracts seen as basic quantities in the bond market, are local martingales when expressed in units of the given numeraire. To this basic market one can then add various derivatives imposing that their prices, expressed in units of the numeraire, are local martingales under Q.

Having made the choice of the OIS curve $T \mapsto p(t, T)$ as the discount curve, consider the instantaneous forward rates $f(t, T) := -\frac{\partial}{\partial T} \log p(t, T)$ and let $r_t = f(t, t)$ be the corresponding short rate at the generic time t. Define the OIS bank account as

$$B_t = \exp\left(\int_0^t r_s ds\right) \tag{1}$$

and, as usual, the standard martingale measure Q as the measure, equivalent to the physical measure P, that is associated to the bank account B_t as numeraire. Hence the arbitrage-free prices of all assets, discounted by B_t, have to be local martingales with respect to Q. For derivative pricing, among them also FRA pricing, it is often more convenient to use, equivalently, the forward measure Q^T associated to the OIS bond $p(t, T)$ as numeraire. The two measures Q and Q^T are related by their Radon–Nikodym density process

$$\left.\frac{dQ^T}{dQ}\right|_{\mathcal{F}_t} = \frac{p(t, T)}{B_t p(0, T)} \qquad 0 \le t \le T. \tag{2}$$

As already mentioned, we shall follow the traditional *martingale modeling*, whereby the model dynamics are assigned under the martingale measure Q. This leads to defining the OIS bond prices according to

$$p(t,T) = E^Q\left\{\exp\left[-\int_t^T r_u du\right] \mid \mathcal{F}_t\right\} \tag{3}$$

after having specified the $Q-$dynamics of r.

Coming now to the FRA contracts, recall that they concern a forward rate agreement, established at a time t for a future interval $[T, T+\Delta]$, where at time $T+\Delta$ the interest corresponding to a floating rate is received in exchange for the interest corresponding to a fixed rate R. There exist various possible conventions concerning the timing of the payments. Here we choose payment in arrears, which in this case means at time $T+\Delta$. Typically, the floating rate is given by the Libor rate and, having assumed payments in arrears, we also assume that the rate is fixed at the beginning of the interval of interest, here at T. Recall that for expository simplicity we had reduced ourselves to a two-curve setup involving just a single Libor for a given tenor Δ. The floating rate received at $T+\Delta$ is therefore the rate $L(T; T, T+\Delta)$, fixed at the inception time T. For a unitary notional, and using the $(T+\Delta)$-forward measure $Q^{T+\Delta}$ as the pricing measure, the arbitrage-free price at $t \leq T$ of the FRA contract is then

$$P^{FRA}(t; T, T+\Delta, R) = \Delta p(t, T+\Delta) E^{T+\Delta}\left\{L(T; T, T+\Delta) - R \mid \mathcal{F}_t\right\}, \tag{4}$$

where $E^{T+\Delta}$ denotes the expectation with respect to the measure $Q^{T+\Delta}$. From this expression it follows that the value of the fixed rate R that makes the contract fair at time t is given by

$$R_t = E^{T+\Delta}\left\{L(T; T, T+\Delta) \mid \mathcal{F}_t\right\} := L(t; T, T+\Delta) \tag{5}$$

and we shall call $L(t; T, T+\Delta)$ the *forward Libor rate*. Note that $L(\cdot; T, T+\Delta)$ is a $Q^{T+\Delta}-$martingale by construction.

In view of developing a model for $L(T; T, T+\Delta)$, recall that, by absence of arbitrage arguments, the classical discrete compounding forward rate at time t for the future time interval $[T, T+\Delta]$ is given by

$$F(t; T, T+\Delta) = \frac{1}{\Delta}\left(\frac{p(t,T)}{p(t,T+\Delta)} - 1\right),$$

where $p(t,T)$ represents here the price of a risk-free zero coupon bond. This expression can be justified also by the fact that it represents the fair fixed rate in a forward rate agreement, where the floating rate received at $T+\Delta$ is

$$F(T; T, T+\Delta) = \frac{1}{\Delta}\left(\frac{1}{p(T,T+\Delta)} - 1\right) \tag{6}$$

and we have

$$F(t;T,T+\Delta) = E^{T+\Delta}\{F(T;T,T+\Delta) \mid \mathcal{F}_t\}. \tag{7}$$

This makes the forward rate coherent with the risk-free bond prices, where the latter represent the expectation of the market concerning the future value of money.

Before the financial crisis, $L(T;T,T+\Delta)$ was assumed to be equal to $F(T;T,T+\Delta)$, an assumption that allowed for various simplifications in the determination of derivative prices. After the crisis $L(T;T,T+\Delta)$ is no longer equal to $F(T;T,T+\Delta)$ and what one considers for $F(T;T,T+\Delta)$ is in fact the *OIS discretely compounded rate*, which is based on the OIS bonds, even though the OIS bonds are not necessarily equal to the risk-free bonds (see Sects. 1.3.1 and 1.3.2 of Grbac and Runggaldier [18] for more details on this issue). In particular, the Libor rate $L(T;T,T+\Delta)$ cannot be expressed by the right-hand side of (6). The fact that $L(T;T,T+\Delta) \neq F(T;T,T+\Delta)$ implies by (5) and (7) that also $L(t;T,T+\Delta) \neq F(t;T,T+\Delta)$ for all $t \leq T$ and this leads to a *Libor-OIS spread* $L(t;T,T+\Delta) - F(t;T,T+\Delta)$.

Following some of the recent literature (see e.g. Kijima et al. [22], Crépey et al. [8], Filipović and Trolle [14]), one possibility is now to keep the classical relationship (6) also for $L(T;T,T+\Delta)$ thereby replacing however the bonds $p(t,T)$ by fictitious risky ones $\bar{p}(t,T)$ that are assumed to be affected by the same factors as the Libor rates. Such a bond can be seen as an average bond issued by a representative bank from the Libor group and it is therefore sometimes referred to in the literature as a *Libor bond*. This leads to

$$L(T;T,T+\Delta) = \frac{1}{\Delta}\left(\frac{1}{\bar{p}(T,T+\Delta)} - 1\right). \tag{8}$$

Recall that, for simplicity of exposition, we consider a single Libor for a single tenor Δ and so also a single fictitious bond. In general, one has one Libor and one fictitious bond for each tenor, i.e. $L^{\Delta}(T;T,T+\Delta)$ and $\bar{p}^{\Delta}(T,T+\Delta)$. Note that we shall model the bond prices $\bar{p}(t,T)$, for all t and T with $t \leq T$, even though only the prices $\bar{p}(T,T+\Delta)$, for all T, are needed in relation (8). Moreover, keeping in mind that the bonds $\bar{p}(t,T)$ are fictitious, they do not have to satisfy the boundary condition $\bar{p}(T,T) = 1$, but we still assume this condition in order to simplify the modeling.

To derive a dynamic model for $L(t;T,T+\Delta)$, we may now derive a dynamic model for $\bar{p}(t,T+\Delta)$, where we have to keep in mind that the latter is not a traded quantity. Inspired by a credit-risk analogy, but also by a common practice of deriving multi-curve quantities by adding a spread over the corresponding single-curve (risk-free) quantities, which in this case is the short rate r_t, let us define then the Libor (risky) bond prices as

$$\bar{p}(t,T) = E^{Q}\left\{\exp\left[-\int_t^T (r_u + s_u)du\right] \mid \mathcal{F}_t\right\}, \tag{9}$$

with s_t representing the short rate spread. In case of default risk alone, s_t corresponds to the hazard rate/default intensity, but here it corresponds more generally to all the factors affecting the Libor rate, namely besides credit risk, also liquidity risk, etc. Notice also that the spread is introduced here from the outset. Having for simplicity considered a single tenor Δ and thus a single $\bar{p}(t, T)$, we shall also consider only a single spread s_t. In general, however, one has a spread s_t^{Δ} for each tenor Δ.

We need now a dynamical model for both r_t and s_t and we shall define this model directly under the martingale measure Q (*martingale modeling*).

3 Short Rate Model

3.1 The Model

As mentioned, we shall consider a dynamical model for r_t and the single spread s_t under the martingale measure Q that, in practice, has to be calibrated to the market. For this purpose we shall consider a factor model with several factors driving r_t and s_t.

The two basic factor model classes for the short rate in the pre-crisis single-curve setup, namely the exponentially affine and the exponentially quadratic model classes, both allow for flexibility and analytical tractability and this in turn allows for closed or semi-closed formulas for linear and optional interest rate derivatives. The former class is usually better known than the latter, but the latter has its own advantages. In fact, for the exponentially affine class one would consider r_t and s_t as given by a linear combination of the factors and so, in order to obtain positivity, one has to consider a square root model for the factors. On the other hand, in the Gaussian exponentially quadratic class, one considers mean reverting Gaussian factor models, but at least some of the factors in the linear combination for r_t and s_t appear as a square. In this way the distribution of the factors remains always Gaussian; in a square-root model it is a non-central χ^2-distribution. Notice also that the exponentially quadratic models can be seen as dual to the square root exponentially affine models.

In the pre-crisis single-curve setting, the exponentially quadratic models have been considered, e.g. in El Karoui et al. [12], Pelsser [29], Gombani and Runggaldier [17], Leippold and Wu [24], Chen et al. [5], and Gaspar [16]. However, since the pre-crisis exponentially affine models are more common, there have also been more attempts to extend them to a post-crisis multi-curve setting (for an overview and details see e.g. Grbac and Runggaldier [18]). A first extension of exponentially quadratic models to a multi-curve setting can be found in Kijima et al. [22] and the present paper is devoted to a possibly full extension.

Let us now present the model for r_t and s_t, where we consider not only the short rate r_t itself, but also its spread s_t to be given by a linear combination of the factors, where at least some of the factors appear as a square. To keep the presentation simple, we shall consider a small number of factors and, in order to model also a possible correlation between r_t and s_t, the minimal number of factors is three. It also follows from some of the econometric literature that a small number of factors may suffice to adequately model most situations (see also Duffee [10] and Duffie and Gârleanu [11]).

Given three independent affine factor processes $\Psi_t^i,\ i = 1, 2, 3$, having under Q the Gaussian dynamics

$$d\Psi_t^i = -b^i \Psi_t^i dt + \sigma^i \, dw_t^i, \quad i = 1, 2, 3, \tag{10}$$

with $b_i, \sigma_i > 0$ and w_t^i, $i = 1, 2, 3$, independent $Q-$Wiener processes, we let

$$\begin{cases} r_t = \Psi_t^1 + (\Psi_t^2)^2 \\ s_t = \kappa \Psi_t^1 + (\Psi_t^3)^2 \end{cases}, \tag{11}$$

where Ψ_t^1 is the common systematic factor allowing for instantaneous correlation between r_t and s_t with correlation intensity κ and Ψ_t^2 and Ψ_t^3 are the idiosyncratic factors. Other factors may be added to drive s_t, but the minimal model containing common and idiosyncratic components requires three factors, as explained above. The common factor is particularly important because we want to take into account the realistic feature of non-zero correlation between r_t and s_t in the model.

Remark 3.1 The zero mean-reversion level is here considered only for convenience of simpler formulas, but can be easily taken to be positive, so that short rates and spreads can become negative only with small probability (see Kijima and Muromachi [21] for an alternative representation of the spreads in terms of Gaussian factors that guarantee the spreads to remain nonnegative and still allows for correlation between r_t and s_t). Note, however, that given the current market situation where the observed interest rates are very close to zero and sometimes also negative, even models with negative mean-reversion level have been considered, as well as models allowing for regime-switching in the mean reversion parameter.

Remark 3.2 For the short rate itself one could also consider the model $r_t = \phi_t + \Psi_t^1 + (\Psi_t^2)^2$ where ϕ_t is a *deterministic shift extension* (see Brigo and Mercurio [2]) that allows for a good fit to the initial term structure in short rate models even with constant model parameters.

In the model (11) we have included a linear term Ψ_t^1 which may lead to negative values of rates and spreads, although only with small probability in the case of models of the type (10) with a positive mean reversion level. The advantage of including this linear term is more generality and flexibility in the model. Moreover, it allows to express $\bar{p}(t, T)$ in terms of $p(t, T)$ multiplied by a factor. This property will lead to an *adjustment factor* by which one can express post-crisis quantities in terms of corresponding pre-crisis quantities, see Morino and Runggaldier [27] in which this idea has been first proposed in the context of exponentially affine short rate models for multiple curves.

3.2 Bond Prices (OIS and Libor Bonds)

In this subsection we derive explicit pricing formulas for the OIS bonds $p(t, T)$ as defined in (3) and the fictitious Libor bonds $\bar{p}(t, T)$ as defined in (9). Thereby, r_t and s_t are supposed to be given by (11) with the factor processes Ψ_t^i evolving under the standard martingale measure Q according to (10). Defining the matrices

$$F = \begin{bmatrix} -b^1 & 0 & 0 \\ 0 & -b^2 & 0 \\ 0 & 0 & -b^3 \end{bmatrix}, \ D = \begin{bmatrix} \sigma^1 & 0 & 0 \\ 0 & \sigma^2 & 0 \\ 0 & 0 & \sigma^3 \end{bmatrix} \tag{12}$$

and considering the vector factor process $\Psi_t := [\Psi_t^1, \Psi_t^2, \Psi_t^3]'$ as well as the multivariate Wiener process $W_t := [w_t^1, w_t^2, w_t^3]'$, where $'$ denotes transposition, the dynamics (10) can be rewritten in synthetic form as

$$d\Psi_t = F\Psi_t dt + D dW_t. \tag{13}$$

Using results on exponential quadratic term structures (see Gombani and Runggaldier [17], Filipović [13]), we have

$$\begin{aligned} p(t, T) &= E^Q\left\{e^{-\int_t^T r_u du} \middle| \mathcal{F}_t\right\} = E^Q\left\{e^{-\int_t^T (\Psi_u^1 + (\Psi_u^2)^2) du} \middle| \mathcal{F}_t\right\} \\ &= \exp\left[-A(t, T) - B'(t, T)\Psi_t - \Psi_t' C(t, T)\Psi_t\right] \end{aligned} \tag{14}$$

and, setting $R_t := r_t + s_t$,

$$\begin{aligned} \bar{p}(t, T) &= E^Q\left\{e^{-\int_t^T R_u du} \middle| \mathcal{F}_t\right\} = E^Q\left\{e^{-\int_t^T ((1+\kappa)\Psi_u^1 + (\Psi_u^2)^2 + (\Psi_u^3)^2) du} \middle| \mathcal{F}_t\right\} \\ &= \exp\left[-\bar{A}(t, T) - \bar{B}'(t, T)\Psi_t - \Psi_t' \bar{C}(t, T)\Psi_t\right], \end{aligned} \tag{15}$$

where $A(t, T)$, $\bar{A}(t, T)$, $B(t, T)$, $\bar{B}(t, T)$, $C(t, T)$ and $\bar{C}(t, T)$ are scalar, vector, and matrix-valued deterministic functions to be determined.

For this purpose we recall the Heath–Jarrow–Morton (HJM) approach for the case when $p(t, T)$ in (14) represents the price of a risk-free zero coupon bond. The HJM approach leads to the so-called HJM drift conditions that impose conditions on the coefficients in (14) so that the resulting prices $p(t, T)$ do not imply arbitrage possibilities. Since the risk-free bonds are traded, the no-arbitrage condition is expressed by requiring $\frac{p(t,T)}{B_t}$ to be a $Q-$martingale for B_t defined as in (1) and it is exactly this martingality property to yield the drift condition. In our case, $p(t, T)$ is the price of an OIS bond that is not necessarily traded and in general does not coincide with the price of a risk-free bond. However, whether the OIS bond is traded or not, $\frac{p(t,T)}{B_t}$ is a $Q-$martingale by the very definition of $p(t, T)$ in (14) (see the first equality in (14)) and so we can follow the same HJM approach to obtain conditions on the coefficients in (14) also in our case.

For what concerns, on the other hand, the coefficients in (15), recall that $\bar{p}(t, T)$ is a fictitious asset that is not traded and thus is not subject to any no-arbitrage condition. Notice, however, that by analogy to $p(t, T)$ in (14), by its very definition given in the first equality in (15), $\frac{\bar{p}(t,T)}{\bar{B}_t}$ is a $Q-$martingale for $\bar{B}_t$ given by $\bar{B}_t := \exp \int_0^t R_u du$. The two cases $p(t, T)$ and $\bar{p}(t, T)$ can thus be treated in complete analogy provided that we use for $\bar{p}(t, T)$ the numeraire $\bar{B}_t$.

We shall next derive from the $Q-$martingality of $\frac{p(t,T)}{B_t}$ and $\frac{\bar{p}(t,T)}{\bar{B}_t}$ conditions on the coefficients in (14) and (15) that correspond to the classical HJM drift condition and lead thus to ODEs for these coefficients. For this purpose we shall proceed by analogy to Sect. 2 in [17], in particular to the proof of Proposition 2.1 therein, to which we also refer for more detail.

Introducing the "instantaneous forward rates" $f(t, T) := -\frac{\partial}{\partial T} \log p(t, T)$ and $\bar{f}(t, T) := -\frac{\partial}{\partial T} \log \bar{p}(t, T)$, and setting

$$a(t, T) := \frac{\partial}{\partial T} A(t, T), \quad b(t, T) := \frac{\partial}{\partial T} B(t, T), \quad c(t, T) := \frac{\partial}{\partial T} C(t, T) \tag{16}$$

and analogously for $\bar{a}(t, T), \bar{b}(t, T), \bar{c}(t, T)$, from (14) and (15) we obtain

$$f(t, T) = a(t, T) + b'(t, T)\Psi_t + \Psi_t' c(t, T)\Psi_t, \tag{17}$$

$$\bar{f}(t, T) = \bar{a}(t, T) + \bar{b}'(t, T)\Psi_t + \Psi_t' \bar{c}(t, T)\Psi_t. \tag{18}$$

Recalling that $r_t = f(t, t)$ and $R_t = \bar{f}(t, t)$, this implies, with $a(t) := a(t, t)$, $b(t) := b(t, t)$, $c(t) := c(t, t)$ and analogously for the corresponding quantities with a bar, that

$$r_t = a(t) + b'(t)\Psi_t + \Psi_t' c(t)\Psi_t \tag{19}$$

and

$$R_t = r_t + s_t = \bar{a}(t) + \bar{b}'(t)\Psi_t + \Psi_t' \bar{c}(t)\Psi_t. \tag{20}$$

Comparing (19) and (20) with (11), we obtain the following conditions where $i, j = 1, 2, 3$, namely

$$\begin{cases} a(t) = 0 \\ b^i(t) = \mathbf{1}_{\{i=1\}} \\ c^{ij}(t) = \mathbf{1}_{\{i=j=2\}} \end{cases} \qquad \begin{cases} \bar{a}(t) = 0 \\ \bar{b}^i(t) = (1 + \kappa)\mathbf{1}_{\{i=1\}} \\ \bar{c}^{ij}(t) = \mathbf{1}_{\{i=j=2\} \cup \{i=j=3\}}. \end{cases}$$

Using next the fact that

$$p(t, T) = \exp\left[-\int_t^T f(t, s)ds\right], \quad \bar{p}(t, T) = \exp\left[-\int_t^T \bar{f}(t, s)ds\right],$$

and imposing $\frac{p(t,T)}{B_t}$ and $\frac{\bar{p}(t,T)}{\bar{B}_t}$ to be $Q-$martingales, one obtains ordinary differential equations to be satisfied by $c(t,T)$, $b(t,T)$, $a(t,T)$ and analogously for the quantities with a bar. Integrating these ODEs with respect to the second variable and recalling (16) one obtains (for the details see the proof of Proposition 2.1 in [17])

$$\begin{cases} C_t(t,T) + 2FC(t,T) - 2C(t,T)DDC(t,T) + c(t) = 0, & C(T,T) = 0 \\ \bar{C}_t(t,T) + 2F\bar{C}(t,T) - 2\bar{C}(t,T)DD\bar{C}(t,T) + \bar{c}(t) = 0, & \bar{C}(T,T) = 0 \end{cases} \tag{21}$$

with

$$c(t) = \begin{bmatrix} 0 & 0 & 0 \\ 0 & 1 & 0 \\ 0 & 0 & 0 \end{bmatrix} \quad \bar{c}(t) = \begin{bmatrix} 0 & 0 & 0 \\ 0 & 1 & 0 \\ 0 & 0 & 1 \end{bmatrix}. \tag{22}$$

The special forms of $F, D, c(t)$ and $\bar{c}(t)$ together with boundary conditions $C(T,T) = 0$ and $\bar{C}(T,T) = 0$ imply that only C^{22}, $\bar{C}^{22}$, $\bar{C}^{33}$ are non-zero and satisfy

$$\begin{cases} C^{22}_t(t,T) - 2b^2C^{22}(t,T) - 2(\sigma^2)^2(C^{22}(t,T))^2 + 1 = 0, & C^{22}(T,T) = 0 \\ \bar{C}^{22}_t(t,T) - 2b^2\bar{C}^{22}(t,T) - 2(\sigma^2)^2(\bar{C}^{22}(t,T))^2 + 1 = 0, & \bar{C}^{22}(T,T) = 0 \\ \bar{C}^{33}_t(t,T) - 2b^3\bar{C}^{33}(t,T) - 2(\sigma^3)^2(\bar{C}^{33}(t,T))^2 + 1 = 0, & \bar{C}^{33}(T,T) = 0 \end{cases} \tag{23}$$

that can be shown to have as solution

$$\begin{cases} C^{22}(t,T) = \bar{C}^{22}(t,T) = \frac{2(e^{(T-t)h^2}-1)}{2h^2+(2b^2+h^2)(e^{(T-t)h^2}-1)} \\ \bar{C}^{33}(t,T) = \frac{2(e^{(T-t)h^3}-1)}{2h^3+(2b^3+h^3)(e^{(T-t)h^3}-1)} \end{cases} \tag{24}$$

with $h^i = \sqrt{4(b^i)^2 + 8(\sigma^i)^2} > 0$, $i = 2, 3$.

Next, always by analogy to the proof of Proposition 2.1 in [17], the vectors of coefficients $B(t,T)$ and $\bar{B}(t,T)$ of the first order terms can be seen to satisfy the following system

$$\begin{cases} B_t(t,T) + B(t,T)F - 2B(t,T)DDC(t,T) + b(t) = 0, & B(T,T) = 0 \\ \bar{B}_t(t,T) + \bar{B}(t,T)F - 2\bar{B}(t,T)DD\bar{C}(t,T) + \bar{b}(t) = 0, & \bar{B}(T,T) = 0 \end{cases} \tag{25}$$

with

$$b(t) = [1, 0, 0] \quad \bar{b}(t) = [(1+\kappa), 0, 0].$$

Noticing similarly as above that only $B^1(t,T)$, $\bar{B}^1(t,T)$ are non-zero, system (25) becomes

$$\begin{cases} B^1_t(t,T) - b^1B^1(t,T) + 1 = 0 & B^1(T,T) = 0 \\ \bar{B}^1_t(t,T) - b^1\bar{B}^1(t,T) + (1+\kappa) = 0 & \bar{B}^1(T,T) = 0 \end{cases} \tag{26}$$

leading to the explicit solution

$$\begin{cases} B^1(t,T) = \frac{1}{b^1}\left(1 - e^{-b^1(T-t)}\right) \\ \bar{B}^1(t,T) = \frac{1+\kappa}{b^1}\left(1 - e^{-b^1(T-t)}\right) = (1+\kappa)B^1(t,T). \end{cases} \tag{27}$$

Finally, $A(t, T)$ and $\bar{A}(t, T)$ have to satisfy

$$\begin{cases} A_t(t,T) + (\sigma^2)^2 C^{22}(t,T) - \frac{1}{2}(\sigma^1)^2(B^1(t,T))^2 = 0, \\ \bar{A}_t(t,T) + (\sigma^2)^2 \bar{C}^{22}(t,T) + (\sigma^3)^2\bar{C}^{33}(t,T) - \frac{1}{2}(\sigma^1)^2(\bar{B}^1(t,T))^2 = 0 \end{cases} \tag{28}$$

with boundary conditions $A(T, T) = 0, \bar{A}(T, T) = 0$. The explicit expressions can be obtained simply by integrating the above equations.

Summarizing, we have proved the following:

Proposition 3.1 *Assume that the OIS short rate r and the spread s are given by (11) with the factor processes Ψ_t^i, $i = 1, 2, 3$, evolving according to (10) under the standard martingale measure Q. The time-t price of the OIS bond $p(t, T)$, as defined in (3), is given by*

$$p(t,T) = \exp[-A(t,T) - B^1(t,T)\Psi_t^1 - C^{22}(t,T)(\Psi_t^2)^2], \tag{29}$$

and the time-t price of the fictitious Libor bond $\bar{p}(t, T)$, as defined in (9), by

$$\begin{aligned} \bar{p}(t,T) &= \exp[-\bar{A}(t,T) - (\kappa+1)B^1(t,T)\Psi_t^1 - C^{22}(t,T)(\Psi_t^2)^2 - \bar{C}^{33}(t,T)(\Psi_t^3)^2] \\ &= p(t,T)\exp[-\tilde{A}(t,T) - \kappa B^1(t,T)\Psi_t^1 - \bar{C}^{33}(t,T)(\Psi_t^3)^2], \end{aligned} \tag{30}$$

where $\tilde{A}(t,T) := \bar{A}(t,T) - A(t,T)$ with $A(t,T)$ and $\bar{A}(t,T)$ given by (28), $B^1(t,T)$ given by (27) and $C^{22}(t,T)$ and $C^{33}(t,T)$ given by (24).

In particular, expression (30) gives $\bar{p}(t, T)$ in terms of $p(t, T)$. Based on this we shall derive in the following section the announced *adjustment factor* allowing to pass from pre-crisis quantities to the corresponding post-crisis quantities.

3.3 Forward Measure

The underlying factor model was defined in (10) under the standard martingale measure Q. For derivative prices, which we shall determine in the following two sections, it will be convenient to work under forward measures, for which, given the single tenor Δ, we shall consider a generic $(T + \Delta)$-forward measure. The density process to change the measure from Q to $Q^{T+\Delta}$ is

$$\mathcal{L}_t := \frac{d\,Q^{T+\Delta}}{d\,Q}\bigg|_{\mathcal{F}_t} = \frac{p(t,T+\Delta)}{p(0,T+\Delta)}\frac{1}{B_t} \tag{31}$$

from which it follows by (29) and the martingale property of $\left(\frac{p(t,T+\Delta)}{B_t}\right)_{t\leq T+\Delta}$ that

$$d\mathcal{L}_t = \mathcal{L}_t\left(-B^1(t,T+\Delta)\sigma^1 dw_t^1 - 2C^{22}(t,T+\Delta)\Psi_t^2\sigma^2 dw_t^2\right).$$

This implies by Girsanov's theorem that

$$\begin{cases} dw_t^{1,T+\Delta} &= dw_t^1 + \sigma^1 B^1(t,T+\Delta)dt \\ dw_t^{2,T+\Delta} &= dw_t^2 + 2C^{22}(t,T+\Delta)\Psi_t^2\sigma^2 dt \\ dw_t^{3,T+\Delta} &= dw_t^3 \end{cases} \tag{32}$$

are $Q^{T+\Delta}$–Wiener processes. From the Q–dynamics (10) we then obtain the following $Q^{T+\Delta}$–dynamics for the factors

$$\begin{aligned} d\Psi_t^1 &= -\left[b^1\Psi_t^1 + (\sigma^1)^2 B^1(t,T+\Delta)\right]dt + \sigma^1 dw_t^{1,T+\Delta} \\ d\Psi_t^2 &= -\left[b^2\Psi_t^2 + 2(\sigma^2)^2 C^{22}(t,T+\Delta)\Psi_t^2\right]dt + \sigma^2 dw_t^{2,T+\Delta} \\ d\Psi_t^3 &= -b^3\Psi_t^3 dt + \sigma^3 dw_t^{3,T+\Delta}. \end{aligned} \tag{33}$$

Remark 3.3 While in the dynamics (10) for Ψ_t^i, $(i=1,2,3)$ under Q we had for simplicity assumed a zero mean-reversion level, under the $(T+\Delta)$-forward measure the mean-reversion level is for Ψ_t^1 now different from zero due to the measure transformation.

Lemma 3.1 *Analogously to the case when $p(t,T)$ represents the price of a risk-free zero coupon bond, also for $p(t,T)$ viewed as OIS bond we have that $\frac{p(t,T)}{p(t,T+\Delta)}$ is a $Q^{T+\Delta}$–martingale.*

Proof We have seen that also for OIS bonds as defined in (3) we have that, with B_t as in (1), the ratio $\frac{p(t,T)}{B_t}$ is a Q–martingale. From Bayes' formula we then have

$$E^{T+\Delta}\left\{\frac{p(T,T)}{p(T,T+\Delta)} \mid \mathcal{F}_t\right\} = \frac{E^Q\left\{\frac{1}{p(0,T+\Delta)}\frac{1}{B_{T+\Delta}}\frac{p(T,T)}{p(T,T+\Delta)}|\mathcal{F}_t\right\}}{E^Q\left\{\frac{1}{p(0,T+\Delta)}\frac{1}{B_{T+\Delta}}|\mathcal{F}_t\right\}}$$

$$= \frac{E^Q\left\{\frac{p(T,T)}{p(T,T+\Delta)}E^Q\left\{\frac{1}{B_{T+\Delta}}|\mathcal{F}_T\right\}|\mathcal{F}_t\right\}}{\frac{p(t,T+\Delta)}{B_t}} = \frac{B_t E^Q\left\{\frac{p(T,T)}{p(T,T+\Delta)}\frac{p(T,T+\Delta)}{B_T}|\mathcal{F}_t\right\}}{p(t,T+\Delta)}$$

$$= \frac{B_t E^Q\left\{\frac{p(T,T)}{B_T}|\mathcal{F}_t\right\}}{p(t,T+\Delta)} = \frac{p(t,T)}{p(t,T+\Delta)},$$

thus proving the statement of the lemma. □

We recall that we denote the expectation with respect to the measure $Q^{T+\Delta}$ by $E^{T+\Delta}\{\cdot\}$. The dynamics in (33) lead to Gaussian distributions for Ψ_t^i, $i = 1, 2, 3$ that, given $B^1(\cdot)$ and $C^{22}(\cdot)$, have mean and variance

$$E^{T+\Delta}\{\Psi_t^i\} = \bar{\alpha}_t^i = \bar{\alpha}_t^i(b^i, \sigma^i) \quad , \quad Var^{T+\Delta}\{\Psi_t^i\} = \bar{\beta}_t^i = \bar{\beta}_t^i(b^i, \sigma^i),$$

which can be explicitly computed. More precisely, we have

$$\begin{cases} \bar{\alpha}_t^1 &= e^{-b^1 t}\left[\Psi_0^1 - \frac{(\sigma^1)^2}{2(b^1)^2} e^{-b^1(T+\Delta)}(1 - e^{2b^1 t}) - \frac{(\sigma^1)^2}{(b^1)^2}(1 - e^{b^1 t})\right] \\ \bar{\beta}_t^1 &= e^{-2b^1 t}(e^{2b^1 t} - 1)\frac{(\sigma^1)^2}{2(b^1)} \\ \bar{\alpha}_t^2 &= e^{-(b^2 t + 2(\sigma^2)^2 \tilde{C}^{22}(t,T+\Delta))}\Psi_0^2 \\ \bar{\beta}_t^2 &= e^{-(2b^2 t + 4(\sigma^2)^2 \tilde{C}^{22}(t,T+\Delta))}\int_0^t e^{2b^2 s + 4(\sigma^2)^2 \tilde{C}^{22}(s,T+\Delta)}(\sigma^2)^2 ds \\ \bar{\alpha}_t^3 &= e^{-b^3 t}\Psi_0^3 \\ \bar{\beta}_t^3 &= e^{-2b^3 t}\frac{(\sigma^3)^2}{2b^3}(e^{2b^3 t} - 1), \end{cases} \tag{34}$$

with

$$\begin{aligned} \tilde{C}^{22}(t, T+\Delta) = & \frac{2(2\log(2b^2(e^{(T+\Delta-t)h^2} - 1) + h^2(e^{(T+\Delta-t)h^2} + 1)) + t(2b^2 + h^2))}{(2b^2 + h^2)(2b^2 - h^2)} \\ & - \frac{2(2\log(2b^2(e^{(T+\Delta)h^2} - 1) + h^2(e^{(T+\Delta)h^2} + 1))}{(2b^2 + h^2)(2b^2 - h^2)} \end{aligned} \tag{35}$$

and $h^2 = \sqrt{(2b^2)^2 + 8(\sigma^2)^2}$, and where we have assumed deterministic initial values Ψ_0^1, Ψ_0^2 and Ψ_0^3. For details of the above computation see the proof of Corollary 4.1.3. in Meneghello [25].

4 Pricing of Linear Interest Rate Derivatives

We have discussed in Sect. 3.2 the pricing of OIS and Libor bonds in the Gaussian, exponentially quadratic short rate model introduced in Sect. 3.1. In the remaining part of the paper we shall be concerned with the pricing of interest rate derivatives, namely with derivatives having the Libor rate as underlying rate. In the present section we shall deal with the basic linear derivatives, namely FRAs and interest rate swaps, while nonlinear derivatives will then be dealt with in the following Sect. 5. For the FRA rates discussed in the next Sect. 4.1 we shall in Sect. 4.1.1 exhibit an *adjustment factor* allowing to pass from the single-curve FRA rate to the multi-curve FRA rate.

4.1 FRAs

We start by recalling the definition of a standard forward rate agreement. We emphasize that we use a text-book definition which differs slightly from a market definition, see Mercurio [26].

Definition 4.1 Given the time points $0 \leq t \leq T < T + \Delta$, a *forward rate agreement* (FRA) is an OTC derivative that allows the holder to lock in at the generic date $t \leq T$ the interest rate between the inception date T and the maturity $T + \Delta$ at a fixed value R. At maturity $T + \Delta$ a payment based on the interest rate R, applied to a notional amount of N, is made and the one based on the relevant floating rate *(generally the spot Libor rate* $L(T; T, T + \Delta)$*)* is received.

Recalling that for the Libor rate we had postulated the relation (8) to hold at the inception time T, namely

$$L(T; T, T + \Delta) = \frac{1}{\Delta}\left(\frac{1}{\bar{p}(T, T + \Delta)} - 1\right),$$

the price, at $t \leq T$, of the FRA with fixed rate R and notional N can be computed under the $(T + \Delta)$-forward measure as

$$\begin{aligned} P^{FRA}&(t; T, T + \Delta, R, N) \\ &= N\Delta p(t, T + \Delta)E^{T+\Delta}\left\{L(T; T, T + \Delta) - R \mid \mathcal{F}_t\right\} \\ &= Np(t, T + \Delta)E^{T+\Delta}\left\{\frac{1}{\bar{p}(T, T + \Delta)} - (1 + \Delta R) \mid \mathcal{F}_t\right\}, \end{aligned} \tag{36}$$

Defining

$$\bar{\nu}_{t,T} := E^{T+\Delta}\left\{\frac{1}{\bar{p}(T, T + \Delta)} \mid \mathcal{F}_t\right\}, \tag{37}$$

it is easily seen from (36) that the *fair rate of the FRA, namely the FRA rate*, is given by

$$\bar{R}_t = \frac{1}{\Delta}\left(\bar{\nu}_{t,T} - 1\right). \tag{38}$$

In the *single-curve case* we have instead

$$R_t = \frac{1}{\Delta}\left(\nu_{t,T} - 1\right), \tag{39}$$

where, given that $\frac{p(\cdot,T)}{p(\cdot,T+\Delta)}$ is a $Q^{T+\Delta}$–martingale (see Lemma 3.1),

$$\nu_{t,T} := E^{T+\Delta}\left\{\frac{1}{p(T, T + \Delta)} \mid \mathcal{F}_t\right\} = \frac{p(t, T)}{p(t, T + \Delta)}, \tag{40}$$

which is the classical expression for the FRA rate in the single-curve case. Notice that, contrary to (37), the expression in (40) can be explicitly computed on the basis of bond price data without requiring an interest rate model.

4.1.1 Adjustment Factor

We shall show here the following:

Proposition 4.1 *We have the relationship*

$$\bar{\nu}_{t,T} = \nu_{t,T} \cdot Ad_t^{T,\Delta} \cdot Res_t^{T,\Delta} \tag{41}$$

with

$$\begin{aligned} Ad_t^{T,\Delta} := E^Q\left\{\frac{p(T,T+\Delta)}{\bar{p}(T,T+\Delta)} \mid \mathscr{F}_t\right\} = E^Q\Big\{\exp\Big[\tilde{A}(T,T+\Delta) \\ + \kappa B^1(T,T+\Delta)\Psi_T^1 + \tilde{C}^{33}(T,T+\Delta)(\Psi_T^3)^2\Big] \mid \mathscr{F}_t\Big\} \end{aligned} \tag{42}$$

and

$$Res_t^{T,\Delta} = \exp\Big[-\kappa\frac{(\sigma^1)^2}{2(b^1)^3}\left(1-e^{-b^1\Delta}\right)\left(1-e^{-b^1(T-t)}\right)^2\Big], \tag{43}$$

where $\tilde{A}(t,T)$ is defined after (30), $B^1(t,T)$ in (27) and $\tilde{C}^{33}(t,T)$ in (24).

Proof Firstly, from (30) we obtain

$$\frac{p(T,T+\Delta)}{\bar{p}(T,T+\Delta)} = e^{\tilde{A}(T,T+\Delta)+\kappa B^1(T,T+\Delta)\Psi_T^1+\tilde{C}^{33}(T,T+\Delta)(\Psi_T^3)^2}. \tag{44}$$

In (37) we now change back from the $(T+\Delta)$-forward measure to the standard martingale measure using the density process $\mathscr{L}_t$ given in (31). Using furthermore the above expression for the ratio of the OIS and the Libor bond prices and taking into account the definition of the short rate r_t in terms of the factor processes, we obtain

$$\begin{aligned} \bar{\nu}_{t,T} &= E^{T+\Delta}\left\{\frac{1}{\bar{p}(T,T+\Delta)}\Big|\mathscr{F}_t\right\} = \mathscr{L}_t^{-1}E^Q\left\{\frac{\mathscr{L}_T}{\bar{p}(T,T+\Delta)}\Big|\mathscr{F}_t\right\} \\ &= \frac{1}{p(t,T+\Delta)}E^Q\left\{\exp\Big(-\int_t^T r_u du\Big)\frac{p(T,T+\Delta)}{\bar{p}(T,T+\Delta)}\Big|\mathscr{F}_t\right\} \\ &= \frac{1}{p(t,T+\Delta)}\exp[\tilde{A}(T,T+\Delta)]E^Q\left\{e^{\tilde{C}^{33}(T,T+\Delta)(\Psi_T^3)^2}\Big|\mathscr{F}_t\right\} \end{aligned}$$

$$
\begin{aligned}
&\cdot E^Q\left\{e^{-\int_t^T (\Psi_u^1+(\Psi_u^2)^2)du} e^{\kappa B^1(T,T+\Delta)\Psi_T^1} \,\middle|\, \mathscr{F}_t\right\} \\
&= \frac{1}{p(t,T+\Delta)} \exp[\tilde{A}(T,T+\Delta)] E^Q\left\{e^{\bar{C}^{33}(T,T+\Delta)(\Psi_T^3)^2} \,\middle|\, \mathscr{F}_t\right\} \\
&\quad \cdot E^Q\left\{e^{-\int_t^T \Psi_u^1 du} e^{\kappa B^1(T,T+\Delta)\Psi_T^1} \,\middle|\, \mathscr{F}_t\right\} E^Q\left\{e^{-\int_t^T (\Psi_u^2)^2 du} \,\middle|\, \mathscr{F}_t\right\}, \qquad (45)
\end{aligned}
$$

where we have used the independence of the factors Ψ^i, $i = 1, 2, 3$ under Q.

Recall now from the theory of affine processes (see e.g. Lemma 2.1 in Grbac and Runggaldier [18]) that, for a process Ψ_t^1 satisfying (10), we have for all $\delta, K \in \mathbb{R}$

$$
E^Q\left\{\exp\left[-\int_t^T \delta\Psi_u^1 du - K\Psi_T^1\right] \mid \mathscr{F}_t\right\} = \exp[\alpha^1(t,T) - \beta^1(t,T)\Psi_t^1], \qquad (46)
$$

where

$$
\begin{cases}
\beta^1(t,T) = Ke^{-b^1(T-t)} - \frac{\delta}{b^1}\left(e^{-b^1(T-t)} - 1\right) \\
\alpha^1(t,T) = \frac{(\sigma^1)^2}{2} \int_t^T (\beta^1(u,T))^2 du.
\end{cases}
$$

Setting $K = -\kappa B^1(T, T+\Delta)$ and $\delta = 1$, and recalling from (27) that $B^1(t,T) = \frac{1}{b^1}\left(1 - e^{-b^1(T-t)}\right)$, this leads to

$$
\begin{aligned}
&E^Q\left\{e^{-\int_t^T \Psi_u^1 du} e^{\kappa B^1(T,T+\Delta)\Psi_T^1} \,\middle|\, \mathscr{F}_t\right\} \\
&= \exp\Bigg[\frac{(\sigma^1)^2}{2}(\kappa B^1(T,T+\Delta))^2 \int_t^T e^{-2b^1(T-u)} du \\
&\quad - \kappa B^1(T,T+\Delta)(\sigma^1)^2 \int_t^T B^1(u,T) e^{-b^1(T-u)} du + \frac{(\sigma^1)^2}{2} \int_t^T (B^1(u,T))^2 du \\
&\quad + \left(\kappa B^1(T,T+\Delta)e^{-b^1(T-t)} - B^1(t,T)\right)\Psi_t^1\Bigg]. \qquad (47)
\end{aligned}
$$

On the other hand, from the results of Sect. 3.2 we also have that, for a process Ψ_t^2 satisfying (10),

$$
E^Q\left\{\exp\left[-\int_t^T (\Psi_u^2)^2 du\right] \mid \mathscr{F}_t\right\} = \exp\left[-\alpha^2(t,T) - C^{22}(t,T)(\Psi_t^2)^2\right],
$$

where $C^{22}(t,T)$ corresponds to (24) and (see (28))

$$
\alpha^2(t,T) = (\sigma^2)^2 \int_t^T C^{22}(u,T) du.
$$

This implies that

$$E^Q\left\{\exp\left[-\int_t^T (\Psi_u^2)^2 du\right] \mid \mathscr{F}_t\right\}$$
$$= \exp\left[-(\sigma^2)^2 \int_t^T C^{22}(u,T)du - C^{22}(t,T)\left(\Psi_t^2\right)^2\right]. \tag{48}$$

Replacing (47) and (48) into (45), and recalling the expression for $p(t,T)$ in (29) with $A(\cdot)$, $B^1(\cdot)$, $C^{22}(\cdot)$ according to (28), (27) and (24) respectively, we obtain

$$\begin{aligned}\bar{\nu}_{t,T} = & \frac{p(t,T)}{p(t,T+\Delta)} e^{\tilde{A}(T,T+\Delta)} E^Q\left[e^{\tilde{C}^{33}(T,T+\Delta)(\Psi_T^3)^2} | \mathscr{F}_t\right] \\ & \cdot \exp\left[\frac{(\sigma^1)^2}{2}(\kappa B^1(T,T+\Delta))^2 \int_t^T e^{-2b^1(T-u)}du + \kappa B^1(T,T+\Delta)e^{-b^1(T-t)}\Psi_t^1\right] \\ & \cdot \exp\left[-\kappa B^1(T,T+\Delta)(\sigma^1)^2 \int_t^T B^1(u,T)e^{-b^1(T-u)}du\right].\end{aligned} \tag{49}$$

We recall the expression (44) for $\frac{p(T,T+\Delta)}{\bar{p}(T,T+\Delta)}$ and the fact that, according to (46), we have

$$\begin{aligned}& E^Q\left\{e^{\kappa B^1(T,T+\Delta)\Psi_T^1} | \mathscr{F}_t\right\} \\ & = \exp\left[\frac{(\sigma^1)^2}{2}(\kappa B^1(T,T+\Delta))^2 \int_t^T e^{-2b^1(T-u)}du + \kappa B^1(T,T+\Delta)e^{-b^1(T-t)}\Psi_t^1\right].\end{aligned}$$

Inserting these expressions into (49) we obtain the result, namely

$$\begin{aligned}\bar{\nu}_{t,T} = & \frac{p(t,T)}{p(t,T+\Delta)} E^Q\left\{\frac{p(T,T+\Delta)}{\bar{p}(T,T+\Delta)} | \mathscr{F}_t\right\} \\ & \cdot \exp\left[-\kappa B^1(T,T+\Delta)(\sigma^1)^2 \int_t^T B^1(u,T)e^{-b^1(T-u)}du\right] \\ = & \frac{p(t,T)}{p(t,T+\Delta)} E^Q\left\{\frac{p(T,T+\Delta)}{\bar{p}(T,T+\Delta)} | \mathscr{F}_t\right\} \\ & \cdot \exp\left[-\frac{\kappa}{b^1}(e^{-b^1\Delta}-1)(\sigma^1)^2\left(\frac{1}{2(b^1)^2}(1-e^{-2b^1(T-t)}) - \frac{1}{(b^1)^2}(1-e^{-b^1(T-t)})\right)\right],\end{aligned} \tag{50}$$

where we have also used the fact that

$$\begin{aligned}\int_t^T B^1(u,T)e^{-b^1(T-u)}du &= \int_t^T \frac{1}{b^1}\left(1-e^{-b^1(T-u)}\right)e^{-b^1(T-u)}du \\ &= -\frac{1}{2(b^1)^2}\left(1-e^{-2b^1(T-t)}\right) + \frac{1}{(b^1)^2}\left(1-e^{-b^1(T-t)}\right).\end{aligned}$$

□

Remark 4.1 The adjustment factor $Ad_t^{T,\Delta}$ allows for some intuitive interpretations. Here we mention only the easiest one for the case when $\kappa = 0$ (independence of r_t and s_t). In this case we have $r_t + s_t > r_t$ implying that $\bar{p}(T, T + \Delta) < p(T, T + \Delta)$ so that $Ad_t^{T,\Delta} \geq 1$. Furthermore, always for $\kappa = 0$, the residual factor has value $Res_t^{T,\Delta} = 1$. All this in turn implies $\bar{\nu}_{t,T} \geq \nu_{t,T}$ and with it $\bar{R}_t \geq R_t$, which is what one would expect to be the case.

Remark 4.2 (*Calibration to the initial term structure*). The parameters in the model (10) for the factors Ψ_t^i and thus also in the model (11) for the short rate r_t and the spread s_t are the coefficients b^i and σ^i for $i = 1, 2, 3$. From (14) notice that, for $i = 1, 2$, these coefficients enter the expressions for the OIS bond prices $p(t, T)$ that can be assumed to be observable since they can be bootstrapped from the market quotes for the OIS swap rates. We may thus assume that these coefficients, i.e. b^i and σ^i for $i = 1, 2$, can be calibrated as in the pre-crisis single-curve short rate models. It remains to calibrate b^3, σ^3 and, possibly the correlation coefficient κ. Via (15) they affect the prices of the fictitious Libor bonds $\bar{p}(t, T)$ that are, however, not observable. One may observe though the FRA rates R_t and $\bar{R}_t$ and thus also $\nu_{t,T}$, as well as $\bar{\nu}_{t,T}$. Via (41) this would then allow one to calibrate also the remaining parameters. This task would turn out to be even simpler if one would have access to the value of κ by other means.

We emphasize that in order to ensure a good fit to the initial bond term structure, a deterministic shift extension of the model or time-dependent coefficients b^i could be considered. We recall also that we have assumed the mean-reversion level equal to zero for simplicity; in practice it would be one more coefficient to be calibrated for each factor Ψ_t^i.

4.2 *Interest Rate Swaps*

We first recall the notion of a *(payer) interest rate swap*. Given a collection of dates $0 \leq T_0 < T_1 < \cdots < T_n$ with $\gamma \equiv \gamma_k := T_k - T_{k-1}$ $(k = 1, \cdots, n)$, as well as a notional amount N, a payer swap is a financial contract, where a stream of interest payments on the notional N is made at a fixed rate R in exchange for receiving an analogous stream corresponding to the Libor rate. Among the various possible conventions concerning the fixing for the Libor and the payment dates, we choose here the one where, for each interval $[T_{k-1}, T_k]$, the Libor rates are fixed in advance and the payments are made in arrears. The swap is thus initiated at T_0 and the first payment is made at T_1. A *receiver swap* is completely symmetric with the interest at the fixed rate being received; here we concentrate on payer swaps.

The arbitrage-free price of the swap, evaluated at $t \leq T_0$, is given by the following expression where, analogously to $E^{T+\Delta}\{\cdot\}$, we denote by $E^{T_k}\{\cdot\}$ the expectation with respect to the forward measure Q^{T_k} $(k = 1, \cdots, n)$

$$
\begin{aligned}
P^{Sw}(t; T_0, T_n, R) &= \gamma \sum_{k=1}^{n} p(t, T_k) E^{T_k} \{L(T_{k-1}; T_{k-1}, T_k) - R | \mathscr{F}_t\} \\
&= \gamma \sum_{k=1}^{n} p(t, T_k) \left(L(t; T_{k-1}, T_k) - R\right). \qquad (51)
\end{aligned}
$$

For easier notation we have assumed the notional to be 1, i.e. $N = 1$.

We shall next obtain an explicit expression for $P^{Sw}(t; T_0, T_n, R)$ starting from the first equality in (51). To this effect, recalling from (24) that $C^{22}(t, T) = \bar{C}^{22}(t, T)$, introduce again some shorthand notation, namely

$$
\begin{aligned}
&A_k := \bar{A}(T_{k-1}, T_k),\ B_k^1 := B^1(T_{k-1}, T_k), \\
&C_k^{22} := C^{22}(T_{k-1}, T_k) = \bar{C}^{22}(T_{k-1}, T_k),\ \bar{C}_k^{33} := \bar{C}^{33}(T_{k-1}, T_k).
\end{aligned} \qquad (52)
$$

The crucial quantity to be computed in (51) is the following one

$$
\begin{aligned}
&E^{T_k}\{\gamma L(T_{k-1}; T_{k-1}, T_k) | \mathscr{F}_t\} = E^{T_k}\left\{\frac{1}{\bar{p}(T_{k-1}, T_k)} | \mathscr{F}_t\right\} - 1 \\
&= e^{A_k} E^{T_k}\{\exp((\kappa + 1) B_k^1 \Psi_{T_{k-1}}^1 + C_k^{22} (\Psi_{T_{k-1}}^2)^2 + \bar{C}_k^{33} (\Psi_{T_{k-1}}^3)^2) | \mathscr{F}_t\} - 1, \qquad (53)
\end{aligned}
$$

where we have used the first relation on the right in (30). The expectations in (53) have to be computed under the measures Q^{T_k}, under which, by analogy to (33), the factors have the dynamics

$$
\begin{aligned}
d\Psi_t^1 &= -\left[b^1 \Psi_t^1 + (\sigma^1)^2 B^1(t, T_k)\right] dt + \sigma^1 dw_t^{1,k} \\
d\Psi_t^2 &= -\left[b^2 \Psi_t^2 + 2(\sigma^2)^2 C^{22}(t, T_k) \Psi_t^2\right] dt + \sigma^2 dw_t^{2,k} \\
d\Psi_t^3 &= -b^3 \Psi_t^3 dt + \sigma^3 dw_t^{3,k}.
\end{aligned} \qquad (54)
$$

where $w^{i,k}$, $i = 1, 2, 3$, are independent Wiener processes with respect to Q^{T_k}. A straightforward generalization of (46) to the case where the factor process Ψ_t^1 satisfies the following affine Hull–White model

$$
d\Psi_t^1 = (a^1(t) - b^1 \Psi_t^1) dt + \sigma^1 dw_t
$$

can be obtained as follows

$$
E^Q\left\{\exp\left[-\int_t^T \delta \Psi_u^1 du - K \Psi_T^1\right] | \mathscr{F}_t\right\} = \exp[\alpha^1(t, T) - \beta^1(t, T) \Psi_t^1], \qquad (55)
$$

with

$$
\begin{cases}
\beta^1(t, T) = K e^{-b^1(T-t)} - \frac{\delta}{b^1}\left(e^{-b^1(T-t)} - 1\right) \\
\alpha^1(t, T) = \frac{(\sigma^1)^2}{2} \int_t^T (\beta^1(u, T))^2 du - \int_t^T a^1(u) \beta^1(u, T) du.
\end{cases} \qquad (56)
$$

We apply this result to our situation where under Q^{T_k} the process Ψ_t^1 satisfies the first SDE in (54) and thus corresponds to the above dynamics with $a^1(t) = -(\sigma^1)^2 B^1(t, T_k)$. Furthermore, setting $K = -(\kappa + 1)\, B_k^1$ and $\delta = 0$, we obtain for the first expectation in the second line of (53)

$$E^{T_k}\{\exp((\kappa + 1)B_k^1 \Psi_{T_{k-1}}^1 | \mathscr{F}_t\} = \exp[\Gamma^1(t, T_k) - \rho^1(t, T_k)\, \Psi_t^1], \tag{57}$$

with

$$\begin{cases} \rho^1(t, T_k) \;= -(\kappa + 1)B_k^1 e^{-b^1(T_k - t)} \\ \Gamma^1(t, T_k) = \frac{(\sigma^1)^2}{2} \int_t^{T_k} \left(\rho^1(u, T_k)\right)^2 du + (\sigma^1)^2 \int_t^{T_k} B^1(u, T_k)\rho^1(u, T_k) du. \end{cases} \tag{58}$$

For the remaining two expectations in the second line of (53) we shall use the following:

Lemma 4.1 *Let a generic process Ψ_t satisfy the dynamics*

$$d\Psi_t = b(t)\Psi_t dt + \sigma\, dw_t \tag{59}$$

with w_t a Wiener process. Then, for all $C \in \mathbb{R}$ such that $E^Q\left\{\exp\left[C\,(\Psi_T)^2\right]\right\} < \infty$, we have

$$E^Q\left\{\exp\left[C\,(\Psi_T)^2\right] \mid \mathscr{F}_t\right\} = \exp\left[\Gamma(t, T) - \rho(t, T)\,(\Psi_t)^2\right] \tag{60}$$

with $\rho(t, T)$ and $\Gamma(t, T)$ satisfying

$$\begin{cases} \rho_t(t, T) + 2b(t)\rho(t, T) - 2(\sigma)^2\,(\rho(t, T))^2 = 0\,; \quad \rho(T, T) = -C \\ \Gamma_t(t, T) = (\sigma)^2 \rho(t, T). \end{cases} \tag{61}$$

Proof An application of Itô's formula yields that the nonnegative process $\Phi_t := (\Psi_t)^2$ satisfies the following SDE

$$d\Phi_t = \left((\sigma)^2 + 2b(t)\,\Phi_t\right) dt + 2\sigma \sqrt{\Phi_t}\, dw_t.$$

We recall that a process Φ_t given in general form by

$$d\Phi_t = (a + \lambda(t)\Phi_t)dt + \eta \sqrt{\Phi_t}\, dw_t,$$

with $a, \eta > 0$ and $\lambda(t)$ a deterministic function, is a CIR process. Thus, $(\Psi_t)^2$ is equivalent in distribution to a CIR process with coefficients given by

$$\lambda(t) = 2b(t) \quad , \quad \eta = 2\sigma \quad , \quad a = (\sigma)^2.$$

From the theory of affine term structure models (see e.g. Lamberton and Lapeyre [23], or Lemma 2.2 in Grbac and Runggaldier [18]) it now follows that

$$\begin{aligned} E^{Q}\left\{\exp\left[C\,(\Psi_T)^2\right] \mid \mathcal{F}_t\right\} &= E^{Q}\left\{\exp\left[C\,\Phi_T\right] \mid \mathcal{F}_t\right\} = \exp\left[\Gamma(t,T) - \rho(t,T)\,\Phi_t\right] \\ &= \exp\left[\Gamma(t,T) - \rho(t,T)\,(\Psi_t)^2\right] \end{aligned}$$

with $\rho(t, T)$ and $\Gamma(t, T)$ satisfying (61).

Corollary 4.1 *When $b(t)$ is constant with respect to time, i.e. $b(t) \equiv b$, so that also $\lambda(t) \equiv \lambda$, then the equations for $\rho(t, T)$ and $\Gamma(t, T)$ in (61) admit an explicit solution given by*

$$\begin{cases} \rho(t,T) = \frac{4bhe^{2b(T-t)}}{4(\sigma)^2he^{2b(T-t)}-1} \quad \text{with} \quad h := \frac{C}{4(\sigma)^2C+4b} \\ \Gamma(t,T) = -(\sigma)^2 \int_t^T \rho(u,T)du. \end{cases} \tag{62}$$

Coming now to the second expectation in the second line of (53) and using the second equation in (54), we set

$$b(t) := -\left[b^2 + 2(\sigma^2)^2 C^{22}(t, T_k)\right],\ \sigma := \sigma^2,\ C = C_k^{22}$$

and apply Lemma 4.1, provided that the parameters b^2 and σ^2 of the process Ψ^2 are such that $C = C_k^{22}$ satisfies the assumption from the lemma. We thus obtain

$$E^{T_k}\{\exp(C_k^{22}(\Psi^2_{T_{k-1}})^2)|\mathcal{F}_t\} = \exp[\Gamma^2(t, T_k) - \rho^2(t, T_k)(\Psi_t^2)^2], \tag{63}$$

with $\rho^2(t, T)$, $\Gamma^2(t, T)$ satisfying

$$\begin{cases} \rho_t^2(t,T) - 2\left[b^2 + 2(\sigma^2)^2C^{22}(t,T_k)\right]\rho^2(t,T) - 2(\sigma^2)^2(\rho^2(t,T))^2 = 0 \\ \rho^2(T_k,T_k) = -C_k^{22} \\ \Gamma^2(t,T) = -(\sigma^2)^2 \int_t^T \rho^2(u,T)du. \end{cases} \tag{64}$$

Finally, for the third expectation in the second line of (53), we may take advantage of the fact that the dynamics of Ψ_t^3 do not change when passing from the measure Q to the forward measure Q^{T_k}. We can then apply Lemma 4.1, this time with (see the third equation in (54))

$$b(t) := -b^3,\ \sigma := \sigma^3,\ C = \bar{C}_k^{33}$$

and ensuring that the parameters b^3 and σ^3 of the process Ψ^3 are such that $C = \bar{C}_k^{33}$ satisfies the assumption from the lemma. Since $b(t)$ is constant with respect to time, also Corollary 4.1 applies and we obtain

$$E^{T_k}\{\exp(\bar{C}_k^{33}(\Psi^3_{T_{k-1}})^2)|\mathcal{F}_t\} = \exp[\Gamma^3(t, T_k) - \rho^3(t, T_k)(\Psi_t^3)^2],$$

where

$$\begin{cases} \rho^3(t,T_k) &= \frac{-4b^3 h_k^3 e^{-2b^3(T_k-t)}}{4(\sigma^3)^2 h_k^3 e^{-2b^3(T_k-t)}-1} \quad \text{with} \quad h_k^3 = \frac{\tilde{C}_k^{33}}{4(\sigma^3)^2 \tilde{C}_k^{33}-4b^3} \\ \Gamma^3(t,T_k) &= -(\sigma^3)^2 \int_t^{T_k} \rho^3(u,T_k)du. \end{cases} \tag{65}$$

With the use of the explicit expressions for the expectations in (53), and taking also into account the expression for $p(t,T)$ in (29), it follows immediately that the arbitrage-free swap price in (51) can be expressed according to the following

Proposition 4.2 *The price of a payer interest rate swap at $t \leq T_0$ is given by*

$$\begin{aligned} P^{Sw}(t;T_0,T_n,R) &= \gamma \sum_{k=1}^{n} p(t,T_k) E^{T_k}\left\{L(T_{k-1};T_{k-1},T_k) - R|\mathcal{F}_t\right\} \\ &= \sum_{k=1}^{n} p(t,T_k)\Big(D_{t,k} e^{-\rho^1(t,T_k)\Psi_t^1 - \rho^2(t,T_k)(\Psi_t^2)^2 - \rho^3(t,T_k)(\Psi_t^3)^2} - (R\gamma+1)\Big) \\ &= \sum_{k=1}^{n} \Big(D_{t,k} e^{-A_{t,k}} e^{-\tilde{B}_{t,k}^1 \Psi_t^1 - \tilde{C}_{t,k}^{22}(\Psi_t^2)^2 - \tilde{C}_{t,k}^{33}(\Psi_t^3)^2} \\ &\qquad - (R\gamma+1) e^{-A_{t,k}} e^{-B_{t,k}^1 \Psi_t^1 - C_{t,k}^{22}(\Psi_t^2)^2}\Big), \end{aligned} \tag{66}$$

where

$$\begin{aligned} &A_{t,k} := A(t,T_k),\ B_{t,k}^1 := B^1(t,T_k),\ C_{t,k}^{22} := C^{22}(t,T_k) \\ &\tilde{B}_{t,k}^1 := B_{t,k}^1 + \rho^1(t,T_k),\ \tilde{C}_{t,k}^{22} := C_{t,k}^{22} + \rho^2(t,T_k),\ \tilde{C}_{t,k}^{33} := \rho^3(t,T_k) \\ &D_{t,k} := e^{A_k} \exp[\Gamma^1(t,T_k) + \Gamma^2(t,T_k) + \Gamma^3(t,T_k)], \end{aligned} \tag{67}$$

with $\rho^i(t,T_k)$, $\Gamma^i(t,T_k)$ $(i=1,2,3)$ determined according to (58), (64), and (65) respectively and with A_k as in (52).

5 Nonlinear/optional Interest Rate Derivatives

In this section we consider the main nonlinear interest rate derivatives with the Libor rate as underlying. They are also called *optional derivatives* since they have the form of an option. In Sect. 5.1 we shall consider the case of caps and, symmetrically, that of floors. In the subsequent Sect. 5.2 we shall then concentrate on swaptions as options on a payer swap of the type discussed in Sect. 4.2.

5.1 Caps and Floors

Since floors can be treated in a completely symmetric way to the caps simply by interchanging the roles of the fixed rate and the Libor rate, we shall concentrate here on caps. Furthermore, to keep the presentation simple, we consider here just a single caplet for the time interval $[T, T+\Delta]$ and for a fixed rate R (recall also that we consider just one tenor Δ). The payoff of the caplet at time $T+\Delta$ is thus $\Delta(L(T; T, T+\Delta) - R)^+$, assuming the notional $N = 1$, and its time-t price $P^{Cpl}(t; T+\Delta, R)$ is given by the following risk-neutral pricing formula under the forward measure $Q^{T+\Delta}$

$$P^{Cpl}(t; T+\Delta, R) = \Delta\, p(t, T+\Delta) E^{T+\Delta}\left\{(L(T; T, T+\Delta) - R)^+ \mid \mathscr{F}_t\right\}.$$

In view of deriving pricing formulas, recall from Sect. 3.3 that, under the $(T+\Delta)-$forward measure, at time T the factors Ψ_T^i have independent Gaussian distributions (see (34)) with mean and variance given, for $i = 1, 2, 3$, by

$$E^{T+\Delta}\{\Psi_t^i\} = \bar{\alpha}_t^i = \bar{\alpha}_t^i(b^i, \sigma^i), \qquad Var^{T+\Delta}\{\Psi_t^i\} = \bar{\beta}_t^i = \bar{\beta}_t^i(b^i, \sigma^i).$$

In the formulas below we shall consider the joint probability density function of $(\Psi_T^1, \Psi_T^2, \Psi_T^3)$ under the $T+\Delta$ forward measure, namely, using the independence of the processes Ψ_t^i, $(i = 1, 2, 3)$,

$$f_{(\Psi_T^1, \Psi_T^2, \Psi_T^3)}(x_1, x_2, x_3) = \prod_{i=1}^{3} f_{\Psi_T^i}(x_i) = \prod_{i=1}^{3} \mathscr{N}(x_i, \bar{\alpha}_T^i, \bar{\beta}_T^i), \tag{68}$$

and use the shorthand notation $f_i(\cdot)$ for $f_{\Psi_T^i}(\cdot)$ in the sequel. We shall also write $\bar{A}, B^1, C^{22}, \bar{C}^{33}$ for the corresponding functions evaluated at $(T, T+\Delta)$ and given in (28), (27) and (24) respectively.

Setting $\tilde{R} := 1 + \Delta R$, and recalling the first equality in (30), the time-0 price of the caplet can be expressed as

$$\begin{aligned} P^{Cpl}(0; T+\Delta, R) &= \Delta\, p(0, T+\Delta) E^{T+\Delta}\left\{(L(T; T, T+\Delta) - R)^+\right\} \\ &= p(0, T+\Delta) E^{T+\Delta}\left\{\left(\frac{1}{\bar{p}(T, T+\Delta)} - \tilde{R}\right)^+\right\} \\ &= p(0, T+\Delta) E^{T+\Delta}\left\{\left(e^{\bar{A} + (\kappa+1)B^1\Psi_T^1 + C^{22}(\Psi_T^2)^2 + \bar{C}^{33}(\Psi_T^3)^2} - \tilde{R}\right)^+\right\} \\ &= p(0, T+\Delta) \int_{\mathbb{R}^3} \left(e^{\bar{A} + (\kappa+1)B^1 x + C^{22}y^2 + \bar{C}^{33}z^2} - \tilde{R}\right)^+ \\ &\quad \cdot f_{(\Psi_T^1, \Psi_T^2, \Psi_T^3)}(x, y, z) d(x, y, z). \end{aligned} \tag{69}$$

To proceed, we extend to the multi-curve context an idea suggested in Jamshidian [19] (where it is applied to the pricing of coupon bonds) by considering the function

$$g(x, y, z) := \exp[\bar{A} + (\kappa+1)B^1 x + C^{22}y^2 + \bar{C}^{33}z^2]. \tag{70}$$

Noticing that $\bar{C}^{33}(T, T+\Delta) > 0$ (see (24) together with the fact that $h^3 > 0$ and $2b^3 + h^3 > 0$), for fixed x, y the function $g(x, y, z)$ can be seen to be continuous and increasing for $z \geq 0$ and decreasing for $z < 0$ with $\lim_{z\to\pm\infty} g(x, y, z) = +\infty$. It will now be convenient to introduce some objects according to the following:

Definition 5.1 Let a set $M \subset \mathbb{R}^2$ be given by

$$M := \{(x, y) \in \mathbb{R}^2 \mid g(x, y, 0) \leq \tilde{R}\} \tag{71}$$

and let M^c be its complement. Furthermore, for $(x, y) \in M$ let

$$\bar{z}^1 = \bar{z}^1(x, y), \quad \bar{z}^2 = \bar{z}^2(x, y)$$

be the solutions of $g(x, y, z) = \tilde{R}$. They satisfy $\bar{z}^1 \leq 0 \leq \bar{z}^2$.

Notice that, for $z \leq \bar{z}^1 \leq 0$ and $z \geq \bar{z}^2 \geq 0$, we have $g(x, y, z) \geq g(x, y, \bar{z}^k) = \tilde{R}$, and for $z \in (\bar{z}^1, \bar{z}^2)$, we have $g(x, y, z) < \tilde{R}$. In M^c we have $g(x, y, z) \geq g(x, y, 0) > \tilde{R}$ and thus no solution of the equation $g(x, y, z) = \tilde{R}$.

In view of the main result of this subsection, given in Proposition 5.1 below, we prove as a preliminary the following:

Lemma 5.1 *Assuming that the (nonnegative) coefficients b^3, σ^3 in the dynamics (10) of the factor Ψ_t^3 satisfy the condition*

$$b^3 \geq \frac{\sigma^3}{\sqrt{2}}, \tag{72}$$

we have that $1 - 2\bar{\beta}_T^3 \bar{C}^{33} > 0$, where $\bar{C}^{33} = \bar{C}^{33}(T, T+\Delta)$ is given by (24) and where $\bar{\beta}_T^3 = \frac{(\sigma^3)^2}{2b^3}(1 - e^{-2b^3T})$ according to (34).

Proof From the definitions of $\bar{\beta}_T^3$ and $\bar{C}^{33}$ we may write

$$1 - 2\bar{\beta}_T^3 \bar{C}^{33} = 1 - \left(1 - e^{-2b^3T}\right) \frac{2\left(e^{\Delta h^3} - 1\right)}{2\frac{b^3h^3}{(\sigma^3)^2} + \frac{b^3}{(\sigma^3)^2}(2b^3 + h^3)\left(e^{\Delta h^3} - 1\right)}. \tag{73}$$

Notice next that $b^3 > 0$ implies that $1 - e^{-2b^3T} \in (0, 1)$ and that $\frac{b^3h^3}{(\sigma^3)^2} \geq 0$. From (73) it then follows that a sufficient condition for $1 - 2\bar{\beta}_T^3 \bar{C}^{33} > 0$ to hold is that

$$2 \leq \frac{b^3}{(\sigma^3)^2}(2b^3 + h^3). \tag{74}$$

Given that, see definition after (24), $h^3 = 2\sqrt{(b^3)^2 + 2(\sigma^3)^2} \geq 2b^3$, the condition (74) is satisfied under our assumption (72). □

Proposition 5.1 *Under assumption (72) we have that the time-0 price of the caplet for the time interval $[T, T+\Delta]$ and with fixed rate R is given by*

$$
\begin{aligned}
P^{Cpl}(0; T+\Delta, R) = p(0, T+\Delta)\Bigg[\int_M & e^{\bar{A}+(\kappa+1)B^1 x+C^{22}(y)^2} \\
& \cdot\Big[\gamma(\bar{\alpha}_T^3, \bar{\beta}_T^3, \bar{C}^{33})\left(\Phi(d^1(x,y)) + \Phi(-d^2(x,y))\right) \\
& - e^{\bar{C}^{33}(\bar{z}^1(x,y))^2}\Phi(d^3(x,y)) + e^{\bar{C}^{33}(\bar{z}^2(x,y))^2}\Phi(-d^4(x,y))\Big] \\
& \times f_1(x)f_2(y)dxdy + \gamma(\bar{\alpha}_T^3, \bar{\beta}_T^3, \bar{C}^{33})\int_{M^c} e^{\bar{A}+(\kappa+1)B^1 x+C^{22}(y)^2} \\
& \times f_1(x)f_2(y)dxdy - \tilde{R}\, Q^{T+\Delta}\left\{(\Psi_T^1, \Psi_T^2) \in M^c\right\}\Bigg],
\end{aligned} \tag{75}
$$

where $\Phi(\cdot)$ is the cumulative standard Gaussian distribution function, M and M^c are as in Definition 5.1,

$$
\begin{cases}
d^1(x,y) := \dfrac{\sqrt{1-2\bar{\beta}_T^3\bar{C}^{33}}\,\bar{z}^1(x,y)-(\bar{\alpha}_T^3-\theta\bar{\beta}_T^3)}{\sqrt{\bar{\beta}_T^3}} \\
d^2(x,y) := \dfrac{\sqrt{1-2\bar{\beta}_T^3\bar{C}^{33}}\,\bar{z}^2(x,y)-(\bar{\alpha}_T^3-\theta\bar{\beta}_T^3)}{\sqrt{\bar{\beta}_T^3}} \\
d^3(x,y) := \dfrac{\bar{z}^1(x,y)-\bar{\alpha}_T^3}{\sqrt{\bar{\beta}_T^3}} \\
d^4(x,y) := \dfrac{\bar{z}^2(x,y)-\bar{\alpha}_T^3}{\sqrt{\bar{\beta}_T^3}}
\end{cases} \tag{76}
$$

with $\theta := \dfrac{\bar{\alpha}_T^3\left(1-1/\sqrt{1-2\bar{\beta}_T^3\bar{C}^{33}}\right)}{\bar{\beta}_T^3}$, which by Lemma 5.1 is well defined under the given assumption (72), and with $\gamma(\bar{\alpha}_T^3, \bar{\beta}_T^3, \bar{C}^{33}) := \dfrac{e^{(\frac{1}{2}(\theta)^2\bar{\beta}_T^3-\bar{\alpha}_T^3\theta)}}{\sqrt{1-2\bar{\beta}_T^3\bar{C}^{33}}}$.

Remark 5.1 Notice that, once the set M and its complement M^c from Definition 5.1 are made explicit, the integrals, as well as the probability in (75), can be computed explicitly.

Proof On the basis of the sets M and M^c we can continue (69) as

$$
\begin{aligned}
P^{Cpl}(0; T+\Delta, R) &= p(0, T+\Delta)\int_{\mathbb{R}^3}\left(e^{\bar{A}+(\kappa+1)B^1 x+C^{22}y^2+\bar{C}^{33}z^2} - \tilde{R}\right)^+ \\
&\cdot f_{(\Psi_T^1,\Psi_T^2,\Psi_T^3)}(x,y,z)d(x,y,z) \\
&= p(0, T+\Delta)\int_{M\times\mathbb{R}}\left(e^{\bar{A}+(\kappa+1)B^1 x+C^{22}y^2+\bar{C}^{33}z^2} - \tilde{R}\right)^+ \\
&\cdot f_{(\Psi_T^1,\Psi_T^2,\Psi_T^3)}(x,y,z)d(x,y,z)
\end{aligned}
$$

$$
\begin{aligned}
&+ p(0, T+\Delta) \int_{M^c \times \mathbb{R}} \left(e^{\bar{A}+(\kappa+1)B^1 x + C^{22} y^2 + \bar{C}^{33} z^2} - \tilde{R} \right)^+ \\
&\cdot f_{(\Psi_T^1, \Psi_T^2, \Psi_T^3)}(x, y, z) d(x, y, z) \\
&=: P^1(0; T+\Delta) + P^2(0; T+\Delta).
\end{aligned} \tag{77}
$$

We shall next compute separately the two terms in the last equality in (77) distinguishing between two cases according to whether $(x, y) \in M$ or $(x, y) \in M^c$.

Case (i): For $(x, y) \in M$ we have from Definition 5.1 that there exist $\bar{z}^1(x, y) \leq 0$ and $\bar{z}^2(x, y) \geq 0$ so that for $z \in [\bar{z}^1, \bar{z}^2]$ we have $g(x, y, z) \leq g(x, y, \bar{z}^k) = \tilde{R}$. For $P^1(0; T+\Delta)$ we now obtain

$$
\begin{aligned}
P^1(0; T+\Delta) &= p(0, T+\Delta) \\
&\cdot \int_M e^{\bar{A}+(\kappa+1)B^1 x + C^{22} y^2} \left(\int_{-\infty}^{\bar{z}^1(x,y)} (e^{\bar{C}^{33} z^2} - e^{\bar{C}^{33} (\bar{z}^1)^2}) f_3(z) dz \right. \\
&\left. + \int_{\bar{z}^2(x,y)}^{+\infty} (e^{\bar{C}^{33} z^2} - e^{\bar{C}^{33} (\bar{z}^2)^2}) f_3(z) dz \right) f_2(y) f_1(x) dy dx.
\end{aligned} \tag{78}
$$

Next, using the results of Sect. 3.3 concerning the Gaussian distribution $f_3(\cdot) = f_{\Psi_T^3}(\cdot)$, we obtain the calculations in (79) below, where, recalling Lemma 5.1, we make successively the following changes of variables: $\zeta := \sqrt{1 - 2\bar{\beta}_T^3 \bar{C}^{33}} z$, $\theta := \frac{\bar{\alpha}_T^3 (1 - 1/\sqrt{1 - 2\bar{\beta}_T^3 \bar{C}^{33}})}{\bar{\beta}_T^3}$, $s := \frac{\zeta - (\bar{\alpha}_T^3 - \theta \bar{\beta}_T^3)}{\sqrt{\bar{\beta}_T^3}}$ and where $d^i(x, y)$, $i = 1, \cdots, 4$ are as defined in (76)

$$
\begin{aligned}
\int_{-\infty}^{\bar{z}^1(x,y)} e^{\bar{C}^{33} z^2} f_3(z) dz &= \int_{-\infty}^{\bar{z}^1(x,y)} e^{\bar{C}^{33} z^2} \frac{1}{\sqrt{2\pi \bar{\beta}_T^3}} e^{-\frac{1}{2} \frac{(z - \bar{\alpha}_T^3)^2}{\bar{\beta}_T^3}} dz \\
&= \int_{-\infty}^{\bar{z}^1(x,y)} \frac{1}{\sqrt{2\pi \bar{\beta}_T^3}} e^{-\frac{1}{2} \frac{(\sqrt{1 - 2\bar{\beta}_T^3 \bar{C}^{33}} z - \bar{\alpha}_T^3)^2}{\bar{\beta}_T^3}} e^{-\frac{\bar{\alpha}_T^3 (\sqrt{1 - 2\bar{\beta}_T^3 \bar{C}^{33}} - 1)}{\bar{\beta}_T^3} z} dz \\
&= \int_{-\infty}^{\sqrt{1 - 2\bar{\beta}_T^3 \bar{C}^{33}} \bar{z}^1(x,y)} \frac{1}{\sqrt{2\pi \bar{\beta}_T^3}} e^{-\frac{1}{2} \frac{(\zeta - \bar{\alpha}_T^3)^2}{\bar{\beta}_T^3}} e^{-\frac{\bar{\alpha}_T^3 (1 - 1/\sqrt{1 - 2\bar{\beta}_T^3 \bar{C}^{33}})}{\bar{\beta}_T^3} \zeta} \frac{1}{\sqrt{1 - 2\bar{\beta}_T^3 \bar{C}^{33}}} d\zeta \\
&= \frac{1}{\sqrt{1 - 2\bar{\beta}_T^3 \bar{C}^{33}}} \int_{-\infty}^{\sqrt{1 - 2\bar{\beta}_T^3 \bar{C}^{33}} \bar{z}^1(x,y)} \frac{1}{\sqrt{2\pi \bar{\beta}_T^3}} e^{-\frac{1}{2} \frac{(\zeta - \bar{\alpha}_T^3)^2}{\bar{\beta}_T^3}} e^{-\theta \zeta} d\zeta \\
&= \frac{e^{(\frac{1}{2}(\theta)^2 \bar{\beta}_T^3 - \bar{\alpha}_T^3 \theta)}}{\sqrt{1 - 2\bar{\beta}_T^3 \bar{C}^{33}}} \int_{-\infty}^{d^1(x,y)} \frac{1}{\sqrt{2\pi}} e^{-\frac{s^2}{2}} ds = \frac{e^{(\frac{1}{2}(\theta)^2 \bar{\beta}_T^3 - \bar{\alpha}_T^3 \theta)}}{\sqrt{1 - 2\bar{\beta}_T^3 \bar{C}^{33}}} \Phi(d^1(x, y)).
\end{aligned} \tag{79}
$$

On the other hand, always using the results of Sect. 3.3 concerning the Gaussian distribution $f_3(\cdot) = f_{\Psi_T^3}(\cdot)$ and making this time the change of variables $\zeta := \frac{(z-\bar{\alpha}_T^3)}{\sqrt{\bar{\beta}_T^3}}$, we obtain

$$\int_{-\infty}^{\bar{z}^1(x,y)} e^{\bar{C}^{33}(\bar{z}^1)^2} f_3(z)dz = e^{\bar{C}^{33}(\bar{z}^1)^2} \int_{-\infty}^{\bar{z}^1(x,y)} \frac{1}{\sqrt{2\pi\bar{\beta}_T^3}} e^{-\frac{1}{2}\frac{(z-\bar{\alpha}_T^3)^2}{\bar{\beta}_T^3}} dz$$

$$= e^{\bar{C}^{33}(\bar{z}^1)^2} \int_{-\infty}^{d^3(x,y)} \frac{1}{\sqrt{2\pi}} e^{-\frac{1}{2}\zeta^2} d\zeta = e^{\bar{C}^{33}(\bar{z}^1)^2} \Phi(d^3(x,y)). \tag{80}$$

Similarly, we have

$$\int_{\bar{z}^2(x,y)}^{+\infty} e^{\bar{C}^{33}z^2} f_3(z)dz = \frac{1}{\sqrt{1-2\bar{\beta}_T^3\bar{C}^{33}}} e^{\left(\frac{1}{2}(\theta)^2\bar{\beta}_T^3 - \bar{\alpha}_T^3\theta\right)} \Phi(-d^2(x,y)) \tag{81}$$

$$\int_{\bar{z}^2(x,y)}^{+\infty} e^{\bar{C}^{33}(\bar{z}^1)^2} f_3(z)dz = e^{\bar{C}^{33}(\bar{z}^2)^2} \Phi(-d^4(x,y)).$$

Case (ii): We come next to the case $(x, y) \in M^c$, for which $g(x, y, z) \geq g(x, y, 0) > \tilde{R}$. For $P^2(0; T + \Delta)$ we obtain

$$\begin{aligned} P^2(0;T+\Delta) &= p(0,T+\Delta)\int_{M^c\times\mathbb{R}} \left(e^{\bar{A}+(\kappa+1)B^1x+C^{22}y^2+\bar{C}^{33}z^2} - \tilde{R}\right) \\ &\quad \cdot f_3(z)f_2(y)f_1(x)dzdydx \\ &= p(0,T+\Delta)\Big(e^{\bar{A}}\int_{M^c} e^{(\kappa+1)B^1x+C^{22}y^2} f_1(x)f_2(y)dxdy \int_{\mathbb{R}} e^{\bar{C}^{33}z^2} f_3(z)dz \\ &\quad - \tilde{R}Q^{T+\Delta}[(\Psi_T^1,\Psi_T^2)\in M^c]\Big) \\ &= p(0,T+\Delta)\Big(e^{\bar{A}}\Big[\int_{M^c} e^{(\kappa+1)B^1x+C^{22}y^2} f_1(x)f_2(y)dxdy\Big] \frac{e^{\left(\frac{1}{2}(\theta^3)^2\bar{\beta}_T^3-\bar{\alpha}_T^3\theta^3\right)}}{\sqrt{1-2\bar{\beta}_T^3\bar{C}^{33}}} \\ &\quad - \tilde{R}Q^{T+\Delta}[(\Psi_T^1,\Psi_T^2)\in M^c]\Big), \end{aligned} \tag{82}$$

where we computed the integral over $\mathbb{R}$ analogously to (79).

Adding the two expressions derived for Cases (i) and (ii), we obtain the statement of the proposition. □

5.2 Swaptions

We start by recalling some of the most relevant aspects of a (payer) swaption. Considering a swap (see Sect. 4.2) for a given collection of dates $0 \leq T_0 < T_1 < \cdots < T_n$, a swaption is an option to enter the swap at a pre-specified initiation date $T \leq T_0$, which is thus also the maturity of the swaption and that, for simplicity of notation, we assume to coincide with T_0, i.e. $T = T_0$. The arbitrage-free swaption price at $t \leq T_0$ can be computed as

$$P^{Swn}(t; T_0, T_n, R) = p(t, T_0)E^{T_0}\left\{\left(P^{Sw}(T_0; T_n, R)\right)^+ | \mathscr{F}_t\right\}, \tag{83}$$

where we have used the shorthand notation $P^{Sw}(T_0; T_n, R) = P^{Sw}(T_0; T_0, T_n, R)$.

We first state the next Lemma, that follows immediately from the expression for $\rho^3(t, T_k)$ and the corresponding expression for h_k^3 in (65).

Lemma 5.2 *We have the equivalence*

$$\rho^3(t, T_k) > 0 \Leftrightarrow h_k^3 \in \left(0, \frac{1}{4(\sigma^3)^2 e^{-2b^3(T_k - t)}}\right). \tag{84}$$

This lemma prompts us to split the swaption pricing problem into two cases:

$$\begin{aligned} &\textbf{Case(1)}: \ h_k^3 < 0 \text{ or } h_k^3 > \frac{1}{4(\sigma^3)^2 e^{-2b^3(T_k - t)}} \\ &\textbf{Case(2)}: \ 0 < h_k^3 < \frac{1}{4(\sigma^3)^2 e^{-2b^3(T_k - t)}}. \end{aligned} \tag{85}$$

Note from the definition of $\rho^3(t, T_k)$ that $h_k^3 \neq \frac{1}{4(\sigma^3)^2 e^{-2b^3(T_k - t)}}$ and that $h_k^3 = 0$ would imply $\bar{C}_k^{33} = 0$ which corresponds to a trivial case in which the factor Ψ^3 is not present in the dynamics of the spread s, hence the inequalities in Case (1) and Case (2) above are indeed strict.

To proceed, we shall introduce some more notation. In particular, instead of only one function $g(x, y, z)$ as in (70), we shall consider also a function $h(x, y)$, more precisely, we shall define here the continuous functions

$$g(x, y, z) := \sum_{k=1}^{n} D_{0,k} e^{-A_{0,k}} e^{-\tilde{B}_{0,k}^1 x - \tilde{C}_{0,k}^{22} y^2 - \tilde{C}_{0,k}^{33} z^2} \tag{86}$$

$$h(x, y) := \sum_{k=1}^{n} (R\gamma + 1) e^{-A_{0,k}} e^{-B_{0,k}^1 x - C_{0,k}^{22} y^2}, \tag{87}$$

with the coefficients given by (67) for $t = T_0$. Note that by a slight abuse of notation we write $D_{0,k}$ for $D_{T_0,k}$ and similarly for other coefficients above, always meaning $t = T_0$ in (67). We distinguish the two cases specified in (85):

For *Case (1)* we have (see (67) and Lemma 5.2) that $\tilde{C}^{33}_{0,k} = \rho^3(T_0, T_k) < 0$ for all $k = 1, \cdots, n$, and so the function $g(x, y, z)$ in (86) is, for given (x, y), monotonically increasing for $z \geq 0$ and decreasing for $z < 0$ with

$$\lim_{z \to \pm\infty} g(x, y, z) = +\infty.$$

For *Case (2)* we have instead that $\tilde{C}^{33}_{0,k} = \rho^3(T_0, T_k) > 0$ for all $k = 1, \cdots, n$ and so the nonnegative function $g(x, y, z)$ in (86) is, for given (x, y), monotonically decreasing for $z \geq 0$ and increasing for $z < 0$ with

$$\lim_{z \to \pm\infty} g(x, y, z) = 0.$$

Analogously to Definition 5.1 we next introduce the following objects:

Definition 5.2 Let a set $\bar{M} \subset \mathbb{R}^2$ be given by

$$\bar{M} := \{(x, y) \in \mathbb{R}^2 \mid g(x, y, 0) \leq h(x, y)\}. \tag{88}$$

Since $g(x, y, z)$ and $h(x, y)$ are continuous, $\bar{M}$ is closed, measurable and connected. Let $\bar{M}^c$ be its complement. Furthermore, we define two functions $\bar{z}^1(x, y)$ and $\bar{z}^2(x, y)$ distinguishing between the two Cases (1) and (2) as specified in (85).

Case (1) If $(x, y) \in \bar{M}$, we have $g(x, y, 0) \leq h(x, y)$ and so there exist $\bar{z}^1(x, y) \leq 0$ and $\bar{z}^2(x, y) \geq 0$ for which, for $i = 1, 2$,

$$\begin{aligned} g(x, y, \bar{z}^i) &= \sum_{k=1}^{n} D_{0,k} e^{-A_{0,k}} e^{-\tilde{B}^1_{0,k} x - \tilde{C}^{22}_{0,k} y^2 - \tilde{C}^{33}_{0,k} (\bar{z}^i)^2} \\ &= \sum_{k=1}^{n} (R\gamma + 1) e^{-A_{0,k}} e^{-B^1_{0,k} x - C^{22}_{0,k} y^2} = h(x, y) \end{aligned} \tag{89}$$

and, for $z \notin [\bar{z}^1, \bar{z}^2]$, one has $g(x, y, z) \geq g(x, y, \bar{z}^i)$.
If $(x, y) \in \bar{M}^c$, we have $g(x, y, 0) > h(x, y)$ so that $g(x, y, z) \geq g(x, y, 0) > h(x, y)$ for all z and we have no points corresponding to $\bar{z}^1(x, y)$ and $\bar{z}^2(x, y)$ above.

Case (2) If $(x, y) \in \bar{M}$, we have, as for Case (1), $g(x, y, 0) \leq h(x, y)$ and so there exist $\bar{z}^1(x, y) \leq 0$ and $\bar{z}^2(x, y) \geq 0$ for which, for $i = 1, 2$, (89) holds. However, this time it is for $z \in [\bar{z}^1, \bar{z}^2]$ that one has $g(x, y, z) \geq g(x, y, \bar{z}^i)$.
If $(x, y) \in M^c$, then we are in the same situation as for Case (1).

Starting from (83) combined with (66) and taking into account the set $\bar{M}$ according to Definition 5.2, we can obtain the following expression for the swaption price at $t = 0$. As for the caps, here too we consider the joint Gaussian distribution $f_{(\Psi^1_{T_0}, \Psi^2_{T_0}, \Psi^3_{T_0})}(x, y, z)$ of the factors under the T_0−forward measure Q^{T_0} and we have

$$
\begin{aligned}
&P^{Swn}(0; T_0, T_n, R) = p(0, T_0) E^{T_0} \left\{ \left(P^{Sw}(T_0; T_n, R) \right)^{+} | \mathcal{F}_0 \right\} \\
&= p(0, T_0) \int_{\mathbb{R}^3} \Big[\sum_{k=1}^{n} D_{0,k} e^{-A_{0,k}} \exp(-\tilde{B}^1_{0,k} x - \tilde{C}^{22}_{0,k} y^2 - \tilde{C}^{33}_{0,k} z^2) \\
&- \sum_{k=1}^{n} (R\gamma + 1) e^{-A_{0,k}} \exp(-B^1_{0,k} x - C^{22}_{0,k} y^2) \Big]^{+} f_{(\Psi^1_{T_0}, \Psi^2_{T_0}, \Psi^3_{T_0})}(x, y, z) dx dy dz \\
&= p(0, T_0) \int_{\bar{M} \times \mathbb{R}} \Big[\sum_{k=1}^{n} D_{0,k} e^{-A_{0,k}} \exp(-\tilde{B}^1_{0,k} x - \tilde{C}^{22}_{0,k} y^2 - \tilde{C}^{33}_{0,k} z^2) \\
&- \sum_{k=1}^{n} (R\gamma + 1) e^{-A_{0,k}} \exp(-B^1_{0,k} x - C^{22}_{0,k} y^2) \Big]^{+} f_{(\Psi^1_{T_0}, \Psi^2_{T_0}, \Psi^3_{T_0})}(x, y, z) dx dy dz \\
&+ p(0, T_0) \int_{\bar{M}^c \times \mathbb{R}} \Big[\sum_{k=1}^{n} D_{0,k} e^{-A_{0,k}} \exp(-\tilde{B}^1_{0,k} x - \tilde{C}^{22}_{0,k} y^2 - \tilde{C}^{33}_{0,k} z^2) \\
&- \sum_{k=1}^{n} (R\gamma + 1) e^{-A_{0,k}} \exp(-B^1_{0,k} x - C^{22}_{0,k} y^2) \Big]^{+} f_{(\Psi^1_{T_0}, \Psi^2_{T_0}, \Psi^3_{T_0})}(x, y, z) dx dy dz \\
&=: P^1(0; T_0, T_n, R) + P^2(0; T_0, T_n, R).
\end{aligned}
\tag{90}
$$

We can now state and prove the main result of this subsection consisting in a pricing formula for swaptions for the Gaussian exponentially quadratic model of this paper. We have

Proposition 5.2 *Assume that the parameters in the model are such that, if h^3_k belongs to Case (1) in (85) and $h^3_k > 0$, then $h^3_k > \frac{1}{4(\sigma^3)^2 e^{-2b^3 T_k}}$. The arbitrage-free price at $t = 0$ of the swaption with payment dates $T_1 < \cdots < T_n$ such that $\gamma = \gamma_k := T_k - T_{k-1}$ $(k = 1, \cdots, n)$, with a given fixed rate R and a notional $N = 1$, can be computed as follows where we distinguish between the Cases (1) and (2) specified in Definition 5.2.*

Case (1) *We have*

$$
\begin{aligned}
P^{Swn}(0; T_0, T_n, R) = p(0, T_0) \Bigg\{ \sum_{k=1}^{n} e^{-A_{0,k}} \Bigg[\int_{\bar{M}} & D_{0,k} \exp(-\tilde{B}^1_{0,k} x - \tilde{C}^{22}_{0,k} y^2) \\
& \cdot \Bigg(\frac{e^{(\frac{1}{2}(\theta_k)^2 \bar{\beta}^3_{T_0} - \bar{\alpha}^3_{T_0} \theta_k)}}{\sqrt{1 + 2\bar{\beta}^3_{T_0} \tilde{C}^{33}_{0,k}}} \Phi(d^1_k(x, y)) - e^{-\tilde{C}^{33}_{0,k} (\bar{z}^1)^2} \Phi(d^2_k(x, y)) \\
& + \frac{e^{(\frac{1}{2}(\theta_k)^2 \bar{\beta}^3_{T_0} - \bar{\alpha}^3_{T_0} \theta_k)}}{\sqrt{1 + 2\bar{\beta}^3_{T_0} \tilde{C}^{33}_{0,k}}} \Phi(-d^3_k(x, y)) - e^{-\tilde{C}^{33}_{0,k} (\bar{z}^2)^2} \Phi(-d^4_k(x, y)) \Bigg)
\end{aligned}
$$

$$\times f_2(y)f_1(x)dydx + \int_{\bar{M}^c}\Bigg(D_{0,k}e^{-\tilde{B}^1_{0,k}x-\tilde{C}^{22}_{0,k}y^2}\frac{e^{\left(\frac{1}{2}(\theta_k)^2\bar{\beta}^3_{T_0}-\bar{\alpha}^3_{T_0}\theta_k\right)}}{\sqrt{1+2\bar{\beta}^3_{T_0}\tilde{C}^{33}_{0,k}}}$$

$$-(R\gamma+1)e^{-B^1_{0,k}x-C^{22}_{0,k}y^2}\Bigg)f_2(y)f_1(x)dydx\Bigg]\Bigg\}. \quad (91)$$

Case (2) *We have*

$$P^{Swn}(0;T_0,T_n,R) = p(0,T_0)\Bigg\{\sum_{k=1}^{n} e^{-A_{0,k}}$$

$$\Bigg[\int_{\bar{M}} D_{0,k}\exp(-\tilde{B}^1_{0,k}x - \tilde{C}^{22}_{0,k}y^2)\Bigg(\frac{e^{\left(\frac{1}{2}(\theta_k)^2\bar{\beta}^3_{T_0}-\bar{\alpha}^3_{T_0}\theta_k\right)}}{\sqrt{1+2\bar{\beta}^3_{T_0}\tilde{C}^{33}_{0,k}}}$$

$$\times\Big[\Phi(d^3_k(x,y)) - \Phi(d^1_k(x,y))\Big] - e^{-\tilde{C}^{33}_{0,k}(\bar{z}^1)^2}\Big[\Phi(d^4_k(x,y))$$

$$-\Phi(d^2_k(x,y))\Big]\Bigg)f_2(y)f_1(x)dydx$$

$$+\int_{\bar{M}^c}\Bigg(D_{0,k}e^{-\tilde{B}^1_{0,k}x-\tilde{C}^{22}_{0,k}y^2}\frac{e^{\left(\frac{1}{2}(\theta_k)^2\bar{\beta}^3_{T_0}-\bar{\alpha}^3_{T_0}\theta_k\right)}}{\sqrt{1+2\bar{\beta}^3_{T_0}\tilde{C}^{33}_{0,k}}}$$

$$-(R\gamma+1)e^{-B^1_{0,k}x-C^{22}_{0,k}y^2}\Bigg)f_2(y)f_1(x)dydx\Bigg]\Bigg\}. \quad (92)$$

The coefficients in these formulas are as specified in (67) for $t = T_0, f_1(x), f_2(x)$ *are the Gaussian densities corresponding to (68) for* $T = T_0$ *and the functions* $d^i_k(x,y)$, *for* $i = 1,\ldots,4$ *and* $k = 1,\ldots,n$, *are given by*

$$\begin{cases} d^1_k(x,y) := \dfrac{\sqrt{1+2\bar{\beta}^3_{T_0}\tilde{C}^{33}_{0,k}}\,\bar{z}^1(x,y)-(\bar{\alpha}^3_{T_0}-\theta_k\bar{\beta}^3_{T_0})}{\sqrt{\bar{\beta}^3_{T_0}}} \\ d^2_k(x,y) := \dfrac{\bar{z}^1(x,y)-\bar{\alpha}^3_{T_0}}{\sqrt{\bar{\beta}^3_{T_0}}} \\ d^3_k(x,y) := \dfrac{\sqrt{1+2\bar{\beta}^3_{T_0}\tilde{C}^{33}_{0,k}}\,\bar{z}^2(x,y)-(\bar{\alpha}^3_{T_0}-\theta_k\bar{\beta}^3_{T_0})}{\sqrt{\bar{\beta}^3_{T_0}}} \\ d^4_k(x,y) := \dfrac{\bar{z}^2(x,y)-\bar{\alpha}^3_{T_0}}{\sqrt{\bar{\beta}^3_{T_0}}} \end{cases} \quad (93)$$

with $\theta_k := \frac{\bar{\alpha}^3_{T_0}\left(1-1/\sqrt{1+2\bar{\beta}^3_{T_0}\tilde{C}^{33}_{0,k}}\right)}{\bar{\beta}^3_{T_0}}$, *for* $k = 1,\ldots,n$, *and where* $\bar{z}^1 = \bar{z}^1(x,y)$, $\bar{z}^2 = \bar{z}^2(x,y)$ *are solutions in* z *of the equation* $g(x,y,z) = h(x,y)$.

In addition, the mean and variance values for the Gaussian factors $(\Psi^1_{T_0}, \Psi^2_{T_0}, \Psi^3_{T_0})$ *are here given by*

$$\begin{cases} \bar{\alpha}^1_{T_0} &= e^{-b^1 T_0}\Psi^1_0 - \frac{(\sigma^1)^2}{2(b^1)^2} e^{-b^1 T_0}(1-e^{2b^1 T_0}) - \frac{(\sigma^1)^2}{(b^1)^2}(1-e^{b^1 T_0})\Big] \\ \bar{\beta}^1_{T_0} &= e^{-2b^1 T_0}(e^{2b^1 T_0}-1)\frac{(\sigma^1)^2}{2(b^1)} \\ \bar{\alpha}^2_{T_0} &= e^{-b^2 T_0}\Psi^2_0 \\ \bar{\beta}^2_{T_0} &= e^{-2b^2 T_0}\int_0^{T_0} e^{2b^2 u + 4(\sigma^2)^2 \bar{C}^{22}(u,T_0)}(\sigma^2)^2 du \\ \bar{\alpha}^3_{T_0} &= e^{-b^3 T_0}\Psi^3_0 \\ \bar{\beta}^3_{T_0} &= e^{-2b^3 T_0}\frac{(\sigma^3)^2}{2b^3}(e^{2b^3 T_0}-1). \end{cases} \tag{94}$$

Remark 5.2 A remark analogous to Remark 5.1 applies here too concerning the sets $\bar{M}$ and $\bar{M}^c$.

Proof First of all notice that, when $h^3_k < 0$ or $h^3_k > \frac{1}{4(\sigma^3)^2 e^{-2b^3 T_k}}$ in Case (1), this implies $1 + 2\bar{\beta}^3_{T_0}\tilde{C}^{33}_{0,k} \geq 0$ (in Case (2) we always have $1 + 2\bar{\beta}^3_{T_0}\tilde{C}^{33}_{0,k} \geq 0$). Hence, the square-root of the latter expression in the various formulas of the statement of the proposition is well-defined. This can be checked, similarly as in the proof of Lemma 5.1, by direct computation taking into account the definitions of $\bar{\beta}^3_{T_0}$ in (94) and of $\tilde{C}^{33}_{0,k}$ in (67) and (65) for $t = T_0$.

We come now to the statement for:

Case 1. We distinguish between whether $(x, y) \in \bar{M}$ or $(x, y) \in \bar{M}^c$ and compute separately the two terms in the last equality in (90).

(i) For $(x, y) \in \bar{M}$ we have from Definition 5.2 that there exist $\bar{z}^1(x, y) \leq 0$ and $\bar{z}^2(x, y) \geq 0$ so that, for $z \notin [\bar{z}^1, \bar{z}^2]$, one has $g(x, y, z) \geq g(x, y, \bar{z}^i)$. Taking into account that, under Q^{T_0}, the random variables $\Psi^1_{T_0}, \Psi^2_{T_0}, \Psi^3_{T_0}$ are independent, so that we shall write $f_{(\Psi^1_{T_0},\Psi^2_{T_0},\Psi^3_{T_0})}(x, y, z) = f_1(x)f_2(y)f_3(z)$ (see also (68) and the line following it), we obtain

$$\begin{aligned} P^1(0; T_0, T_n, R) = p(0, T_0)\Big[\sum_{k=1}^{n} D_{0,k}e^{-A_{0,k}} \int_{M} \exp(-\tilde{B}^1_{0,k}x - \tilde{C}^{22}_{0,k}y^2) \\ \cdot\Big(\int_{-\infty}^{\bar{z}^1(x,y)} \exp(-\tilde{C}^{33}_{0,k}z^2)f_3(z)dz \\ - \int_{-\infty}^{\bar{z}^1(x,y)} \exp(-\tilde{C}^{33}_{0,k}(\bar{z}^1)^2)f_3(z)dz \\ + \int_{\bar{z}^2(x,y)}^{+\infty} \exp(-\tilde{C}^{33}_{0,k}z^2)f_3(z)dz \\ - \int_{\bar{z}^2(x,y)}^{+\infty} \exp(-\tilde{C}^{33}_{0,k}(\bar{z}^2)^2)f_3(z)dz\Big)f_2(y)f_1(x)dydx\Big]. \end{aligned} \tag{95}$$

By means of calculations that are completely analogous to those in the proof of Proposition 5.1, we obtain, corresponding to (79)–(81) respectively and with the same meaning of the symbols, the following explicit expressions for the integrals in the last four lines of (95), namely

$$\int_{-\infty}^{\bar{z}^1(x,y)} e^{-\tilde{C}^{33}_{0,k}z^2} f_3(z)dz = \frac{e^{\left(\frac{1}{2}(\theta_k)^2\bar{\beta}^3_{T_0} - \bar{\alpha}^3_{T_0}\theta_k\right)}}{\sqrt{1 + 2\bar{\beta}^3_{T_0}\tilde{C}^{33}_{0,k}}}\Phi(d^1_k(x, y)), \tag{96}$$

$$\int_{-\infty}^{\bar{z}^1(x,y)} e^{-\tilde{C}^{33}_{0,k}(\bar{z}^1)^2} f_3(z)dz = e^{-\tilde{C}^{33}_{0,k}(\bar{z}^1)^2}\Phi(d^2_k(x, y)), \tag{97}$$

and, similarly,

$$\begin{aligned} \int_{\bar{z}^2(x,y)}^{+\infty} e^{-\tilde{C}^{33}_{0,k}z^2} f_3(z)dz &= \frac{e^{\left(\frac{1}{2}(\theta_k)^2\bar{\beta}^3_{T_0} - \bar{\alpha}^3_{T_0}\theta_k\right)}}{\sqrt{1 + 2\bar{\beta}^3_{T_0}\tilde{C}^{33}_{0,k}}}\Phi(-d^3_k(x, y)), \\ \int_{\bar{z}^2(x,y)}^{+\infty} e^{-\tilde{C}^{33}_{0,k}(\bar{z}^2)^2} f_3(z)dz &= e^{-\tilde{C}^{33}_{0,k}(\bar{z}^2)^2}\Phi(-d^4_k(x, y)), \end{aligned} \tag{98}$$

where the $d^i_k(x, y)$, for $i = 1, \ldots, 4$ and $k = 1, \ldots, n$, are as specified in (93).

(ii) If $(x, y) \in \bar{M}^c$ then, according to Definition 5.2 we have $g(x, y, z) \geq g(x, y, 0) > h(x, y)$ for all z. Noticing that, analogously to (96),

$$\int_{\mathbb{R}} e^{-\tilde{C}^{33}_{0,k}\zeta^2} f_3(\zeta)d\zeta = \frac{e^{\left(\frac{1}{2}(\theta_k)^2\bar{\beta}^3_{T_0} - \bar{\alpha}^3_{T_0}\theta_k\right)}}{\sqrt{1 + 2\bar{\beta}^3_{T_0}\tilde{C}^{33}_{0,k}}}$$

we obtain the following expression

$$\begin{aligned} P^2(0; T_0, T_n, R) &= p(0, T_0)\sum_{k=1}^{n} e^{-A_{0,k}}\Big[\int_{\bar{M}^c\times\mathbb{R}}\Big(D_{0,k}e^{-\bar{B}^1_{0,k}x - \tilde{C}^{22}_{0,k}y^2 - \tilde{C}^{33}_{0,k}z^2} \\ &\quad - (R\gamma + 1)e^{-B^1_{0,k}x - C^{22}_{0,k}y^2}\Big)f_3(z)f_2(y)f_1(x)dzdydx\Big] \\ &= p(0, T_0)\sum_{k=1}^{n} e^{-A_{0,k}}\Big[D_{0,k}\Big(\int_{M^c} e^{-\bar{B}^1_{0,k}x - \tilde{C}^{22}_{0,k}y^2} f_2(y)f_1(x)dydx\Big) \\ &\quad \times \frac{e^{\left(\frac{1}{2}(\theta_k)^2\bar{\beta}^3_{T_0} - \bar{\alpha}^3_{T_0}\theta_k\right)}}{\sqrt{1 + 2\bar{\beta}^3_{T_0}\tilde{C}^{33}_{0,k}}} - (R\gamma + 1)\Big(\int_{\bar{M}^c} e^{-B^1_{0,k}x - C^{22}_{0,k}y^2} f_2(y)f_1(x)dydx\Big)\Big]. \end{aligned} \tag{99}$$

Adding the two expressions in (i) and (ii) we obtain the statement for Case 1.

Case (2). Also for this case we distinguish between whether $(x, y) \in \bar{M}$ or $(x, y) \in \bar{M}^c$ and, again, compute separately the two terms in the last equality in (90).

(i) For $(x, y) \in \bar{M}$ we have that there exist $\bar{z}^1(x, y) \le 0$ and $\bar{z}^2(x, y) \ge 0$ so that, contrary to Case 1), one has $g(x, y, z) \ge g(x, y, \bar{z}^i)$ when $z \in [\bar{z}^1, \bar{z}^2]$. It follows that

$$\begin{aligned}
P^1(0; T_0, T_n, R) &= p(0, T_0)\Bigg[\sum_{k=1}^{n} D_{0,k} e^{-A_{0,k}} \int_{\bar{M}} \exp(-\tilde{B}^1_{0,k}x - \tilde{C}^{22}_{0,k}y^2) \\
&\quad \cdot \Bigg(\int_{\bar{z}^1(x,y)}^{\bar{z}^2(x,y)} \exp(-\tilde{C}^{33}_{0,k}z^2) f_3(z)dz \\
&\quad - \int_{\bar{z}^1(x,y)}^{\bar{z}^2(x,y)} \exp(-\tilde{C}^{33}_{0,k}(\bar{z}^1)^2) f_3(z)dz\Bigg) f_2(y) f_1(x) dy dx\Bigg] \\
&= p(0, T_0)\Bigg[\sum_{k=1}^{n} D_{0,k} e^{-A_{0,k}} \int_{\bar{M}} \exp(-\tilde{B}^1_{0,k}x - \tilde{C}^{22}_{0,k}y^2) \\
&\quad \cdot \Bigg(\frac{e^{\left(\frac{1}{2}(\theta_k)^2 \bar{\beta}^3_{T_0} - \bar{\alpha}^3_{T_0}\theta_k\right)}}{\sqrt{1 + 2\bar{\beta}^3_{T_0}\tilde{C}^{33}_{0,k}}} \Big(\Phi(d^3_k(x, y)) - \Phi(d^1_k(x, y))\Big) \\
&\quad - e^{-\tilde{C}^{33}_{0,k}(\bar{z}^1)^2} \Big(\Phi(d^4_k(x, y)) - \Phi(d^2_k(x, y))\Big)\Bigg) f_2(y) f_1(x) dy dx\Bigg],
\end{aligned} \tag{100}$$

where we have made use of (96) and (97), (98).

(ii) For $(x, y) \in \bar{M}^c$ we can conclude exactly as we did it for Case (1) and, by adding the two expressions in (i) and (ii), we obtain the statement also for Case (2).

Acknowledgements The KPMG Center of Excellence in Risk Management is acknowledged for organizing the conference "Challenges in Derivatives Markets - Fixed Income Modeling, Valuation Adjustments, Risk Management, and Regulation".

References

1. Bormetti, G., Brigo, D., Francischello, M., Pallavicini, A.: Impact of multiple curve dynamics in credit valuation adjustments under collateralization. Preprint, arXiv:1507.08779 (2015)
2. Brigo, D., Mercurio, F.: Interest Rate Models – Theory and Practice, 2nd edn. Springer, Berlin (2006)
3. Brigo, D., Pallavicini, A., Perini, D.: Funding, collateral and hedging: uncovering the mechanics and the subtleties of funding valuation adjustments. Preprint, arXiv:1210.3811, 2012
4. Brigo, D., Morini, M., Pallavicini, A.: Counterparty Credit Risk, Collateral and Funding: With Pricing Cases for All Asset Classes. Wiley, New Jersey (2013)
5. Chen, L., Filipović, D., Poor, H.V.: Quadratic term structure models for risk-free and defaultable rates. Math. Financ. **14**, 515–536 (2004)
6. Crépey, S.: Bilateral counterparty risk under funding constraints - Part II: CVA. Math. Financ. **25**(1), 23–50 (2015)
7. Crépey, S., Douady, R.: LOIS: credit and liquidity. Risk Mag. pp. 82–86 (2013)
8. Crépey, S., Grbac, Z., Nguyen, H.N.: A multiple-curve HJM model of interbank risk. Math. Financ. Econ. **6**(3), 155–190 (2012)
9. Crépey, S., Bielecki, T.R., Brigo, D.: Counterparty Risk and Funding–A Tale of Two Puzzles. Financial Mathematics Series. Chapman & Hall/CRC, Boca Raton (2014)

10. Duffee, G.: Estimating the price of default risk. Rev. Financ. Stud. **12**, 197–226 (1999)
11. Duffie, D., Gârleanu, N.: Risk and valuation of collateralized debt obligations. Financ. Anal. J. **57**, 41–59 (2001)
12. El Karoui, N., Myneni, R., Viswanathan, R.: Arbitrage pricing and hedging of interest rate claims with state variables, theory and applications. Working Paper (1992)
13. Filipović, D.: Separable term structures and the maximal degree problem. Math. Financ. **12**, 341–349 (2002)
14. Filipović, D., Trolle, A.B.: The term structure of interbank risk. J. Financ. Econ. **109**(3), 707–733 (2013)
15. Gallitschke, J., Müller, S., Seifried, F.T.: Post-crisis interest rates: XIBOR mechanics and basis spreads. Preprint, SSRN/2448657 (2014)
16. Gaspar, R.M.: General quadratic term structures for bond, futures and forward prices. SSE/EFI Working paper Series in Economics and Finance, p. 559 (2004)
17. Gombani, A., Runggaldier, W.J.: A filtering approach to pricing in multifactor term structure models. Int. J. Theor. Appl. Financ. **4**, 303–320 (2001)
18. Grbac, Z., Runggaldier, W.J.: Interest Rate Modeling: Post-Crisis Challenges and Approaches. Springer Briefs in Quantitative Finance. Springer International Publishing (2015)
19. Jamshidian, F.: An exact bond option pricing formula. J. Financ. **44**, 205–209 (1989)
20. Kenyon, C.: Short-rate pricing after the liquidity and credit shocks: including the basis. Risk Mag. pp. 83–87 (2010)
21. Kijima, M., Muromachi, Y.: Reformulation of the arbitrage-free pricing method under the multi-curve environment. Preprint (2015)
22. Kijima, M., Tanaka, K., Wong, T.: A multi-quality model of interest rates. Quant. Financ. **9**(2), 133–145 (2009)
23. Lamberton, D., Lapeyre, B.: Introduction to Stochastic Calculus Applied to Finance. Chapman and Hall/CRC, Boca Raton (2007)
24. Leippold, M., Wu, L.: Asset pricing under the quadratic class. J. Financ. Quant. Anal. **37**(2), 271–291 (2002)
25. Meneghello, L.: Interest rate derivatives pricing in multicurve factor models. Master Thesis, University of Padova (2014)
26. Mercurio, F.: LIBOR market models with stochastic basis. Preprint, SSRN/1563685 (2010)
27. Morino, L., Runggaldier, W.J.: On multicurve models for the term structure. In: Dieci, R., He, X.Z., Hommes, C. (eds.) Nonlinear Economic Dynamics and Financial Modelling, pp. 275–290. Springer, Berlin (2014)
28. Pallavicini, A., Brigo, D.: Interest-rate modelling in collateralized markets: multiple curves, credit-liquidity effects, CCPs. Preprint, arXiv:1304.1397 (2013)
29. Pelsser, A.: A tractable yield-curve model that guarantees positive interest rates. Rev. Deriv. Res. **1**, 269–284 (1997)

2

Multi-Curve Construction: Definition, Calibration, Implementation and Application of Rate Curves

Christian P. Fries

Abstract In this chapter we discuss the definition, construction, interpolation and application of *curves*. We will discuss discount curves, a tool for the valuation of deterministic cash-flows and forward curves, a tool for the valuation of linear cash-flows of an index. A curve is mainly a tool to interpolate certain basic financial products (zero coupon bonds, FRAs) with respect to maturity date and fixing date, such that it can be used to value products, which can be represented as linear functions of possibly interpolated values of a discount or forward curve. For this, the chosen interpolation method and interpolation entity plays an important role. Distinguishing forward curves from discount curves (representing the collateralization of the forward) motivates an alternative interpolation method, namely interpolation of the forward value (the product of the forward and the discount factor). In addition, treating forward curves as native curves (instead of representing them by pseudo-discount curves) will avoid other problems, like that of overlapping instruments. Besides the interpolation, we discuss the calibration of the curves for which we give a generic object-oriented implementation in Fries (Curve calibration. Object-oriented reference implementation, 2010–2015, [11]). We give some numerical results, which have been obtained using this implementation and conclude with a remark on how to define term-structure models (analog to a LIBOR market model) based on the definition of the performance index of an accrual account associated with a discount curve.

Keywords Multi-curve construction · Interest rate curves · Interest rate curve interpolation · Cross-currency curves · Term structure models

C.P. Fries (✉)
DZ BANK AG, Frankfurt, Germany
e-mail: email@christian fries.de

C.P. Fries
Department of Mathematics, LMU Munich, Munich, Germany

1 Introduction

Dynamic multi-curve term structure models, as the one discussed in this book, often use given interest rate curves as initial data. The classical (single curve) example is the HJM oder LMM model, where

$$\mathrm{d}f(t,T) = \mu(t,T)\mathrm{d}t + \Sigma(t,T)\mathrm{d}W(t), \qquad f(t_0,T) = f_0(T).$$

While research on multi-curve interest rates models was and is very active, see, e.g., [5, 6, 15, 20–22], references therein and the other chapters of in this book, the construction of the initial interest rate curve, here $f_0(T)$, naturally does not get a similar strong attention. However, a good curve construction is of high importance for practitioners, since it has a strong impact on the delta-hedge (that is, the first-order interest rate risk).

The market standard of (forward) curve construction is to calibrate an interpolated curve to given market instruments, often via an iterative procedure (bootstrapping). With respect to the interpolation of (interest rate) forward curves, a common approach is to represent a forward curve in terms of (pseudo-)discount factors (aka. synthetic discount factors) and apply an interpolation scheme on these discount factors. While this approach is in general not backed by an economic concept, it also introduces several (self-made) problems, e.g., the interpolation of (so-called) overlapping instruments, see Sect. 5.3.

In this paper we focus on the curve construction, provide an open source implementation and suggest appealing alternative interpolation schemes motivated from the multi-curve setup: direct interpolation of the forward curve or direct interpolation of the forward value curve, where the forward value is the product of a forward and the associated discount factor. While linear interpolation of the forward is a common scheme,[1] the interpolation of the forward value appears to be a new approach.

Nevertheless, the paper puts both methods on a solid foundation by deriving the schemes from the multi-curve definition of forward curves. Both interpolation schemes ease some of the complications associated with synthetic discount factors.

Once the curves and interpolations are defined, we are considering the problem of calibrating a set of curves to given market quotes. The value of an instrument is in general determined by a whole collection of curves, e.g., one or two discount curves and zero or more forward curves. To simplify the implementation, we define a generalized swap, which allows to represent most calibration instruments (FRAs, swaps, tenor basis swaps, cross-currency swaps, etc.) by a single class.

[1] Some trading systems, like Murex, do offer it as an option.

2 Foundations, Assumptions, Notation

Under well-known assumptions the valuation of a future cash flow can be written as an expectation,[2] that is the time t_0-value $V(t_0)$ is

$$V(t_0) = N(t_0) \cdot \mathrm{E}^{\mathbb{Q}^N}\left(\frac{V(T)}{N(T)} \mid \mathscr{F}_{t_0}\right) \quad \text{for } t_0 \leq T, \tag{1}$$

where $V(T)$ is the time T cash-flow, N is the value process of a traded asset (or collateral account) which can serve as a *numéraire* and $\mathbb{Q}^N$ is the equivalent martingale measure associated with N. Equation (1) is the starting point for *curve construction* in the following sense: If the above valuation formula holds, then the value of a linear function of future cash-flows is the linear function of the values of the single cash flows. In other words: we can represent the valuation of so-called linear products by a *basis* consisting of the values of elementary products. This basis of elementary products is the set of curves, where "the curve" is formed by the parameter T.

Note that here and in the following, we consider the valuation for a fixed t_0. We are not concerned with the description of a dynamic model (describing $t \mapsto V(t)$ as a stochastic process).

Definition 1 Let I denote an index, that is, $I(T)$ is an $\mathscr{F}_T$-measurable random variable and $d > 0$ is some payment offset, then we define the (time t_0-)valuation curve with respect to T as the map

$$T \mapsto C(T) := N(t_0) \cdot \mathrm{E}^{\mathbb{Q}^N}\left(\frac{I(T)}{N(T+d)} \mid \mathscr{F}_{t_0}\right). \tag{2}$$

For $I \equiv 1$ and $d = 0$ the curve in (2) represents the curve of (synthetical) zero-coupon bond prices $T \mapsto P(T; t_0)$, also known as *discount curve*.[3] For arbitrary indices I (with fixed payment offset d[4]), the curve $T \mapsto C(T)/P(T; t_0)$ is known as the *forward curve*. Obviously both curves depend on N and t_0.

Note that the specific stochastic behavior of I and N does not play a role when looking at t_0 only in the sense that we are only interested in the time t_0-expectation. That is, we could define $t \mapsto N(t)$ and $t \mapsto I(t)$ to be $\mathscr{F}_{t_0}$-measurable for all times t and still generate any given discount curve and forward curve, respectively. There

[2]Since we are only considering the linearity of the valuation at a fixed time t_0, we just require that some fundamental theorem of asset pricing holds, for example, assuming that the price processes are locally bounded semi-martingales and the *no free lunch with vanishing risk* condition holds, [7].

[3]We will use the notation $P(T; t)$ (instead of the more common $P(t, T)$) for a the time-t value of zero-coupon bond maturing in T, since we consider $t = t_0$ as fixed. Sometimes we even drop the argument and just write $P(T)$. Similar for forward curves. The curves considered here are parametrized by T for a fixed time t.

[4]In practice the payment offset may depend on t_0 and T due to business day adjustments. Our implementation handles this, but to ease notation we drop the dependence here.

is no arbitrage constraint with respect to t yet, since for different t the index $I(t)$ represents different assets (underlyings).

Thus, with respect to the processes $1/N$ and I/N we just require that they fulfill regularity assumptions such that (2) exists.[5]

On the other hand, the interpretation of the curve as a curve of valuations in the sense of (2) does play a role, when we consider the construction of the curve via interpolation of observed market prices. Here, the linearity of the expectation operator E allows to link market prices to different points of the curve.

Curves, like discount curves and forward curves solve, among others, two important problems:

- Valuation of linear instruments. This is performed by decomposing instruments into the value of single cash flows (zero coupon bonds and FRAs), which then allows to synthesize the valuation of linear functions of the individual cash flows (e.g., swaps).
- Valuation of a time T cash-flow as interpolation of valuations of cash flows at discrete times $\{T_i\}_{i=0}^{n}$ (where $T_i \geq t_0$ for all i), e.g., swaps referencing cash flows on illiquid maturities.

Thus, curves are simply a methodology to interpolate on the cash flows with respect to their payment time.[6] Apart from this, the curves also represent the initial data for advanced term structure models (like the LIBOR market model). Hence, careful construction of curves is also key to (interest rate) derivatives valuation, when interpolated curves are the initial values of a dynamic model.

For details on the evolution of multi-curve construction see the recent book by Henrard, [18] (citing a preprint of the present paper). A very detailed description of multi-curve bootstrapping, which also details market conventions and convexity adjustments of the calibration instruments, can be found in [2]. For market conventions also see [17]. Here, we do not consider a possible convexity adjustment due to different market conventions (they should be part of the valuation formulas) and rather focus on the curves and their interpolation schemes. Also, we do not need to consider a bootstrapping, since we set up the calibration as a system of equations passed to a multi-dimensional optimization algorithm.

Usually (and here), the curves are used to interpolate at the fixed time t_0 only. If a curve interpolation should also be used for times $t > t_0$ within a dynamic multi-curve model, then this may impose additional constraints on the admissible interpolations schemes. For example, (2) implies that linear interpolation of time-t zero-coupon bond prices for $t > t_0$ implies linear interpolation of the time-t zero-coupon bond prices, which in turn implies a special interpolation of forward rates in a LIBOR market model, see Sect. 19.5 in [10]. In this case the linear interpolation of the discount curve and forward value curve would not introduce an arbitrage violation, given that

[5] For example, let $1/N$ and I/N be Itô stochastic processes with integrable drift and bounded quadratic variation.

[6] This also applies to forward curve, see below, although in these cases there is also an associated fixing time of an index and it is maybe more consistent to parametrize the curve w.r.t. the fixing of the index.

the interpolation points are the same for all times. In practice term-structure models are often constructed with their own curve interpolations, such that the interpolation used for the initial data differs from the interpolation used for the simulated curves (while the model is still calibrated and arbitrage-free given that the drift is specified accordingly). In the following we focus on the interpolation of the initial data—that is, the time-t_0 curves, which is of greater importance for the deltas of interpolated products, where only the linear part matters.

In the above valuation formula (1) it is assumed that V and N are expressed in the same currency. If the two are in different currency, one of them has to be converted by an exchange rate, which we will denote by FX. Let V be in currency U_2 and the numéraire N in currency U_1, then the valuation formula is given by

$$V(t_0) = FX^{\frac{U_2}{U_1}}(t_0) \cdot N(t_0) \cdot \mathrm{E}^{\mathbb{Q}^N}\left(\frac{V(T)}{FX^{\frac{U_2}{U_1}}(T) \cdot N(T)} \mid \mathscr{F}_{t_0}\right),$$

where $FX^{\frac{U_2}{U_1}}(t)$ denotes the time t exchange rate for one unit of currency U_1 into one unit of currency U_2. Furthermore, $FX^{\frac{U_1}{U_2}} = \left(FX^{\frac{U_2}{U_1}}\right)^{-1}$.

As discussed in [12], the valuation of a collateralized claim can be written as an expectation with respect to a specific numéraire, namely the collateral account $N = N^{\mathsf{C}}$.[7] We denote the currency of the collateral numéraire by [C]. Let U denote the currency of the cash flow $V(T)$. Assume that the cash flow $V(T)$ is collateralized by units of N^{C}. In this case the Eq. (1) holds with the numéraire $N = N^{\mathsf{C}}$, $U_2 = U$, $U_1 = [C]$ (given that $V(t)$ is the collateral amount in the account N^{C}).

Remark 1 From the above we see that collateralization in a different currency can be interpreted twofold:

1. We may consider a payment converted to collateral currency and valued with respect to the collateral numéraire N^{C}, or, alternatively,
2. we may consider a payment in the currency U collateralized with respect to the collateral account $N^{U,\mathsf{C}} := FX^{\frac{U}{[\mathsf{C}]}} \cdot N^{\mathsf{C}}$.

We will adopt the latter interpretation, which will also make the valuation look more consistent[8]

$$V(t_0) = N^{U,\mathsf{C}}(t_0) \cdot \mathrm{E}^{\mathbb{Q}^{U,N^{\mathsf{C}}}}\left(\frac{V(T)}{N^{U,\mathsf{C}}(T)} \mid \mathscr{F}_{t_0}\right). \tag{3}$$

Note that this interpretation will then give rise to a new discount curve: the discount curve associated with $N^{U,\mathsf{C}}$, being the discount curve of a foreign currency (U) cash flow collateralized by a C.

[7] See also [8, 14].

[8] As has been noted in [12], the measures agree, i.e., $\mathbb{Q}^{U,N^{\mathsf{C}}} = \mathbb{Q}^{N^{\mathsf{C}}}$.

Remark 2 For an uncollateralized product the role of the collateral account is taken by the funding account and the corresponding numéraire is the funding account. Since the valuation formulas are identical to the case of a "special" collateral account (agreeing with the funding account), we will consider an uncollateralized product as a product with a different collateralization.

In the following we use the notation U for the currency unit of a cash flow, i.e., we may consider $U = 1€$ or $U = 1\$$. We will need this notation only when we consider cross-currency basis swaps. The symbols V and N (as well as P defined below) will denote value processes including the corresponding currency unit, e.g., $V(t_0) = 0.25€$. The symbol V refers to the value of the product under consideration, while N denotes the numéraire, e.g., the OIS accrued collateral account. The symbol X denotes a real number while I denotes a real valued stochastic process, both can be considered as rates, i.e., unit-less indices, e.g., $X = 2.5\,\%$. For example X will denote the fix rate in a swap, I will denote the floating rate index in a swap, U denotes the currency unit of the two legs, N will be used to define the discount factor and the value of the swap. The value of the swap is then denoted by V.

3 Discount Curves

Consider a fixed constant cash flow X, paid in currency U in time T, collateralized by an account C. Since X is a constant and the expectation operator is linear, we can express the time-t_0 value $V(t_0)$ of this cash flow as

$$V(t_0) \;=\; X \cdot P^{U,\mathsf{C}}(T; t_0), \tag{4}$$

where

$$P^{U,\mathsf{C}}(T; t_0) \;:=\; N^{U,\mathsf{C}}(t_0) \cdot \mathrm{E}^{\mathbb{Q}^{N^{U,\mathsf{C}}}}\left(\frac{1 \cdot U}{N^{U,\mathsf{C}}(T)} \mid \mathscr{F}_{t_0}\right) \tag{5}$$

defines the value of a theoretical zero coupon bond. Note that Eq. (4) can be used in two ways. First, for given market prices we may determine $P^{U,\mathsf{C}}(T; t_0)$—that is we calibrate the curve $T \mapsto P^{U,\mathsf{C}}(T; t_0)$. Second, for given $P^{U,\mathsf{C}}(T; t_0)$ we may value a constant cash flow.

This defines the discount curve:

Definition 2 Let $P^{U,\mathsf{C}}(T; t_0)$ denote the time t_0 value expressed in currency unit U of a unit cash-flow of 1 unit of the currency U in T, collateralized by a collateral account C. In this case we call $T \mapsto P^{U,\mathsf{C}}(T; t_0)$ given by (5) the *discount curve* for cash flows in currency U collateralized by the account C.

Remark 3 By assumption (of a frictionless no-arbitrage market, (1)) the value of a fixed constant future cash-flow X is a linear function of its amount. Hence, we have that the time t_0 value of a cash flow X in T and currency U, collateralized with an account C is

$$X \cdot P^{U,\mathsf{C}}(T; t_0).$$

In other words, the discount curve allows us to valuate all fixed (deterministic) cash flows in a given currency, collateralized by a given account.

The discount factor $P^{U,\mathsf{C}}(T; t_0)$ represents the price of an (idealized) zero-coupon bond. Although a zero-coupon bond is usually not a market-traded asset, we may represent market-traded coupon bonds as a linear combination of zero-coupon bonds, and vice versa. If C denotes some cash-collateral account, there is no such thing as a collateralized bond, but in that case $P^{U,\mathsf{C}}(T; t_0)$ has the natural interpretation of representing the time-t value of a collateralized unit currency time-T cash flow. In any case, $P^{U,\mathsf{C}}(T; t_0)$ can be considered a linear function of traded asset (within its collateralization scheme).

4 Forward Curves

The same approach can now be applied to a payoff of a cash flow $X \cdot I(T_1)$, paid in currency U in time T_2 ($T_1 \leq T_2$), collateralized by account C, where X is a constant and I is an adapted process representing index.[9] Its value is

$$V(t_0) = N^{U,\mathsf{C}}(t_0) \cdot \mathrm{E}^{\mathbb{Q}^{N^{U,\mathsf{C}}}} \left(\frac{X \cdot I(T_1) \cdot U}{N^{U,\mathsf{C}}(T_2)} \mid \mathscr{F}_{t_0} \right).$$

We can express the value as $V(t_0) = X \cdot F_I^{U,\mathsf{C}}(T_1, T_2; t_0) \cdot P^{U,\mathsf{C}}(T_2; t_0)$, where

$$F_I^{U,\mathsf{C}}(T_1, T_2; t_0) = N^{U,\mathsf{C}}(t_0) \cdot \mathrm{E}^{\mathbb{Q}^{N^{U,\mathsf{C}}}} \left(\frac{I(T_1) \cdot U}{N^{U,\mathsf{C}}(T_2)} \mid \mathscr{F}_{t_0} \right) / P^{U,\mathsf{C}}(T_2; t_0). \tag{6}$$

This definition allows us to derive $F_I^{U,\mathsf{C}}(T_1, T_2; t_0)$ from given market prices. Conversely, given $P^{U,\mathsf{C}}(T_2; t_0)$ and $F_I^{U,\mathsf{C}}(T_1, T_2; t_0)$ we may value all linear payoff functions of $I(T_1)$ paid in T_2.

In (6) the forward depends on the fixing time T_1 and the payment time T_2. However, the offset of the payment time from the fixing time $d = T_2 - T_1$ can be viewed as a property of the index (a constant) and hence, the forward represents a curve $T \mapsto F_I^{U,\mathsf{C}}(T, T+d; t_0)$.

Definition 3 Let $t \mapsto I(t)$ denote an index, that is I is an adapted stochastic real valued process. Let

$$V_I^{U,\mathsf{C}}(T, T+d; t_0) := N^{U,\mathsf{C}}(t_0) \cdot \mathrm{E}^{\mathbb{Q}^{N^{U,\mathsf{C}}}} \left(\frac{I(T) \cdot U}{N^{U,\mathsf{C}}(T+d)} \mid \mathscr{F}_{t_0} \right)$$

[9] Examples for I are LIBOR rates or the performance of an EONIA accrual account.

denote the time t_0-value of a payment of $I(T)$ paid in $T+d$ in currency U, collateralized by an account C (where $d \geq 0$). We assume that I and N is such that the expectation exists for all T. Then we define the *forward of a payment of $I(T)$ paid in $T+d$ in currency U, collateralized by an account C* as

$$F_I^{U,\mathsf{C}}(T;t_0) := \frac{V_I^{U,\mathsf{C}}(T,T+d;t_0)}{P^{U,\mathsf{C}}(T+d;t_0)}.$$

Remark 4 The forward curve allows us to value a future payment of the index I by

$$V_I^{U,\mathsf{C}}(T,T+d;t_0) = F_I^{U,\mathsf{C}}(T;t_0) \cdot P^{U,\mathsf{C}}(T+d;t_0)$$

and by assumption (of a frictionless no-arbitrage market, (1)), the forward curve allows us to evaluate all linear cash flows $X \cdot I$ (in currency U, collateralized by an account C) by $X \cdot F_I^{U,\mathsf{C}}(T;t_0) \cdot P^{U,\mathsf{C}}(T+d;t_0)$.

Note that $F_I^{U,\mathsf{C}}$ is not a classical single curve forward rate, related to some discount curve. Due to our definition of the forward curve, the curve includes all valuation effects related to the index, in particular a possible convexity adjustment. For example: if we would consider an in-arrears index and an in-advance index we would obtain two different forward curves which differ by the in-arrears convexity adjustment!

4.1 Performance Index of a Discount Curve (or "Self-Discounting")

The OIS swap pays the performance of an account, accruing with the overnight rate, that is:

Definition 4 (*Overnight Index Swap*) Let $N^{\mathsf{C}}(t)$ denote the account accruing at the overnight rate $r(t)$, $N^{\mathsf{C}}(t_0) = 1U$, i.e. on a given time discretization (accrual periods) $\{t_i\}_{i=0}^n$

$$N^{\mathsf{C}}(t_k) := \prod_{i=0}^{k}(1+r(t_i)\Delta t_i) \approx \exp\left(\int_{t_0}^{t_k} r(s)\mathrm{d}s\right).$$

The overnight index swap pays a fix coupon and receives the performance I_i^{C} of the accrual account, that is

$$I_i^{\mathsf{C}}(T_i,T_{i+1}) := \frac{N^{\mathsf{C}}(T_{i+1})}{N^{\mathsf{C}}(T_i)} - 1.$$

in T_{i+1} with a quarterly tenor $T_0, T_1, \ldots$.

The time-t_0 linear forward of the index above is $\frac{P^{U,\mathsf{C}}(T_i;t_0)-P^{U,\mathsf{C}}(T_{i+1};t_0)}{P^{U,\mathsf{C}}(T_{i+1};t_0)}$ (and dividing by $T_{i+1} - T_i$ this gives the linear forward rate). Hence, this is the same situation as for single curve interest rate theory swaps.

The OIS swap is collateralized with respect to the account N^{C}. Due to this, it is sometimes called "self-discounted". However, we may give an appealing alternative view, defining the forward curve from the discount curve (and not the other way around):

Let us consider a discount factor curve $P^{U,\mathsf{C}}(T;t)$ as seen in time t. The curve allows the definition of a special index, namely the performance rate of the collateral account C in currency U over a period of period length d:
Let $I^{\mathsf{C}}(T_i) := \frac{1-P^{U,\mathsf{C}}(T_i+d;T_i)}{P^{U,\mathsf{C}}(T_i+d;T_i)}$, where $P^{U,\mathsf{C}}(T_i+d;T_i)$ is the discount factor for the maturity $T_i + d$ as seen in time T_i. The index $I^{\mathsf{C}}(T_i)$ is the payment we have to receive in $T_i + d$ collateralized with respect to the collateral account C, such that $1 + I^{\mathsf{C}}(T_i)$ in T_{i+1} has the same value as 1 in T_i. This index has a special property, namely that its forward can be expressed in terms of the discount factor curve $P^{U,\mathsf{C}}$ too: The time t_0 forward of $I^{\mathsf{C}}(T_i)$ is $F^{U,\mathsf{C}}(T_i;t_0)$ where

$$\begin{aligned} F^{U,\mathsf{C}}(T_i;t_0) \cdot P^{U,\mathsf{C}}(T_i+d;t_0) &= N^{U,\mathsf{C}}(t_0) \cdot \mathrm{E}^{\mathbb{Q}^{N^{U,\mathsf{C}}}}\left(\frac{I^{\mathsf{C}}(T_i)\cdot U}{N^{U,\mathsf{C}}(T_i+d)} \mid \mathscr{F}_{t_0}\right) \\ &= P^{U,\mathsf{C}}(T_i;t_0) - P^{U,\mathsf{C}}(T_i+d;t_0). \end{aligned}$$

Consequently this index has the special property that its forward can be expressed by the associated discount factors evaluated at different maturities.

Definition 5 (*Forward associated with a Discount Curve*) Let $P^{U,\mathsf{C}}(T_i+d;t_0)$ denote a discount curve. For a given period length d we define the forward $F^{d,U,\mathsf{C}}(T_i;t_0)$ as

$$F^{d,U,\mathsf{C}}(T_i;t_0) := \frac{P^{U,\mathsf{C}}(T_i;t_0) - P^{U,\mathsf{C}}(T_i+d;t_0)}{P^{U,\mathsf{C}}(T_i+d;t_0)\cdot d}. \tag{7}$$

$F^{d,U,\mathsf{C}}(T_i;t_0)$ is the forward associated with the performance index of $P^{U,\mathsf{C}}$ over a period of length d.

Remark 5 The above definition relates a forward curve and discount factor curve. Note however, that we define a forward from a discount factor curve and that this definition is backed by a clear interpretation of the underlying index. Conversely, we may define a discount curve from a forward curve "implicitly" such that the relation (7) holds. Note however, that a generalization of this relation should be considered with care, since the associated product may not exist.

The definition above is an idealization in the sense that we assume that interval points over which the performance is measured correspond to the payment dates. In practice (EONIA is an example) there might be some small deviations from this assumption (e.g. payment offsets of a few days). In this case (7) does not hold (but may be still considered an approximation).

Products like the OIS swaps are sometimes called "self-discounting" since the discounting is performed on a curve corresponding to the index they fix. From the above, we find an alternative (and maybe more natural) interpretation, namely that the swap pays the performance index of its collateral account, i.e., it pays the index associated with the discount curve.

5 Interpolation of Curves

In this section we consider a discount curve $P^{U,\mathsf{C}}$ and an associated forward curve $F^{U,\mathsf{C}}$. To simplify notation we set $D(T) := P^{U,\mathsf{C}}(T; t_0)$ and $F(T) := F^{U,\mathsf{C}}(T; t_0)$.

Forwards and discount factors are linked together by Definition 3, which says that the time-t_0 value of a forward contract $V(t_0, T)$ with fixing in T is the product of the forward $F(T)$ and the associated discount factor $D(T+d)$, i.e., $V(t_0, T) = F(T) \cdot D(T+d)$. Note that $T \mapsto V(t_0, T)$ and $T \mapsto D(T)$ are *value curves*, i.e., for a fixed T the quantities $V(t_0, T)$ and $D(T)$ are values of financial products. However, $F(T)$ is a derived quantity, the forward.

Since V and D represent values of financial products, there is a natural interpretation for a linear interpolation of different values $V(T_i)$ and of different values of $D(T_i)$, since this would correspond to a portfolio of such products. Note that defining an interpolation method for V and D implies a (possible more complex) interpolation method of F.

On the other hand, it is common practice to define an interpolation method for a rate curve (both forward curve and discount factor curve) via zero rates, sometimes even regardless of the nature of the curve, which then implies the interpolation of the value curves D and V. Some of these interpolations will result in natural interpolations on the value process V, others not. Other examples for interpolations of F and D are:

- log-linear interpolation of the forward, log-linear interpolation of the discount factor: the case is equivalent to log-linear interpolation of the value.
- linear interpolation of the forward, log-linear interpolation of the discount factor: the case is equivalent with a linear interpolation of the value, with an interpolation weight being a function of the discount factor ratio.

In [16] interpolations on the discount factors, on the logarithm of discount factors, on the yield and directly on the forwards were discussed. Highlighting some disadvantages of cubic splines, they introduced two new interpolation methods (monotone convex spline and minimal cubic spline) which overcome most of the shortfalls of the other interpolations. In [19] some issues of these methods were pointed out, favoring a harmonic spline interpolation. In [1] a modified Bessel spline on the logarithm of the discount factors was proposed.

Based on the formal setup presented in the present paper, the stability of cumulated error of a dynamic hedge was considered as a criterion for the interpolation methods and compared for a large collection of methods in [13].

At this point, we would like to stress the importance of the *interpolation entity*, that is, whether we interpolate on a forward or on a synthetic discount factor (in the sense of Definition 5). While the interpolation method (e.g., *linear* compared to *spline*) is often in the focus (discussing locality versus smoothness, [16]), the choice of the interpolation entity has a strong impact on the delta hedge, see Table 1.

Depending on the application, it is popular to represent a curve by a parametric curve. This is done especially for discount curves. Examples are the Nelson–Siegel (NS) and the Nelson–Siegel–Svensson (NSS) parametrization. Our benchmark implementation in [11] allows to use NS or NSS in the calibration.[10]

5.1 *Implementing the Interpolation of a Curve: Interpolation Method and Interpolation Entities*

In this paper we focus on interpolation schemes based on given interpolation points. Implementing the interpolation of a curve that way, it is convenient to distinguish the *interpolation method*, e.g., linear interpolation of interpolation points $\{(T_i, x_i)\}$, and the *interpolation entity*, that is, a (bijective) transformation from (T, x) to the actual curve. For example, for discount curves one might consider a linear interpolation of the zero rate. In this case the interpolation method is *linear interpolation* and the interpolation entity is $(T, x(T)) = (T, \frac{\log(D(T))}{T})$ for $T > 0$, where D denotes the discount curve. Given $0 < T_i \leq T \leq T_{i+1}$ and discount factors $D(T_j)$, a linear interpolation of the zero rates would then imply the interpolation

$$D(T) := \exp\left(\left(\frac{T - T_i}{T_{i+1} - T_i}\frac{\log(D(T_{i+1}))}{T_{i+1}} + \frac{T_{i+1} - T}{T_{i+1} - T_i}\frac{\log(D(T_i))}{T_i}\right) \cdot T\right).$$

In our benchmark implementation [11], this functionality is provided for a large number of interpolation methods (constant, linear, Akima, spline, etc.) and interpolation entities (value, log-value, log-value-per-time) by the class `net.finmath.marketdata.model.curves.Curve`.[11] For forward curves we provide two additional interpolation entities: forward and synthetic discount factor (see below).

5.2 *Interpolation Time*

For both, parametric curves (like NSS) and non-parametric interpolation schemes, it is important to specify the convention used to transform product maturities (dates) to real numbers (time T). For example, we might use a daycount convention (like

[10] See http://finmath.net/finmath-lib/apidocs/net/finmath/marketdata/model/curves/DiscountCurveNelsonSiegelSvensson.html.

[11] See http://finmath.net/finmath-lib/apidocs/net/finmath/marketdata/model/curves/Curve.html.

ACT/365) and measure T as a daycount fraction between evaluation date and maturity date, that is $T := \mathrm{dcf}(\text{evaluation date, maturity date})$. Clearly, a change in the time parametrization will change the interpretation of the curve parameters (for a parametric curve). Also, some daycount convention actually introduces non-linear time transformations.

5.3 *Interpolation of Forward Curves*

5.3.1 The Classical Approach

For forward curves, a common approach is to consider an interpolation of the forward as an independent entity (like for the discount curve). For interest rate forwards, a popular interpolation scheme (coming from the single curve interpretation of interest rates forwards) is to represent the forward in terms of synthetic discount factors. That is, if d denotes a period length associated with the forward and if $F(T_i)$ is given for $T_i = i \cdot d$, then one might consider interpolation of (pseudo-)discount factor $D^F(T_i) := \prod_{k=0}^{i-1}(1 + F(T_k) \cdot d)^{-1}$, possibly considering another transformation on $D^F(T)$ to define the actual interpolation entity. See [3] for a corresponding multi-curves bootstrap algorithm.

It is obvious that this definition of the interpolation entity for forward curve is complex, results in problems for non-equidistant interpolation points and is—without further assumptions—not backed by a meaningful interpretation. First, in a multi-curve setup this approach lacks an economic justification. Second, it may introduce problems:

- The common approach of a linear interpolation of the logarithm of the synthetic discount factor representing the forward curve results in an almost piecewise constant interpolation of the forward, see [13]. This may result into "jumps" when products are aging.
- The use of synthetic discount factors defines a forward with fixing time T in terms of (interpolated) discount factors at times T and $T + d$ (where d is the period length). The method is a common practice (also considered in [1]). However, considering forwards for overlapping periods, this may introduce oscillations and result in implausible delta-hedges (see Table 1).

5.3.2 Alternative Interpolation Schemes for Forward Curves

The definition of the forward curve in the multi-curve setup suggests an appealing alternative for the creation of an interpolated forward: Like a discount factor curve, the curve $V(T) = F(T) \cdot D(T + d)$ represents the value of a financial product. Hence, we may consider the interpolation of V like we did for the curve D. For example, if we consider linear interpolation of the value curve V, we interpolate the forward curve F by considering the interpolation entity $F(T) \cdot D(T + d)$ with a given discount curve D, i.e., we have

$$F(T) := \frac{1}{D(T+d)} \left(\frac{T - T_i}{T_{i+1} - T_i} F(T_{i+1}) D(T_{i+1} + d) + \frac{T_{i+1} - T}{T_{i+1} - T_i} F(T_i) D(T_i + d) \right)$$

for $T_i \leq T \leq T_{i+1}$ and given points $F(T_j)$.

Given that log-linear interpolation is a popular interpolation scheme for discount curves one may consider log-linear interpolation of V. This interpolation scheme has the restriction that the forward is required to be positive. Since negative interest rates are possible, this interpolation scheme is not appropriate for interest rate curves.

5.4 *Assessment of the Interpolation Method*

The assessment of the quality of performance of an interpolation method is difficult. Some basic criteria (like continuity, locality, etc.) have been reviewed in [16]. Locality, i.e., how does a local change in input data affect the curve, is a desired property from a hedging perspective. In [13] a long-term dynamic hedging is used to asses the performance of an interpolation scheme. The results in [13] suggest that among the local methods, linear interpolation of the forward curve and log-linear interpolation of the discount curve were the best performing schemes when using the cumulated dynamic hedge error as a primary criterion.

6 Implementation of the Calibration of Curves

A curve (discount curve or forward curve) is used to encode values of market instruments. A forward curve together with its associated discount curve, allows to value all linear products (linear payoffs) in the corresponding currency under the corresponding collateralization.

The standard way to calibrate a curve is, hence, to obtain given market values of (linear) instruments (e.g., swaps). For each market value a single "point" in a single curve is calibrated. Hence the total number of calibrated curve interpolation points (aggregated across all curves) equals the number of market instruments.

By "sorting" and combining the calibration instruments, the corresponding equations can be brought into the form of a system of equations with a triangular structure, i.e., the value of the nth calibration instrument only depends on the first n curve points. This allows for an iterative construction of the curve.

However, here (and in the associated reference implementation [11]) we propose the calibration of the curves using a multi-variate optimization algorithm, like the Levenberg–Marquardt algorithm or a Differential Evolution algorithm. This approach brings several advantages, e.g., the freedom to specify the calibration instruments and the ability to extend the approach to over-determined systems of equations.

In addition, we can handle the case of curve-interdependence, for example to calibrate certain discount curves from cross-currency swaps. This comes at the cost of slower performance in terms of required calculation time.

What remains is to specify the valuation equations for the calibration instruments. To simplify implementation, we may generalize the definition of a "swap" comprising plain swaps, tenor basis swaps and cross-currency swaps.

6.1 Generalized Definition of a Swap

Many of the following calibration instruments (from OIS swaps to cross-currency basis-swaps) fit under a generalized definition of a swap. The swap consists of two legs. Each leg consists of several periods $[T_i, T_{i+1}]$. To ease notation, we do not distinguish between period start time, period end time, fixing time of the index and payment time. We assume that for the period $[T_i, T_{i+1}]$ index fixing is in T_i and payment is in T_{i+1}. This is done purely to ease notation, the generalization to distinguished times is straightforward.

Definition 6 (*Swap Leg*) A swap leg pays a multiple α of the index I fixed in T_i plus some fixed payment X, both in currency unit U collateralized by the collateral account C and paid in time T_{i+1}. Here α and X are constants (possibly zero). The value of the swap leg can be expressed in terms of forwards and discount factors as

$$V^{U,\mathsf{C}}_{SwapLeg}(\alpha I, X, \{T_i\}_{i=0}^{n}) = \sum_{i=0}^{n-1} \left(\alpha F^{U,\mathsf{C}}(T_i) + X\right) \cdot P^{U,\mathsf{C}}(T_{i+1}),$$

where $F^{U,\mathsf{C}}$ denotes the forward curve of the index I paid in currency U collateralized with respect to C and $P^{U,\mathsf{C}}$ denotes the corresponding discount curve.

A swap leg with notional exchange has the payments as in Definition 6 together with an additional payment of -1 in T_i and $+1$ in T_{i+1}. The value of the swap leg with notional exchange can be expressed in terms of forwards and discount factors as

$$V^{U,\mathsf{C}}_{SwapLeg}(\alpha I, X, \{T_i\}_{i=0}^{n}) = \sum_{i=0}^{n-1} \Big(\left(\alpha F^{U,\mathsf{C}}(T_i) + X\right) \cdot P^{U,\mathsf{C}}(T_{i+1}) + P^{U,\mathsf{C}}(T_{i+1}) - P^{U,\mathsf{C}}(T_i)\Big),$$

where $F^{U,\mathsf{C}}$ denotes the forward curve of the index I paid in currency U collateralized with respect to C and $P^{U,\mathsf{C}}$ denotes the corresponding discount curve.

Definition 7 (*Swap*) A swap exchanges the payments of two swap legs, the receiver leg and the payer leg. We allow that the legs have different indices, different fixed payments, different payment times, different currency units, but are collateralized with respect to the same account C. The swaps receive a swap leg with value $V^{U_1,\mathsf{C}}_{SwapLeg}(\alpha_1 I_1, X_1, \{T^1_i\}^{n_1}_{i=0})$ and pay a leg with value $V^{U_2,\mathsf{C}}_{SwapLeg}(\alpha_2 I_2, X_2, \{T^2_i\})$. Since the currency unit of the two legs may be different, the value of the swap in currency U_1 is

$$V_{Swap} = V^{U_1,\mathsf{C}}_{SwapLeg}(\alpha_1 I_1, X_1, \{T^1_i\}^{n_1}_{i=0}) - V^{U_2,\mathsf{C}}_{SwapLeg}(\alpha_2 I_2, X_2, \{T^2_i\}^{n_2}_{i=0}) \cdot FX^{\frac{U_1}{U_2}}$$

Many instruments can be represented (and hence valued) in this form. We will now list a few of them.

6.2 Calibration of Discount Curve to Swap Paying the Collateral Rate (aka. Self-Discounted Swaps)

Discount curves can be calibrated to swaps paying the performance index of their collateral account. For example, a swap as in Definition 7 where both legs pay in the same currency $U = U_1 = U_2$. In a receiver swap the receiver leg pays a fixed rate C, and the payer leg pays an index I. Thus the value of the swap can be expressed in terms of the discount factors $P^{U,\mathsf{C}}(T_{i+1}; t)$ only, which allows to calibrate this curve using these swaps. Overnight index swaps are an example.

For the swap paying the performance of the collateral account we have

$$\begin{aligned}
X_1 &= C = \text{const.} = \text{given}, \; X_2 = 0, \\
F^{U_1,\mathsf{C}}_1(T^1_i; t_0) &= 0, \qquad F^{U_2,\mathsf{C}}_2(T^2_i; t_0) = \frac{P^{U,\mathsf{C}}(T^2_i; t_0) - P^{U,\mathsf{C}}(T^2_{i+1}; t_0)}{P^{U,\mathsf{C}}(T^2_{i+1}; t_0)(T^2_{i+1} - T^2_i)}, \\
P^{U_1,\mathsf{C}}_1 &= P^{U,\mathsf{C}} = \text{calibrated}, \; P^{U_2,\mathsf{C}}_2 = P^{U,\mathsf{C}} = \text{calibrated}.
\end{aligned}$$

In a situation where the number of interpolation points matches the number of swaps (e.g., a bootstrapping), we calibrate the time T discount factor $P^{U,\mathsf{C}}(T; t_0)$ with $T = \max(T^1_n, T^2_n)$ being the last payment time from a given swap.

6.3 Calibration of Forward Curves

Given a calibrated discount curve $P^{U,\mathsf{C}}$ we consider a swap with payments in currency U collateralized with respect to the account C, paying some index I and receiving some fixed cash flow C. An example is swaps paying the 3M LIBOR rate. For such a swap we have

$$\begin{aligned}
&X_1 = C = \text{const.} = \text{given}, X_2 = 0,\\
&F_1^{U_1,\mathsf{C}}(T_i^1) = 0, \qquad F_2^{U_2,\mathsf{C}}(T_i^2) = F^{U,\mathsf{C}}(T_i^2) = \text{calibrated},\\
&P_1^{U_1,\mathsf{C}} = P^{U,\mathsf{C}} = \text{given}, \qquad P_2^{U_2,\mathsf{C}} = P^{U,\mathsf{C}} = \text{given}.
\end{aligned}$$

From one such swap we calibrate the time T forward $F^{U,\mathsf{C}}(T)$ of $I(T)$ with $T = T_{n-1}^2$ (the last fixing time).

Given a calibrated discount curve $P^{U,\mathsf{C}}$ and a calibrate forward curve $F_1^{U,\mathsf{C}}$ belonging to the index I_1, both in currency U and collateralized with respect to the account C, we consider a swap collateralized with respect to the account C, paying some index $I_2 = I$ in currency U, receiving the index I_1 in currency U. An example is tenor basis swaps paying the 6M LIBOR rate, receiving the 3M LIBOR rate. For such a swap we have

$$\begin{aligned}
&X_1 = C_1 = \text{const.} = \text{given}, \qquad X_2 = C_2 = \text{const.} = \text{given},\\
&F_1^{U_1,\mathsf{C}}(T_i^1) = F_1^{U,\mathsf{C}}(T_i^1) = \text{given}, F_2^{U_2,\mathsf{C}}(T_i^2) = F_2^{U,\mathsf{C}}(T_i^2) = \text{calibrated},\\
&P_1^{U_1,\mathsf{C}} = P^{U,\mathsf{C}} = \text{given}, \qquad P_2^{U_2,\mathsf{C}} = P^{U,\mathsf{C}} = \text{given}.
\end{aligned}$$

From one such swap we calibrate the time T forward $F_2^{U,\mathsf{C}}(T)$ of $I(T)$ with $T = T_{n-1}^2$ (the last fixing time of index I_2).

6.4 *Calibration of Discount Curves When Payment and Collateral Currency Differ*

6.4.1 Fixed Payment in Other Currency

Given a calibrated discount curve $P^{U_1,\mathsf{C}}$ we consider a swap collateralized with respect to the account C, paying some index I_1 in currency U_1, and receiving some fixed cash flow C_2 in currency U_2. An example for such a swap is a cross-currency swap paying floating index I in collateral currency and receiving fixed C_2 in a different currency.[12] For such a swap we have

$$\begin{aligned}
&X_1 = C_1 = \text{const.} = \text{given}, \qquad X_2 = C_2 = \text{const.} = \text{given},\\
&F_1^{U_1,\mathsf{C}}(T_i^1) = F_1^{U_1,\mathsf{C}}(T_i^1) = \text{given}, F_2^{U_2,\mathsf{C}}(T_i^2) = 0,\\
&P_1^{U_1,\mathsf{C}} = P^{U_1,\mathsf{C}} = \text{given}, \qquad P_2^{U_2,\mathsf{C}} = P^{U_2,\mathsf{C}} = \text{calibrated}.
\end{aligned}$$

We calibrate the discount factor $P^{U_2,\mathsf{C}}(T; t_0)$ with $T = T_n^2$ (last payment time in currency U_2).

[12] Usually cross-currency swaps exchange two floating indices, we will consider this case below.

6.4.2 Float Payment in Other Currency

If instead of a fixed payment we have that an index I_2 is paid in an other currency U_2 we may encounter the problem that the swap has two unknowns, namely the discount curve $P^{U_2,\mathsf{C}}$ for payments in currency U_2 collateralized with respect to C and the forward curve $F_2^{U_2,\mathsf{C}}$ of the index I_2 paid in currency U_2 collateralized with respect to C. The two curves can be obtained jointly from two different swaps: first a fix-versus-float swaps in currency U_2 collateralized by C, and second, a cross-currency swap exchanging the index I_2 with an index I_1 in currency U_1 for which the forward $F_1^{U_1,\mathsf{C}}$ is known. For the first instrument we denote the fixed payment by C_1, C_2. For the second instrument we denote the fixed payment by s_1, s_2 (usually a spread). For the first instrument we have

$$\begin{aligned} X_1 &= C_1 = \text{const.} = \text{given}, & X_2 &= C_2 = \text{const.} = \text{given}, \\ F_1^{U_1,\mathsf{C}}(T_i^1) &= 0, & F_2^{U_2,\mathsf{C}}(T_i^2) &= F_2^{U_2,\mathsf{C}}(T_i^2) = \text{calibrated}, \\ P_1^{U_1,\mathsf{C}} &= P_2^{U_2,\mathsf{C}} = \text{calibrated}, & P_2^{U_2,\mathsf{C}} &= \text{calibrated}. \end{aligned}$$

For the second swap we have

$$\begin{aligned} X_1 &= s_1 = \text{const.} = \text{given}, & X_2 &= s_2 = \text{const.} = \text{given}, \\ F_1^{U_1,\mathsf{C}}(T_i^1) &= F_1^{U_1,\mathsf{C}}(T_i^1) = \text{given}, & F_2^{U_2,\mathsf{C}}(T_i^2) &= F_2^{U_2,\mathsf{C}}(T_i^2) = \text{calibrated}, \\ P_1^{U_1,\mathsf{C}} &= \text{given}, & P_2^{U_2,\mathsf{C}} &= \text{calibrated}. \end{aligned}$$

We calibrate the discount factor $P^{U_2,\mathsf{C}}(T;t_0)$ with $T = T_n^2$ and the forward $F_2^{U_2,\mathsf{C}}(\mathrm{T})$ with $T = T_{n-1}^2$.

Often market data are not available to calibrate the forward $F_2^{U_2,\mathsf{C}}$, but the forward $F_2^{U_2,\mathsf{C}_2}$ collateralized with respect to a different account C_2 is available. The two forwards differ by a possible convexity adjustment. One possible approximation (which would follow from the assumption that forwards are independent of their collateralization) is to use $F_2^{U_2,\mathsf{C}} \approx F_2^{U_2,\mathsf{C}_2}$.

The joint calibration of the two curves can be decomposed into two independent calibration steps, which would then allow to re-use a traditional bootstrap algorithm, see, e.g., [4].

Calibration of Discount Curves as Spread Curves

We consider a swap leg with notional exchange and tenor $\{T_i\}_{i=0}^n$, paying an index I plus some constant $X = s(T_n) = const.$ Here $s(T_n)$ has the interpretation of a maturity-dependent spread. If this leg is in currency U and with respect to a collateral account (here funding account) D, then its value is

$$V_{SwapLeg}^{U,\mathsf{D}}(\alpha I, X, \{T_i\}_{i=0}^n) = \sum_{i=0}^{n-1} \Big(\big(\alpha F^{U,\mathsf{D}}(T_i) + X\big) \cdot P^{U,\mathsf{D}}(T_{i+1}) \\ + P^{U,\mathsf{D}}(T_{i+1}) - P^{U,\mathsf{D}}(T_i) \Big) .$$

An example of such an instrument is an (uncollateralized) floating rate bond, paying a 3M rate plus some spread. If we assume that the forward $F^{U,\mathsf{D}}(T_i)$ is known, this instrument can be used to calibrate the discount curve $P^{U,\mathsf{D}}$. In fact $I+X$ represents the performance of the funding account associated with $P^{U,\mathsf{D}}$.

If the forward $F^{U,\mathsf{D}}(T_i)$ is not known, we encounter the same problem as for cross-currency swaps, namely that the forward curve $F^{U,\mathsf{D}}(T_i)$ and the discount curve $P^{U,\mathsf{D}}$ need to be calibrated jointly to two instruments. The first one is a swap which is collateralized with respect to the funding account D, i.e., it is an uncollateralized swap. The second is the funding floater.

For the first instrument, the uncollateralized swap, we have

$$\begin{aligned} X_1 &= C_1 = \text{const.} = \text{given}, \; X_2 = C_2 = \text{const.} = \text{given}, \\ F_1^{U,\mathsf{D}}(T_i^1) &= 0 = \text{given}, \quad F_2^{U,\mathsf{D}}(T_i^2) = F^{U,\mathsf{D}}(T_i^2) = \text{calibrated}, \\ P_1^{U,\mathsf{D}} &= P^{U,\mathsf{D}} = \text{calibrated}, \; P_2^{U,\mathsf{D}} = P^{U,\mathsf{D}}. \end{aligned}$$

For the second instrument, the funding floating rate bond (uncollateralized swap leg with notional exchange) we have

$$\begin{aligned} X_1 &= S = \text{const.} = \text{given}, \\ F_1^{U,\mathsf{D}}(T_i^1) &= F^{U,\mathsf{D}}(T_i^1) = \text{calibrated}, \\ P_1^{U,\mathsf{D}} &= P^{U,\mathsf{D}} = \text{calibrated}. \end{aligned}$$

Remark 6 The calibration of the funding curve $P^{U,\mathsf{D}}$ is analog to the calibration of the cross-currency discount curve $P^{U_2,\mathsf{C}}$.

In the above, we consider the *funding floater* as a floating rate bond. Note however, that bonds (in contrast to swaps) do not permit negative coupons, hence they have an implicit floor. There are ways to solve this problem: either one has to incorporate an option premium in the calibration procedure (which does require a model for the volatility) or one considers only market data of fixed bonds together with uncollateralized swaps (which likely requires some assumption since usually this calibration instrument is not observed). See the following section.

6.5 Lack of Calibration Instruments (for Difference in Collateralization)

The calibration of cross-currency curves (forward curve and discount curves for currency U_2 with collateralization in currency U_1, see Sect. 6.4) and the calibration of un-collateralized curves (forward curves and discount curves for uncollateralized products, see section "Calibration of Discount Curves as Spread Curves") may require market data which are not available, e.g., the forward of an index I paid in currency U_2 collateralized in a different currency or by a different account. This issue has been pointed out by [14].

In this case the curve can be obtained by adding additional assumptions. Two simple examples are:

- the market rates are assumed to be independent of the type of collateralization, or
- the forward rates are assumed to be independent of the type of collateralization.

The two assumptions lead to different results, since they imply different correlations which will lead to different (convexity) adjustments. For details on the example see [11], where a sample calculation with assuming identical market rates for 3M swaps collateralized in USD-OIS or EUR-OIS results in a difference of around 1 or 2 basis points (0.01 %) for the forward curves.

6.6 Implementation

The definition of the various calibration instruments indicated that an iterative bootstrapping algorithm (there the curve is built in a step-by-step process solving only one dimensional problems in one variable) is no longer straightforward. This is due to the interdependence of discount and forward curves. While this problem may be solved in some cases via a pre-processing (see [4]), we suggest a different route: we propose to solve the calibration problem via a single optimization run on the full multi-dimensional problem. This also allows to calibrate curve in the sense of a best fit in cases where we use more calibration instruments than curve points, resulting in an overdetermined system.

We provide an object-oriented implementation at [11] implementing the Java classes for `Curves`, `DiscountCurves`, `ForwardCurves`, `Solver`, `SwapLeg` and `Swap`.

A detailed discussion of the implementation can be found in the associated JavaDocs and is left out here to shorten the presentation.

7 Redefining Forward Rate Market Models

Having discussed the setup of curves, we would like to conclude with a remark on how the curves are integrated into term-structure models, specifically, how the multi-curve setup harmonizes with a classical single curve standard LIBOR market model, which can then be extended to a fully multi-curve model.

If N^{C} denotes an accrual account, i.e., N^{C} is a process with $N^{\mathrm{C}}(t_0) = 1U$ (e.g., a collateral account), then N^{C} defines a discount curve, namely the discount curve $T \mapsto P^{U,\mathrm{C}}(T; t_0) =: P^{\mathrm{C}}(T; t_0)$ of fixed payments made in T, valued in t and collateralized by units of N^{C}.

Now let $\{T_i\}$ denote a given tenor discretization. As shown in Sect. 4.1 the period-$[T_i, T_{i+1}]$ performance index $I^{\mathrm{C}}(T_i, T_{i+1})$ of the an accrual account, i.e., $I^{\mathrm{C}}(T_i, T_{i+1}; T_i) := \frac{N^{\mathrm{C}}(T_{i+1})}{N^{\mathrm{C}}(T_i)} - 1$ has the property that its time t *forward* (of a payment of $I^{\mathrm{C}}(T_i, T_{i+1})$ made in T_{i+1}, collateralized in units of N^{C}) (following the definition of a forward from Definition 3) is given as $F^{U,\mathrm{C}}(T_i, T_{i+1}; t) := \frac{P^{\mathrm{C}}(T_i;t)-P^{\mathrm{C}}(T_{i+1};t)}{P^{\mathrm{C}}(T_{i+1};t_0)}$.

This relation allows us to create a term-structure model for the curve P^{C} which has the same structural properties as a standard single curve (LIBOR) market model. This model is given by a joint modeling of the processes $L_i(t) := \frac{F^{U,\mathrm{C}}(T_i,T_{i+1};t)}{T_{i+1}-T_i}$, e.g., as log-normal processes under the measure $\mathbb{Q}^{N^{\mathrm{C}}}$ and the additional assumption that the process $P^{\mathrm{C}}(T_i; t)$ is deterministic on its short period $t \in (T_{i-1}, T_i]$.

From these two assumptions it follows that the processes L_i have the structure of a standard LIBOR market model and $\mathbb{Q}^{N^{\mathrm{C}}}$ corresponds to the spot measure. Indeed we have $\prod_{j=0}^{i-1} 1 + L_j(T_j) \cdot (T_{j+1} - T_j) = N^{\mathrm{C}}(T_i)$.

What we have described is how to use the standard LIBOR market model as a term structure model for the collateral account N^{C} (e.g., the OIS curve). Now, modeling all other rates (including LIBOR) can be performed by modeling (possibly stochastic) spreads over this curve. This is analog to a defaultable market model.

An alternative is to start with a stochastic model for the forward rates, where now the forward curve defines the initial value of the model SDEs, and then define the discount curve (numéraire) via deterministic or stochastic spreads. This approach has a practical advantage, since for LIBOR rates implied volatilities are more liquid than for OIS rates. See, e.g., [20] and references therein. An implementation of the standard LMM with a deterministic adjustment for the discount curve is provided by the author at [9].

8 Some Numerical Results

8.1 *Impact of the Interpolation Entity of a Forward Curve on the Delta Hedge*

Using our reference implementation [11], we investigate the interpolation of forward curves using different interpolation methods and interpolation entities. While interpolation of (synthetic) discount factors is—motivated from its single curve origin—a very popular interpolation method, it may result in very implausible deltas, if the curve is constructed from overlapping instruments. Table 1 shows the delta of an 8x11 FRA calculated on a curve constructed from 0x3, 1x4, 2x5, 3x6, 4x7, 5x8, 6x9, 7x10, 9x12 FRA (note that the 8x11 is missing in the curve construction). The plausible hedge would be to use the adjacent 7x10 and 9x12 FRAs. Using the interpolation entity `DISCOUNTFACTOR` we find non-zero deltas for instruments prior to the 7x10 FRA, summing up to zero. This effect stems from the error propagation inherent in the definition of the interpolation entity. The interpolation entity `FORWARD` does not show this effect.

Table 1 The delta of an 7Mx10M FRA with respect to different calibration instruments, where the 7Mx10M FRA is not part of the calibration instruments, hence interpolates

Risk Factor	Delta of an 7Mx10M FRA using the interpolation entity	
	DISCOUNTFACTOR (%)	FORWARD (%)
0Dx3M	44.5	0.0
1Mx4M	−95.9	0.0
2Mx5M	52.4	0.0
3Mx6M	44.0	0.0
4Mx7M	−97.0	0.0
5Mx8M	52.4	0.0
6Mx9M	47.6	48.4
7Mx10M	0.0	0.0
8Mx11M	51.9	51.6
9Mx12M	0.0	0.0

Different interpolation entities result in very different delta hedges. The popular interpolation entity of a synthetic discount factor results in counterintuitive hedges. The interpolation method is LINEAR in both cases. It is the choice of the interpolation entity which introduces the effect

8.2 Impact of the Lack of Calibration Instruments for the Case of a Foreign Swap Collateralized in Domestic Currency

Based on the curve framework and the calibration instruments defined in this paper and implemented at [11] we have investigated the impact of the assumptions, which had to be made due to the lack of calibration instruments for foreign currency swaps. Since a foreign currency swap collateralized in domestic currency is (currently) not a liquid instrument, the *foreign forward with respect to domestic collateralization* cannot be calibrated. Hence, a model assumption is required. Two possible assumptions are: (1) the forward rate is independent from its collateralization—that is, use the foreign forward curve derived from instruments collateralized in *foreign* currency, or, (2) the market (swap) rates are independent from its collateralization—that is, use the foreign market (par-)swap rates form foreign currency swaps collateralized in foreign currency together with a domestic currency discount curve to calibrate a foreign currency forward rate curve with respect to domestic collateralization. Both approaches result in different forward curves. The impact can be assessed using the spreadsheet available at [11]. For 2012 market data the difference for an USD forward curve collateralized in EUR can be found to be around two basis points. While the first assumption (re-using the forward curve) is likely the more natural one, and maybe a market standard, the calculation shows that the assumption has a considerable impact on the resulting curve, see Fig. 1.

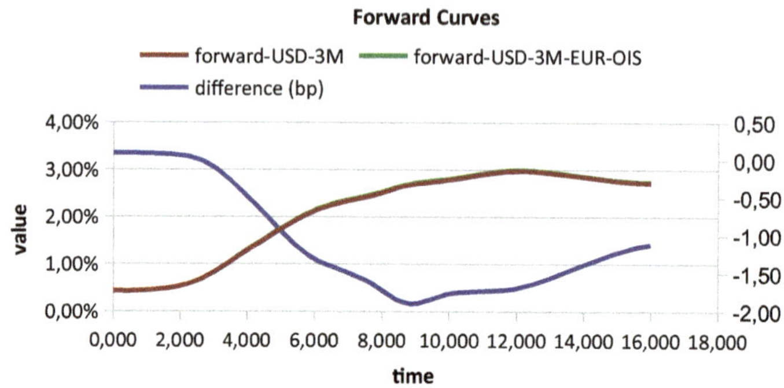

Fig. 1 Forward curve (USD-3M) calibrated from swaps with different collateralization (USD-OIS and EUR-OIS) assuming independence of the market rates of from the type of collateralization

8.3 Impact of the Interpolation Scheme on the Hedge Efficiency

Also based on the framework presented here, the impact of the different interpolation schemes has been investigated in [13], where indication was found that among the local interpolation schemes, it is indeed better to use a different interpolation scheme for forward curves than for discount curves. For details we refer to [13].

9 Conclusion

We have presented the re-definition of discount curves and forward curves, which clearly distinguishes the two as different objects (with some relation for the special case of OIS curves). This re-definition results in curves, representing values with well-defined economic interpretations. We then discussed some interpolation schemes for these curves, where our re-definition suggests to apply different interpolation schemes for discount and forward curves. This stands in contrast to the classical approach where a forward curve had been represented via synthetic discount factors, using the same interpolation schemes for both types of curves.

We have presented the calibration, defining the calibration instruments. Based on this, we provide an open source, object-oriented implementation at [11].[13]

Based on this benchmark implementation it was possible to assess the impact of assumptions, which had to be made due to the lack of calibration instruments, e.g.,

[13] A complete description of the implementation is given at http://www.finmath.net/finmath-lib, including source code and numerical examples. They are left out in this paper.

for the case of cross-currency swaps, and the impact of the different interpolation schemes. Indication was found that it is better to use a different interpolation scheme for forward curves than for discount curves. With respect to delta hedges one should favor forward interpolation over synthetic discount factor interpolation. Among forward interpolation, linear interpolation performed well with respect to the hedge performance.

Acknowledgements The KPMG Center of Excellence in Risk Management is acknowledged for organizing the conference "Challenges in Derivatives Markets - Fixed Income Modeling, Valuation Adjustments, Risk Management, and Regulation".

References

1. Ametrano, F.M., Bianchetti, M.: Bootstrapping the illiquidity: multiple yield curves construction for market coherent forward rates estimation. Ohio State University (2000)
2. Ametrano, F.M., Bianchetti, M.: Everything you always wanted to know about multiple interest rate curve bootstrapping but were afraid to ask. Preprint (2013)
3. Chibane, M., Selvaraj, J.P., Sheldon, G.: Building curves on a good basis. Social Scientific Research Network (2009). http://ssrn.com/abstract=1394267
4. Clark, J.: Constructing a non-USD swap discounting curve with USD collateral. http://www.edurisk.ie
5. Crépey, S., Grbac, Z., Nguyen, H., Skovmand, D.: A Lévy HJM multiple-curve model with application to CVA computation. Quant. Financ. **15**(3), 401–419 (2015)
6. Cuchiero, C., Fontana, C., Gnoatto, A.: A general HJM framework for multiple yield curve modeling. Financ. Stoch. **6**, 397 (2016)
7. Delbaen, F., Schachermayer, W.: A general version of the fundamental theorem of asset pricing. Math. Annalen **300**, 463–520 (1994)
8. Fillipovic, D., Trolle, A.B.: The term structure of interbank risk. J. Financ. Econ. **109**(3), 707–733 (2012)
9. Fries, C.P.: Libor market model. Object oriented reference implementation 2004–2015. http://www.finmath.net/topics/libormarketmodel
10. Fries, C.P.: Mathematical Finance. Theory, Modeling, Implementation. Wiley, Hoboken (2007). http://www.christian-fries.de/finmath/book
11. Fries, C.P.: Curve calibration. Object oriented reference implementation 2010–2015. http://www.finmath.net/topics/curvecalibration
12. Fries, C.P.: Funded replication: fund exchange process and the valuation with different funding-accounts (cross-currency analogy to funding revisited). Wilmott **63**, 36–41 (2013). http://papers.ssrn.com/abstract=2115839
13. Fries, C.P., Plum, C.: Interest rate curve interpolations and their assessment via hedge simulations. Preprint (2015). http://ssrn.com/abstract=2635903
14. Fujii, M., Shimadaz, Y., Takahashi, A.: A note on construction of multiple swap curves with and without collateral (2010)
15. Grbac, Z., Papapantoleon, A., Schoenmakers, J., Skovmand, D.: Affine LIBOR models with multiple curves: theory, examples and calibration. SIAM. J. Financ. Math. **6**(1), 984–1025 (2015)
16. Hagan, P.S., West, G.: Interpolation methods for curve construction. Appl. Math. Financ. **13**(2), 89–129 (2006)
17. Henrard, M.: Interest rate instruments and market conventions guide. OpenGamma (2013)

18. Henrard, M.: Interest Rate Modelling in the Multi-Curve Framework: Foundations, Evolution and Implementation. Palgrave Macmillan, Basingstoke (2014)
19. Le Floc'h, F.: Stable interpolation for the yield curve. Social Scientific Research Network (2013)
20. Mercurio, F.: LIBOR market models with stochastic basis. Bloomberg Education and Quantitative Research Paper, (2010-05-FRONTIERS) (2010)
21. Mercurio, F.: Modern LIBOR market models: using different curves for projecting rates and discounting. Bloomberg Education and Quantitative Research Paper, 13(1), 113–137 (2010)
22. Moreni, M., Pallavicini, A.: Parsimonious HJM modelling for multiple yield-curve dynamics. Quant. Financ. **14**(2), 199–210 (2014)

3

Simultaneous Hedging of Regulatory and Accounting CVA

Christoph Berns

Abstract As a consequence of the recent financial crisis, Basel III introduced a new capital charge, the CVA risk charge to cover the risk of future CVA fluctuations (CVA volatility). Although Basel III allows for hedging the CVA risk charge, mismatches between the regulatory (Basel III) and accounting (IFRS) rules lead to the fact that hedging the CVA risk charge is challenging. The reason is that the hedge instruments reducing the CVA risk charge cause additional Profit and Loss (P&L) volatility. In the present article, we propose a solution which optimizes the CVA risk charge and the P&L volatility from hedging.

Keywords CVA risk charge · Accounting CVA · Hedging · Optimization

1 Introduction

Counterparty credit risk is the risk that a counterparty in a derivatives transaction will default prior to expiration of the trade and will therefore not be able to fulfill its contractual obligations. Before the recent financial crisis many market participants believed that some counterparties will never fail ("too big to fail") and therefore counterparty risk was generally considered as not significant. This view changed due to the bankruptcy of Lehman Brothers during the financial crisis and market participants realized that even major banks can fail. For that reason, counterparty risk is nowadays considered to be significant for investment banks. The International Financial Reporting Standards (IFRS) demand that the fair value of a derivative incorporates the credit quality of the counterparty. This is achieved by a valuation adjustment which is commonly referred to as credit valuation adjustment (CVA), see e.g. [3–5]. The CVA is part of the IFRS P&L, i.e. losses (gains) caused by changes of the counterparties credit quality reduce (increase) the balance sheet equity.

Basel III requires a capital charge for future changes of the credit quality of derivatives, i.e. CVA volatility. Banks can either use a standardized approach to

C. Berns (✉)
KPMG AG, Am Flughafen, 60549 Frankfurt am Main, Germany
e-mail: christophberns@kpmg.com

compute this capital charge or an internal model [2]. The latter charge is commonly referred to as CVA risk charge. Many banks have implemented a CVA desk in order to manage actively their CVA risk. CVA desks buy CDS protection on the capital markets to hedge the counterparty credit risk of uncollateralized derivatives which have been bought by the ordinary trading desks. Recognizing that banks actively manage CVA positions, Basel III allows for hedging the CVA risk charge using credit hedges such as single name CDSs and CDS indexes. However, the recognition of hedges is different depending on whether the standardized approach or an internal model is used [2].

Summarizing, we can look at counterparty credit risk from two different perspectives: the regulatory (Basel III) and the accounting (IFRS) one. Depending whether we consider counterparty risk from a regulatory or accounting perspective, different valuation methods are applied for this risk. In general, the regulatory treatment of counterparty risk is more conservative than the accounting one, cf. [6]. The difference between the regulatory and the accounting treatment of counterparty risk causes the following problem in hedging the CVA risk charge: eligible hedge instruments such as CDSs would lead to a reduction of the CVA risk charge. On the other hand, under IFRS, a CDS is recognized as a derivative and thus accounted at fair value through profit and loss and therefore introducing further P&L volatility.

The current accounting and regulatory rules expose banks to the situation that they cannot achieve regulatory capital relief and low P&L volatility simultaneously. Deutsche Bank, for instance, has largely hedged the CVA risk charge in the first half of 2013. The hedging strategy that reduced the CVA risk charge has caused large losses due to additional P&L volatility, cf. [7]. This example illustrates the mismatch between the regulatory and accounting treatment of CVA.[1] The mismatch demands for a trade-off between these two regimes, cf. [8]. For this reason, we propose in this article an approach which leads to an optimal allocation between CVA risk charge reduction and P&L volatility. Our considerations are restricted to the standardized CVA risk charge.

We start with an explanation of the standardized CVA risk charge, i.e. the regulatory treatment of CVA. Afterwards, we show that the standardized CVA charge can be interpreted as a (scaled) volatility/variance of a portfolio of normally distributed positions. This interpretation reveals the modeling assumptions of the regulator and will be crucial for the later considerations. In a next step, we explain the counterparty risk modeling from an accounting perspective and we compute the impact of the hedge instruments (used to reduce the CVA risk charge) to the overall P&L volatility, assuming that the risk factor returns are normally distributed. Without the mismatch between the regulatory and the accounting regime, the hedge instruments would move anti-correlated to the corresponding accounting CVAs and the resulting common volatility would be small. Due to the mismatch, the CVA and the hedge instrument changes will not offset completely. For this reason we introduce a

---

[1]Due to the exclusion of DVA from the Basel III regulatory calculation, the mismatch potentially intensifies.

synthetic[2] total volatility σ_{syn} consisting basically of the sum of the additional accounting P&L volatility σ_{hed} caused by fair value changes of the hedge instruments (hedge P&L volatility) and the regulatory CVA volatility $\sigma_{CVA,reg}$ (i.e. basically the CVA risk charge)[3]:

$$\sigma_{syn}^2 = \sigma_{hed}^2 + \sigma_{CVA,reg}^2. \tag{1}$$

Hence, (1) defines a steering variable describing the common effects of CVA risk charge hedging and resulting P&L volatility. One should mention that formula (1) may suggest statistical independence of the two quantities. However, there exists a dependence in the following sense: both the regulatory CVA volatility and the hedge P&L volatility depend on the hedge amount. The more we hedge, the smaller the $\sigma_{CVA,reg}$. On the other hand, the more we hedge, the larger the σ_{hed}. The definition of the synthetic volatility as a sum of σ_{hed}^2 and $\sigma_{CVA,reg}^2$ can be motivated by the following consideration: the term $\sigma_{CVA,reg}^2$ is related to the regulatory capital demand for CVA risk. The other term, σ_{hed}^2, can be interpreted as capital demand for market risk of the hedge instruments. Although the hedge instruments are excluded from the regulatory capital demand computation for market risk, they potentially reduce the balance sheet equity and therefore may reduce the available regulatory capital. The sum in (1) is now motivated by the additivity of the total capital demand.

In the following we will consider σ_{syn} as function of the hedge amount and search for its minimum. The hedge amount minimizing σ_{syn} leads to the optimal allocation between CVA risk charge relief and P&L volatility. We will derive analytical solutions. The discussion of several special cases will provide an intuitive understanding of the optimal allocation. For technical reasons we exclude index hedges in the derivation of the optimal hedge strategy. However, it is easy to generalize the results to the case where index hedges are allowed.

2 Counterparty Risk from a Regulatory Perspective: The Standardized CVA Risk Charge

In this section we introduce the standardized CVA risk charge. A detailed explanation of all involved parameters is given in the Basel III document [2]. The formula for the standardized CVA risk charge is prescribed by the regulator and is used to determine the amount of regulatory capital which banks must hold in order to absorb possible losses caused by future deteriorations of the counterparties credit quality. We will see that the standardized CVA risk charge can be interpreted as volatility (i.e. standard deviation) of a normally distributed random variable. More precisely, we will show that the CVA risk charge can be interpreted as the 99 % quantile of a portfolio of

---

[2] We use the word synthetic since σ_{syn} mixes a volatility measured in regulatory terms and a volatility measured in accounting terms.

[3] This connection will be explained later.

positions subject to normally distributed CVA changes (i.e. CVA P&L) only. This gives some insights into the regulators modeling assumptions for future CVA. It is worth to mention that the regulators modeling assumptions may hold or not hold. A detailed look at the regulators modeling assumptions can be found in [6].

In order to be prepared for later computations, we introduce in this section some notations and recall some facts about normally distributed random variables.

The standardized CVA risk charge K is given by [2]:

$$K = \beta\sqrt{h}\Phi^{-1}(q) \tag{2}$$

with

- $h = 1$, the 1-year time horizon,
- Φ the cumulative distribution function of the standard normal distribution
- $q = 99\,\%$ the confidence level and
- β defined by[4]

$$\begin{aligned}\beta^2 = &\left(\sum_{i=1}^{n} 0.5 \cdot \omega_i \left(M_i EAD_i - M_i^{hed} B_i\right) - \omega_{ind} M_{ind} B_{ind}\right)^2 \\ &+ \sum_{i=1}^{n} 0.75 \cdot \omega_i^2 \left(M_i EAD_i - M_i^{hed} B_i\right)^2\end{aligned} \tag{3}$$

with

- ω_i a weight depending on the rating of the counterparty i, n is the number of counterparties
- M_i, M_i^{hed}, and M_{ind} the effective maturities for the ith netting set (corresponding to counterparty i), the hedged instrument for counterparty i and the index hedge
- EAD_i the discounted regulatory exposure w.r.t. counterparty i
- B_i, B_{ind} the discounted hedge notional amounts invested in the hedge instrument (CDS) for counterparty i and the index hedge.

Formula (2) is determined by the regulator. In order to get a better understanding of this formula, we will derive a stochastic interpretation of it. Before that, we need to recall a fact about normal distributions: if the random vector $\vec{X}$ has a multivariate normal distribution, i.e. $\vec{X} \sim \mathcal{N}(0, \Sigma)$ with mean 0 and covariance matrix Σ, then, for a deterministic vector $\vec{a}$, the scalar product

$$\langle \vec{a}, \vec{X} \rangle := \sum_i a_i X_i \tag{4}$$

[4]For simplicity we consider only one index hedge. The results in this article can easily be generalized to more than one index hedge.

has a univariate normal distribution with mean 0 and variance

$$\sigma^2 = \langle \vec{a}, \Sigma \vec{a} \rangle. \tag{5}$$

Now we are able to derive the stochastic interpretation of the CVA risk charge, more precise the interpretation as volatility.

2.1 *Standardized CVA Risk Charge as Volatility*

In this section we will show that the regulators' modeling assumptions behind the standardized CVA risk charge are given by normally distributed CVA returns which are aggregated by using a one-factor Gaussian copula model.[5] We consider n counterparties. By R_i, we denote the (one year) CVA P&L (i.e. those P&L effects caused by CVA changes) w.r.t. counterparty i.

Lemma 1 *If one assumes $R_i \sim \mathcal{N}(0, \sigma_i^2)$ and further, if one assumes that the random vector*[6]

$$\vec{R} = (R_1, \ldots, R_n)^t$$

is distributed according to a one-factor Gaussian copula model, i.e. $\vec{R} \sim \mathcal{N}(0, \Gamma)$ with $\Gamma_{ii} = \sigma_i^2$ and $\Gamma_{ij} = \rho\sigma_i\sigma_j$ with ρ independent of i and j for $i \neq j$, then the 99 % quantile of the distribution of $\vec{R}$ is equal to the CVA risk charge (2).

Proof Using (4) and (5), we find that the aggregated CVA return (common CVA P&L) $R_{CVA,reg} := \sum_{i=1}^{n} R_i = \langle \vec{1}, \vec{R} \rangle$[7] has the distribution $\mathcal{N}(0, \sigma_{CVA,reg}^2)$ with

$$\sigma_{CVA,reg}^2 = \langle \vec{1}, \Gamma \vec{1} \rangle = \sum_{i,j=1}^{n} \Gamma_{i,j} = \left(\sqrt{\rho} \sum_{i=1}^{n} \sigma_i \right)^2 + (1-\rho) \sum_{i=1}^{n} \sigma_i^2 \tag{6}$$

If we compare the above expression with (3), we see that this expression is equal to β^2 (with $B_{ind} = 0$, i.e. no index hedges) if we set $\rho = 0.25$ and $\sigma_i = \omega_i(M_i EAD_i - M_i^{hed} B_i)$. The quantile interpretation of the CVA risk charge (i.e. Formula (2)) follows from standard properties of the normal distribution.

The above lemma shows that the standardized CVA risk charge is basically the volatility of the sum $\sum_i R_i$ of n normally distributed random variables. The normally distributed random variables are equicorrelated: $\rho(R_i, R_j) = 0.25$. Each CVA return R_i has the volatility

$$\sigma_i = \omega_i(M_i EAD_i - M_i^{hed} B_i). \tag{7}$$

---

[5] This is a very strong assumption that might not be true in reality.

[6] By $\cdot^t$ we denote the transpose of a vector/matrix.

[7] By $\vec{1}$ we denote the vector $(1, \ldots, 1)^t$.

Hence, buying credit protection on counterparty i reduces the corresponding CVA volatility. If we assume $M_i = M_i^{hed}$, the optimal hedge w.r.t. counterparty i is given by a CDS with notional amount B_i equals

$$B_i = EAD_i. \tag{8}$$

3 Counterparty Risk from an Accounting Perspective

As explained in the introduction, counterparty risk from an accounting perspective is quantified by a fair value adjustment called credit valuation adjustment (CVA). The CVA reduces the present value (PV) of a derivatives portfolio in order to incorporate counterparty risk:

$$PV = PV_{riskfree} - CVA,$$

whereby $PV_{riskfree}$ denotes the market value of the portfolio without counterparty risk and CVA is the adjustment to reflect counterparty risk. For the modeling of CVA, banks have some degrees of freedom. Typically, the accounting CVA is computed by means of the following formula (see e.g. [4]):

$$CVA = \int_0^T D(t)EE(t)dP(t) \tag{9}$$

with T the effective maturity of the derivatives portfolio, $D(t)$ the risk-free discount curve, $EE(t) = E[\max\{0, PV(t)\}]$ the (risk-neutral) expected positive exposure at (future time point) t, and $dP(t)$ is the (risk-neutral) default probability of the counterparty in the infinitesimal interval $[t, t+dt]$. For the implementation of (9), a discretization of the integral is necessary. Many banks assume a constant EE profile (i.e. $EE(t) = EE^*$ for all t). In that case, (9) simplifies to

$$CVA = EE^* \int_0^T D(t)dP(t). \tag{10}$$

Further, the (risk-neutral) default probabilities are typically modeled by a hazard rate model, i.e. one assumes that the default time is exponentially distributed with parameter λ. Using this assumption, we can write:

$$CVA = \lambda EE^* \int_0^T D(t)e^{-\lambda t}dt. \tag{11}$$

The approximation (11) will be helpful in the next section, where we describe the hedging of CVA from an accounting perspective

3.1 CVA Hedging from an Accounting Perspective

In previous sections we have seen that the regulatory CVA hedging (i.e. CVA risk charge hedging) can be achieved by buying credit protection. Effectively, (7) says that the regulatory exposure is reduced by the notional amount of the bought credit protection. At this place, we describe CVA hedging from an accounting perspective.

Let us consider a derivatives portfolio with a single counterparty. In order to hedge the corresponding counterparty risk, one can buy, for example, a single name CDS such that the CVA w.r.t. the counterparty together with the CDS is Delta neutral (i.e. up to first order, CVA movements are neutralized by the CDS movements). The condition for Delta neutrality is

$$\Delta CVA = \Delta CDS \tag{12}$$

whereby Δ describes the derivative of the CVA and CDS respectively (w.r.t. the credit spread of the counterparty). To be more precise, the default leg of the CDS should compensate the CVA movements. Using a standard valuation model for a CDS (see e.g. [4]) and computing the derivatives in (12), it is easy to see that (12) is equivalent to

$$B = EE^*, \tag{13}$$

i.e. the optimal hedge amount is given by EE^*. Typically, EE^* is given by the average of the expected positive exposures $EE(t)$ at future time points t:

$$EE^* = \frac{1}{T}\int_0^T EE(t)dt. \tag{14}$$

If we compare (13) with (8) we see that the optimal hedge notional amount for hedging CVA risk from a regulatory perspective is the regulatory exposure EAD, while the optimal hedge notional amount for hedging accounting CVA risk is given by EE^*. In general it holds $EAD > EE^*$, due to conservative assumptions made by the regulator[8] (we refer to [6] for a detailed comparison of these two quantities). Thus, hedging CVA risk differs whether it is considered from an accounting or a regulatory perspective. This mismatch causes additional P&L volatility in the accounting framework, if the CVA risk is hedged from a regulatory perspective (i.e. if the CVA risk charge is hedged).

Finally we remark that we can write the CVA sensitivities $\Delta_{CVA} = \frac{d}{ds}CVA$ as

$$\Delta_{CVA} = EE^* \Delta_{CDS}, \tag{15}$$

whereby Δ_{CDS} is the sensitivity of (the default leg of) a CDS with notional amount $B = 1$.

---

[8] For example, the alpha multiplier in the IMM context overstates the EAD by a factor of 1.4. Further, the non-decreasing constraint to the exposure profile leads to an overstatement, see [6] for details.

4 Portfolio P&L

As explained above, the hedge instruments reduce the (regulatory) counterparty credit risk. But they may cause new market risk due to additional P&L volatility. However, although in accordance with Basel III eligible hedge instruments are excluded from market risk RWA calculations, the additional P&L volatility of the hedge instruments leads to fluctuations in reported equity. In order to describe the effects of hedging to the overall P&L, we introduce in the present section the corresponding framework. We divide the overall P&L in different parts: the P&L of the hedge instruments, the P&L of the remaining positions, and the CVA P&L. The framework will be helpful later on, when we want to quantify the impact of the CVA risk charge hedges to the accounting P&L.

4.1 *Portfolio P&L Without CVA*

Let us assume that a bank holds derivatives with n different counterparties for which single name CDS exists. The bank has to decide to which extent it hedges the counterparty risk w.r.t. these counterparties by either single name CDS or index hedges. By Σ we denote the correlation matrix (of dimension $N \times N$, $N > n$) of all risk factors r_i, $i = 1, \ldots, N$ the banks (trading) portfolio is exposed to. Without loss of generality, we assume that the correlations between the CDS of the considered n counterparties are given by the first $n \times n$ components of Σ, i.e. $\Sigma_{i,j} = \rho(CDS_i, CDS_j)$, $i, j = 1, \ldots, n$. Further, $\Sigma_{n+1,i}$ denotes the correlation between the index hedge and the CDS on counterparty $i \in \{1, \ldots, n\}$. The whole portfolio Π of the bank contains the hedge instruments (CDS and index hedge) as well as other instruments (e.g. bonds): $\Pi = \Pi_{hed} \cup \Pi_{rest}$. The sub-portfolio Π_{hed} is driven by the credit spreads of the counterparties. Note that Π_{rest} may depend on some of these credit spreads as well. In the following, we will assume the P&L of the portfolio Π is given by:

$$P\&L = \sum_{i=1}^{n} (B_i \Delta_i + \Delta_{i,rest}) dr_i + B_{ind} \Delta_{ind} dr_{ind} + \sum_{j=n+2}^{N} \Delta_j dr_j, \tag{16}$$

whereby Δ_i denotes the sensitivity of CDS_i w.r.t. the corresponding credit spread, $\Delta_{i,rest}$ denotes the sensitivity of the remaining positions which are sensitive w.r.t. the credit spread of counterparty i as well,[9] B_i (resp. B_{ind}) denotes the notional of CDS_i (resp. the notional of the index hedge), and dr_i describes the change of the risk factor r_i (the first n risk factors are the credit spreads) in the considered time period.

[9]For example, if Π_{rest} contains a bond emitted by the counterparty i, then (ignoring the Bond-CDS Basis) $\Delta_{i,rest} = -\Delta_i$).

4.2 Impact with CVA

This section extends the above considerations to the case where we allow for a CVA component. We define the total P&L as the difference between the P&L given by (16) and the CVA P&L:

$$P\&L_{tot} = P\&L - P\&L_{CVA}, \tag{17}$$

whereby $P\&L_{CVA}$ is defined in a similar manner as in (16)[10]:

$$P\&L_{CVA} = \sum_{i=1}^{n+1} \Delta_{i,CVA} dr_i. \tag{18}$$

In (18), the risk factors r_i are the same risk factors which appear in the first $n+1$ summands of (16). This is because the CVAs are driven by the same risk factors as the corresponding hedge instruments. Recall that in a setup where counterparty risk is completely hedged, the P&L of the hedge instruments is canceled out by the P&L of the CVAs. This is the case, if the corresponding sensitivity is equal. In Sect. 3.1 we have shown how one can achieve this (using the condition of Delta neutrality) by choosing the right hedge notional amounts.

4.3 Impact of CVA Risk Charge Hedging on the Accounting P&L Volatility

The additional P&L volatility caused by the hedge instruments is basically given by the residual volatility of the hedge instruments which is not canceled by the CVAs. In order to derive an expression for this volatility, we start with the derivation of the volatility of the total portfolio P&L. The residual volatility will consist of those parts of the total volatility which are sensitive w.r.t. the hedge instruments.

In order to proceed, we have to introduce the following notations: the vector $\vec{\Delta}_{CVA} \in \mathbb{R}^{n+1}$ contains the CVA sensitivities and the return vector $\vec{dr} \in \mathbb{R}^N$ describes the changes of the N risk factors the trading book is exposed to. We further introduce the sensitivity vectors[11] $\vec{\Delta} = (\Delta_1, \ldots, \Delta_{ind}, \ldots, \Delta_N)^t \in \mathbb{R}^N$

---

[10] We consider only the credit spreads as risk factors. Exposure movements due to changes in market risk factors are not considered. This is unproblematic for the considerations in this article since we will end up with dynamic CVA hedging strategy (cf. Sect. 5) which incorporates the exposure changes.

[11] The first n components of $\vec{\Delta}$ are the CDS sensitivities w.r.t. credit spread changes and the $n+1$th component is the sensitivity of the index hedge.

and[12] $\vec{\Delta}_{rest} = (\Delta_{1,rest}, \ldots, \Delta_{n,rest})^t \in \mathbb{R}^n$, the notional vector $\vec{B} = (B_1, \ldots, B_n, B_{ind})^t \in \mathbb{R}^{n+1}$ and the diagonal matrix $Q_\Delta = diag(\Delta_1, \ldots, \Delta_n, \Delta_{ind}) \in \mathbb{R}^{(n+1)\times(n+1)}$.

Lemma 2 *If we assume that the portfolio P&L is given by (17) and if we further assume $\vec{dr} \sim \mathcal{N}(0, \Sigma)$ (for some correlation matrix Σ), then the squared volatility (i.e. the variance) of (17) is given by*[13]

$$\begin{aligned}\sigma^2_{P\&L_{tot}} =& \left\langle \begin{pmatrix} Q_\Delta \vec{B} \\ \vec{0} \end{pmatrix} \Sigma \begin{pmatrix} Q_\Delta \vec{B} \\ \vec{0} \end{pmatrix} \right\rangle + \left\langle \begin{pmatrix} \vec{\Delta}_{CVA} \\ \vec{0} \end{pmatrix} \Sigma \begin{pmatrix} \vec{\Delta}_{CVA} \\ \vec{0} \end{pmatrix} \right\rangle \\ &+ \left\langle \begin{pmatrix} \vec{\Delta}_{rest} \\ \vec{\Delta}_{N-n-1} \end{pmatrix} \Sigma \begin{pmatrix} \vec{\Delta}_{rest} \\ \vec{\Delta}_{N-n-1} \end{pmatrix} \right\rangle - 2\left\langle \begin{pmatrix} Q_\Delta \vec{B} \\ \vec{0} \end{pmatrix} \Sigma \begin{pmatrix} \vec{\Delta}_{CVA} \\ \vec{0} \end{pmatrix} \right\rangle \\ &+ 2\left\langle \begin{pmatrix} Q_\Delta \vec{B} \\ \vec{0} \end{pmatrix} \Sigma \begin{pmatrix} \vec{\Delta}_{rest} \\ \vec{\Delta}_{N-n-1} \end{pmatrix} \right\rangle - 2\left\langle \begin{pmatrix} \vec{\Delta}_{rest} \\ \vec{\Delta}_{N-n-1} \end{pmatrix} \Sigma \begin{pmatrix} \vec{\Delta}_{CVA} \\ \vec{0} \end{pmatrix} \right\rangle. \end{aligned} \tag{19}$$

Proof With the above defined vectors, we can write:

$$\begin{aligned} P\&L_{tot} &= \langle Q_\Delta \vec{B} - \vec{\Delta}_{CVA}, \vec{dr}_{n+1} \rangle + \langle \vec{\Delta}_{rest}, \vec{dr}_{n+1} \rangle + \langle \vec{\Delta}_{N-n-1}, \vec{dr}_{N-n-1} \rangle \\ &= \left\langle \begin{pmatrix} Q_\Delta \vec{B} \\ \vec{0}_{N-n-1} \end{pmatrix} - \begin{pmatrix} \vec{\Delta}_{CVA} \\ \vec{0}_{N-n-1} \end{pmatrix} + \begin{pmatrix} \vec{\Delta}_{rest} \\ \vec{\Delta}_{N-n-1} \end{pmatrix}, \vec{dr} \right\rangle \\ &= \langle \vec{a} - \vec{b} + \vec{c}, \vec{dr} \rangle \end{aligned} \tag{20}$$

whereby $\vec{dr}_{n+1}$ denotes the $n+1$-dimensional vector consisting of the first $n+1$ components of $\vec{dr}$, $\vec{dr}_{N-n-1}$ consists of the remaining $N-n-1$ components of $\vec{dr}$, $\vec{\Delta}_{N-n-1}$ denotes the vector of the remaining $N-n-1$ sensitivities, and $\vec{0}_{N-n-1}$ is the $N-n-1$-dimensional vector whose components are all equal to 0.[14] Clearly, the vectors $\vec{a}$, $\vec{b}$ and $\vec{c}$ coincide with the respective summands of the left hand side of the scalar product in (20). If we use $\vec{dr} \sim \mathcal{N}(0, \Sigma)$, it follows from (4) to (5):

$$\begin{aligned} \sigma^2_{P\&L_{tot}} &= \langle \vec{a} - \vec{b} + \vec{c}, \Sigma(\vec{a} - \vec{b} + \vec{c}) \rangle \\ &= \langle \vec{a}, \Sigma\vec{a} \rangle + \langle \vec{b}, \Sigma\vec{b} \rangle + \langle \vec{c}, \Sigma\vec{c} \rangle - 2\langle \vec{a}, \Sigma\vec{b} \rangle + 2\langle \vec{a}, \Sigma\vec{c} \rangle - 2\langle \vec{c}, \Sigma\vec{b} \rangle. \end{aligned} \tag{21}$$

If we plug in the expressions for $\vec{a}$, $\vec{b}$ and $\vec{c}$, we obtain (19). □

In order to be prepared for later computations, we will further simplify Expression (19). To this end, we introduce the following notations: by Σ_{n+1} we denote the $(n+1) \times (n+1)$ matrix consisting of the first $n+1$ column and row entires of Σ only, i.e. $\Sigma_{i,j}$, $i, j = 1, \ldots n+1$. The matrix $\Sigma_{N,n+1}$ is the $N \times (n+1)$ matrix

[12]The vector $\vec{\Delta}_{rest}$ contains the n sensitivities w.r.t. credit spread changes of those trading book positions which are different from the CDSs used for hedging but are sensitive w.r.t. to the credit spreads of the hedge instruments as well.

[13]The vector $\vec{\Delta}_{N-n-1}$ is defined in the proof.

[14]In the following, we will omit the index $N-n-1$ and simply write $\vec{0}$.

obtained from Σ by deleting the last $N - n - 1$ columns and $\Sigma^t_{N,n+1}$ denotes its transpose matrix. With this notation and using that $\vec{0}$ cancels many components in (19), we can write:

$$\begin{aligned}\sigma^2_{P\&L_{tot}} &= \langle Q_\Delta \vec{B}, \Sigma_{n+1} Q_\Delta \vec{B}\rangle + \langle \vec{\Delta}_{CVA}\Sigma_{n+1}, \vec{\Delta}_{CVA}\rangle - 2\langle Q_\Delta \vec{B}, \Sigma_{n+1}\vec{\Delta}_{CVA}\rangle \\ &+ 2\left\langle \vec{B}, Q_\Delta \Sigma^t_{N,n+1}\begin{pmatrix}\vec{\Delta}_{rest}\\ \vec{\Delta}_{N-n-1}\end{pmatrix}\right\rangle - 2\left\langle \vec{\Delta}_{CVA}, \Sigma^t_{N,n+1}\begin{pmatrix}\vec{\Delta}_{rest}\\ \vec{\Delta}_{N-n-1}\end{pmatrix}\right\rangle \\ &+ \left\langle \begin{pmatrix}\vec{\Delta}_{rest}\\ \vec{\Delta}_{N-n-1}\end{pmatrix} \Sigma \begin{pmatrix}\vec{\Delta}_{rest}\\ \vec{\Delta}_{N-n-1}\end{pmatrix}\right\rangle.\end{aligned} \tag{22}$$

In (22), the first summand describes the volatility of the hedge instruments if they are considered as isolated from the remaining positions (i.e. those positions which are different from the hedge instruments). Analogously, the other quadratic terms (i.e. the second and the last summand in (22)) represent the volatility of the CVA and the remaining positions respectively. The cross terms (third, fourth, and fifth summand) describe the interactions between the volatility of the hedge instruments, the CVA and the remaining positions. For example, the third term describes the interaction between the CVA and the hedge instruments.

The P&L volatility σ^2_{hed} caused by the hedge instruments is given by those terms of (22) which depend on the hedge instruments, i.e. those terms which depend on $\vec{B}$. These are the first, the third, and the fourth term of (22), i.e.

$$\sigma^2_{hed} = \langle Q_\Delta \vec{B}, \Sigma_{n+1} Q_\Delta \vec{B}\rangle - 2\langle Q_\Delta \vec{B}, \Sigma_{n+1}\vec{\Delta}_{CVA}\rangle + 2\left\langle \vec{B}, Q_\Delta \Sigma^t_{N,n+1}\begin{pmatrix}\vec{\Delta}_{rest}\\ \vec{\Delta}_{N-n-1}\end{pmatrix}\right\rangle. \tag{23}$$

The other terms of (22) describe the volatility caused by the remaining positions.

In order to simplify the notation, we write σ^2_{hed} in the following way:

$$\sigma^2_{hed} = \langle A\vec{B}, \vec{B}\rangle + \langle \vec{B}, \vec{b}\rangle \tag{24}$$

with

$$A = Q_\Delta \Sigma_{n+1} Q_\Delta \tag{25}$$

and

$$\vec{b} = Q_\Delta \Sigma^t_{N,n+1}\begin{pmatrix}\vec{\Delta}_{rest}\\ \vec{\Delta}_{N-n-1}\end{pmatrix} - Q_\Delta \Sigma_{n+1}\vec{\Delta}_{CVA}. \tag{26}$$

Note that σ^2_{hed} is not simply given by a quadratic form but also incorporates a linear part. The quadratic form describes the volatility of a portfolio consisting of the hedge instruments, while the linear part describes the correlations of the hedge instruments with the remaining positions and with the CVAs.

4.3.1 Definition of the Steering Variable

We now define a steering variable aiming to define a unified framework for CVA risk charge hedging and P&L volatility. The steering variable is given by a synthetic volatility consisting of the sum of the regulatory CVA volatility and the volatility of the accounting P&L caused by the hedge instruments:

$$\sigma_{syn}^2 = \sigma_{CVA,reg}^2 + \sigma_{hed}^2. \tag{27}$$

The synthetic volatility unifies both the regulatory and the accounting framework. It can be considered as a function of the hedge notional amounts. The minimum of $\sigma_{tot,syn}^2$ describes the optimal allocation between CVA risk charge reduction and P&L volatility. Note that $\sigma_{tot,syn}^2$ contains now the matrices Γ and Σ, who describe the correlations between the same risk factors. This mismatch can be resolved, if the advanced CVA risk charge is used [2]. However, the use of different CVA sensitivities cannot be resolved. The most significant differences arise due to different exposure definitions: while the exposures EAD_i contained in the regulatory CVA sensitivities are based on the effective EPE and multiplied by the alpha multiplier (for IMM banks), this is not the case for the exposures used to compute the accounting CVA sensitivities. In general, these mismatches will lead to smaller accounting CVA sensitivities. Thus, a complete hedging of the CVA risk charge leads to an overhedged accounting CVA. See [6] for a complete description of the sources of the mismatch. Another source of potential overhedging is the following: if accounting CVA is already hedged by instruments which are not eligible hedge instruments in the sense of Basel III, additional hedge instruments are necessary for the hedging of the CVA risk charge. These hedge instruments will cause additional P&L volatility, since their offsetting counterparts (i.e. the CVAs) are not present (since they are already hedged).

5 Determination of the Optimal Hedge Strategy

This section describes concretely how the mismatch between the regulatory regime and the accounting regime can be mitigated. The result will be a dynamic CVA hedging strategy based on an optimization principle of the steering variable introduced in the previous section. We will ignore index hedges but all results can easily be generalized to the case where index hedges are included.

As opposed to the previous sections, the vector $\vec{B}$ will not contain the component B_{ind} in this section. As explained before, we want to minimize the synthetic volatility[15]

$$\sigma_{syn}^2(\vec{B}) = \sigma_{hed}^2(\vec{B}) + \sigma_{CVA}^2(\vec{B}) \tag{28}$$

[15] We ignore the index *tot*.

as a function of $\vec{B}$. The component B_i^* of the minimum $\vec{B}^*$ describes the optimal notional amounts of CDS_i, used to hedge the counterparty risk w.r.t. counterparty i. We now determine $\vec{B}^*$ by computing the zeros of the first derivative of σ^2_{syn}.

Theorem 1 *Under the same assumptions as in Lemma 2, the minimum $\vec{B}^*$ of (28) is given by*[16]

$$\vec{B}^* = H^{-1}\vec{f} \tag{29}$$

with

$$H := 2(A + Q_{M^{hed}} \Gamma Q_{M^{hed}}) \tag{30}$$

and

$$\vec{f} := 2Q_{M^{hed}} \Gamma Q_M \overrightarrow{EAD} - \vec{b}. \tag{31}$$

Proof In order to keep the display of the computations clear, we introduce the diagonal matrices $Q_M := diag(\omega_1 M_1, \ldots, \omega_n M_n)$ and $Q_{M^{hed}} := diag(\omega_1 M_1^{hed}, \ldots, \omega_n M_n^{hed})$ and the n-dimensional vector $\overrightarrow{EAD}$ whose components are given by the counterparty exposures. Using these definitions, we can write:

$$\sigma^2_{CVA} = \langle Q_M \overrightarrow{EAD} - Q_{M^{hed}}\vec{B}, \Gamma(Q_M \overrightarrow{EAD} - Q_{M^{hed}}\vec{B})\rangle. \tag{32}$$

whereby Γ describes the constant correlation between the CVAs (all diagonal elements given by 1). Using (32) and (24), we can write:

$$\begin{aligned}
\frac{\partial \sigma^2_{syn}}{\partial \vec{B}} &= \frac{\partial}{\partial \vec{B}}(\langle A\vec{B}, \vec{B}\rangle + \langle \vec{b}, \vec{B}\rangle) \\
&\quad + \frac{\partial}{\partial \vec{B}}\langle Q_{M^{hed}}\vec{B}, \Gamma Q_{M^{hed}}\vec{B}\rangle \\
&\quad - 2\frac{\partial}{\partial \vec{B}}\langle Q_{M^{hed}}\vec{B}, \Gamma Q_M \overrightarrow{EAD}\rangle \\
&= 2A\vec{B} + \vec{b} + 2Q_{M^{hed}}\Gamma Q_{M^{hed}}\vec{B} - 2Q_{M^{hed}}\Gamma Q_M \overrightarrow{EAD} \\
&= H\vec{B} - \vec{f},
\end{aligned} \tag{33}$$

where we have used the notations (30) and (31). This shows (29). Further, we note that the matrix H is derived from correlation matrices and therefore positive semi-definite. As a result, H is indeed invertible. Moreover, it holds

$$\frac{\partial^2 \sigma^2_{syn}}{\partial^2 \vec{B}} = H.$$

Hence, the second derivative of σ^2_{syn} is positive semi-definite and B^* is indeed a minimum.

[16] All terms are introduced in the proof.

Remark The implementation of the optimal hedge strategy works as follows: one has to compute on a regular basis (e.g. daily, weekly, etc.) the optimal solution (29). To do this one needs the CVA sensitivities,[17] the trading book sensitivities, and the correlation matrix of the risk factors.[18] Afterwards, the CVA desk needs to buy credit protection described by the optimal solution. This reduces the capital demand for counterparty risk and (by construction) minimizes the accounting P&L of the bought credit protection.

The approach presented in this article is based on many simplifying assumptions and restricted to the standardized CVA risk charge. Obviously, one could relax these assumptions and apply a comparable optimization principle. In such a case, it would possibly be hard to derive an analytical solution. Instead, one would obtain a numerical solution.

5.1 Special Cases

For illustration purposes, we consider the case $n = 1$, i.e. the special case of a single netting set. In that case both H and $\vec{f}$ are scalars:

$$H = 2\Delta^2 \Sigma_{1,1} + 2\omega^2 (M^{hed})^2$$

and

$$f = 2\omega^2 M M^{hed} EAD + 2\Delta\Delta_{CVA}\Sigma_{1,1} - \left(\Delta\Sigma_{1,1}\Delta_{rest} + \Delta \sum_{j=2}^{N} \Sigma_{1,j}\Delta_j \right), \tag{34}$$

whereby Δ describes the sensitivity of the hedge instrument of the considered counterparty, Δ_{rest} the sensitivity of the remaining positions (i.e. all positions without the CDS used for hedging purposes), Δ_{CVA} the sensitivity of accounting CVA and Δ_j are the sensitivities to the risk factors of the remaining positions. Thus, the optimal solution is

$$B^* = \frac{2\omega^2 M M^{hed} EAD + 2\sigma^2 \Delta\Delta_{CVA} - \left(\Delta\sigma^2 \Delta_{rest} + \Delta \sum_{j=2}^{N} \Sigma_{1,j}\Delta_j \right)}{2\Delta^2\sigma^2 + 2\omega^2 (M^{hed})^2} \tag{35}$$

where we have used that $\Sigma_{1,1}$ is equal to the volatility σ^2 of the hedge instrument. First, in order to get a better understanding of B^*, let us assume that the risk factor (credit spread) of the hedge instrument is independent of the remaining positions, i.e.

[17] Banks which actively manage their CVA risk usually compute these sensitivities.

[18] Larger banks usually have these data available, e.g. for market risk management purposes.

$\Delta_{rest} = 0$ and $\Sigma_{1,j} = 0$, for $j = 2, \ldots, N$. In that case (35) (we assume additionally $M = M^{hed}$) becomes

$$B^* = \frac{2\omega^2 M^2 EAD + 2\Delta\Delta_{CVA}\sigma^2}{2\omega^2 M^2 + 2\Delta^2\sigma^2}. \tag{36}$$

We see already that B^* is (at least from a certain volatility level) a decreasing function in σ^2, as we would expect it. Obviously, if we ignore the fact that the hedge instrument introduces further volatility (i.e. we assume $\sigma^2 = 0$), it holds

$$B^* = EAD.$$

It is easy to see that this is the optimal hedge amount if we minimize the CVA risk charge alone. As explained above, the most significant differences between the IFRS CVA and the regulatory CVA are the different exposure computation methodologies. In (36), these differences are reflected in EAD and Δ_{CVA}: while EAD is based on the regulatory methodology, Δ_{CVA} is based on accounting CVA methodology.[19] For illustration purposes, let us assume that Δ_{CVA} is based on the same exposure methodology as the regulatory CVA sensitivities (and that the modeling assumptions Sect. 3 holds). This means, that cf. (15)

$$\Delta_{CVA} = EAD\Delta, \tag{37}$$

i.e. we use the regulatory exposure EAD in (15) instead of the economical exposure EE^*. If we plug in (37) in (36), we obtain:

$$B^* = \frac{(2\omega^2 M^2 + 2\Delta^2\sigma^2)EAD}{2\omega^2 M^2 + 2\Delta^2\sigma^2} = EAD. \tag{38}$$

Thus, if we ignore the mismatch between the accounting and the regulatory CVA, the optimal hedge solution is given by the optimal hedge solution of the CVA risk charge only. If we include the mismatch, we can approximate the accounting CVA sensitivity by (cf. (15))

$$\Delta_{CVA} = EE^*\Delta. \tag{39}$$

As explained in Sect. 4.3.1, EE^* is smaller than EAD. Using (36) and (39) yields:

$$B^* = \frac{2\omega^2 M^2 EAD + 2\Delta\sigma^2 EE^*}{2\omega^2 M^2 + 2\Delta^2\sigma^2} < \frac{2\omega^2 M^2 EAD + 2\Delta\sigma^2 EAD}{2\omega^2 M^2 + 2\Delta^2\sigma^2} = EAD. \tag{40}$$

Hence, the mismatch leads to a smaller optimal hedge amount than the current regulatory exposure.

[19] Note that Δ_{CVA} depends on the exposure as well (while Δ is based on a unit exposure, cf. (16)). But this exposure is computed based on accounting methodology. This is the main source of differences between the accounting and regulatory regimes.

We remark that it cannot be excluded that B^* becomes negative. This is the case if the risk factors of the remaining positions are strongly correlated to the risk factor of the hedge instrument. In such a situation it seems to be reasonable to set $B^* = 0$.

Acknowledgements The KPMG Center of Excellence in Risk Management is acknowledged for organizing the conference "Challenges in Derivatives Markets - Fixed Income Modeling, Valuation Adjustments, Risk Management, and Regulation".

References

1. Basel Committee on Banking Supervision: International Convergence of Capital Measurement and Capital Standards (2006)
2. Basel Committee on Banking Supervision: A Global Regulatory Framework for More Resilient Banks and Banking Systems (2010)
3. Brigo, D., Morini, M., Pallavicini, A.: Counterparty Credit Risk Collateral and Funding. Wiley, Chichester (2013)
4. Gregory, J.: Counterparty Credit Risk. Wiley, Chichester (2012)
5. Kenyon, C., Stamm, R.: Discounting, LIBOR CVA and Funding. Palgrave Macmillan, Basingstoke (2012)
6. Pykhtin, M.: Model Foundations of the Basel III Standardized CVA Charge. Risk Magazine, London (2012)
7. Carver, L.: Capital or P&L? Deutsche Bank Losses Highlight CVA Trade-Off. Risk Magazine, London (2013)
8. Schubert, D.: How to Hedge CVA Without Being Hurt. Risk Magazine, London (2014)

4

Capital Optimization through an Innovative CVA Hedge

Michael Hünseler and Dirk Schubert

Abstract One of the lessons of the financial crisis as of late was the inherent credit risk attached to the value of derivatives. Since not all derivatives can be cleared by central counterparties, a significant amount of OTC derivatives will be subject to increased regulatory capital charges. These charges cover both current and future unexpected losses; the capital costs for derivatives transactions can become substantial if not prohibitive. At the same time, capital optimization through CDS hedging of counterparty risks will result in a hedge position beyond the economic risk ("over-hedging") required to meet Basel II/III rules. In addition, IFRS accounting rules again differ from Basel, creating a mismatch when hedging CVA. Even worse, CVA hedging using CDS may introduce significant profit and loss volatility while satisfying the conditions for capital relief. An innovative approach to hedging CVA aims to solve these issues.

Keywords CVA · Hedging · CDS · Contingent financial guarantee · Risk charges · OTC derivatives

1 Preface

In the following the nexus between credit risk (counterparty risk), liquidity, and market risk is analyzed and a solution with respect to CVA hedging of OTC derivative contracts is proposed.

The starting point is the consideration of collateral and its respective recognition in different but "basic" financial instruments like repos and (partially un-) collateralized

M. Hünseler (✉)
Credit Portfolio Management, Assenagon Asset Management S.A., Zweigniederlassung München, Prannerstrae 8, 80333 Munich, Germany
e-mail: michael.huenseler@assenagon.com

D. Schubert
Financial Services KPMG AG Wirtschaftsprüfungsgesellschaft, The Squaire, Am Flughafen, 60549 Frankfurt am Main, Germany
e-mail: dschubert@kpmg.com

OTC derivative contracts as well as the comparison to corresponding uncollateralized financial instruments like money market loans or uncollateralized OTC derivative contracts. The role of collateral is analyzed with respect to its legal basis, its treatment in Financial Accounting (IFRS, refer to [4]) and regulatory reporting according to Basel II/III (cf. [1, 2]).

The analysis leads to a definition of the concept of liquidity and its relation to the use of collateral in financial markets. As will be shown, the concept of liquidity, inherent in the legal framework related to collateral of basic financial instruments, can be considered as a transformation of secured into unsecured financing and vice versa. Moreover, with respect to the associated valuation and risk the liquidity transformation exhibits similarities to the concept of wrong-way risk. The transformation of unsecured into secured financing can be used to derive new types of financial instruments, e.g. in the application to CVA hedging issues of OTC derivative contracts. In this case the hedging instrument also solves the issue of disentangling funding value adjustments (FVA) and counterparty value adjustments (CVA), which is intensively discussed by practitioners in context with the pricing of OTC derivatives.

2 The Role of Collateral in OTC Contracts and Its Legal Basis

In the following the main legal basis with respect to the role of collateral is outlined.

2.1 The Role of Legal Versus Economic Ownership

There are two main properties which are of relevance in connection with the role of collateral, the transfer of legal ownership (i.e. the possibility of "re-hypothecation") in contrast to the economic ownership and the value of the collateral.

By entering into a repurchase agreement the legal title to the securities is transferred to the counterparty but economically the securities stay with the selling counterparty since the buying counterparty has the obligation to compensate the selling counterparty for income (manufactured payments) associated with the securities and to redeliver the securities. In case of an Event of Default, both obligations terminate. The treatment in an Event of Default provides that the residual claim is settled in cash and determined taking into account the cash side as well as the value of the collateral. In this case the obligation to redeliver securities transferred as collateral expires and the buying counterparty remains the legal owner. Thus the price risk of the collateral (uncertainty of value) is entirely borne by the legal owner.

In case of (only) economic ownership, e.g. a pledge, this is not necessarily the case, since the treatment in an Event of Default differs as e.g. this kind of "collateral" is part of the bankrupt/legal estate and therefore underlying the insolvency procedure.

Despite these legal differences, the regulatory rules according to Basel II/III and the accounting rules under IFRS also require different treatment of collateral. In general IFRS follows the economic ownership concept irrespective of the legal basis of the collateral while Basel II/III rather follows the legal ownership concept.

2.2 Affected Market Participants

Not all market participants are affected by the same accounting and regulatory rules. Banks have to follow IFRS and Basel II/III rules, while e.g. investment funds are not affected by Basel II/III rules but are governed by investment fund legislation, e.g. UCITS directive. These different legal frameworks for market participants impact the usage of collateral in OTC contracts, e.g. the assets of an investment fund under UCITS represent special assets and the use of repos and cash collateral is limited. In addition, these investment funds have no access to sources of liquidity other than the capital paid which limits the use of cash and the provision of cash collateral in context of derivatives exposure. For example, cash collateral received from OTC derivative contracts has to be kept in segregated accounts and cannot be used for any kind of (reverse) repo transaction. Alternatively, the use of a custodian for optimizing the provision of cash collateral can be considered.

2.3 Financial Instruments Involving Collateral and Standard Legal Frameworks (Master Agreements)

Analyzing the legal basis of collateral facilitates the definition of liquidity and liquidity transformation.

2.3.1 Derivatives Under ISDA Master Agreement

The type and use of collateral are governed in the CSA (credit support annex), which represents an integral part of the ISDA Master Agreement framework[1] and cannot be considered separately. The ISDA Master Agreement forms the legal framework and is applicable for the individual derivative contracts supplemented by the CSA. For example, default netting in the Event of Default (default of a counterparty) is governed by the ISDA Master Agreement including the netting of the collateral which in turn is defined in the CSA. The CSA defines the type(s) of collateral and the terms of margining/posting, while the transfer of the legal ownership is governed in the ISDA Master Agreement. In general ISDA Master Agreements contracted under English Law provide the legal transfer of ownership of the collateral while ISDA Master

[1] ISDA®, International Swaps and Derivatives Association, Inc., 2002 Master Agreement.

Agreements contracted under New York Law do not. In the latter re-hypothecation, i.e. the re-use of the received collateral for counterparties is prohibited.

In case of ISDA Master Agreements under English Law the derivative contracts are terminated in case of an Event of Default and the collateral is taken into account in order to determine the residual claim. The determination of the residual claim is performed independently from the estate of the insolvent party.

2.3.2 Repos Under GMRA

A repo or repurchase agreement under GMRA[2] can economically be seen as a collateralized loan and is typically motivated by the request for cash. In case of repurchase agreements, the legal title to the securities provided as collateral is transferred to the counterparty (buyer) in exchange of the desired cash (purchase price). The credit risk and liquidity of the underlying securities determine the haircut in the valuation of the collateral. Adverse changes in the inherent credit risk of the securities are offset by an increase in haircut and induce in terms of margining additional posting of collateral to the counterparty. At maturity the securities are legally transferred back to original owner (seller) in exchange for the agreed cash amount (repurchase price). In case of a counterparty's default the securities are not returned and the recovery risk of the securities is borne by their legal owner (the buyer).

2.3.3 Securities Lending Under GSLMA

In contrast to a repo, a securities lending under GSLMA[3] is motivated by the need for securities but is (commonly) also a secured financing transaction since the securities as well as the collateral are legally transferred to the respective counterparty. In the secured case the collateral can be cash or other securities.

2.4 Credit and Counterparty Risk Related to Collateral

Consider the case that Bank 1 and Bank 2 enter into a repo transaction, where Bank 2 receives cash from Bank 1 in return for securities. There are two features of importance: Bank 1 needs cash funding, which requires an assumption with respect to the sources of funding, e.g. central bank, deposits. The corresponding assumption represents a component in determining the profitability of the repo. An additional feature is the inherent wrong-way risk within the repo transaction. In this case the

---

[2]Sifma, Securities Industry and Financial Markets Association and ICMA, International Capital Market Association, 2011 version Global Master Repurchase Agreement.

[3]ISLA, International Securities Lending Association, Global Master Securities Lending Agreement, Version: January 2010.

wrong-way risk for Bank 1 is defined as an adverse correlation (positive in the example above) between counterparty credit risk toward Bank 2 and market value of the collateral (securities). Assuming a long position in the underlying securities (collateral) for Bank 1, the wrong-way risk constitutes a decrease in value of the securities (collateral) and a simultaneous decrease in credit worthiness of Bank 2. In this case the risk for Bank 1 is the failure of Bank 2 in balancing the collateral posting. Since in a repo transaction the legal ownership is transferred to Bank 1, the net risk position comprises the price risk (in the Event of Default of Bank 2) associated with the collateral (securities) including the haircut and the cash claim (cash loan). A similar rationale holds in case of a short position in securities (collateral) since an event of default affects the ability to post as well as to return posted collateral. Similar considerations hold in case of a (partially) collateralized OTC derivative transaction, e.g. an interest rate swap.

3 Terms of Liquidity and Definition of Liquidity Transformation

Dealing with the concept of liquidity reveals that the term is not defined consistently or not uniformly in financial regulations. A natural way is to adopt legal definitions.

3.1 Terms of Liquidity

There is a variety of definitions for the term liquidity, e.g. meeting payment obligations (liquidity of an entity), liquid marketable securities (ability to buy and sell financial instruments), etc. The analysis above reveals the interdependence of "liquidity" and counterparty credit risk, respectively credit risk. As such liquidity of an entity can be considered as the relatively measured ability for a bank to raise cash from a credit line or in return of collateral which in turn is dependent on the liquidity of financial instruments. The collateral itself is only accepted if the price of the collateral can be reliably determined, e.g. it is traded with sufficient frequency on an active market.

3.2 Comparison of Secured and Unsecured Financing

The best way to illustrate the concept formation of liquidity respectively liquidity transformation is the comparison of unsecured and secured financing in case of a default event. Continuing the example above, the following comparison considers Bank 1 as cash provider.

1. Financial action

Secured:	Exchange of cash versus collateral
Unsecured:	Paying out cash of a loan granted

2. Prerequisite and term of liquidity

Secured:	"Liquid" collateral (price of collateral can be reliably determined)
Unsecured:	Credit line loan illiquid - not marketable

3. Net (relative) risk position in case of default

Secured:	Market value of collateral: Default Probability (issuer of the security received as collateral) × recovery rate of collateral × amount of collateral (proximate representation via haircut)
Unsecured:	Recovery rate of cash loan × exposure at default (EAD)

4. Relation to estate of insolvent party

Secured:	Only residual claim part of the estate of the insolvent party but amount of residual claim is determined independently of the estate of the insolvent party
Unsecured:	Entirely part of the estate of the insolvent party

5. Risk

Secured:	Credit risk of collateral issuer, correlation between counterparty risk and price of collateral (wrong-way risk in an adverse case)
Unsecured:	Credit risk with respect to the borrower

Note that in the comparison above the net (relative) risk position in both cases, for secured and unsecured financing, involves a recovery rate but the associated risk relates to different counterparties. In case of secured financing the default risk is coupled with the recovery risk (price risk) of the collateral and the risk position can be settled promptly in case of a default while in case of the unsecured financing the settlement of the recovery depends on the insolvency process.

This comparison in particular shows that the credit risk toward the counterparty in the unsecured financing transaction being rather illiquid is opposed to the market value risk of the received collateral which is assumed to be liquid in the secured case plus the correlation of this risk and the credit risk of the issuer of the securities taken as collateral. In the adverse case this risk correlation is also known as "wrong way risk".

3.3 Liquidity Transformation

Accordingly considering liquidity as an absolute quantity is not useful but as a relative quantity: a relation between secured financing and unsecured financing, which we term liquidity transformation. This transformation is not independent from credit respective counterparty risk, since each type of financing is associated with a different type of credit risk. The liquidity transformation is dependent on the type of entity and cannot be considered separately from its legal status. A bank has different access and a higher degree of freedom to assign liquidity irrespective of the purpose than, e.g. an investment fund.

4 New Approach to CVA Hedging

The new CVA hedging approach outlined below represents a response to current challenges in banking regulation and reveals the importance of liquidity transformation. The legal-based background described above can be used to explain current challenges of banking industry if in addition to prevailing market conditions the regulatory and financial accounting environments are taken into account. Recent environmental changes have immediate impact on banking business activities concerning counterparty risk and can be summarized as follows:

Regulatory and Accounting Aspects	Business Impact
• CCR (counterparty credit risk) is under scrutiny of regulators and financial accounting standard setters. • Increased regulatory requirements on bilateral collateralization and clearing. • Increased (regulatory) capital requirements for banks. • Increased P/L volatility due to IFRS fair value accounting rules (e.g. recognition of CVA).	• Increased (regulatory) capital affects resp. limits banking business. • Intensified application of credit risk mitigation by netting, collateralization and hedging. • Increased demand for secured (collateralized) transactions • Increased demand for (liquid / high quality) collateral. • Increased demand for optimization of collateral.

4.1 *Issue*

During the financial crises regulators and financial accounting setters notified the relevance of counterparty credit risk in OTC derivative contracts. In response to this relevance several regulatory (legislative) initiatives have been undertaken like central clearing, increased regulatory capital, etc. These impacted the business of banking industry in several ways: intensified use of credit risk mitigation techniques and increased demand for secured transactions (demand for collateral, cf. also [3]).

Despite the environmental changes credit risk mitigation is and remains essential to continue banking business. Considering equity as a scarce source, banks are forced to tighten their credit exposure in order to offset the increase in capital charges due to increased costs for CCR and other factors. The tightening of credit exposure limits banking business and increases the demand for credit risk mitigation techniques (including hedging).

The mentioned regulatory changes induce tremendous costs for the banking industry. Therefore, managing credit risk by commonly used CDS hedging strategies becomes expensive in presence of the banking regulation, so credit risk management will be rearranged, e.g. more offsetting positions, avoiding exposures (reducing limits) or transferred ("outsourced") outside the regulated banking sector, so e.g. investment funds are in a favorable position to manage a bank's risks. This also holds for counterparty credit risk following the idea to transfer counterparty credit risk to market participants outside the banking sector that are in the situation to manage this risk economically at lower cost than banks.

Additionally banking industry is faced with various different regulations. With respect to counterparty credit risk a bank is confronted with conflicting objectives resulting from regulatory requirements, i.e. Basel II/III, and financial accounting rules. Therefore, under current regulatory and accounting requirements banks cannot manage counterparty credit risk (CCR) of derivatives uniformly in respect of capital requirements and P/L volatility. This results from the fact that the hedging of counterparty credit risk exposure (in terms of Basel II/III requirements) requires the hedging of current and future changes of exposure, while IFRS only considers current exposure. So a bank is required to hedge more than the current exposure ("overhedging") in terms of Basel II/III. But since hedging is mainly carried out by derivatives as CDS, these CDS cause P/L volatility under IFRS, since derivatives are recognized at fair value through P/L.

As described above secured and unsecured financing is common practice in finance industry and can be observed in counterparty credit risk of OTC derivative contracts. As illustrated below in an uncollateralized OTC derivative trade between Bank A and counterparty B, the parties enter into an unsecured financing relationship. If the market value of the derivative trades of Bank A against counterparty B increases then Bank A is exposed to counterparty credit risk (CVA risk). Bank A implicitly provides counterparty B an illiquid credit line in the sense, that the positive exposure amount ("market value") is recognized as an asset which becomes a legal claim in the Event of Default. This exposure is not a tradable asset but needs to be funded thus it could be interpreted as an illiquid asset. In comparison to standard banking credit business, this credit line is unlimited and varies with the market value of the underlying derivative trades, which implies also unlimited funding. The current focus of discussions and research concentrates on measuring counterparty credit risk by exposure and default probability modeling (CVA risk) and the assignment of the appropriate discount rate for the OTC derivative trades reflecting the FVA. The discussed approaches share the following assumptions:

1. No market segmentation between collateralized and uncollateralized OTC derivative trades.
2. The application of the absence of arbitrage principle, which in particular assumes the unlimited use of liquidity by market participants.
3. Liquidity risk and credit risk cannot be decoupled.
4. The coincidence of counterparty credit risk and credit risk, which can be both hedged by the same type of hedging instruments (credit default swaps (CDS), contingent credit default swaps (CCDS)).
5. The absence of transaction costs, which are represented by regulatory costs (e.g. CVA risk charges according to Basel II/III) and reported earnings volatility under IFRS stemming from fair value accounting of counterparty fair value adjustments and derivative valuation.

These ideal assumptions are not necessarily met in reality, therefore alternative approaches have to be explored.

4.2 Solution

Since banks with significant activities in derivatives markets can be affected quite heavily by the aforementioned issues, a workable solution should solve the build-in conflict of regulatory and accounting requirements. As a result, the solution contributes to an improved competitiveness of the bank in the context of derivative risk management, derivatives' pricing, and support the bank in conducting derivatives business which will ultimately benefit the economy as a whole. Consequently, a potential solution is about developing a financial instrument ("credit risk mitigating instrument") which reduces the Basel II/III CCR capital requirements and CVA risk charge without resulting in additional P/L volatility under IFRS. Such a financial instrument represents a solution to the issues described above since it creates:

- A market for counterparty credit risk exposure
  The positive exposure of an (un-) collateralized derivative portfolio can be considered as an illiquid asset in contrast, e.g. to a liquid issuance of a bank.
- A new asset type—make the derivative claim a tradable asset
  The idea is to make this exposure tradable in exchange for collateral by means of an instrument like Collateral Support Annex (CSA) which directly refers to the possibly varying positive exposure of a derivative portfolio.
- An active market involving banks and investment funds
  In order to increase liquidity and to avoid only a shift of capital charges from one institution to another due to hedging activities for the taken credit risk a transfer to a market participant outside the banking sector is considered.

The outlinc of a solution follows the liquidity transformation. The unsecured financing for OTC derivatives would be represented by uncollateralized OTC derivatives while secured financing requires corresponding posting of collateral. Pursuing the

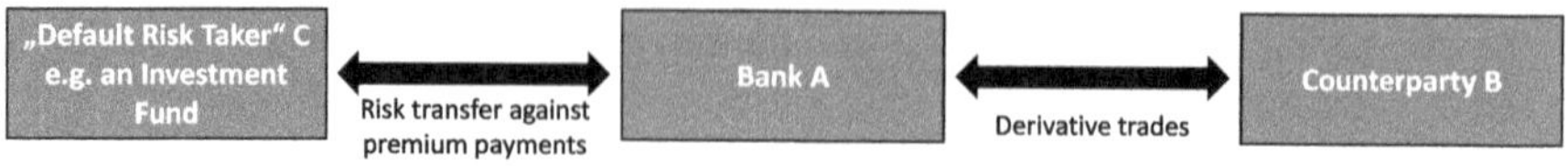

Fig. 1 Secured OTC derivative transaction

aim of decoupling liquidity and counterparty risk, at least three parties are necessary to involve as demonstrated in the analysis on repos above. Therefore, the aim could not be achieved by cash collateralized bilateral OTC derivatives commonly used in the interbank market, since there is still a one-to-one correspondence between liquidity requirements (e.g. cash collateral postings) and counterparty risk. Additionally a bilateral CSA assumes that both counterparties have unlimited access to liquidity, which represents a difficulty if counterparty B is a corporate according to its limited access to collateral/cash. Therefore a secured financing transaction for CVA hedging has to be structured differently.

The secured financing transaction outlined in Fig. 1 involves a third party "Default Risk Taker" C, who is posting collateral to Bank A on behalf of counterparty B, i.e. whenever the value of the derivative trade is positive for Bank A. This transaction represents a tri-party CSA and works similar to a margining. The transaction between "Default Risk Taker" C and Bank A is an asymmetric contract, since if the value of the derivative trade is negative for Bank A, no collateral is provided to or by Bank A. In case of a default of counterparty B the posted collateral is not returned to "Default Risk Taker C". The structure described above represents the appropriate complement for a bilateral uncollateralized OTC derivative transaction.

The structure reveals the concept of liquidity transformation including a decoupling of liquidity and counterparty risk, since by using the contract the unsecured financing transaction is transformed into a secured financing transaction. Referring to the comparison of unsecured and secured financing described above (cf. Sect. 2.3), the proposed structure goes one step further by linking both market segments and transforming liquidity within one single transaction. By definition of the liquidity transformation, the transaction exchanges different types of credit risk.

4.3 Application

The table in Fig. 2 shows the contemplation of the new CVA hedge structure (cash collateral with contingent financial guarantee, "CCCFG"; for more detail refer to [5]) to existing credit risk mitigation techniques applied in the banking industry. Its main features are summarized as follows:

- The proposed structure represents a credit risk mitigating instrument, which reduces the Basel II/III CCR capital requirements CVA risk charge, since the cash collateral provided by a third party is permitted under Basel II/III requirements and reduces the exposure according to Basel II/III.

Aspects	Netting	Bilateral Collateralization	Credit Default Swap (CDS) based hedges	Contingent CDS
Economics	Reduction of the risk position by netting of exposures	Counterparty risk is reduced by posted (cash) collateral	Hedges of the counterparty default risk	Hedges of the counterparty default and exposure risk
Operational	▪ Legally enforceable ▪ Default netting (ISDA standard)	▪ Changes in OTC derivative contracts (CSA) ▪ Requires liquidity (an issue for corporates)	▪ Delta Hedging required ▪ Liquid CDS	▪ No Delta Hedging required ▪ Less liquid than CDS
Financial Accounting (IFRS)	IAS 32 requires simultaneous payment- and default netting	Posted collateral reduces fair value volatility	Fair value accounting through P&L	Fair value accounting through P&L
Regulatory (Basel II/III)	Basel differs from IFRS due to default netting	Reduces derivative exposure (credit risk mitigation)	Credit risk mitigation if requirements are met	Credit risk mitigation if requirements are met

Fig. 2 Current and new approaches for credit risk mitigation in banking industry

- Accordingly there is immediate regulatory capital relief, which results in an immediate saving respectively reduction of the cost of equity.
- The proposed structure simultaneously qualifies as a contingent financial guarantee such that there is no additional P/L volatility under IFRS. In particular the financial guarantee accounting under IFRS applies to the proposed structure by considering the case of default. In case of a default of OTC derivatives contracted under ISDA the final claim is determined. The financial guarantee under IFRS comes into effect only at default—not before—and "guarantees" the value of the final claim, which is recognized at amortized cost and physically transferred to counterparty C in return for cash to Bank A. The final claim takes into account the posted collateral until the Event of Default. For a more detailed description refer to [5].
- As becomes apparent from the table above the new CVA hedge structure is a separate financial instrument. This cash collateral with contingent financial guarantee ("CCCFG") differs from a "traditional" CDS/CCDS, since the collateral postings are directly related to the counterpartys exposure. In case of a CCDS the cash collateral refers to the CCDS contract itself reflecting its value and there is no direct legal link to the exposure subject to hedging by the CCDS. Additionally CCDS represents derivatives in terms of IFRS and not necessarily qualify as credit risk mitigation instrument under Basel II/III. If a CCDS qualifies as credit risk mitigation instrument it applies to the Basel II/III PD, while the CCCFG directly affects the exposure.
- Operationally the new CVA hedging instrument is more effective and less costly than CDS delta hedging approaches, since a constant adjustment of a hedging position using CDS induces transaction costs and depends also on the gamma of the risk position. Accordingly the hedge position is never "perfect".

- The approach is flexible with respect to counterparty risk profiles, since it applies to linear and nonlinear exposure profiles.
- The legal framework of the approach is based on ISDA, which ensures the operational effectiveness in terms of legal certainty and the recognition in front office IT systems in order to process the transaction.
- It has to be noticed that investment funds have to observe certain rules and regulations which come with the specific fund format and domicile. For example, funds fulfilling the highest standards are limited to invest in eligible assets which are characterized by sufficient liquidity in order to ensure that the fund is in a position to meet potential redemptions. Bilateral transactions that are illiquid by definition require a buy-and-hold investment strategy which may not be suitable for all investment funds.

4.4 Example

In the following for the sake of simplicity only a qualitative example is provided, since by comparing the induced costs the CVA hedge already indicates its profitability.

- Bank A holds a portfolio of uncollateralized derivatives (e.g. interest rate swaps (IRS)) with Counterparty B (e.g. a corporate) a netting set is considered.[4]
- Bank A enters into a CVA hedge transaction with Investment Fund C who is taking over credit (counterparty credit risk of B) and market risk and provides liquidity with reference to the uncollateralized derivative transaction(s) between Bank A and Counterparty B in terms of the cash collateral postings to Bank A. The transaction between Investment Fund C and Bank A is a unilateral (asymmetric) collateral contract in favour of Bank A (and on behalf of Counterparty B). The transaction chart follows Fig. 1.
- In the following table the impact for Bank A with and without CVA hedge is summarized:

With respect to the risk illustrated in the first line in the table above, the CVA hedge transaction mitigates entirely the risk of Bank A by transferring the risk to investment fund C. This results from the posted cash collateral of Investment Fund C to Bank A on behalf of counterparty C. Comparing the induced costs (second line in the table above) reveals that the (uncollateralized) derivative business is exposed to regulatory and cost of equity charges as well as funding costs. In case of the CVA hedge transaction all these costs are inapplicable, since the posted cash collateral by Investment Fund C to Bank A on behalf of counterparty B leads to entire regulatory capital and cost of capital relief and serves as funding to the derivative exposure between Bank A and counterparty B. On the other hand Bank A pays a fee to Investment Fund C for taking over the counterparty credit risk of B and also interest

[4]In order to keep legal and operational complexity in an event of default low one netting set is considered.

Bank A	without CVA Hedge	with CVA Hedge
Risk	▪ **Counterparty Credit Risk of B,** ▪ **Market Risk and** ▪ **Liquidity/Funding Provision**	0
Induced Costs	▪ **Costs related to Counterparty Credit Risk B** ▪ **Cost of Equity on Regulatory Capital** (Basel II/III charges)) ▪ **Costs associated with the Leverage Ratio (Basel III)** ▪ **Costs of Funding costs** (depending on Bank A's rating and funding model assumption)	▪ **CVA hedge spread („fee payment")** ▪ **Interest on received cash collateral**
Cash Flows	▪ **No Default:** derivative payments ▪ **Default:** residual claim times recovery rate	▪ **No Default:** derivative payments, fee payment, receive cash collateral, pay interest on cash collateral, repayment of collateral at maturity (since exposure reduces to zero). ▪ **Default**: physical delivery of residual claim vs. keeping posted cash collateral and receiving difference payment up to the amount of residual claim

Fig. 3 Comparison derivatives exposure with and without CVA Hedge transaction from bank A's perspective

on the posted cash collateral. Describing the associated cash flow profiles the two situations, default and non-default of the counterparty, are distinguished (third line in the table above). While in case without CVA hedge structure the cash profiles are straightforward, with CVA hedge transaction in addition fee and interest payments on the collateral have to be considered in the non-default situation. In the event of default of counterparty B, the residual claim of the transaction is physically delivered to Investment Fund C in return for cash equal to the notional of the residual claim. This procedure follows standard ISDA rules (Fig. 3).

5 Conclusion

The new CVA hedging instrument is used in order to transfer counterparty credit risk to entities which are able to manage the risk on an economic basis at lower cost. Investment funds can act as "credit risk taker" and manage counterparty credit exposure at a lower cost than banks, since investment funds are not subject to regulatory capital requirements according to Basel II/III. It has to be noted though that an implementation of the solution described above requires an intense capability and knowledge of dealing with derivatives at the risk taking investment funds. On the other hand, since investment funds are not subject to the same regulations as those for banks described above they may become a natural partner for banks in this context.

The proposed structure bridges the difference between capital rules and financial accounting standards in order to optimize capital requirements and charges for CVA. This is achieved by its liquidity transformation property—the liquidity and credit risk transformation of the counterparty's exposure—and by meeting the Basel II/III and

IFRS requirements: simultaneous CCR capital and CVA risk charge relief as well as reduced P/L volatility in IFRS resulting from CVA accounting. While the objective outlined herein is predominantly to provide a suitable solution for CVA issues in context of derivatives transactions, it may also create interesting opportunities for investors of the risk taking investment funds.

This solution also contributes to valuation and the discussion on FVA and CVA, since it requires the pricing of the collateral between counterparties "at arm's length". This price determines the discount rate by applying the absence of arbitrage principle. As a consequence FVA is disentangled from CVA by using the proposed structure as a mean.

Acknowledgements The KPMG Center of Excellence in Risk Management is acknowledged for organizing the conference "Challenges in Derivatives Markets - Fixed Income Modeling, Valuation Adjustments, Risk Management, and Regulation".

References

1. Basel Committee on Banking Supervision: International Convergence of Capital Measurement and Capital Standards (2006)
2. Basel Committee on Banking Supervision: Basel III: A Global Regulatory Framework for More Resilient Banks and Banking Systems (2011)
3. Hünseler, M.: Credit Portfolio Management. Palgrave Macmillan, London (2013)
4. International Accounting Standards Board: International Financial Reporting Standards (IFRS) (2015)
5. Schubert, D.: How to hedge CVA without getting hurt, pp. 76–79. Risk Magazine, September Issue (2014)

5

Option Pricing and Sensitivity Analysis in the Lévy Forward Process Model

Ernst Eberlein, M'hamed Eddahbi and Sidi Mohamed Lalaoui Ben Cherif

Abstract The purpose of this article is to give a closed Fourier-based valuation formula for a caplet in the framework of the Lévy forward process model which was introduced in Eberlein and Özkan, Financ. Stochast. 9:327-348, 2005, [5]. Afterwards, we compute Greeks by two approaches which come from totally different mathematical fields. The first is based on the integration-by-parts formula, which lies at the core of the application of the Malliavin calculus to finance. The second consists in using Fourier-based methods for pricing derivatives as exposed in Eberlein, Quantitative Energy Finance, 2014, [3]. We illustrate the results in the case where the jump part of the underlying model is driven by a time-inhomogeneous Gamma process and alternatively by a Variance Gamma process.

Keywords Option valuation · Lévy forward process model · Fourier transform · Time-inhomogeneous Lévy processes · Malliavin calculus · Greeks and sensitivity analysis

---

We acknowledge financial support from the Federal Foreign Office of Germany which has been granted within a program of the German Academic Exchange Service (DAAD).

E. Eberlein (✉)
Department of Mathematical Stochastics, University of Freiburg, Eckerstr. 1,
79104 Freiburg im Breisgau, Germany
e-mail: eberlein@stochastik.uni-freiburg.de

M. Eddahbi
Faculty of Sciences and Techniques, Department of Mathematics,
Cadi Ayyad University, B.P. 549, Marrakech, Morocco
e-mail: m.eddahbi@uca.ma

S.M. Lalaoui Ben Cherif
Faculty of Sciences Semlalia, Department of Mathematics, Cadi Ayyad University,
B.P. 2390, Marrakech, Morocco
e-mail: mohamed.lalaoui@ced.uca.ac.ma

1 Introduction

To compute expectations which arise as prices of derivative products is a key issue in quantitative finance. The effort which is necessary to get these values depends to a high degree on the sophistication of the model approach which is used. Simple models such as the classical geometric Brownian motion lead to easy-to-evaluate formulas for expectations but entail at the same time a high model risk. As has been shown in numerous studies, the empirical return distributions which one can observe are far from normality. This is true for all categories of financial markets: equity, fixed income, foreign exchange as well as credit markets (see e.g. Eberlein and Keller (1995) [4] for the analysis of stock price data and Eberlein and Kluge (2007) [7] for data from fixed income markets). A first step to reduce model risk and to improve the performance of the model consists in introducing volatility as a stochastic quantity. Some of the stochastic volatility models became quite popular. Nevertheless one must be aware that the distributions which diffusion processes with non-deterministic coefficients generate on a given time horizon are not known. They can only be determined approximately on the basis of simulations of process paths. In order to get more realistic distributions, an excellent choice is to replace the driving Brownian motion in classical models by a suitably chosen Lévy process. This can also be interpreted in the sense that instead of making volatility stochastic one can go over to a stochastic clock. The reason is that many Lévy processes can be obtained as time-changed Brownian motions. For example, the Variance Gamma process results when one replaces linear time by a Gamma process as subordinator. Of course, one can also consider both: a more powerful driver and stochastic volatility.

Lévy processes are in a one-to-one correspondence to the rich class of infinitely divisible distributions and at the same time analytically well tractable. Due to the higher number of available parameters, this class of distributions is flexible enough to allow a much better fit to empirical return distributions. The systematic error which results from the assumption of normality is avoided. The generating distribution of a Lévy process shows up as the distribution of increments of length one. Consequently, any distribution which one gets by fitting a parametrized subclass to empirical return data can be implemented not only approximately but exactly into Lévy-driven models. Suitably parametrized model classes which have been used successfully so far are driven by generalized hyperbolic, normal inverse Gaussian (NIG), or Variance Gamma (VG) processes, just to mention a few.

As noted above, advanced models with superior statistical properties require more demanding numerical methods. Efficient and accurate algorithms are crucial in this context, in particular for calibration purposes. For pricing of derivatives the historical distribution, which can be derived from price data of the underlying and which is used for risk management, is of less interest. Calibration usually means to estimate the risk-neutral distribution parameters. In other words, one exploits price data of derivatives. In most cases this is given in terms of volatilities. Whereas years ago calibration was usually done overnight, many trading desks recalibrate nowadays on an intraday basis. During a calibration procedure in each iteration step a large number of model prices have to be computed and compared to market prices. A method which almost always works to get the corresponding expectations is Monte Carlo simulation. Its disadvantage is that it is computationally intensive and therefore too slow for many purposes. Another classical approach is to represent prices as solutions of partial differential equations (PDEs) which in the case of Lévy processes with jumps become partial integro–differential equations (PIDEs). This approach, which is based on the Feynman–Kac formula, applies to a wide range of valuation problems, in particular it allows to compute prices of American options as well. Nevertheless, the numerical solution of PIDEs rests on sophisticated discretization methods and corresponding programs. In this paper we concentrate on the third, namely the Fourier-based approach.

To manage portfolios of derivatives, traders have to understand how sensitive prices of derivative products are with respect to changes in the underlying parameters. For this purpose they need to know the Greeks which are given by the partial derivatives of the pricing functional with respect to those parameters. Usually Greeks are estimated by means of a finite difference approximation. Two kinds of errors are produced this way: the first one comes from the approximation of the derivative by a finite difference and the second one results from the numerical computation of the expectation. To eliminate one of the sources of error, Fournié et al. (1999) [9] adopted a new approach which consists in shifting the differential operator from the pricing functional to the diffusion kernel. This procedure results in an expectation operator applied to the payoff multiplied by a random weight function.

In the following we focus on a discrete tenor interest rate model which has been introduced in Eberlein and Özkan (2005) [5]. This so-called Lévy forward process model is driven by a time-inhomogeneous Lévy process and is developed on the basis of a backward induction that is necessary to get the LIBOR rates in a convenient homogeneous form. A major advantage of the forward process approach is that it is invariant under the measure change in the sense that the driving process remains a time-inhomogeneous Lévy process. Moreover, the measure changes do not only have the invariance property but in addition they are analytically and consequently also numerically much simpler compared to the corresponding measure changes in the so-called LIBOR model. The reason is that in each induction step the forward process itself represents up to a norming constant the density process on which the measure change is based. As a consequence, any approximation such as the 'frozen drift' approximation or more sophisticated versions of it are completely avoided. This means that the approximation error with which one has to struggle in the LIBOR approach does not show up in the forward process approach.

Another important aspect is that in the latter model the increments of the driving process translate directly into increments of the LIBOR rates. This is not the case for the LIBOR model where the increments of the LIBOR rates are proportional to the corresponding increments of the driving process scaled with the current value of the LIBOR rate. Expressed in terms of the terminology which will be developed in Sects. 2 and 3 this means that in the Lévy LIBOR model

$$L(t+\Delta t, T_k) - L(t, T_k) \sim L(t, T_k)\left(L^{T_{k+1}}_{t+\Delta t} - L^{T_{k+1}}_t\right), \tag{1}$$

whereas in the Lévy forward process model

$$L(t+\Delta t, T_k) - L(t, T_k) \sim \delta_k^{-1}\left(L^{T_{k+1}}_{t+\Delta t} - L^{T_{k+1}}_t\right). \tag{2}$$

The fact that the increments of the LIBOR rate process do not depend on current LIBOR values, translates into increased flexibility and a superior model performance of the forward process approach.

In addition to the differences in mathematical properties there is a fundamental economic difference. The forward process approach allows for negative interest rates as well as for negative starting values. This is of crucial importance in particular in the current economic environment where negative rates are common. Models where by construction interest rates stay strictly positive are not able to produce realistic valuations for a large collection of interest rate derivatives in a deflationary or near-deflationary environment.

As far as the calculation of Greeks in this setting is concerned, we refer to Glasserman and Zhao (1999) [12], Glasserman (2004) [11], and Fries (2007) [10] where some treatment of this issue is given. The classical diffusion-based LIBOR market model offers a high degree of analytical tractability. However, this model cannot reproduce the phenomenon of changing volatility smiles along the maturity axis. In order to gain more flexibility in a first step one can replace the driving Brownian motion by a (time-homogeneous) Lévy process. However, one observes that the shape of the volatility surface produced by cap and floor prices is too sophisticated in order to be matched with sufficient accuracy by a model which is driven by a time-homogeneous process. To achieve a more accurate calibration of the model across different strikes and maturities one has to use the more flexible class of time-inhomogeneous Lévy processes (see e.g. Eberlein and Özkan (2005) [5] and Eberlein and Kluge (2006) [6]). Graphs in the latter paper show in particular that interest rate models driven by time-inhomogeneous Lévy processes are able to reproduce implied volatility curves (smiles) observed in the market across all maturities with high accuracy. If one restricts the approach to (time-homogeneous) Lévy processes as drivers, the smiles flatten out too fast at longer maturities. Consequently, we have analytical—the invariance under measure changes—as well as statistical reasons to choose time-inhomogeneous Lévy processes as drivers. In implementations of the model already a rather mild form of time-inhomogeneity turns out to be sufficient. Typically one has to glue together three pieces of (time-homogeneous) Lévy processes in order to cover the full range of maturities with sufficient accuracy. In terms of parameters this means that instead of three or four one uses nine or twelve parameters.

The first goal of this paper is to give a closed Fourier-based valuation formula for a caplet in the framework of the Lévy forward process model. The second aim is to study sensitivities. We discuss two approaches for this purpose. The first is based on the integration-by-parts formula, which lies at the core of the application of the Malliavin calculus to finance as developed in Fournié et al. (1999) [9], León et al.

(2002) [14], Petrou (2008) [17], Yablonski (2008) [19]. This approach is appropriate if the driving process has a diffusion component. The second approach which covers purely discontinuous drivers as well relies on Fourier-based methods for pricing derivatives. For a survey of Fourier-based methods see Eberlein (2014) [3]. We illustrate the result by applying the formula to the pricing of a caplet where the jump-part of the underlying model is driven by a time-inhomogeneous Gamma process and alternatively by a Variance Gamma process.

2 The Lévy Forward Process Model

Let $0 = T_0 < T_1 < \cdots < T_{n-1} < T_n = T^*$ denote a discrete tenor structure and set $\delta_k = T_{k+1} - T_k$ for all $k \in \{0, \ldots, n-1\}$. Because we proceed by backward induction, let us use the notation $T_i^* := T_{n-i}$ and $\delta_i^* = \delta_{n-i}$ for $i \in \{1, \ldots, n\}$. For zero-coupon bond prices $B(t, T_i^*)$ and $B(t, T_{i-1}^*)$, the forward process is defined by

$$F(t, T_i^*, T_{i-1}^*) = \frac{B(t, T_i^*)}{B(t, T_{i-1}^*)}. \tag{3}$$

Hence, modeling forward processes means specifying the dynamics of ratios of successive bond prices. Let $(\Omega; \mathscr{F}=\mathscr{F}_{T^*}; \mathbb{F}; \mathbb{P}_{T^*})$ be a complete stochastic basis where $\mathbb{P}_{T^*}$ should be regarded as the forward martingale measure for the settlement date $T^* > 0$ and the filtration $\mathbb{F}=(\mathscr{F}_t)_{t\in[0,T^*]}$ satisfies the usual conditions. Consider a time-inhomogeneous Lévy process L^{T^*} defined on $(\Omega; \mathscr{F}=\mathscr{F}_{T^*}; \mathbb{F}; \mathbb{P}_{T^*})$ starting at 0 with local characteristics (b^{T^*}, c, F^{T^*}) such that the drift term $b_s^{T^*} \in \mathbb{R}$, the volatility coefficient c_s and the Lévy measure $F_s^{T^*}$ satisfy the following conditions

$$\exists\, \sigma > 0,\ \ \forall\, s \in [0, T^*]:\ \ c_s\ >\ \sigma,\ \ F_s^{T^*}(\{0\})\ =\ 0 \tag{4}$$

and

$$\int_0^{T^*} \left(|b_s^{T^*}| + |c_s| + \int_{\mathbb{R}} \left(|x|^2 \wedge 1\right) F_s^{T^*}(dx) \right) ds < \infty. \tag{5}$$

We impose as usual a further integrability condition. Note that the processes which we will define later, are by construction martingales and therefore every single random variable has to be integrable.

Assumption 2.1 ($\mathbb{EM}$) There exists a constant $M > 1$ such that

$$\int_0^{T^*} \int_{\{|x|>1\}} \exp(ux) F_s^{T^*}(dx)ds < \infty,\ \ \forall\, u \in [-M, M]. \tag{6}$$

Under ($\mathbb{EM}$) the random variable $L_t^{T^*}$ has a finite expectation and its law is given by the characteristic function

$$\mathbb{E}\left[e^{\mathrm{i}uL_t^{T^*}}\right] = \exp\left(\int_0^t \left(\mathrm{i}ub_s^{T^*} - \frac{1}{2}u^2 c_s + \int_{\mathbb{R}} \left(e^{\mathrm{i}ux} - 1 - \mathrm{i}ux\right) F_s^{T^*}(dx)\right) ds\right). \quad (7)$$

Furthermore, the process L^{T^*} is a special semimartingale, and thus its canonical representation has the simple form

$$L_t^{T^*} = \int_0^t b_s^{T^*} ds + \int_0^t \sqrt{c_s} dW_s^{T^*} + \int_0^t \int_{\mathbb{R}} x\widetilde{\mu}^{L^{T^*}}(ds, dx), \quad (8)$$

where $(W_t^{T^*})_{t\geq 0}$ is a $\mathbb{P}_{T^*}$-standard Brownian motion and $\widetilde{\mu}^{L^{T^*}} := \mu^{L^{T^*}} - \nu^{T^*}$ is the $\mathbb{P}_{T^*}$-compensated random measure of jumps of L^{T^*}. As usual, $\mu^{L^{T^*}}$ denotes the random measure of jumps of L^{T^*} and $\nu^{T^*}(ds, dx) := F_s^{T^*}(dx)ds$ the $\mathbb{P}_{T^*}$-compensator of $\mu^{L^{T^*}}$. We denote by θ_s the cumulant function associated with the process L^{T^*} as given in (8) with local characteristics (b^{T^*}, c, F^{T^*}), that is, for appropriate $z \in \mathbb{C}$

$$\theta_s(z) = zb_s^{T^*} + \frac{z^2}{2}c_s + \int_{\mathbb{R}} \left(e^{zx} - 1 - zx\right) F_s^{T^*}(dx), \quad (9)$$

where c and F^{T^*} are free parameters, whereas the drift characteristic b^{T^*} will later be chosen to guarantee that the forward process is a martingale. The following ingredients are needed.

Assumption 2.2 ($\mathbb{LR}$.1) For any maturity T_i^* there is a bounded, deterministic function $\lambda(\cdot, T_i^*) : [0,\ T^*] \longmapsto \mathbb{R}$ which represents the volatility of the forward process $F(\cdot, T_i^*, T_{i-1}^*)$. These functions satisfy

$\lambda(s, T_i^*) > 0, \forall s \in [0, T_i^*]$ and $\lambda(s, T_i^*) = 0$ for $s > T_i^*$ for any maturity T_i^*, $\sum_{i=1}^{n-1} \lambda(s, T_i^*) \leq M, \quad \forall s \in [0,\ T^*]$ where M is the constant from Assumption ($\mathbb{EM}$).

Assumption 2.3 ($\mathbb{LR}$.2) The initial term structure of zero-coupon bond prices $B(0, T_i^*)$ is strictly positive for all $i \in \{1, \ldots, n\}$.

We begin to construct the forward process with the most distant maturity and postulate

$$F(t, T_1^*, T^*) = F(0, T_1^*, T^*) \exp\left(\int_0^t \lambda(s, T_1^*) dL_s^{T^*}\right). \quad (10)$$

One forces this process to become a $\mathbb{P}_{T^*}$-martingale by choosing b^{T^*} such that

$$\int_0^t \lambda(s, T_1^*) b_s^{T^*} ds = -\frac{1}{2} \int_0^t c_s \lambda^2(s, T_1^*) ds - \int_0^t \int_{\mathbb{R}} \left(e^{x\lambda(s,T_1^*)} - 1 - x\lambda(s, T_1^*) \right) \nu^{T^*}(ds, dx). \quad (11)$$

Then the forward process $F(\cdot, T_1^*, T^*)$ can be given as a stochastic exponential

$$F(t, T_1^*, T^*) = F(0, T_1^*, T^*) \mathscr{E}_t \left(Z(\cdot, T_1^*) \right) \quad (12)$$

with

$$Z(t, T_1^*) = \int_0^t \sqrt{c_s} \lambda(s, T_1^*) dW_s^{T^*} + \int_0^t \int_{\mathbb{R}} (e^{x\lambda(s,T_1^*)} - 1) \widetilde{\mu}^{L^{T^*}}(ds, dx). \quad (13)$$

Since the forward process $F(\cdot, T_1^*, T^*)$ is a $\mathbb{P}_{T^*}$-martingale, we can use it as a density process and define the forward martingale measure $\mathbb{P}_{T_1^*}$ by setting

$$\frac{d\mathbb{P}_{T_1^*}}{d\mathbb{P}_{T^*}} = \frac{F(T_1^*, T_1^*, T^*)}{F(0, T_1^*, T^*)} = \mathscr{E}_{T_1^*} \left(Z(\cdot, T_1^*) \right). \quad (14)$$

By the semimartingale version of Girsanov's theorem (see Jacod and Shiryaev (1987) [13])

$$W_t^{T_1^*} := W_t^{T^*} - \int_0^t \sqrt{c_s} \lambda(s, T_1^*) ds \quad (15)$$

is a $\mathbb{P}_{T_1^*}$-standard Brownian motion and

$$\nu^{T_1^*}(dt, dx) := e^{x\lambda(s,T_1^*)} \nu^{T^*}(dt, dx) = e^{x\lambda(s,T_1^*)} F_s^{T^*}(dx) ds \quad (16)$$

is the $\mathbb{P}_{T_1^*}$-compensator of $\mu^{L^{T^*}}$.

Continuing this way one gets the forward processes $F(\cdot, T_i^*, T_{i-1}^*)$ such that for all $i \in \{1, \ldots, n\}$

$$F(t, T_i^*, T_{i-1}^*) = F(0, T_i^*, T_{i-1}^*) \exp \left(\int_0^t \lambda(s, T_i^*) dL_s^{T_{i-1}^*} \right). \quad (17)$$

The drift term $b^{T_{i-1}^*}$ is chosen in such a way that the forward process $F(\cdot, T_i^*, T_{i-1}^*)$ becomes a martingale under the forward measure $\mathbb{P}_{T_{i-1}^*}$, that is

$$\int_0^t \lambda(s, T_i^*) b_s^{T_{i-1}^*} ds = -\frac{1}{2} \int_0^t c_s \lambda^2(s, T_i^*) ds - \int_0^t \int_{\mathbb{R}} \left(e^{x\lambda(s,T_i^*)} - 1 - x\lambda(s, T_i^*) \right) \nu^{T_{i-1}^*}(ds, dx). \quad (18)$$

We propose the following choice for the functions $b^{T^*_{i-1}}$ for all $i \in \{1, \dots, n\}$

$$\begin{cases} b_s^{T^*_{i-1}} = -\dfrac{c_s}{2}\lambda(s, T_i^*) - \displaystyle\int_{\mathbb{R}} \left(\dfrac{e^{x\lambda(s,T_i^*)} - 1}{\lambda(s, T_i^*)} - x \right) F_s^{T^*_{i-1}}(dx), \; 0 \le s < T_i^* \\ b_s^{T^*_{i-1}} = 0, \qquad\qquad s \ge T_i^*. \end{cases} \tag{19}$$

The driving process $L^{T^*_{i-1}}$ becomes therefore

$$\begin{aligned} L_t^{T^*_{i-1}} &= -\int_0^t \left(\frac{c_s}{2}\lambda(s, T_i^*) + \int_{\mathbb{R}} \left(\frac{e^{x\lambda(s,T_i^*)} - 1}{\lambda(s, T_i^*)} - x \right) F_s^{T^*_{i-1}}(dx) \right) ds \\ &\quad + \int_0^t \sqrt{c_s} dW_s^{T^*_{i-1}} + \int_0^t \int_{\mathbb{R}} x(\mu^{T^*} - \nu^{T^*_{i-1}})(ds, dx) \end{aligned} \tag{20}$$

under the successive forward measures $\mathbb{P}_{T_i^*}$ which are given by the recursive relation

$$\begin{cases} \dfrac{d\mathbb{P}_{T_i^*}}{d\mathbb{P}_{T^*_{i-1}}} = \dfrac{F(T_i^*, T_i^*, T^*_{i-1})}{F(0, T_i^*, T^*_{i-1})} = \mathcal{E}_{T_i^*}\left(Z(\cdot, T_i^*)\right), \quad i \in \{1, \dots, n\} \\ \mathbb{P}_{T_0^*} = \mathbb{P}_{T^*} \end{cases} \tag{21}$$

with

$$Z(t, T_i^*) = \int_0^t \sqrt{c_s}\lambda(s, T_i^*) dW_s^{T^*_{i-1}} + \int_0^t \int_{\mathbb{R}} (e^{x\lambda(s,T_i^*)} - 1)\widetilde{\mu}^{L^{T^*_{i-1}}}(ds, dx), \tag{22}$$

where $(W_t^{T^*_{i-1}})_{t \ge 0}$ is a $\mathbb{P}_{T^*_{i-1}}$-standard Brownian motion such that

$$\begin{cases} W_t^{T_i^*} = W_t^{T^*_{i-1}} - \displaystyle\int_0^t \sqrt{c_s}\lambda(s, T_i^*) ds, \quad i \in \{1, \dots, n\} \\ W_t^{T_0^*} = W_t^{T^*}. \end{cases} \tag{23}$$

$\widetilde{\mu}_{i-1}^{L^{T^*}} := \mu^{L^{T^*}} - \nu^{T^*_{i-1}}$ is the $\mathbb{P}_{T^*_{i-1}}$-compensated random measure of jumps of L^{T^*} and $\nu^{T^*_{i-1}}(ds, dx) = F_s^{T^*_{i-1}}(dx)ds$ is the $\mathbb{P}_{T^*_{i-1}}$-compensator of $\mu^{L^{T^*}}$ such that

$$\begin{cases} F_s^{T_i^*}(dx) = e^{x\lambda(s,T_i^*)} F_s^{T^*_{i-1}}(dx), \quad i \in \{1, \dots, n\} \\ F_s^{T_0^*}(dx) = F_s^{T^*}(dx). \end{cases} \tag{24}$$

Setting $\Lambda^i(s) := \sum_{j=1}^{i} \lambda(s, T_j^*)$, we conclude that for all $i \in \{1, \dots, n\}$

$$W_t^{T_i^*} = W_t^{T^*} - \int_0^t \sqrt{c_s}\Lambda^i(s)ds \tag{25}$$

and

$$F_s^{T_i^*}(dx) = \exp\left(x\Lambda^i(s)\right) F_s^{T^*}(dx). \tag{26}$$

Note that the coefficients $\sqrt{c_s}\Lambda^i(s)$ and $\exp(x\Lambda^i(s))$, which appear in this measure change, are deterministic functions and therefore the measure change is structure preserving, i.e. the driving process is still a time-inhomogeneous Lévy process after the measure change.

Since the forward process $F(\cdot, T_i^*, T_{i-1}^*)$ is by construction a $\mathbb{P}_{T_{i-1}^*}$-martingale, the process $\frac{F(\cdot,T_i^*,T_{i-1}^*)}{F(0,T_i^*,T_{i-1}^*)}$, which is the density process

$$\left.\frac{d\mathbb{P}_{T_i^*}}{d\mathbb{P}_{T_{i-1}^*}}\right|_{\mathscr{F}_t} = \frac{F(t, T_i^*, T_{i-1}^*)}{F(0, T_i^*, T_{i-1}^*)} \tag{27}$$

is a $\mathbb{P}_{T_{i-1}^*}$-martingale as well. By iterating the relation (21) we get on $\mathscr{F}_{T_{i-1}^*}$

$$\begin{aligned}\frac{d\mathbb{P}_{T_{i-1}^*}}{d\mathbb{P}_{T^*}} &= \frac{B(0, T^*)}{B(0, T_{i-1}^*)} \prod_{j=1}^{i-1} F(T_{i-1}^*, T_j^*, T_{j-1}^*) \\ &= \exp\left(\sum_{j=1}^{i-1} \int_0^{T_{i-1}^*} \lambda(s, T_j^*) dL_s^{T_{j-1}^*}\right).\end{aligned} \tag{28}$$

Applying Proposition III.3.8 of Jacod and Shiryaev (1987) [13], we see that its restriction to $\mathscr{F}_t$ for $t \in [0, T_i^*]$

$$\left.\frac{d\mathbb{P}_{T_i^*}}{d\mathbb{P}_{T^*}}\right|_{\mathscr{F}_t} = \frac{B(0, T^*)}{B(0, T_i^*)} \prod_{j=1}^{i} F(t, T_j^*, T_{j-1}^*) \tag{29}$$

is a $\mathbb{P}_{T^*}$-martingale.

3 Fourier-Based Methods for Option Pricing

We will derive an explicit valuation formula for standard interest rate derivatives such as caps and floors in the Lévy forward process model. Since floor prices can be derived from the corresponding put-call-parity relation we concentrate on caps. Recall that a cap is a sequence of call options on subsequent LIBOR rates. Each single option is called a caplet. The payoff of a caplet with strike rate K and maturity T_i^* is

$$\delta_i^* \left(L(T_i^*, T_i^*) - K\right)^+, \tag{30}$$

where the payment is made at time point T_{i-1}^*. The forward LIBOR rates $L(T_i^*, T_i^*)$ are the discretely compounded, annualized interest rates which can be earned from investment during a future interval starting at T_i^* and ending at T_{i-1}^* considered at the time point T_i^*. These rates can be expressed in terms of the forward prices as follows

$$L(T_i^*, T_i^*) = \frac{1}{\delta_i^*}\left(F(T_i^*, T_i^*, T_{i-1}^*) - 1\right). \tag{31}$$

Its time-0-price, denoted by $Cplt_0(T_i^*, K)$, is given by

$$Cplt_0(T_i^*, K) = B(0, T_{i-1}^*)\delta_i^* \mathbb{E}_{\mathbb{P}_{T_{i-1}^*}}\left[\left(L(T_i^*, T_i^*) - K\right)^+\right]. \tag{32}$$

Instead of basing the pricing on the Lévy LIBOR model one can use the Lévy forward process approach (see Eberlein and Özkan (2005) [5]). It is then more natural to write the pricing formula (32) in the form

$$Cplt_0(T_i^*, K) = B(0, T_{i-1}^*)\mathbb{E}_{\mathbb{P}_{T_{i-1}^*}}\left[\left(F(T_i^*, T_i^*, T_{i-1}^*) - \widetilde{K}_i\right)^+\right], \tag{33}$$

where $\widetilde{K}_i := 1 + \delta_i^* K$. From (17), the forward process $F(\cdot, T_i^*, T_{i-1}^*)$ is given by

$$\begin{aligned} F(T_i^*, T_i^*, T_{i-1}^*) &= F(0, T_i^*, T_{i-1}^*) \exp\left(\int_0^{T_i^*} b_s^{T_{i-1}^*} \lambda(s, T_i^*) ds\right) \\ &\quad \times \exp\left(\int_0^{T_i^*} \sqrt{c_s}\lambda(s, T_i^*) dW_s^{T_{i-1}^*}\right) \\ &\quad \times \exp\left(\int_0^{T_i^*} \int_{\mathbb{R}} x\lambda(s, T_i^*)\widetilde{\mu}_{i-1}^{L^{T^*}}(ds, dx)\right). \end{aligned} \tag{34}$$

Using the relations (25) and (26) we obtain for $t \in [0, T_i^*]$

$$F(t, T_i^*, T_{i-1}^*) = F(0, T_i^*, T_{i-1}^*) \exp\left(\int_0^t \lambda(s, T_i^*) dL_s^{T^*} + d(t, T_i^*)\right), \tag{35}$$

where

$$d(t, T_i^*) = \int_0^t \lambda(s, T_i^*) \left[b_s^{T_{i-1}^*} - b_s^{T^*} - \Lambda^{i-1}(s)c_s \right] ds$$
$$- \int_0^t \lambda(s, T_i^*) \int_{\mathbb{R}} x \left(e^{x\Lambda^{i-1}(s)} - 1 \right) F_s^{T^*}(dx) ds. \tag{36}$$

Remember that on $\mathscr{F}_{T_{i-1}^*}$

$$\frac{d\mathbb{P}_{T_{i-1}^*}}{d\mathbb{P}_{T^*}} = \exp\left(\sum_{j=1}^{i-1} \int_0^{T_{i-1}^*} \lambda(s, T_j^*) dL_s^{T^*} + \sum_{j=1}^{i-1} d(T_{i-1}^*, T_j^*) \right). \tag{37}$$

Keeping in mind Assumption 2.2 ($\mathbb{LR}$.1), we find

$$\exp\left(-\sum_{j=1}^{i-1} d(T_{i-1}^*, T_j^*) \right) = \mathbb{E}_{\mathbb{P}_{T^*}} \left[\exp\left(\int_0^{T_{i-1}^*} \Lambda^{i-1}(s) dL_s^{T^*} \right) \right]. \tag{38}$$

Using Proposition 8 in Eberlein and Kluge (2006) [6], we find

$$\exp\left(-\sum_{j=1}^{i-1} d(T_{i-1}^*, T_j^*) \right) = \exp\left(\int_0^{T_{i-1}^*} \theta_s \left(\Lambda^{i-1}(s) \right) ds \right). \tag{39}$$

Consequently,

$$\frac{d\mathbb{P}_{T_{i-1}^*}}{d\mathbb{P}_{T^*}} = \exp\left(\int_0^{T_{i-1}^*} \Lambda^{i-1}(s) dL_s^{T^*} - \int_0^{T_{i-1}^*} \theta_s \left(\Lambda^{i-1}(s) \right) ds \right). \tag{40}$$

Knowing that the process $\left(\frac{F(\cdot, T_i^*, T_{i-1}^*)}{F(0, T_i^*, T_{i-1}^*)} \right)$ is a $\mathbb{P}_{T_{i-1}^*}$-martingale, we reach

$$\exp(-d(T_i^*, T_i^*)) = \mathbb{E}_{\mathbb{P}_{T_{i-1}^*}} \left[\exp\left(\int_0^{T_i^*} \lambda(s, T_i^*) dL_s^{T^*} \right) \right]. \tag{41}$$

Hence,

$$\begin{aligned} &\exp(-d(T_i^*, T_i^*)) \\ &= \exp\left(-\int_0^{T_i^*} \theta_s \left(\Lambda^{i-1}(s) \right) ds \right) \mathbb{E}_{\mathbb{P}_{T^*}} \left[\exp\left(\int_0^{T_i^*} \Lambda^i(s) dL_s^{T^*} \right) \right] \\ &= \exp\left(\int_0^{T_i^*} \left[\theta_s \left(\Lambda^i(s) \right) - \theta_s \left(\Lambda^{i-1}(s) \right) \right] ds \right). \end{aligned} \tag{42}$$

Thus,

$$d(T_i^*, T_i^*) = \int_0^{T_i^*} \left[-\theta_s\left(\Lambda^i(s)\right) + \theta_s\left(\Lambda^{i-1}(s)\right)\right] ds. \tag{43}$$

Define the random variable $X_{T_i^*}$ as the logarithm of $F(T_i^*, T_i^*, T_{i-1}^*)$. Therefore,

$$X_{T_i^*} = \ln\left(F(0, T_i^*, T_{i-1}^*)\right) + \int_0^{T_i^*} \lambda(s, T_i^*) dL_s^{T^*} + d(T_i^*, T_i^*). \tag{44}$$

Proposition 3.1 *Suppose there is a real number $R \in (1, 1+\varepsilon)$ such that the moment-generating function of $X_{T_i^*}$ with respect to $\mathbb{P}_{T_{i-1}^*}$ is finite at R, i.e. $M_{X_{T_i^*}}(R) < \infty$, then*

$$\begin{aligned}
\mathrm{Cplt}_0(T_i^*, K) = {} & \frac{\widetilde{K}_i B(0, T_{i-1}^*)}{2\pi} \int_{\mathbb{R}} \left\{ \left(\frac{F(0, T_i^*, T_{i-1}^*)}{\widetilde{K}_i} \right)^{R+iu} \right. \\
& \times \exp\left(\int_0^{T_i^*} \int_{\mathbb{R}} e^{x\Lambda^{i-1}(s)} \left[\left(e^{(R+\mathrm{i}u)x\lambda(s,T_i^*)} - 1 \right) - (R+\mathrm{i}u)\left(e^{x\lambda(s,T_i^*)} - 1 \right) \right] F_s^{T^*}(dx) ds \right) \\
& \left. \times \exp\left(\int_0^{T_i^*} \frac{c_s}{2}(R+\mathrm{i}u)(R+\mathrm{i}u-1)\lambda^2(s, T_i^*) ds \right) \right\} \frac{du}{(R+\mathrm{i}u)(R+\mathrm{i}u-1)}.
\end{aligned} \tag{45}$$

Proof The time-0-price of the caplet with strike rate K and maturity T_i^* has the form

$$\begin{aligned}
Cplt_0(T_i^*, K) &= B(0, T_{i-1}^*) \mathbb{E}_{\mathbb{P}_{T_{i-1}^*}} \left[\left(e^{X_{T_i^*}} - \widetilde{K}_i \right)^+ \right] \\
&= B(0, T_{i-1}^*) \mathbb{E}_{\mathbb{P}_{T_{i-1}^*}} \left[f\left(X_{T_i^*} \right) \right],
\end{aligned} \tag{46}$$

where the function $f : \mathbb{R} \to \mathbb{R}^+$ is defined by $f(x) = (e^x - \widetilde{K}_i)^+$.

Applying Theorem 2.2 in Eberlein et al. (2010) [8] (by the definition of $X_{T_i^*}$ we have $s = 0$ here), we get

$$Cplt_0(T_i^*, K) = \frac{B(0, T_{i-1}^*)}{2\pi} \int_{\mathbb{R}} M_{X_{T_i^*}}(R+\mathrm{i}u) \hat{f}(-u+\mathrm{i}R) du, \tag{47}$$

where the Fourier transform $\hat{f}$ is given by

$$\hat{f}(-u+\mathrm{i}R) = \frac{\widetilde{K}_i^{1-R-\mathrm{i}u}}{(R+\mathrm{i}u)(R+\mathrm{i}u-1)} \tag{48}$$

and the moment-generating function $M_{X_{T_i^*}}$ is given by

$$\begin{aligned} M_{X_{T_i^*}}(R+\mathrm{i}u) &= \mathbb{E}_{\mathbb{P}_{T_{i-1}^*}}\left[\exp\left((R+\mathrm{i}u)X_{T_i^*}\right)\right] \\ &= \left(F(0,T_i^*,T_{i-1}^*)\right)^{R+\mathrm{i}u}\exp\left((R+\mathrm{i}u)d(T_i^*,T_i^*)\right) \\ &\quad\times\mathbb{E}_{\mathbb{P}_{T_{i-1}^*}}\left[\exp\left(\int_0^{T_i^*}(R+\mathrm{i}u)\lambda(s,T_i^*)dL_s^{T^*}\right)\right]. \end{aligned} \tag{49}$$

Making a change of measure, we find

$$\begin{aligned} M_{X_{T_i^*}}(R+\mathrm{i}u) &= \left(F(0,T_i^*,T_{i-1}^*)\right)^{R+\mathrm{i}u}\exp\left((R+\mathrm{i}u)d(T_i^*,T_i^*)\right) \\ &\quad\times\frac{\mathbb{E}_{\mathbb{P}_{T^*}}\left[\exp\left(\int_0^{T_i^*}\left((R+\mathrm{i}u)\lambda(s,T_i^*)+\Lambda^{i-1}(s)\right)dL_s^{T^*}\right)\right]}{\mathbb{E}_{\mathbb{P}_{T^*}}\left[\exp\left(\int_0^{T_i^*}\Lambda^{i-1}(s)dL_s^{T^*}\right)\right]}. \end{aligned} \tag{50}$$

Using Proposition 8 in Eberlein and Kluge (2006) [6], we can prove easily that

$$\begin{aligned} M_{X_{T_i^*}}(R+\mathrm{i}u) &= \left(F(0,T_i^*,T_{i-1}^*)\right)^{R+\mathrm{i}u} \\ &\quad\times\exp\left((R+\mathrm{i}u)\int_0^{T_i^*}\left[-\theta_s\left(\Lambda^i(s)\right)+\theta_s\left(\Lambda^{i-1}(s)\right)\right]ds\right) \\ &\quad\times\frac{\exp\left(\int_0^{T_i^*}\theta_s\left((R+\mathrm{i}u)\lambda(s,T_i^*)+\Lambda^{i-1}(s)\right)ds\right)}{\exp\left(\int_0^{T_i^*}\theta_s\left(\Lambda^{i-1}(s)\right)ds\right)} \\ &= \left(F(0,T_i^*,T_{i-1}^*)\right)^{R+\mathrm{i}u}\exp\left(\int_0^{T_i^*}\theta_s\left((R+\mathrm{i}u)\lambda(s,T_i^*)+\Lambda^{i-1}(s)\right)ds\right) \\ &\quad\times\exp\left(\int_0^{T_i^*}\left[(-R-\mathrm{i}u)\theta_s\left(\Lambda^i(s)\right)-(1-R-\mathrm{i}u)\theta_s\left(\Lambda^{i-1}(s)\right)\right]ds\right). \end{aligned} \tag{51}$$

Taking into account the choice of the drift coefficient in (19), the cumulant function θ_s (see (9)) and the moment-generating function $M_{X_{T_i^*}}$, respectively, become

$$\begin{aligned} \theta_s(R+\mathrm{i}u) &= (R+\mathrm{i}u)\int_{\mathbb{R}}\left(\frac{e^{x(R+\mathrm{i}u)}-1}{R+\mathrm{i}u}-\frac{(e^{x\lambda(s,T_1^*)}-1)}{\lambda(s,T_1^*)}\right)F_s^{T^*}(dx) \\ &\quad+\frac{c_s}{2}(R+\mathrm{i}u)\left(R+\mathrm{i}u-\lambda(s,T_1^*)\right) \end{aligned} \tag{52}$$

and

$$M_{X_{T_i^*}}(R+\mathrm{i}u) = \left(F(0,T_i^*,T_{i-1}^*)\right)^{R+\mathrm{i}u}\exp\left(\int_0^{T_i^*}\frac{c_s}{2}(R+\mathrm{i}u)(R+\mathrm{i}u-1)\lambda^2(s,T_i^*)ds\right)$$

$$\times \exp\left(\int_0^{T_i^*}\int_{\mathbb{R}} e^{x\Lambda^{i-1}(s)}\left(e^{(R+\mathrm{i}u)x\lambda(s,T_i^*)}-1\right)F_s^{T^*}(dx)ds\right)$$
$$\times \exp\left(-(R+\mathrm{i}u)\int_0^{T_i^*}\int_{\mathbb{R}} e^{x\Lambda^{i-1}(s)}\left(e^{x\lambda(s,T_i^*)}-1\right)F_s^{T^*}(dx)ds\right). \quad (53)$$

Finally, from (48) and (53) we conclude that

$$Cplt_0(T_i^*,K)=\frac{\widetilde{K}_i B(0,T_{i-1}^*)}{2\pi}\int_{\mathbb{R}}\left\{\left(\frac{F(0,T_i^*,T_{i-1}^*)}{\widetilde{K}_i}\right)^{R+\mathrm{i}u}\right.$$
$$\times \exp\left(\int_0^{T_i^*}\int_{\mathbb{R}} e^{x\Lambda^{i-1}(s)}\left[\left(e^{(R+\mathrm{i}u)x\lambda(s,T_i^*)}-1\right)-(R+\mathrm{i}u)\left(e^{x\lambda(s,T_i^*)}-1\right)\right]F_s^{T^*}(dx)ds\right)$$
$$\left.\times \exp\left(\int_0^{T_i^*}\frac{c_s}{2}(R+\mathrm{i}u)(R+\mathrm{i}u-1)\lambda^2(s,T_i^*)ds\right)\right\}\frac{du}{(R+\mathrm{i}u)(R+\mathrm{i}u-1)}. \quad (54)$$

4 Sensitivity Analysis

4.1 Greeks Computed by the Malliavin Approach

In this section we present an application of the Malliavin calculus to the computation of Greeks within the Lévy forward process model. We refer to the literature, for example Di Nunno et al. (2008) [2] as well as Nualart (2006) [15] for details on the theoretical aspects of Malliavin calculus. Another important reference is Yablonski (2008) [19]. See also the Appendix for a short presentation of definitions and results used in the sequel. The forward process $F(t,T_i^*,T_{i-1}^*)$ under the forward measures $\mathbb{P}_{T_{i-1}^*}$ can be written as stochastic exponential

$$F(t,T_i^*,T_{i-1}^*)=F(0,T_i^*,T_{i-1}^*)\mathscr{E}_t\left(Z(\cdot,T_i^*)\right) \quad (55)$$

with

$$Z(t,T_i^*)=\int_0^t\sqrt{c_s}\lambda(s,T_i^*)dW_s^{T_{i-1}^*}+\int_0^t\int_{\mathbb{R}}(e^{x\lambda(s,T_i^*)}-1)\widetilde{\mu}^{L^{T_{i-1}^*}}(ds,dx). \quad (56)$$

Expressed in a differential form we get the $\mathbb{P}_{T_{i-1}^*}$-dynamics

$$\frac{dF(t,T_i^*,T_{i-1}^*)}{F(t-,T_i^*,T_{i-1}^*)}=\sqrt{c_t}\lambda(t,T_i^*)dW_t^{T_{i-1}^*}+\int_{\mathbb{R}}(e^{x\lambda(t,T_i^*)}-1)\widetilde{\mu}^{L^{T_{i-1}^*}}(dt,dx), \quad (57)$$

where $F(t-,T_i^*,T_{i-1}^*)$ is the pathwise left limit of $F(\cdot,T_i^*,T_{i-1}^*)$ at the point t.

As in the classical Malliavin calculus we are able to associate the solution of (57) with the process $Y(t, T_i^*, T_{i-1}^*) := \frac{\partial F(t,T_i^*,T_{i-1}^*)}{\partial F(0,T_i^*,T_{i-1}^*)}$; called the first variation process of $F(t, T_i^*, T_{i-1}^*)$. The following proposition provides a simpler expression for the Malliavin derivative operator $D_{r,0}$ when applied to the forward process rates $F(t, T_i^*, T_{i-1}^*)$ (see Di Nunno et al. (2008) [2], Theorem 17.4 and Yablonski (2008) [19], Definition 17. for details). We will denote the domain of the operator $D_{r,0}$ in $L^2(\Omega)$ by $\mathbb{D}^{1,2}$, meaning that $\mathbb{D}^{1,2}$ is the closure of the class of smooth random variables $\mathscr{S}$ (see (100) in the Appendix).

Proposition 4.1 *Let $F(t, T_i^*, T_{i-1}^*)_{t\in[0,T^*]}$ be the solution of (57). Then $F(t, T_i^*, T_{i-1}^*) \in \mathbb{D}^{1,2}$ and the Malliavin derivative is given by*

$$\begin{aligned} &D_{r,0}F(t, T_i^*, T_{i-1}^*) \\ &\quad = Y(t, T_i^*, T_{i-1}^*)Y(r-, T_i^*, T_{i-1}^*)^{-1}F(r-, T_i^*, T_{i-1}^*)\lambda(r, T_i^*)\sqrt{c_r}\mathbf{1}_{\{r\leq t\}}. \end{aligned} \tag{58}$$

4.1.1 Variation in the Initial Forward Price

In this section, we provide an expression for the *Delta*, the partial derivative of the expectation $Cplt_0(T_i^*, K)$ with respect to the initial condition $F(0, T_i^*, T_{i-1}^*)$ which is given by

$$\Delta(F(0, T_i^*, T_{i-1}^*)) = \frac{\partial Cplt_0(T_i^*, K)}{\partial F(0, T_i^*, T_{i-1}^*)}. \tag{59}$$

The derivative with respect to the initial LIBOR rate is then an easy consequence.

$$\begin{aligned} \Delta(L(0, T_i^*)) &= \frac{\partial Cplt_0(T_i^*, K)}{\partial L(0, T_i^*)} \\ &= \Delta(F(0, T_i^*, T_{i-1}^*))\frac{\partial F(0, T_i^*, T_{i-1}^*)}{\partial L(0, T_i^*)} \\ &= \delta_i^* \Delta(F(0, T_i^*, T_{i-1}^*)), \end{aligned} \tag{60}$$

since

$$L(0, T_i^*) = \frac{1}{\delta_i^*}\left(F(0, T_i^*, T_{i-1}^*) - 1\right). \tag{61}$$

Let us define the set

$$\widetilde{T}_i = \left\{h_i \in L^2([0, T_i^*]) : \int_0^{T_i^*} h_i(u)du = 1\right\}. \tag{62}$$

Proposition 4.2 *For all functions $h_i \in \widetilde{T}_i$, we have*

$$\begin{aligned}\Delta(F(0,T_i^*,T_{i-1}^*)) = \frac{B(0,T_{i-1}^*)}{F(0,T_i^*,T_{i-1}^*)}\mathbb{E}_{\mathbb{P}_{T^*}}\Big[&\left(F(T_i^*,T_i^*,T_{i-1}^*)-\widetilde{K}_i\right)^+\\ &\times\exp\left(\int_0^{T_i^*}\Lambda^{i-1}(s)dL_s^{T^*}-\int_0^{T_i^*}\theta_s\left(\Lambda^{i-1}(s)\right)ds\right)\\ &\times\left(\int_0^{T_i^*}\frac{h_i(u)dW_u^{T^*}}{\lambda(u,T_i^*)\sqrt{c_u}}-\int_0^{T_i^*}\frac{h_i(u)\Lambda^{i-1}(u)du}{\lambda(u,T_i^*)}\right)\Big]. \end{aligned}\quad (63)$$

Proof We consider a more general payoff of the form $H(F(T_i^*,T_i^*,T_{i-1}^*))$ such that $H:\mathbb{R}\longrightarrow\mathbb{R}$ is a locally integrable function satisfying

$$\mathbb{E}_{\mathbb{P}_{T_{i-1}^*}}\left[H(F(T_i^*,T_i^*,T_{i-1}^*))^2\right]<\infty\cdot \quad (64)$$

First, assume that H is a continuously differentiable function with compact support. Then we can differentiate inside the expectation and get

$$\begin{aligned}\Delta_H(F(0,T_i^*,T_{i-1}^*)) &:= \frac{\partial\mathbb{E}_{\mathbb{P}_{T_{i-1}^*}}\left[H(F(T_i^*,T_i^*,T_{i-1}^*))\right]}{\partial F(0,T_i^*,T_{i-1}^*)}\\ &= \mathbb{E}_{\mathbb{P}_{T_{i-1}^*}}\left[H'(F(T_i^*,T_i^*,T_{i-1}^*))\frac{\partial F(T_i^*,T_i^*,T_{i-1}^*)}{\partial F(0,T_i^*,T_{i-1}^*)}\right]\\ &= \mathbb{E}_{\mathbb{P}_{T_{i-1}^*}}\left[H'(F(T_i^*,T_i^*,T_{i-1}^*))Y(T_i^*,T_i^*,T_{i-1}^*)\right].\end{aligned}\quad (65)$$

Using Proposition 4.1 we find for any $h_i \in \widetilde{T}_i$

$$Y(T_i^*,T_i^*,T_{i-1}^*)=\int_0^{T_i^*}D_{u,0}F(T_i^*,T_i^*,T_{i-1}^*)\frac{h_i(u)Y(u-,T_i^*,T_{i-1}^*)du}{F(u-,T_i^*,T_{i-1}^*)\lambda(u,T_i^*)\sqrt{c_u}}. \quad (66)$$

From the chain rule (see Yablonski (2008) [19], Proposition 4.8) we find

$$\begin{aligned}\Delta_H(F(0,T_i^*,T_{i-1}^*)) &= \mathbb{E}_{\mathbb{P}_{T_{i-1}^*}}\Big[\int_0^{T_i^*}H'(F(T_i^*,T_i^*,T_{i-1}^*))D_{u,0}F(T_i^*,T_i^*,T_{i-1}^*)\\ &\qquad\times\frac{h_i(u)Y(u-,T_i^*,T_{i-1}^*)du}{F(u-,T_i^*,T_{i-1}^*)\lambda(u,T_i^*)\sqrt{c_u}}\Big]\\ &= \mathbb{E}_{\mathbb{P}_{T_{i-1}^*}}\Big[\int_0^{T_i^*}D_{u,0}H(F(T_i^*,T_i^*,T_{i-1}^*))\\ &\qquad\times\frac{h_i(u)Y(u-,T_i^*,T_{i-1}^*)du}{F(u-,T_i^*,T_{i-1}^*)\lambda(u,T_i^*)\sqrt{c_u}}\Big]\end{aligned}$$

$$= \mathbb{E}_{\mathbb{P}_{T^*_{i-1}}}\left[\int_0^{T_i^*}\int_{\mathbb{R}} D_{u,x} H(F(T_i^*, T_i^*, T_{i-1}^*)) \times \frac{h_i(u)Y(u-, T_i^*, T_{i-1}^*)du\delta_0(dx)}{F(u-, T_i^*, T_{i-1}^*)\lambda(u, T_i^*)\sqrt{c_u}}\right], \tag{67}$$

where $\delta_0(dx)$ is the Dirac measure at 0.

By the definition of the Skorohod integral $\delta(\cdot)$ (see Yablonski (2008) [19], Sect. 5), we reach

$$\begin{aligned}
&\Delta_H(F(0, T_i^*, T_{i-1}^*)) \\
&= \mathbb{E}_{\mathbb{P}_{T^*_{i-1}}}\left[H(F(T_i^*, T_i^*, T_{i-1}^*))\delta\left(\frac{h_i(\cdot)Y(\cdot-, T_i^*, T_{i-1}^*)\delta_0(\cdot)}{F(\cdot-, T_i^*, T_{i-1}^*)\lambda(\cdot, T_i^*)\sqrt{c_\cdot}}\right)\right].
\end{aligned} \tag{68}$$

However, the stochastic process

$$\left(\frac{h_i(u)Y(u-, T_i^*, T_{i-1}^*)}{F(u-, T_i^*, T_{i-1}^*)\lambda(u, T_i^*)\sqrt{c_u}}\right)_{0\le u\le T_i^*} \tag{69}$$

is a predictable process, thus the Skorohod integral coincides with the Itô stochastic integral and we get

$$\begin{aligned}
&\Delta_H(F(0, T_i^*, T_{i-1}^*)) \\
&= \mathbb{E}_{\mathbb{P}_{T^*_{i-1}}}\left[H(F(T_i^*, T_i^*, T_{i-1}^*))\int_0^{T_i^*} \frac{h_i(u)Y(u-, T_i^*, T_{i-1}^*)dW_u^{T^*_{i-1}}}{F(u-, T_i^*, T_{i-1}^*)\lambda(u, T_i^*)\sqrt{c_u}}\right].
\end{aligned} \tag{70}$$

By Lemma 12.28. p. 208 in Di Nunno et al. (2008) [2] the result (70) holds for any locally integrable function H such that

$$\mathbb{E}_{\mathbb{P}_{T^*_{i-1}}}\left[H(F(T_i^*, T_i^*, T_{i-1}^*))^2\right] < \infty. \tag{71}$$

In particular, if one takes

$$H(F(T_i^*, T_i^*, T_{i-1}^*)) = B(0, T_{i-1}^*)\left(F(T_i^*, T_i^*, T_{i-1}^*) - \widetilde{K}_i\right)^+, \tag{72}$$

we can express the derivatives of the expectation $Cplt_0(T_i^*, K, \delta_i^*)$ with respect to the initial condition $F(0, T_i^*, T_{i-1}^*)$ in the form of a weighted expectation as follows

$$\begin{aligned}
\Delta(F(0, T_i^*, T_{i-1}^*)) = B(0, T_{i-1}^*)\mathbb{E}_{\mathbb{P}_{T^*_{i-1}}}\Bigg[&\left(F(T_i^*, T_i^*, T_{i-1}^*) - \widetilde{K}_i\right)^+ \\
&\times \int_0^{T_i^*} \frac{h_i(u)Y(u-, T_i^*, T_{i-1}^*)dW_u^{T^*_{i-1}}}{\lambda(u, T_i^*)\sqrt{c_u}F(u-, T_i^*, T_{i-1}^*)}\Bigg].
\end{aligned} \tag{73}$$

We show easily that

$$Y(u-, T_i^*, T_{i-1}^*) = \frac{F(u-, T_i^*, T_{i-1}^*)}{F(0, T_i^*, T_{i-1}^*)}, \tag{74}$$

hence

$$\begin{aligned} &\Delta(F(0, T_i^*, T_{i-1}^*)) \\ &= \frac{B(0, T_{i-1}^*)}{F(0, T_i^*, T_{i-1}^*)} \mathbb{E}_{\mathbb{P}_{T_{i-1}^*}} \left[\left(F(T_i^*, T_i^*, T_{i-1}^*) - \widetilde{K}_i\right)^+ \int_0^{T_i^*} \frac{h_i(u) dW_u^{T_{i-1}^*}}{\lambda(u, T_i^*)\sqrt{c_u}} \right]. \end{aligned} \tag{75}$$

In accordance with (25) we can write

$$W_t^{T_{i-1}^*} = W_t^{T^*} - \int_0^t \Lambda^{i-1}(s)\sqrt{c_s} ds. \tag{76}$$

By making a measure change using the fact (see (40)) that

$$\left.\frac{d\mathbb{P}_{T_{i-1}^*}}{d\mathbb{P}_{T^*}}\right|_{\mathscr{F}_{T_i^*}} = \exp\left(\int_0^{T_i^*} \Lambda^{i-1}(s) dL_s^{T^*} - \int_0^{T_i^*} \theta_s\left(\Lambda^{i-1}(s)\right) ds\right), \tag{77}$$

we end up with

$$\begin{aligned} \Delta(F(0, T_i^*, T_{i-1}^*)) = {} & \frac{B(0, T_{i-1}^*)}{F(0, T_i^*, T_{i-1}^*)} \mathbb{E}_{\mathbb{P}_{T^*}} \Bigg[\left(F(T_i^*, T_i^*, T_{i-1}^*) - \widetilde{K}_i\right)^+ \\ & \times \exp\left(\int_0^{T_i^*} \Lambda^{i-1}(s) dL_s^{T^*} - \int_0^{T_i^*} \theta_s\left(\Lambda^{i-1}(s)\right) ds\right) \\ & \times \left(\int_0^{T_i^*} \frac{h_i(u) dW_u^{T^*}}{\lambda(u, T_i^*)\sqrt{c_u}} - \int_0^{T_i^*} \frac{h_i(u)\Lambda^{i-1}(u)}{\lambda(u, T_i^*)} du\right) \Bigg]. \end{aligned} \tag{78}$$

4.2 Greeks Computed by the Fourier-Based Valuation Method

Thanks to the Fourier-based valuation formula obtained in (45) and the structure of the forward process model as an exponential semimartingale, we can calculate readily the Greeks. We focus on the variation to the initial condition, i.e. Delta.

Proposition 4.3 *Suppose there is a real number* $R \in (1, 1+\varepsilon)$ *such that the moment-generating function of* $X_{T_i^*}$ *with respect to* $\mathbb{P}_{T_{i-1}^*}$ *is finite at* R, *i.e.* $M_{X_{T_i^*}}(R) < \infty$, *then*

$$\begin{aligned}\Delta(F(0,T_i^*,T_{i-1}^*)) = {} & \frac{B(0,T_{i-1}^*)}{2\pi}\int_{\mathbb{R}}\Bigg\{\left(\frac{F(0,T_i^*,T_{i-1}^*)}{\widetilde{K}_i}\right)^{R+iu-1} \\ & \times \exp\left(\int_0^{T_i^*}\int_{\mathbb{R}} e^{x\Lambda^{i-1}(s)}\left(e^{(R+iu)x\lambda(s,T_i^*)}-1\right)F_s^{T^*}(dx)ds\right) \\ & \times \exp\left(-\int_0^{T_i^*}\int_{\mathbb{R}} e^{x\Lambda^{i-1}(s)}(R+iu)\left(e^{x\lambda(s,T_i^*)}-1\right)F_s^{T^*}(dx)ds\right) \\ & \times \exp\left(\int_0^{T_i^*}\frac{c_s}{2}(R+iu)(R+iu-1)\lambda^2(s,T_i^*)ds\right)\Bigg\}\frac{du}{R+iu-1}. \end{aligned} \tag{79}$$

Proof Based on the Sect. 4 in Eberlein et al. (2010) [8], this proposition can be shown easily.

4.3 Examples

4.3.1 Variance Gamma Process (VG)

We suppose that the jump component of the driving process L^{T^*} (see (8)) is described by a Variance Gamma process with the Lévy density ν given by

$$\nu(dx) = F_{VG}(x)dx \tag{80}$$

such that

$$F_{VG}(x) := \frac{1}{\eta|x|}\exp\left(\frac{\theta}{\sigma^2}x - \frac{1}{\sigma}\sqrt{\frac{2}{\eta}+\frac{\theta^2}{\sigma^2}}|x|\right), \tag{81}$$

where (θ, σ, η) are the parameters such that $\theta \in \mathbb{R}$, $\sigma > 0$ and $\eta > 0$.

Let us put $B = \frac{\theta}{\sigma^2}$ and $C = \frac{1}{\sigma}\sqrt{\frac{2}{\eta}+\frac{\theta^2}{\sigma^2}}$ and get

$$F_{VG}(x) = \frac{\exp(Bx - C|x|)}{\eta|x|}. \tag{82}$$

In this case, the moment-generating function $M_{X_{T_i^*}}$ is given by

$$M_{X_{T_i^*}}(z) = \left(F(0,T_i^*,T_{i-1}^*)\right)^z \exp\left(\int_0^{T_i^*}\left(\frac{c_s z}{2}(z-1)\lambda^2(s,T_i^*) + I^{VG}(s,z)\right)ds\right), \tag{83}$$

where the generalized integral $I^{VG}(s,z)$ is given by

$$I^{VG}(s,z) := \int_{\mathbb{R}} \left(e^{x\left(z\lambda(s,T_i^*)+\Lambda^{i-1}(s)\right)} - e^{x\Lambda^{i-1}(s)}\right) F_{VG}(x)dx \\ -\int_{\mathbb{R}} z\left(e^{x\Lambda^{i}(s)} - e^{x\Lambda^{i-1}(s)}\right) F_{VG}(x)dx. \tag{84}$$

Now substituting $F_{VG}(x)$ by its explicit expression we get

$$\begin{aligned} I^{VG}(s,z) &= \int_{\mathbb{R}} \left(e^{x\left(z\lambda(s,T_i^*)+\Lambda^{i-1}(s)\right)} - e^{x\Lambda^{i-1}(s)}\right) \exp\left(Bx - C|x|\right) \frac{dx}{\eta|x|} \\ &\quad - \int_{\mathbb{R}} z\left(e^{x\Lambda^{i}(s)} - e^{x\Lambda^{i-1}(s)}\right) \exp\left(Bx - C|x|\right) \frac{dx}{\eta|x|} \\ &= \int_0^{+\infty} \left(e^{x\left(z\lambda(s,T_i^*)+\Lambda^{i-1}(s)\right)} - e^{x\Lambda^{i-1}(s)}\right) \exp\left(Bx - Cx\right) \frac{dx}{\eta x} \\ &\quad - \int_0^{+\infty} z\left(e^{x\Lambda^{i}(s)} - e^{x\Lambda^{i-1}(s)}\right) \exp\left(Bx - Cx\right) \frac{dx}{\eta x} \\ &\quad - \int_{-\infty}^{0} \left(e^{x\left(z\lambda(s,T_i^*)+\Lambda^{i-1}(s)\right)} - e^{x\Lambda^{i-1}(s)}\right) \exp\left(Bx + Cx\right) \frac{dx}{\eta x} \\ &\quad + \int_{-\infty}^{0} z\left(e^{x\Lambda^{i}(s)} - e^{x\Lambda^{i-1}(s)}\right) \exp\left(Bx + Cx\right) \frac{dx}{\eta x}, \end{aligned}$$

or

$$\begin{aligned} I^{VG}(s,z) &= \int_0^{+\infty} \left[\frac{e^{\left(z\lambda(s,T_i^*)+\Lambda^{i-1}(s)+B-C\right)x} - e^{\left(\Lambda^{i-1}(s)+B-C\right)x}}{\eta x}\right] dx \\ &\quad - \int_0^{+\infty} \left[z\frac{e^{\left(\Lambda^{i}(s)+B-C\right)x} - e^{\left(\Lambda^{i-1}(s)+B-C\right)x}}{\eta x}\right] dx \\ &\quad - \int_{-\infty}^{0} \left[\frac{e^{\left(z\lambda(s,T_i^*)+\Lambda^{i-1}(s)+B+C\right)x} - e^{\left(\Lambda^{i-1}(s)+B+C\right)x}}{\eta x}\right] dx \\ &\quad + \int_{-\infty}^{0} \left[z\frac{e^{\left(\Lambda^{i}(s)+B+C\right)x} - e^{\left(\Lambda^{i-1}(s)+B+C\right)x}}{\eta x}\right] dx \\ &= \int_0^{+\infty} \left[\frac{e^{\left(z\lambda(s,T_i^*)+\Lambda^{i-1}(s)+B-C\right)x} - e^{\left(\Lambda^{i-1}(s)+B-C\right)x}}{\eta x}\right] dx \\ &\quad - \int_0^{+\infty} \left[z\frac{e^{\left(\Lambda^{i}(s)+B-C\right)x} - e^{\left(\Lambda^{i-1}(s)+B-C\right)x}}{\eta x}\right] dx \\ &\quad + \int_0^{+\infty} \left[\frac{e^{-\left(z\lambda(s,T_i^*)+\Lambda^{i-1}(s)+B+C\right)x} - e^{-\left(\Lambda^{i-1}(s)+B+C\right)x}}{\eta x}\right] dx \\ &\quad - \int_0^{+\infty} \left[z\frac{e^{-\left(\Lambda^{i}(s)+B+C\right)x} - e^{-\left(\Lambda^{i-1}(s)+B+C\right)x}}{\eta x}\right] dx. \end{aligned}$$

Using the notations

$$\alpha_i(s,z) = -\left(z\lambda(s,T_i^*) + \Lambda^{i-1}(s) + B - C\right), \tag{85}$$
$$\beta_i(s) = -\left(\Lambda^{i-1}(s) + B - C\right), \tag{86}$$
$$\gamma_i(s) = -\left(\Lambda^{i}(s) + B - C\right), \tag{87}$$

we end up with

$$I^{VG}(s,z) = \int_0^{+\infty}\left[\frac{e^{-\alpha_i(s,z)x} - e^{-\beta_i(s)x}}{x} - z\frac{e^{-\gamma_i(s)x} - e^{-\beta_i(s)x}}{x}\right]dx$$
$$+ \int_0^{+\infty}\left[\frac{e^{-(2C-\alpha_i(s,z))x} - e^{-(2C-\beta_i(s))x}}{x} - z\frac{e^{-(2C-\gamma_i(s))x} - e^{-(2C-\beta_i(s))x}}{x}\right]dx.$$

Using Frullani's integral (see for details Ostrowski (1949) [16]), we can show that, if $\alpha \in \mathbb{C}$ and $\beta \in \mathbb{C}$ such that $\mathscr{Re}(\alpha) > 0, \mathscr{Re}(\beta) > 0$ and $\frac{\beta}{\alpha} \in \mathbb{C} \setminus \mathbb{R}^-$ where $\mathbb{R}^- =]-\infty; 0]$,

$$I_{(\alpha,\beta)} := \int_0^{+\infty}\frac{e^{-\alpha x} - e^{-\beta x}}{x}dx = Log\left(\frac{\beta}{\alpha}\right), \tag{88}$$

where Log is the principal value of the logarithm. Consequently

$$\begin{aligned}
I^{VG}(s,z) &= Log\left(\frac{\beta_i(s)}{\alpha_i(s,z)}\right) - zLog\left(\frac{\beta_i(s)}{\gamma_i(s)}\right) \\
&\quad + Log\left(\frac{2C-\beta_i(s)}{2C-\alpha_i(s,z)}\right) - zLog\left(\frac{2C-\beta_i(s)}{2C-\gamma_i(s)}\right) \\
&= Log\left(\frac{\beta_i(s)}{\alpha_i(s,z)}\right) + Log\left(\frac{2C-\beta_i(s)}{2C-\alpha_i(s,z)}\right) \\
&\quad -z\left(Log\left(\frac{\beta_i(s)}{\gamma_i(s)}\right) + Log\left(\frac{2C-\beta_i(s)}{2C-\gamma_i(s)}\right)\right) \\
&= Log\left(\frac{\beta_i(s)\,(2C-\beta_i(s))}{\alpha_i(s,z)\,(2C-\alpha_i(s,z))}\right) - zLog\left(\frac{\beta_i(s)\,(2C-\beta_i(s))}{\gamma_i(s)\,(2C-\gamma_i(s))}\right).
\end{aligned}$$

The moment-generating function $M_{X_{T_i^*}}$ becomes

$$\begin{aligned}
M_{X_{T_i^*}}(z) &= \left(F(0,T_i^*,T_{i-1}^*)\right)^z \exp\left(\int_0^{T_i^*}\frac{c_s z}{2}(z-1)\lambda^2(s,T_i^*)ds\right) \\
&\quad \times \exp\left(\int_0^{T_i^*} Log\left(\frac{\beta_i(s)\,(2C-\beta_i(s))}{\alpha_i(s,z)\,(2C-\alpha_i(s,z))}\right)ds\right) \\
&\quad \times \exp\left(-\int_0^{T_i^*} zLog\left(\frac{\beta_i(s)\,(2C-\beta_i(s))}{\gamma_i(s)\,(2C-\gamma_i(s))}\right)ds\right)
\end{aligned}$$

or

$$
\begin{aligned}
M_{X_{T_i^*}}(R+\mathrm{i}u) &= \left(F(0,T_i^*,T_{i-1}^*)\right)^{R+\mathrm{i}u} \\
&\times \exp\left(\int_0^{T_i^*} \frac{c_s}{2}(R+\mathrm{i}u)(R+\mathrm{i}u-1)\lambda^2(s,T_i^*)ds\right) \\
&\times \exp\left(\int_0^{T_i^*} Log\left(\frac{\beta_i(s)\,(2C-\beta_i(s))}{\alpha_i(s,R+\mathrm{i}u)\,(2C-\alpha_i(s,R+\mathrm{i}u))}\right)ds\right) \\
&\times \exp\left(-\int_0^{T_i^*} (R+\mathrm{i}u)Log\left(\frac{\beta_i(s)\,(2C-\beta_i(s))}{\gamma_i(s)\,(2C-\gamma_i(s))}\right)ds\right).
\end{aligned}
$$

The valuation formula becomes

$$
\begin{aligned}
Cplt_0(T_i^*,K) &= \frac{B(0,T_{i-1}^*)}{2\pi}\int_{\mathbb{R}} \frac{\widetilde{K}_i^{1-R-\mathrm{i}u} M_{X_{T_i^*}}(R+\mathrm{i}u)}{(R+\mathrm{i}u)(R+\mathrm{i}u-1)}du \\
&= \frac{\widetilde{K}_i B(0,T_{i-1}^*)}{2\pi}\int_{\mathbb{R}} \left\{\left(\frac{F(0,T_i^*,T_{i-1}^*)}{\widetilde{K}_i}\right)^{R+\mathrm{i}u}\right. \\
&\times \exp\left(\int_0^{T_i^*} \frac{c_s}{2}(R+\mathrm{i}u)(R+\mathrm{i}u-1)\lambda^2(s,T_i^*)ds\right) \\
&\times \exp\left(\int_0^{T_i^*} Log\left(\frac{\beta_i(s)\,(2C-\beta_i(s))}{\alpha_i(s,R+\mathrm{i}u)\,(2C-\alpha_i(s,R+\mathrm{i}u))}\right)ds\right) \\
&\times \exp\left.\left(-\int_0^{T_i^*} (R+\mathrm{i}u)Log\left(\frac{\beta_i(s)\,(2C-\beta_i(s))}{\gamma_i(s)\,(2C-\gamma_i(s))}\right)ds\right)\right\}\frac{du}{(R+\mathrm{i}u)(R+\mathrm{i}u-1)}. \qquad (89)
\end{aligned}
$$

The *Delta* is given by

$$
\begin{aligned}
\Delta(F(0,T_i^*,T_{i-1}^*)) &= \frac{B(0,T_{i-1}^*)}{2\pi}\int_{\mathbb{R}} \left\{\left(\frac{F(0,T_i^*,T_{i-1}^*)}{\widetilde{K}_i}\right)^{R+\mathrm{i}u-1}\right. \\
&\times \exp\left(\int_0^{T_i^*} \frac{c_s}{2}(R+\mathrm{i}u)(R+\mathrm{i}u-1)\lambda^2(s,T_i^*)ds\right) \\
&\times \exp\left(\int_0^{T_i^*} Log\left(\frac{\beta_i(s)\,(2C-\beta_i(s))}{\alpha_i(s,R+\mathrm{i}u)\,(2C-\alpha_i(s,R+\mathrm{i}u))}\right)ds\right) \\
&\times \exp\left.\left(-\int_0^{T_i^*} (R+\mathrm{i}u)Log\left(\frac{\beta_i(s)\,(2C-\beta_i(s))}{\gamma_i(s)\,(2C-\gamma_i(s))}\right)ds\right)\right\}\frac{du}{R+\mathrm{i}u-1}. \qquad (90)
\end{aligned}
$$

4.3.2 Inhomogeneous Gamma Process (IGP)

We suppose that the jump component of the driving process L^{T^*}, is described by an inhomogeneous Gamma process (IGP), which has been introduced by Berman (1981) [1] as follows

Definition 4.4 Let $A(t)$ be a nondecreasing function from $\mathbb{R}^+ \longrightarrow \mathbb{R}^+$ and $B > 0$. A Gamma process with shape function A and scale parameter B is a stochastic process $(L_t)_{t \geq 0}$ on $\mathbb{R}^+$ such that:

1. $L_0 = 0$;
2. Independent increments: for every increasing sequence of time points $t_0, \ldots, t_n$, the random variables $L_{t_0}, L_{t_1} - L_{t_0}, \ldots, L_{t_n} - L_{t_{n-1}}$ are independent;
3. for $0 \leq s < t$, the distribution of the random variable $L_t - L_s$ is given by the Gamma distribution $\Gamma(A(t) - A(s); B)$.

We suppose that the shape function A is differentiable, hence we can write

$$A(t) = A(0) + \int_0^t \dot{A}(s)ds \tag{91}$$

for all $t \in \mathbb{R}^+$ where $\dot{A}$ denotes the derivative of A. In this case, the Lévy density of the Gamma process L is given by

$$F_s^G(x) = \dot{A}(s)\frac{e^{-Bx}}{x}\mathbf{1}_{\{x>0\}}. \tag{92}$$

The moment-generating function (53) has the form

$$\begin{aligned}
M_{X_{T_i^*}}(z) &= \left(F(0, T_i^*, T_{i-1}^*)\right)^z \exp\left(\int_0^{T_i^*} \frac{c_s z}{2}(z-1)\lambda^2(s, T_i^*)ds\right) \\
&\quad \times \exp\left(\int_0^{T_i^*} \int_{\mathbb{R}} e^{x\Lambda^{i-1}(s)} \left[\left(e^{zx\lambda(s,T_i^*)} - 1\right) - z\left(e^{x\lambda(s,T_i^*)} - 1\right)\right] F_s^G(x)dxds\right) \\
&= \left(F(0, T_i^*, T_{i-1}^*)\right)^z \exp\left(\int_0^{T_i^*} \frac{c_s z}{2}(z-1)\lambda^2(s, T_i^*)ds\right) \\
&\quad \times \exp\left(\int_0^{T_i^*} \dot{A}(s) \int_{\mathbb{R}} e^{x\Lambda^{i-1}(s)} \left(e^{zx\lambda(s,T_i^*)} - 1\right) \frac{e^{-Bx}}{x}\mathbf{1}_{\{x>0\}}dxds\right) \\
&\quad \times \exp\left(-z\int_0^{T_i^*} \dot{A}(s) \int_{\mathbb{R}} e^{x\Lambda^{i-1}(s)} \left(e^{x\lambda(s,T_i^*)} - 1\right) \frac{e^{-Bx}}{x}\mathbf{1}_{\{x>0\}}dxds\right) \\
&= \left(F(0, T_i^*, T_{i-1}^*)\right)^z \exp\left(\int_0^{T_i^*} \left(\frac{c_s z}{2}(z-1)\lambda^2(s, T_i^*) + \dot{A}(s)I^G(s,z)\right) ds\right),
\end{aligned}$$

where

$$\begin{aligned}
I^G(s, z) = &\int_0^{+\infty} \frac{e^{\left(z\lambda(s,T_i^*)+\Lambda^{i-1}(s)-B\right)x} - e^{\left(\Lambda^{i-1}(s)-B\right)x}}{x}dx \\
&- \int_0^{+\infty} z\frac{e^{\left(\Lambda^{i}(s)-B\right)x} - e^{\left(\Lambda^{i-1}(s)-B\right)x}}{x}dx.
\end{aligned}$$

Setting

$$\alpha_i(s,z) = -\left(z\lambda(s,T_i^*) + \Lambda^{i-1}(s) - B\right), \tag{93}$$

$$\beta_i(s) = -\left(\Lambda^{i-1}(s) - B\right), \tag{94}$$

$$\gamma_i(s) = -\left(\Lambda^{i}(s) - B\right) \tag{95}$$

and using Frullani's integral, we find that

$$\begin{aligned} I^G(s,z) &= \int_0^{+\infty}\left[\frac{e^{-\alpha_i(s,z)x} - e^{-\beta_i(s)x}}{x} - z\frac{e^{-\gamma_i(s)x} - e^{-\beta_i(s)x}}{x}\right]dx \\ &= Log\left(\frac{\beta_i(s)}{\alpha_i(s,z)}\right) - zLog\left(\frac{\beta_i(s)}{\gamma_i(s)}\right) \\ &= Log\left(\frac{\Lambda^{i-1}(s) - B}{z\lambda(s,T_i^*) + \Lambda^{i-1}(s) - B}\right) - zLog\left(\frac{\Lambda^{i-1}(s) - B}{\Lambda^{i}(s) - B}\right). \end{aligned}$$

Therefore, we get the form

$$\begin{aligned} M_{X_{T_i^*}}(z) &= \left(F(0,T_i^*,T_{i-1}^*)\right)^z \exp\left(\int_0^{T_i^*}\frac{c_s z}{2}(z-1)\lambda^2(s,T_i^*)ds\right) \\ &\quad\times \exp\left(\int_0^{T_i^*}\dot{A}(s)Log\left(\frac{\Lambda^{i-1}(s) - B}{z\lambda(s,T_i^*) + \Lambda^{i-1}(s) - B}\right)ds\right) \\ &\quad\times \exp\left(-z\int_0^{T_i^*}\dot{A}(s)Log\left(\frac{\Lambda^{i-1}(s) - B}{\Lambda^{i}(s) - B}\right)ds\right) \end{aligned}$$

or

$$\begin{aligned} M_{X_{T_i^*}}(R+\mathrm{i}u) &= \left(F(0,T_i^*,T_{i-1}^*)\right)^{R+\mathrm{i}u} \\ &\quad\times \exp\left(\int_0^{T_i^*}\frac{c_s}{2}(R+\mathrm{i}u)(R+\mathrm{i}u-1)\lambda^2(s,T_i^*)ds\right) \\ &\quad\times \exp\left(\int_0^{T_i^*}\dot{A}(s)Log\left(\frac{\Lambda^{i-1}(s) - B}{(R+\mathrm{i}u)\lambda(s,T_i^*) + \Lambda^{i-1}(s) - B}\right)ds\right) \\ &\quad\times \exp\left(-(R+\mathrm{i}u)\int_0^{T_i^*}\dot{A}(s)Log\left(\frac{\Lambda^{i-1}(s) - B}{\Lambda^{i}(s) - B}\right)ds\right). \end{aligned}$$

The valuation formula becomes

$$\begin{aligned} Cplt_0(T_i^*,K) &= \frac{B(0,T_{i-1}^*)}{2\pi}\int_{\mathbb{R}}\frac{\widetilde{K}_i^{1-R-\mathrm{i}u}M_{X_{T_i^*}}(R+\mathrm{i}u)}{(R+\mathrm{i}u)(R+\mathrm{i}u-1)}du \\ &= \frac{\widetilde{K}_i B(0,T_{i-1}^*)}{2\pi}\int_{\mathbb{R}}\frac{du}{(R+\mathrm{i}u)(R+\mathrm{i}u-1)}\left\{\left(\frac{F(0,T_i^*,T_{i-1}^*)}{\widetilde{K}_i}\right)^{R+\mathrm{i}u}\right. \end{aligned}$$

$$\times \exp\left(\int_0^{T_i^*} \frac{c_s}{2}(R+\mathrm{i}u)(R+\mathrm{i}u-1)\lambda^2(s,T_i^*)ds\right)$$
$$\times \exp\left(\int_0^{T_i^*} \dot{A}(s)Log\left(\frac{\Lambda^{i-1}(s)-B}{(R+\mathrm{i}u)\lambda(s,T_i^*)+\Lambda^{i-1}(s)-B}\right)ds\right)$$
$$\times \exp\left(-\int_0^{T_i^*}(R+\mathrm{i}u)\dot{A}(s)Log\left(\frac{\Lambda^{i-1}(s)-B}{\Lambda^{i}(s)-B}\right)ds\right)\Bigg\}. \tag{96}$$

The Greek *Delta* is given by

$$\Delta(F(0,T_i^*,T_{i-1}^*)) = \frac{B(0,T_{i-1}^*)}{2\pi}\int_{\mathbb{R}}\Bigg\{\left(\frac{F(0,T_i^*,T_{i-1}^*)}{\widetilde{K}_i}\right)^{R+\mathrm{i}u-1}$$
$$\times \exp\left(\int_0^{T_i^*} \frac{c_s}{2}(R+\mathrm{i}u)(R+\mathrm{i}u-1)\lambda^2(s,T_i^*)ds\right)$$
$$\times \exp\left(\int_0^{T_i^*} \dot{A}(s)Log\left(\frac{\Lambda^{i-1}(s)-B}{(R+\mathrm{i}u)\lambda(s,T_i^*)+\Lambda^{i-1}(s)-B}\right)ds\right)$$
$$\times \exp\left(-\int_0^{T_i^*}(R+\mathrm{i}u)\dot{A}(s)Log\left(\frac{\Lambda^{i-1}(s)-B}{\Lambda^{i}(s)-B}\right)ds\right)\Bigg\}\frac{du}{R+\mathrm{i}u-1}. \tag{97}$$

Acknowledgments The KPMG Center of Excellence in Risk Management is acknowledged for organizing the conference "Challenges in Derivatives Markets - Fixed Income Modeling, Valuation Adjustments, Risk Management, and Regulation".

A Appendix

A.1 Isonormal Lévy Process (ILP)

Let μ and ν be σ-finite measures without atoms on the measurable spaces $(\mathrm{T},\mathscr{A})$ and $(\mathrm{T}\times \mathrm{X}_0,\mathscr{B})$, respectively. Define a new measure

$$\pi(dt,dz) := \mu(dt)\delta_\Theta(dz) + \nu(dt,dz) \tag{98}$$

on a measurable space $(\mathrm{T}\times\mathrm{X},\mathscr{G})$, where $\mathrm{X}=\mathrm{X}_0\cup\{\Theta\}$, $\mathscr{G}=\sigma(\mathscr{A}\times\{\Theta\},\mathscr{B})$ and $\delta_\Theta(dz)$ is the measure which gives mass one to the point Θ. We assume that the Hilbert space $\mathrm{H} := \mathrm{L}^2(\mathrm{T}\times\mathrm{X},\mathscr{G},\pi)$ is separable.

Definition A.1 We say that a stochastic process $\mathrm{L}=\{\mathrm{L}(h), h\in\mathrm{H}\}$ defined on a complete probability space $(\Omega,\mathscr{F},P)$ is an isonormal Lévy process (or Lévy process on H) if the following conditions are satisfied:

1. The mapping $h \longrightarrow L(h)$ is linear;

2. $\mathrm{E}[e^{ixL(h)}] = \exp(\Psi(x,h))$, where $\Psi(x,h)$ is equal to

$$\int_{\mathrm{T}\times\mathrm{X}} \left((e^{\mathrm{i}xh(t,z)} - 1 - \mathrm{i}xh(t,z))\mathbf{1}_{\mathrm{X}_0}(z) - \frac{1}{2}x^2h^2(t,z)\mathbf{1}_{\Theta}(z) \right) \pi(dt,dz). \quad (99)$$

A.2 The Derivative Operator

Let $\mathscr{S}$ denote the class of smooth random variables, that is the class of random variables ξ of the form

$$\xi = f(L(h_1), \ldots, L(h_n)), \quad (100)$$

where f belongs to $C_b^\infty(\mathbb{R}^n)$, $h_1, \ldots, h_n$ are in H, and $n \geq 1$. The set $\mathscr{S}$ is dense in $L^p(\Omega)$ for any $p \geq 1$.

Definition A.2 The stochastic derivative of a smooth random variable of the form (100) is the H-valued random variable $D\xi = \{D_{t,x}\xi, (t,x) \in T \times X\}$ given by

$$\begin{aligned} D_{t,x}\xi = & \sum_{k=1}^{n} \frac{\partial f}{\partial y_k}(L(h_1), \ldots, L(h_n))h_k(t,x)\mathbf{1}_{\Theta}(x) \\ & + (f(L(h_1) + h_1(t,x), \ldots, L(h_n) + h_n(t,x)) \\ & - f(L(h_1), \ldots, L(h_n)))\, \mathbf{1}_{X_0}(x). \end{aligned} \quad (101)$$

We will consider $D\xi$ as an element of $L^2(T \times X \times \Omega) \cong L^2(\Omega; H)$; namely $D\xi$ is a random process indexed by the parameter space $T \times X$.

1. If the measure ν is zero or $h_k(t,x) = 0$, $k = 1, \ldots, n$ when $x \neq \Theta$ then $D\xi$ coincides with the Malliavin derivative (see, e.g. Nualart (2006) [15] Definition 1.2.1 p.38).
2. If the measure μ is zero or $h_k(t,x) = 0$, $k = 1, \ldots, n$ when $x = \Theta$ then $D\xi$ coincides with the difference operator (see, e.g. Picard (1996) [18]).

A.3 Integration by Parts Formula

Theorem A.3 *Suppose that ξ and η are smooth random variables and $h \in H$. Then*

1.

$$\mathrm{E}[\xi L(h)] = \mathrm{E}[\langle D\xi; h\rangle_H]; \quad (102)$$

$$\mathrm{E}[\xi \eta L(h)] = \mathrm{E}[\eta \langle D\xi; h\rangle_H] + \mathrm{E}[\xi \langle D\eta; h\rangle_H] + \mathrm{E}[\langle D\eta; h\mathbf{1}_{X_0} D\xi\rangle_H]. \quad (103)$$

As a consequence of the above theorem we obtain the following result:

The expression of the derivative $D\xi$ given in (101) does not depend on the particular representation of ξ in (100).
The operator D is closable as an operator from $L^2(\Omega)$ to $L^2(\Omega; H)$.

We will denote the closure of D again by D and its domain in $L^2(\Omega)$ by $\mathbb{D}^{1,2}$.

A.4 The Chain Rule

Proposition A.4 (see Yablonski (2008), Proposition 4.8) *Suppose $F = (F_1, F_2, \ldots, F_n)$ is a random vector whose components belong to the space $\mathbb{D}^{1,2}$. Let $\phi \in \mathscr{C}^1(\mathbb{R}^n)$ be a function with bounded partial derivatives such that $\phi(F) \in \mathrm{L}^2(\Omega)$. Then $\phi(F) \in \mathbb{D}^{1,2}$ and*

$$D_{t,x}\phi(F) = \begin{cases} \sum_{i=1}^{n} \frac{\partial \phi}{\partial x_i}(F) D_{t,\Theta} F_i; & x = \Theta \\ \phi(F_1 + D_{t,x}F_1, \ldots, F_n + D_{t,x}F_n) - \phi(F_1, \ldots, F_n); & x \neq \Theta. \end{cases} \quad (104)$$

A.5 Regularity of Solutions of SDEs Driven by Time-Inhomogeneous Lévy Processes

We focus on a class of models in which the price of the underlying asset is given by the following stochastic differential equation (see Di Nunno et al. [2] and Petrou [17] for details)

$$\begin{aligned} dS_t &= b(t, S_{t-})dt + \sigma(t, S_{t-})dW_t \\ &\quad + \int_{\mathbb{R}_0} \varphi(t, S_{t-}, z)\tilde{N}(dt, dz), \\ S_0 &= x, \end{aligned} \quad (105)$$

where $\mathbb{R}_0 := \mathbb{R}^d \setminus \{0_{\mathbb{R}^d}\}$, $x \in \mathbb{R}^d$, $\{W_t, 0 \le t \le T\}$ is an m-dimensional standard Brownian motion, $\tilde{N}$ is a compensated Poisson random measure on $[0, T] \times \mathbb{R}_0$ with compensator $\nu_t(dz)dt$. The coefficients $b : \mathbb{R}^+ \times \mathbb{R}^d \longrightarrow \mathbb{R}^d$, $\sigma : \mathbb{R}^+ \times \mathbb{R}^d \longrightarrow \mathbb{R}^d \times \mathbb{R}^m$ and $\varphi : \mathbb{R}^+ \times \mathbb{R}^d \times \mathbb{R} \longrightarrow \mathbb{R}^d \times \mathbb{R}$, are continuously differentiable with bounded derivatives and the family of positive measures $(\nu_t)_{t\in[0,T]}$ satisfies $\int_0^T (\int_{\mathbb{R}_0} (\|z\|^2 \wedge 1)\nu_t(dz))dt < \infty$ and $\nu_t(\{0\}) = 0$. The coefficients are assumed to satisfy the following linear growth condition

$$\|b(t,x)\|^2 + \|\sigma(t,x)\|^2 + \int_{\mathbb{R}_0} \|\varphi(t,x,z)\|^2 \nu_t(dz) \leq C(1+\|x\|^2), \qquad (106)$$

for all $t \in [0, T]$, $x \in \mathbb{R}^d$, where C is a positive constant. Furthermore, we suppose that there exists a function $\rho : \mathbb{R} \longrightarrow \mathbb{R}$ with

$$\sup_{0 \leq t \leq T} \int_{\mathbb{R}_0} |\rho(z)|^2 \nu_t(dz) < \infty, \qquad (107)$$

and a positive constant K such that

$$\|\varphi(t,x,z) - \varphi(t,y,z)\| \leq K|\rho(z)|\|x-y\|, \qquad (108)$$

for all $t \in [0, T]$, $x, y \in \mathbb{R}^d$ and $z \in \mathbb{R}_0$.

In the sequel we provide a theorem which proves that under specific conditions the solution of a stochastic differential equation belongs to the domain $\mathbb{D}^{1,2}$.

Theorem A.5 *Let $(S_t)_{t\in[0,T]}$ be the solution of (105). Then $S_t \in \mathbb{D}^{1,2}$ for all $t \in [0, T]$ and the derivative $D_{r,0}S_t$ satisfies the following linear equation*

$$\begin{aligned} D_{r,0}S_t &= \int_r^t \frac{\partial b}{\partial x}(u, S_{u-}) D_{r,0}S_{u-} du + \sigma(r, S_{r-}) \\ &+ \int_r^t \frac{\partial \sigma}{\partial x}(u, S_{u-}) D_{r,0}S_{u-} dW_u \\ &+ \int_r^t \int_{\mathbb{R}_0} \frac{\partial \varphi}{\partial x}(u, S_{u-}, y) D_{r,0}S_{u-} \tilde{N}(du, dy) \end{aligned} \qquad (109)$$

for $0 \leq r \leq t$ a.e. and $D_{r,0}S_t = 0$ a.e. otherwise.

As in the classical Malliavin calculus we are able to associate the solution of (105) to the first variation process $Y_t := \nabla_x S_t$. Then, we will also provide a specific expression for $D_{r,0}S_t$, the Wiener directional derivative of the S_t.

Proposition A.6 *Let $(S_t)_{t\in[0,T]}$ be the solution of (105). Then the derivative satisfies the following equation*

$$D_{r,0}S_t = Y_t Y_{r-}^{-1} \sigma(r, S_{r-}) \mathbf{1}_{\{r \leq t\}} \ \ a.e. \qquad (110)$$

where $(Y_t)_{t\in[0,T]}$ is the first variation process of $(S_t)_{t\in[0,T]}$.

References

1. Berman, M.: Inhomogeneous and modulated gamma processes. Biometrika **68**, 143–152 (1981)
2. Di Nunno, G., Øksendal, B., Proske, F.: Malliavin Calculus for Lévy Processes with Applications to Finance. Springer, Berlin (2008)
3. Eberlein, E.: Fourier-based valuation methods in mathematical finance. In: Benth, F.E., Kholodnyi, V.A., Laurence, P. (eds.) Quantitative Energy Finance, pp. 85–114. Springer, New York (2014)
4. Eberlein, E., Keller, U.: Hyperbolic distributions in finance. Bernoulli **1**(3), 281–299 (1995)
5. Eberlein, E., Özkan, F.: The Lévy LIBOR model. Financ. Stochast. **9**, 327–348 (2005)
6. Eberlein, E., Kluge, W.: Exact pricing formulae for caps and swaptions in a Lévy term structure model. J. Comput. Financ. **9**(2), 99–125 (2006)
7. Eberlein, E., Kluge, W.: Calibration of Lévy term structure models. In: Fu, M., Jarrow, R., Yen, J.-Y., Elliott, R. (eds.) Advances in Mathematical Finance, Applied and Numerical Harmonic Analysis, pp. 147–172. Birkhäuser, Boston (2007)
8. Eberlein, E., Glau, K., Papapantoleon, A.: Analysis of Fourier transform valuation formulas and applications. Appl. Math. Financ. **17**, 211–240 (2010)
9. Fournié, E., Lasry, J.-M., Lebuchoux, J., Lions, P.-L., Touzi, N.: Applications of Malliavin calculus to Monte Carlo methods in finance. Financ. Stochast. **3**(4), 391–412 (1999)
10. Fries, C.: Mathematical Finance: Theory, Modeling, Implementation. Wiley, Chichester (2007)
11. Glasserman, P.: Monte Carlo Methods in Financial Engineering. Springer, New York (2004)
12. Glasserman, P., Zhao, X.: Fast Greeks by simulation in forward LIBOR models. J. Comput. Financ. **3**(1), 5–39 (1999)
13. Jacod, J., Shiryaev, A.N.: Limit Theorems for Stochastic Processes. Springer, Berlin (1987)
14. León, J.A., Solé, J.L., Utzet, F., Vives, J.: On Lévy processes, Malliavin calculus and market models with jumps. Financ. Stochast. **6**, 197–225 (2002)
15. Nualart, D.: The Malliavin Calculus and Related Topics, 2nd edn. Springer, Berlin (2006)
16. Ostrowski, A.M.: On some generalizations of the Cauchy-Frullani integral. Proc. Natl. Acad. Sci. **35**, 612–615 (1949)
17. Petrou, E.: Malliavin calculus in Lévy spaces and applications to finance. Electron. J. Probab. **13**(27), 852–879 (2008)
18. Picard, J.: On the existence of smooth densities for jump processes. Probab. Theory Related Fields **105**(4), 481–511 (1996)
19. Yablonski, A.: The calculus of variations for processes with independent increments. Rocky Mt. J. Math. **38**(2), 669–701 (2008)

6

Inside the EMs Risky Spreads and CDS-Sovereign Bonds Basis

Vilimir Yordanov

Abstract The paper considers a no-arbitrage setting for pricing and relative value analysis of risky sovereign bonds. The typical case of an emerging market country (EM) that has bonds outstanding both in foreign hard currency (Eurobonds) and local soft currency (treasuries) is inspected. The resulting two yield curves give rise to a credit and currency spread that need further elaboration. We discuss their proper measurement and also derive and analyze the necessary no-arbitrage conditions that must hold. Then we turn attention to the CDS-Bond basis in this multi-curve environment. For EM countries the concept shows certain specifics both in theoretical background and empirical performance. The paper further focuses on analyzing these peculiarities. If the proper measurement of the basis in the standard case of only hard currency debt being issued is still problematic, the situation is much more complicated in a multi-curve setting when a further contingent claim on the sovereign risk in the face of local currency debt curve appears. We investigate the issue and provide relevant theoretical and empirical input.

Keywords HJM · Foreign debt · Domestic debt · Z-Spread · CDS-Bond basis

1 Introduction

Local currency debt of EM sovereigns became a hot topic both for practitioners and academics in the recent years. Major investment banks and asset managers consider it a separate asset class and publish regularly special local currency investment reports. A joint working group of IMF, WB, EBRD, and OECD demonstrated recently an official interest in a thorough investigation of this market segment and support for its development, thus forming a strict policy agenda. It was recognized that not only do the local bonds complete the market and thus bring market efficiency, but also

V. Yordanov (✉)
Vienna Graduate School of Finance, Vienna, Austria
e-mail: research@vjord.com

V. Yordanov
Karlsruhe Institute of Technology, Karlsruhe, Germany

they could act as a shock absorber to the volatile capital inflows. Furthermore, they provide flexibility to the governments in financing their budget deficit. However, these instruments are not well understood from a no-arbitrage point of view and a formal setting is lacking. Such a setting would provide not only a better picture for their inherent risk-return characteristics, but would also be an indispensable tool for market research and strategy. The aim of this paper is exactly to focus attention on the large set of open questions the local currency debt gives rise to and lay the ground for a formal relative value analysis with a special emphasis on the CDS-Bond basis.

The paper begins with our general modeling no-arbitrage approach under an HJM reduced credit risk setting. It serves as a basis and gives a financial engineering intuition about the nature of the problem. The default of the sovereign is represented as the first jump of a counting process. For the dynamics of the interest rates and the exchange rate we use jump diffusions controlling the jumps and correlations in a suitable way, so that we have high precision in capturing the structural macrofinancial effects. We derive the no-arbitrage conditions that must hold in that multi-curve environment and then analyze their informational content. Then we turn to an application related to correctly extracting the credit and currency spreads and measuring the CDS-Bond basis on a broader scope. This provides basic building blocks for relative value trades under presence of the local currency yield curve which could serve as an additional pillar.

The literature on integrating the foreign and domestic debt of a risky sovereign in a consistent way is at a nascent stage both from an academic and practitioners' point of view. Related technically but different in essence is the work of Ehlers and Schönbucher [9] who give a reduced form model for CDS of an obligor denominated in different currencies which accounts for dependence between the exchange rate and the credit spread. Eberlain and Koval [8] give a high generalization of the cross-currency term structure models, but similarly they deal only with hard currencies. Regarding the CDS-Bond basis, Berd et al. [2] provide a thorough analysis of the shortcomings of the Z-spread as a risky spread metric.[1] Alizalde et al. [10] further discuss the issue and provide extensive simulations. Interesting new measures for the basis are given in Bernhard and Mai [3] which need further elaboration and development. However, all these references deal with the single-curve case with an extension to the multi-curve case pending.

2 Local Currency Bonds No-Arbitrage HJM Setting

In this section we first lay the foundations in brief for pricing of risky debt in a general reduced form setting. Then we add the local currency debt into the picture and discuss the risky spreads. We conclude by derivation and analysis of the no-arbitrage conditions.

[1] The Z-spread represents a simple shift of the discounting risk-free curve so that the price of the risky bond is attained.

2.1 Risky Bonds Under Marked Point Process

The first task is to model default in a suitable way. We start with the most general formulation and then modify it appropriately. We consider a filtered probability space $(\Omega, (G_t)_{t\geq 0}, P)$ which supports an n-dimensional Brownian motion $W^P = (W_1, W_2, \ldots, W_n)$ under the objective probability measure P and a marked point process $\mu : \left(\Omega, B(R^+), \varepsilon\right) \to R^+$ with markers (τ_i, X_i) representing the jump times and their sizes in a measurable space (E, ε), where $E = [0, 1]$ and by ε we denote the Borel subsets of E. We assume that $\mu(\omega; dt, dx)$ has a separable compensator of the form:

$$\upsilon : \left(\Omega, B(R^+), \varepsilon\right) \to R^+ \quad \text{and} \quad \upsilon(\omega; dt, dx) = h(\omega; t)F_t(\omega; dx)dt,$$

where $h(\omega; t) = \int_{R^+} \upsilon(\omega; t, dx)$ is a G_t measurable intensity and the marks have a conditional distribution of the jumps of $F_t(\omega; dx)$. Thus, we have the identity $\int_E F_t(\omega; dx) = 1$. Furthermore, we can define the total loss function $L(\omega; t) = \int_0^t \int_E l(\omega; s, x)\mu(\omega; ds, dx)$ and the recovery $R(\omega; t) = 1 - \int_0^t \int_E l(\omega; s, x)\mu(\omega; ds, dx)$. The function $l(\omega; t, x)$ scales the marks in a suitable way, and having control over it, we can define it such that our model is tractable enough. We define also the sum of the jumps by $S(\omega; t) = \int_0^t \int_E x\mu(\omega; ds, dx)$ and their number by $N(\omega; t) = \int_0^t \int_E \mu(\omega; ds, dx)$.

Effectively, the marked point process as a sequence of random jumps (τ_i, X_i) is characterized by the probability measure $\mu(\omega; dt, dx)$, which gives the number of jumps with size dx in a small time interval of dt. The compensator $\upsilon(\omega; t, dx)$ provides a full probability characterization of the process. It incorporates in itself two effects. On one hand, we have the intensity $h(\omega; t)dt$, which gives the conditional probability of jump of the process in a small time interval of dt incorporating the whole market information up to t. On the other hand, we have the conditional distribution $F_t(\omega; dx)$ of the markers X in case of a jump realization.

We can look at the jumps of the marked point process as sequential defaults of an obligor at random times τ_i that lead to losses X_i at each of them. They can also be considered a set of restructuring events leading to losses for the creditors. Under this general setting, the prices of the riskless and risky bonds are given by:

- **Riskless bond**:

$$P(t, T) = E^Q\left(\exp\left(-\int_t^T r(s)ds\right) | G_t\right) = \exp\left(-\int_t^T f(t, s)ds\right) \tag{1}$$

- **Risky bond**:

$$
\begin{aligned}
P^*(t,T) &= E^Q\left(\exp\left(-\int_t^T r(s)ds\right)R(\omega;T)|G_t\right)\\
&= R(t)\exp\left(-\int_t^T f^*(t,s)ds\right),
\end{aligned} \tag{2}
$$

where $r(t)$, $f(t,T)$, and $f^*(t,T)$ are the riskless spot, riskless forward, and risky forward rates respectively.

Depending on how we specify the convention of recovery, we can get further simplification of the formulas. However, this should be well motivated and come either from the legal definitions of the debt contracts or their economic grounding.

Under a recovery of market value (RMV) setting, default is a percentage mark down, q, from the previous recovery. So we have $R(\omega;\tau_i) = (1 - q(\omega;\tau_i, X_i))$ $R(\omega;\tau_i-)$ and $l(\omega;\tau_i)$ has the form $l(\omega;\tau_i) = -q(\omega;\tau_i,X_i) \times R(\omega;\tau_i-)$. This definition allows us to write:

$$
\begin{aligned}
\mu(\omega,dt,dx) &= \sum_{s>0} 1_{\{\Delta N(\omega,s)\neq 0\}}\delta_{(s,\Delta N(\omega,s))}(dt,dx)\\
dR(\omega;t) &= -R(\omega;t)\int_E q\,(\omega;t,x)\,\mu(\omega;dt,dx);\ R(\omega;0)=1
\end{aligned}
$$

and if we assume no jumps of the intensity and the risk-free rate at default times (contagion effects), we have no change for the risk-free bond pricing formula and for the risky one and as in [13] we get:

$$
\begin{aligned}
P^{*RMV}(t,T) &= E^Q\left(\exp\left(-\int_t^T r(s)ds\right)R(\omega;T)|G_t\right)\\
&= R(t)E^Q\left(\exp\left(-\int_t^T (r(s)+h(s)\int_E q\,(\omega;s,x)\,F_s(dx))ds\right)|G_t\right)\\
&= R(t)\exp\left(-\int_t^T f^{*RMV}(t,s)ds\right)
\end{aligned} \tag{3}
$$

Note that within this setting there is no "last default". The intensity is defined for the whole marked point process and not just for a concrete single default time, so it does not go to zero after default realizations. This combined with the fact that intensity is continuous makes the market filtration G_t behave like a background filtration in the pricing formulas. So we can avoid using the generalized Duffie, Schroder, and Skiadas [7] formula. Furthermore, we can denote $q_e(t) = \int_E q\,(\omega;t,x)\,F_t(dx)$ to be the expected loss. So we have that the pricing formula is dependent on the generalized intensity $h(t)q_e(t)$. Due to the multiplicative nature of the last expression, only from market information, as discussed in Schönbucher (2003), we cannot distinguish between the pure intensity effect $h(t)$ and the recovery induced one $q_e(t)$.

Under a recovery of par (RP) setting, in case of default, the recovery is a separate fixed or random quantity independent of the default indicator and the risk-free rate. So we have $E = \{0, 1 - R(\omega)\}$ and $\upsilon(\omega; dt, dx) = h(\omega; t)(1 - R_e)dt$ with $R_e = E^Q(R(\omega) \mid G_t)$. Since we have just one jump, we can write:

$$\mu(\omega, dt, dx) = 1_{\{\Delta N(\omega,t)\neq 0\}}\delta_{(t,\Delta N(\omega,t))}(dt, dx)$$

The bond price is:

$$\begin{aligned} P^{*RP}(t,T) &= E^Q\left(\exp\left(-\int_t^T r(s)ds\right)\left(R(\omega)\,1_{\{\tau\leq T\}} + 1_{\{\tau>T\}}\right)|G_t\right) \\ &= 1_{\{\tau>t\}}\exp\left(-\int_t^T f^{*RP}(t,s)ds\right) \end{aligned} \quad (4)$$

In contrast to RMV, here, as discussed in Schönbucher (2003), he can distinguish between the pure intensity and recovery induced effects.

2.2 *Model Formulation*

In this section we develop our HJM model for pricing of local and foreign currency bonds of a risky country. However, before this being done formally, it is essential to elaborate on the nature of the problem. Although we do not put here explicitly macrofinancial structure, but just proxy it by jumps and correlations, it, by all means, stays in the background and must be conceptually considered.

2.2.1 General Notes

A risky emerging market country can have bonds denominated both in local and foreign currency that give rise to two risky yield curves and risky spreads—credit and currency. Generally, the latter arise due to the possibility of the respective credit events to occur and their severity. To investigate them, formal assumptions are needed both on their characteristics and interdependence.

We will consider that the two types of debt have different priorities. The country is first engaged to meeting the foreign debt obligation from its limited international reserves. The impossibility of this being done leads to default or restructuring. In both cases, we have a credit event according to the ISDA classification. The foreign debt has a senior status. The spread that arises reflects the credit risk of the country. It is a function of: (1) the probability of the credit event to occur; (2) the expected loss given default; (3) the risk aversion of the market participants to the credit event.

The domestic debt economically stands differently. It reflects the priority of the payments in hard currency and it incurs instantly the losses in case of default of the country. So this debt is the first to be affected by a default and is subordinated. Technically, the credit event can be avoided under a flexible exchange rate regime because the country can always make a debt monetization and pay the amounts due in local currency taking advantage of the fact that there is no resource constraint on it. However, the price for this is inflation pick-up and exchange rate depreciation. This leads to real devaluation of the domestic debt. It is exactly the seigniorage and the dilution effect that cause the loss in the value.[2] This resembles the case of a firm issuing more equity to avoid default. The spread of the domestic debt over the foreign one forms the currency spread. Its nature is very broad, and it is not only due to the currency mismatch. Namely, it is a function of: (1) the probability of the credit event to occur and the need for monetization; (2) the negative side effect of the credit event on the exchange rate by a sudden depreciation of the latter; (3) the volatility of the exchange rate; (4) the expected depreciation of the exchange rate without taking into consideration the monetization; (5) the risk aversion of market participants to the credit event and the need for monetization, the sudden exchange rate depreciation and its size; (6) the risk aversion of the market participants to the volatility of the exchange rate. All these effects are captured by our model.

2.2.2 Multi-currency Risky Bonds Model

We use the setting of Sect. 2.1 modified to a multi-currency debt. Firstly, we consider the case of no monetization and then analyze the case with monetization. Secondly, to avoid using an additional marked point process, and thus a second intensity, the default on the foreign debt is modeled indirectly. Namely, we assume that default on domestic debt leads to default on foreign debt, but due to the different priority of the two, we have just different losses incurred, respectively recoveries. This means that by controlling recoveries we control default and the inherent subordination without imposing too much structure. If the default on the domestic debt is so strong that it leads to a default on the foreign debt as well, we incur zero recovery on the domestic debt and some positive one on the foreign debt. If the insolvency is mild, we have a loss only on the domestic debt, so we incur some positive recovery on the domestic debt and a full recovery on the foreign debt. Thirdly, for notational purposes, we take as a benchmark Germany and EUR as the base hard currency. Lastly, we employ the recovery of market value assumption. The reason for this is twofold. On one hand, in that way, we are consistent with the HJM methodology of Schönbucher [12] for a single risky curve under RMV and produce parsimonious no-arbitrage conditions for the extension to a multi-curve environment. On the other

[2] This pattern can be observed historically for almost all EM countries resorting to a galloping inflation to avoid a nominal domestic debt default. The Russian default of 1998 somehow seems to be a partial notable exception where there was along with the inflation surge an actual default on certain ruble (RUR) bonds—GKOs and OFZs.

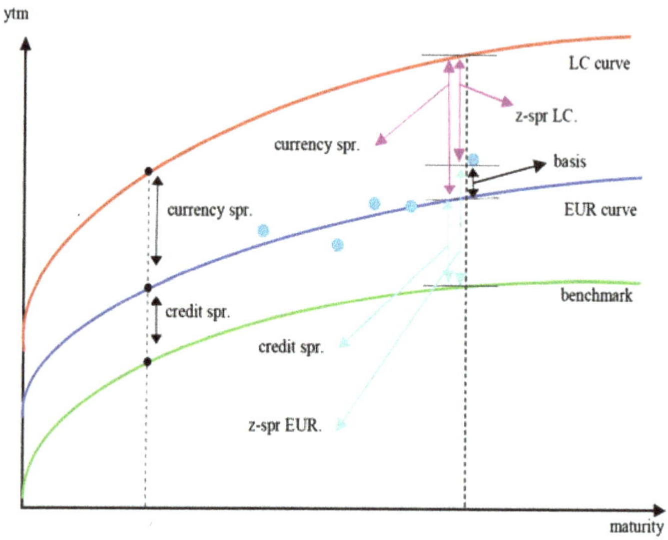

Fig. 1 Risky spreads

hand, as pointed out in Bonnaud et al. [5], for bonds denominated in a different currency than the numerator employed in discounting, the RMV assumption should be the working engine. Their argument is exactly as ours above, in case of default, the sovereign would rather dilute by depreciating the exchange rate and thus the remaining cash flows of the bond produce in essence the RMV structure. Moreover, rather than using EUR denominated bonds, we could take advantage of the CDS quotes and produce synthetic bonds having an RMV recovery structure. Using them is actually preferable for empirical work since major academic studies argue that it is the CDS market that first captures the market information about the credit risk stance of the risky sovereign. Furthermore, with a few exceptions, if the EM sovereigns have in most cases both well developed local currency treasury markets and are subject to CDS quotation, they do have only few Eurobonds outstanding. Figure 1 represents the typical situation the risky sovereign faces.

Mathematical formulation We continue with the model setup. Firstly, we give the suitable notation and assumptions. Then we move to the derivation of the no-arbitrage conditions and the pricing.

- **Notation**
  $f_{EUR}(t, T)$—nominal forward rate, EUR, Ger.
  $f^*_{EUR}(t, T)$—nominal forward rate, EUR, EM
  $f^*_{LC}(t, T)$—nominal forward rate in LC, EM
  $r_{EUR}(t)$—nominal short rate, EUR, Ger.
  $r^*_{EUR}(t)$—nominal short rate, EUR, EM
  $r^*_{LC}(t)$—nominal short rate in LC, EM
  $h^*_{EUR}(t, T) = f^*_{EUR}(t, T) - f_{EUR}(t, T)$—credit spr., EM

$h^*_{LC,EUR}(t,T) = f^*_{LC}(t,T) - f^*_{EUR}(t,T)$—currency spr., EM
$h^*_{LC}(t,T) = f^*_{LC}(t,T) - f_{EUR}(t,T)$—general currency spr., EM
$P_{EUR}(t,T) = \exp(-\int_t^T f_{EUR}(t,s)ds)$—bond, EUR, Ger.
$P^*_{f,EUR}(t,T) = R_{f,EUR}(t)\exp(-\int_t^T f^*_{EUR}(t,s)ds)$—for. bond price., EUR, EM
$P^*_{d,LC}(t,T) = R_{d,LC}(t)\exp(-\int_t^T f^*_{LC}(t,s)ds)$—dom. bond price., LC, EM
$B_{EUR}(t) = \exp(\int_0^t r_{EUR}(s)ds)$—bank account, EUR, Ger.
$B^*_{f,EUR}(t) = R_{f,EUR}(t)\exp(\int_0^t r^*_{EUR}(s)ds)$—for. bank account, EUR, EM
$B^*_{d,LC}(t) = R_{d,LC}(t)\exp(\int_0^t r^*_{LC}(s)ds)$—dom. bank account, LC, EM
$X(t)$—exchange rate, EUR for 1 LC, $\widetilde{X}(t)$—exchange rate, LC for 1 EUR
$R_{f,EUR}(t)$—bond recovery, EUR, EM, $R_{d,LC}(t)$—bond recovery, LC, EM

We use the asterisk to denote risk, the first letter (d or f) to denote domestic or foreign debt, and finally the currency of denomination is shown as EUR or LC.[3]

- **Currency denominations**
  $P^*_{d,EUR}(t,T) = X(t)P^*_{d,LC}(t,T)$—dom. bond, EUR
  $P^*_{f,LC}(t,T) = \widetilde{X}(t)P^*_{f,EUR}(t,T)$—for. bond, LC
  $B^*_{d,EUR}(t) = X(t)B^*_{d,LC}(t)$—dom. bank account, EUR
  $B^*_{f,LC}(t) = \widetilde{X}(t)B^*_{f,EUR}(t)$—for. bank account, LC
- **Intensities**

Foreign debt, EUR:

Intensity:	$h_{EUR}(t) = h(t)$
Compensator:	$h_{EUR}(t)q_{e,EUR}(t) = h(t)\int_E q_{f,EUR}(\omega; t, x)\, F_t(dx)$

Domestic debt, LC:

Intensity:	$h_{LC}(t) = h(t)$
Compensator:	$h_{LC}(t)q_{e,LC}(t) = h(t)\int_E q_{d,LC}(\omega; t, x)\, F_t(dx)$

The compensator (generalized intensity) characterizes default. Controlling in a suitable way the recovery, we can control the compensator and thus the default event. We turn attention now to the dynamics of the instruments under consideration.

- **Forward rates**
  $df_{EUR}(t,T) = \alpha_{EUR}(t,T)dt + \sum_{i=1}^n \sigma_{EUR,i}(t,T)dW_i^P(t)$
  $df^*_{EUR}(t,T) = \alpha^*_{EUR}(t,T)dt + \sum_{i=1}^n \sigma^*_{EUR,i}(t,T)dW_i^P(t)$
  $+\int_E \delta^*_{EUR}(x,t,T)\mu(dx,dt)$

---

[3]It must be further noted that we actually used standard definitions for the risky forward rates as in Schönbucher [12]. Namely, $f^*_{EUR/LC}(t,T) = -\frac{\partial}{\partial T}\log P^*_{f,EUR/d,LC}(t,T)$ with terminal conditions $P^*_{f,EUR/d,LC}(T,T) = R_{f,EUR/d,LC}(T)$. The risky bank accounts economically just represent a unit of currency invested at the respective short rates and continuously rolled over accounting for any default losses. However, since the forward rates, resp. the bonds, are our basic modeling object, it would be more precise to consider the bank accounts derived quantities from them similar to Björk et al. [4] without going here deeper into the modified technical details.

$df^*_{LC}(t,T) = \alpha^*_{LC}(t,T)dt + \sum_{i=1}^{n} \sigma^*_{LC,i}(t,T)dW_i^P(t)$
$+\int_E \delta^*_{LC}(x,t,T)\mu(dx,dt)$
We assume that in case of default there is a market turmoil leading to a jump in both curves. At maturity T, the EUR curve jumps by a size of $\int_E \delta^*_{EUR}(x,t,T)\mu(dx,dt)$, and that of the local currency by $\int_E \delta^*_{LC}(x,t,T)\mu(dx,dt)$. The terms $\delta^*_{EUR}(x,t,T)$ and $\delta^*_{LC}(x,t,T)$ show the jump sizes of the respective curves for every maturity. As indicated at the beginning of the section, everywhere we will work under the market filtration G_t so both the Brownian motions and the point process are adapted to it.

- **Recoveries**

  $\frac{dR_{f,EUR}(t)}{R_{f,EUR}(t)} = -\int_E q_{f,EUR}(x,t)\mu(dx,dt)$

  $\frac{dR_{d,LC}(t)}{R_{d,LC}(t)} = -\int_E q_{d,LC}(x,t)\mu(dx,dt)$

  After each default we have a devaluation of the respective bond by an expected value of $\int_E q_{f/d}(x,t)\mu(dx,dt)$. The stochasticity of the loss is captured by the random jump size $q(.,.)$ as elaborated in Sect. 2.1.

- **Bank accounts**

  $\frac{dB_{EUR}(t)}{B_{EUR}(t)} = r_{EUR}(t)dt$

  $\frac{dB^*_{f,EUR}(t)}{B^*_{f,EUR}(t)} = r^*_{EUR}(t)dt - \int_E q_{f,EUR}(x,t)\mu(dx,dt)$

  $\frac{dB^*_{d,LC}(t)}{B^*_{d,LC}(t)} = r^*_{LC}(t)dt - \int_E q_{d,LC}(x,t)\mu(dx,dt)$

- **Exchange rate**

  $\frac{dX(t)}{X(t)} = \alpha_X(t)dt + \sum_{i=1}^{n} \sigma_{X,i}(t)dW_i^P(t) - \int_E \delta_X(x,t)\mu(dx,dt)$
  We assume that in case of default the market turmoil causes an exchange rate devaluation by $\int_E \delta_X(x,t)\mu(dx,dt)$.

- **Bond prices**

  $P_{EUR}(t,T) = \exp(-\int_t^T f_{EUR}(t,s)ds) = E^{Q^f}(\exp(-\int_t^T r_{EUR}(s)ds)|G_t)$

  $P^*_{f,EUR}(t,T) = R_{f,EUR}(t)\exp(-\int_t^T f^*_{EUR}(t,s)ds)$

  $= E^{Q^f}(\exp(-\int_t^T r_{EUR}(s)ds)R_{f,EUR}(T)|G_t)$

  $P^*_{d,EUR}(t,T) = P^*_{d,LC}(t,T)X(t) = R_{d,LC}(t)X(t)\exp(-\int_t^T f^*_{LC}(t,s)ds)$

  $= E^{Q^f}(\exp(-\int_t^T r_{EUR}(s)ds)R_{d,LC}(T)X(T)|G_t)$

  It must be emphasized that the effects of exchange rate, recovery, and the expected devaluation sizes are incorporated in the respective forward rates of the bonds. Furthermore, the expectations are taken under Q^f, the foreign risk-neutral measure.

- **Arbitrage**

  Under standard regularity conditions, for the system to be free of arbitrage, all traded assets denominated in euro must have a rate of return r_{EUR} under Q^f. This means that the processes:

$$\frac{P_{EUR}(t,T)}{B_{EUR}(t)}, \frac{B^*_{f,EUR}(t)}{B_{EUR}(t)}, \frac{P^*_{f,EUR}(t,T)}{B_{EUR}(t)}, \frac{B^*_{d,LC}(t)X(t)}{B_{EUR}(t)}, \frac{P^*_{d,LC}(t,T)X(t)}{B_{EUR}(t)}$$

  must be local martingales under Q^f. For our purposes being martingales would be enough.
  Taking the stochastic differentials of the upper expressions, omitting the technicalities to the appendix, we can get the respective no-arbitrage conditions.

- Spreads:

$$r^*_{EUR}(t) - r_{EUR}(t) = h(t)\varphi_{q_{f,EUR}}(t) \tag{5.1}$$

$$\begin{aligned} &r^*_{LC}(t) - r^*_{EUR}(t) = -\alpha_X(t) - \phi(t)\sigma_X(t) \\ &+h(t)(\varphi_{\delta_X}(t) - \varphi_{q_{d,LC},\delta_X}(t) + \varphi_{q_{d,LC}}(t) - \varphi_{q_{f,EUR}}(t)) \end{aligned} \tag{5.2}$$

- Drifts:

  $\alpha_{EUR}(t,T) = \sigma_{EUR}(t,T)\int_t^T \sigma_{EUR}(t,v)dv - \sigma_{EUR}(t,T)\phi(t)$

  $\alpha^*_{EUR}(t,T) = \sigma^*_{EUR}(t,T)\int_t^T \sigma^*_{EUR}(t,v)dv - \sigma^*_{EUR}(t,T)\phi(t)$
  $+h_{EUR}(t)\varphi_{\theta^*_{EUR}}^{q_{f,EUR},\delta_X}(t)$

  $\alpha^*_{LC}(t,T) = \sigma^*_{LC}(t,T)\int_t^T \sigma^*_{LC}(t,v)dv - \sigma^*_{LC}(t,T)\phi(t) - \sigma^*_{LC}(t,T)\sigma_X(t,T)$
  $+h_{LC}(t)\varphi_{\theta^*_{LC}}^{q_{d,LC},\delta_X}(t)$,

  where we have used the notation:

  $\theta^*_{EUR} = \exp(-\int_t^T \delta^*_{EUR}(x,t,s)ds)$, $\theta^*_{LC} = \exp(-\int_t^T \delta^*_{LC}(x,t,s)ds)$
  $\varphi_{a.b,\ldots}^{x,y,\ldots}(t) = \int_E (ab\ldots)((1-x)(1-y)\ldots)\Phi(t,x)F_t(dx)$

  and used vector notation and scalar products where necessary for simplicity.

  By $\Phi(t,x)$ and $\phi(t)$ we denoted the Girsanov's kernels of the counting process and the Brownian motion respectively when changing the probability measure from P to Q^f. The term $\varphi(t)$ represents the scaled expected jump sizes of the counting process. We can give the interpretation that $\phi(t)$ is the market price of diffusion risk and $\varphi(t)$ is the market price of jump risk. Parametrizing the volatilities and the market prices of risk, as well as imposing suitable dynamics for $h(t)$, we give a full characterization of our system. Furthermore, the intensity could be a function of the underlying processes of the rates, so we could get correlation between the intensity, the interest rates, and the exchange rate.

Spreads diagnostics from a reduced form point of view It is important to give a deeper interpretation of the no-arbitrage conditions and see which factors drive the credit and currency spreads. Despite the heavy notation, the analysis actually goes fluently. The drift equations give the modified HJM drift restrictions. The slight change from the classical riskless case is due to the jumps that arise. Equation (5.1) shows that the credit risk is proportional to the intensity of default and the scaled expected LGD by the coefficient controlling the risk aversion. The higher they are, the higher the spread is. Equation (5.2) gives the currency spread. It arises due to two main reasons. Firstly, the intensity of default and the difference between the two *LGDs* in local currency and euro, scaled by the coefficient for the risk aversion, act as in the previous case. They also make explicit the subordination. Secondly, the expected local currency depreciation, its volatility, and the risk aversion to diffusion risk act similarly to the standard uncovered interest parity (UIP) relationship. The higher they are, the higher the spread is. It is both important and interesting to note that inflation does not appear directly and it influences the spreads, as the next section shows, only through a secondary channel.

Monetization The analysis so far considered a loss of $1 - R_{d,LC}(T)$ on default of the domestic debt. However, if a full monetization is applied, then we would have $R_{d,LC}(T) = 1$ and thus $\varphi_{q_{d,LC}}(t) = 0$ and $\varphi_{q_{d,LC},\delta_X}(t) = 0$. If such a monetary injection is neutral to nominal values, it is certainly not to real ones. Devaluation arises due to the negative market sentiment following the default and the higher amount of money in circulation. Its effect can be measured differently based on what we take as a base—the price index or the exchange rate. Most naturally, we can expect both of them to depreciate due to the structural macrolinks that exist between these variables. For quantifying the amount we would need a macromodel which is beyond the scope of the reduced form model presented. The latter only shows what characteristics the market prices in general without imposing concrete macrolinks among them. Depending on what the base is, we would have a direct estimation of certain type of indicators and an indirect one of the rest up to their structural influence on the former. If the inflation is taken as a base, then we would have the comparison of inflation indexed bonds to the non-indexed ones. The spread between them would give an estimate for the expected inflation. Unfortunately, such an analysis is unrealistic due to the fact that such bonds are issued very rarely by emerging market countries. If the exchange rate is taken as a base, then we would have the comparison of domestic debt bonds to foreign debt bonds. The spread between them would give an estimate for the currency risk and the devaluation effect. The estimate for the inflation would be indirect and based on hypothetical structural links.

Whether the country would monetize or declare a formal default is based on strategic considerations. It is a matter of structural analysis which option it would take. By all means, its decision is priced. In case of default, the pricing formula is Eq. (5.2). In case of monetization, we would have a jump in the exchange rate. Let us denote its size by $\widehat{\delta_X}$. It will be different from the no-monetization one, δ_X, due to the different regimes that are followed, and we would thus get:

$$r^*_{LC}(t) - r^*_{EUR}(t) = h(t)(\varphi_{\widehat{\delta}_X}(t) - \varphi_{q_{f,EUR}}(t)) - \alpha_X(t) - \phi(t)\sigma_X(t) \quad (6)$$

There is no a priori no-arbitrage argument that $\varphi_{\widehat{\delta}_X}(t) = \varphi_{\delta_X}(t) - \varphi_{q_{d,LC},\delta_X}(t) + \varphi_{q_{d,LC}}(t)$ must hold so that the two scenarios are equivalent.[4] The only information we get from the market is an estimate for the generalized intensity being $h(t)\varphi_{\widehat{\delta}_X}(t)$ or $h(t)(\varphi_{\delta_X}(t) - \varphi_{q_{d,LC},\delta_X}(t) + \varphi_{q_{d,LC}}(t))$ but not knowing which possible scenario will be realized.

3 CDS-Bond Basis

3.1 General Notes

The setting we built gives us an alternative for evaluating the CDS-Bond basis. This is represented in Fig. 1. There the LC zero-coupon yield curve is built by employing local currency treasuries and an appropriate smoothing method. The EUR zero-coupon yield curve is built by employing CDS quotes with the maths represented in the sequel. Along with the curves, there are few Eurobonds represented in light blue colored dots. Both credit and currency spreads can be computed for them employing a standard Z-spread methodology. Despite its various shortcomings, as discussed in Berd et al. [2] and Elizalde et al. [10], it allows us to have a certain measure for the spreads and it is widely accepted by practitioners. Subtracting from the yield curves' implied credit and currency spreads the bond implied spreads, we get two alternative specifications for the CDS-Bonds basis. Several things need a comment.

Firstly, the two basis measures are not equal by default. The one representing the credit spread is subject to Z-spread measurement based on a parallel shift of the benchmark curve. So it depends on the whole benchmark curve and has nothing to do with the LC one. Vice versa, the basis implied by the LC curve is subject to Z-spread measurement based on a parallel shift of the LC curve. So it depends on the whole *LC* curve, but has nothing to do with the benchmark one. This provides intuition how the introduction of the LC curve brings additional information in the picture and provides more market completeness that must be utilized in relative value trades.

Secondly, as mentioned above, the EUR curve is built by utilizing CDS quotes. As shown below, in the procedure employed, an assumption is needed for the recovery scheme. What it should be depends on our purposes. On one hand, if we would like to just extract the credit and currency spreads from the yield curves and calibrate a reduced form model,[5] it would be convenient to employ the setting from Sect. 2. So

[4]This is a delicate issue. As indicated, a further structural analysis is needed for a complete answer. The crucial point is that the two scenarios affect in a different way the monetary base. It will have a neutral effect on the macro variables in general and the risky spreads in particular only in case the economy is at the macro potential. Exactly when that is not the case, we can expect that the two scenarios will not be equivalent. A further elaboration on these issues from a structural point of view could be found in Yordanov [15, 16].

[5]We postpone the factors to build realization of the model from Sect. 2 so that it becomes operative for calibration and consequent further analysis to the forthcoming follow-up paper of Yordanov [17].

an RMV assumption for the EUR curve is the most appropriate one since the same assumption is imposed also for the LC curve and when subtracting the corresponding zero yields, we subtract apples from apples. On the other hand, if we like to extract the basis, we must be careful since the Eurobonds are priced under a firmly established RP assumption. So for a standard calculation via a Z-spread based on the benchmark curve we need an RP built EUR curve to be consistent. With the many problems of the Z-spread, it would be definitely bad to add further ones coming from a recovery assumption inconsistency which would only further contribute to an imprecise basis measurement. For a calculation via a Z-spread based on the LC curve, we should not use the RMV LC curve but a modified one. From the RMV LC curve we need to build an RP one and then compute the Z-spread and the basis to be consistent.

3.2 *Technical Notes*

Here we provide the technical notes regarding the above discussion.

- **EUR curve**
  Using OIS differential discounting as in Doctor and Goulden [6], we could modify[6] the standard CDS bootstrap procedure of ISDA and extract at time t the $T-$maturity default probabilities $p^R_{EUR}(t,T)$ under a recovery assumption of R. Then we would get in a straightforward way the EUR zero coupon yields (ytm) and credit spreads (spr) under RMV and RP:

  - **RMV**:

    $\mathrm{spr}^{RMV,R}_{EUR}(t,T) = -\frac{(1-R)\log(1-p^R_{EUR}(t,T))}{T-t}$

    $\mathrm{ytm}^{RMV,R}_{EUR}(t,T) = \mathrm{spr}^{RMV,R}_{EUR}(t,T) + \exp(-y_{EUR}(t,T)(T-t))$

  - **RP**:

    $\mathrm{spr}^{RP,R}_{EUR}(t,T) = -\frac{\log(Rp^R_{EUR}(t,T)+1-p^R_{EUR}(t,T))}{T-t}$

    $\mathrm{ytm}^{RP,R}_{EUR}(t,T) = \mathrm{spr}^{RP,R}_{EUR}(t,T) + \exp(-y_{EUR}(t,T)(T-t)),$

    where $y_{EUR}(t,T)$ is the $T-$maturity zero yield of the riskless benchmark curve (e.g. German bunds).

- **LC curve**

  - **RMV**:

    $\mathrm{ytm}^{RMV,R}_{LC}(t,T)$–observed from the market

---

[6]The OIS discounting should be given a special comment since there is still no consensus on how to bootstrap OIS swaps to form the discount factors for the CDS swap bootstrap. The problem comes from the presence of gaps for certain maturities. A possible specification is given in West [14].

$$\mathrm{spr}^{RMV,R}_{LC,EUR}(t,T) = \mathrm{ytm}^{RMV,R}_{LC}(t,T) - \mathrm{ytm}^{RMV,R}_{EUR}(t,T)$$

$$p^{R}_{LC}(t,T) = 1 - \exp\left(-\frac{\mathrm{spr}^{RMV,R}_{LC,EUR}(t,T)}{1-R}(T-t)\right)$$

- **RP**:

$$\mathrm{spr}^{RP,R}_{LC,EUR}(t,T) = -\frac{\log(Rp^{R}_{LC}(t,T)+1-p^{R}_{LC}(t,T))}{T-t}$$

$$\mathrm{ytm}^{RP,R}_{LC}(t,T) = \mathrm{spr}^{RP,R}_{LC,EUR}(t,T) + \mathrm{ytm}^{RP,R}_{EUR}(t,T)$$

Note that similarly to the EUR curve procedure, the LC curve one relies on the premise that both the RMV and RP cases must share the same $p^{R}_{LC}(t,T)$, which stands for the probability of default on the LC debt. However, according to the analysis we had in Sect. 2 on the no-arbitrage conditions, due to the monetization, such probability actually does not formally exist. Here it is only a derived quantity since although we assume the same point process as a driver of default on both the LC and EUR debt, we can control the compensator by changing the recoveries. However, we could just take the formulas above for the RP spread as definitions. Taking the limit case of zero EUR debt, they would be entirely consistent to the RP in case of EUR debt, thus providing a justification for our method.

3.3 *CDS-Bond Basis Empirics*

For illustration we provide visualization of the Z-spread measured basis according to the two alternative ways for a set of European EM countries. They are chosen so that they have both Eurobonds outstanding in EUR and a liquid LC curve. The data sources are: Bloomberg, Datastream, and CBonds. We build the LC curves by employing the Bloomberg BFV curves. Since they are par curves, see Lee [11], we transform them to zero-coupon yield ones. For spreads extraction we use both EUR and USD denominated CDS. We give preference to the former, but in case of missing quotes we use USD quotes instead by making a quanto adjustment using cross currency basis swaps. The countries under focus are: Bulgaria (BGN), Czech Rep. (CZK), Hungary (HUF), Lithuania (LTL), Poland (PLN), Romania (RON), and Slovakia (SKK).

Since there are plenty of bonds outstanding, aggregate measures are presented based on duration weighting. The events: 1—GM turmoil of May 09, 2005, 2—Liquidity crisis of August 09, 2007, 3—Bear Sterns default of March 14, 2008, 4—Lehman default of September 15, 2008, 5—Greek turmoil of April 23, 2010, 6—August 5, 2011—the US rating downgrade, 7—06 May, 2012—ECB refi-rate woes are marked by the vertical dashed lines.

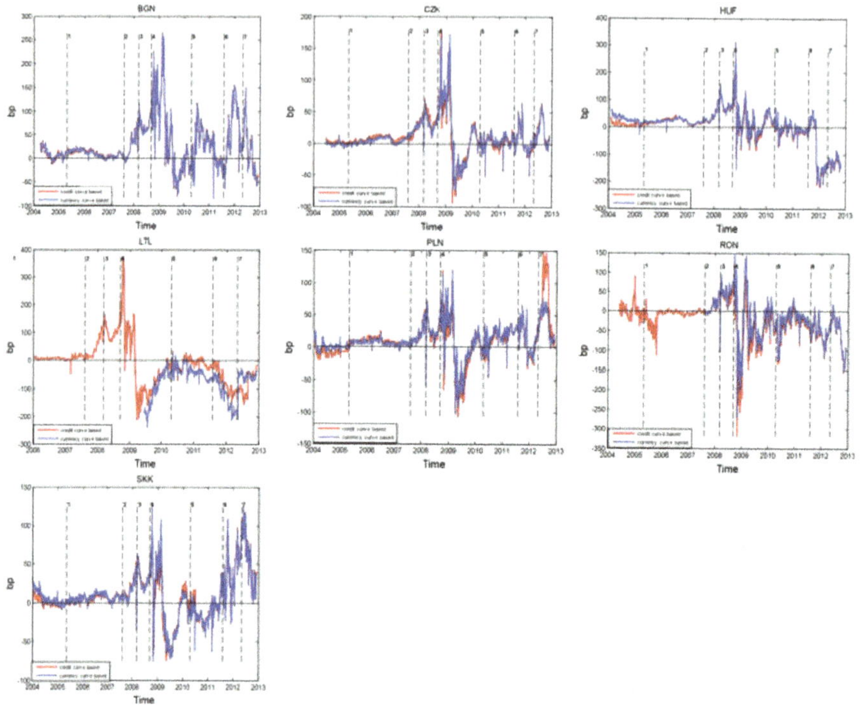

Fig. 2 CDS-Bond basis across countries

The short conclusion from the patterns in Fig. 2 is that the bonds provide important input for extracting the credit and currency spreads. The two alternative basis formulations preserve general shape similarity, but still give different results that should not be underestimated. This is not surprising since the outcome is driven by the difference in shapes between the benchmark and the LC curves. Market strategists and arbitrage traders have a large scope for interpretations and trades design.

4 Conclusion

The paper considers the credit and currency spreads of a risky EM country. The necessary no-arbitrage conditions are derived and their informational content is analyzed. An application of the setting is made to proper building of the foreign and local currency yield curves of a sovereign as well as to providing ideas for relative value diagnostics in a multi-currency framework. In that direction, an alternative measure for the CDS-Bond basis is discussed when the local currency curve is employed as a pillar. The aim of the paper is both to point out the rich opportunities the setting gives for market-related research that could be of use to strategists and policy officers and to make the first several steps toward investigating such opportunities.

Acknowledgements The KPMG Center of Excellence in Risk Management is acknowledged for organizing the conference "Challenges in Derivatives Markets - Fixed Income Modeling, Valuation Adjustments, Risk Management, and Regulation".

Appendix

Here we briefly elaborate on the derivation of Eqs. (5.1) and (5.2). Applying the Girsanov's theorem and the Ito's Lemma for jump diffusions to Eq. (2), we get the dynamics:

$$\begin{aligned}\frac{dP^*_{f,EUR}(t,T)}{P^*_{f,EUR}(t,T)} &= \left(-\int_t^T \alpha^*_{EUR}(t,s)ds + r^*_{EUR}(t) + \frac{1}{2}\left\|\int_t^T \sigma^*_{EUR}(t,s)ds\right\|^2\right)dt \\ &\quad - \left(\int_t^T \sigma^*_{EUR}(t,s)ds\right)dW^P(t) \\ &\quad + \int_E (1-q_{f,EUR}(x,t))\left(\exp\left(-\int_t^T \delta^*_{EUR}(x,t,s)ds\right)-1\right)\mu(dx,dt) \\ &\quad - \int_E q_{f,EUR}(x,t)\mu(dx,dt)\end{aligned}$$

$$\begin{aligned}\frac{dP^*_{d,LC}(t,T)}{P^*_{d,LC}(t,T)} &= \left(-\int_t^T \alpha^*_{LC}(t,s)ds + r^*_{LC}(t) + \frac{1}{2}\left\|\int_t^T \sigma^*_{LC}(t,s)ds\right\|^2\right)dt \\ &\quad - \left(\int_t^T \sigma^*_{LC}(t,s)ds\right)dW^P(t) \\ &\quad + \int_E (1-q_{d,LC}(x,t))\left(\exp\left(-\int_t^T \delta^*_{LC}(x,t,s)ds\right)-1\right)\mu(dx,dt) \\ &\quad - \int_E q_{d,LC}(x,t)\mu(dx,dt)\end{aligned}$$

Furthermore, we have the dynamics of the exchange rate:

$$\frac{dX(t)}{X(t)} = \alpha_X(t)dt + \sum_{i=1}^n \sigma_{X,i}(t)dW_i^P(t) - \int_E \delta_X(x,t)\mu(dx,dt)$$

So using the no-arbitrage conditions and equating the expected local drifts to the risk-free rate, we get the results shown.

References

1. Bai, J., Collin-Dufresne, P.: The CDS-Bond Basis During the Financial Crisis of 2007–2009. WP SSRN.2024531 (2011)
2. Berd, A., Mashal, R., Wang, P.: Definig. Estimating and Using Credit Term Structures, Lehman Brothers Research (2004)
3. Bernhart, G., Mai, J.: Negative Basis Measurement: Finding the Holy Scale. XAIA Investment Research (2012)
4. Björk, T., Di Masi, G., Kabanov, Y., Runggaldier, W.: Towards a general theory of bond markets. Financ. Stoch. **1**, 141–174 (1997)
5. Bonnaud, J., Carlier, L., Laurent, J., Vila, J.: Sovereign recovery schemes: discounting and risk management issues. In: 29th International Conference of the French Finance Association (AFFI) (2012)
6. Doctor, S., Goulden, J.: Differential Discounting for CDS. JPMorgan Europe Credit Research (2012)
7. Duffie, D., Schroder, M., Skiadas, C.: Recursive Valuation of Defaultable Securities and the Timing of Resolution Uncertainty. WP 195, Kellog Graduate School of Management, Department of Finance, Northwestern University (1994)
8. Eberlein, E., Koval, N.: A cross-currency Lévy market model. Quant. Financ. **6**, 465–480 (2006)
9. Ehlers, P., Schönbucher, P.: The Influence of FX Risk on Credit Spreads. WP, ETH Zurich (2006)
10. Elizalde, A., Doctor, S., Saltuk, Y.: Bond-CDS Basis Handbook. JPMorgan Research (2009)
11. Lee, M.: Bloomberg fair value market curves. In: International Bond Conference, Taipei (2007)
12. Schönbucher, P.: Term structure of defaultable bonds. Rev. Deriv. Stud. Special Issue: Credit Risk **2**(2/3), 161–192 (1998)
13. Schönbucher, P.: Credit Derivatives Pricing Models: Models. Wiley, Pricing and Implementation (2003)
14. West, G., Post-crisis methods for bootstrapping the yield curve. WP, Financial Modelling Agency (2011). http://finmod.co.za/OIS%20Curve.pdf
15. Yordanov, V.: Risky Sovereign Capital Structure: Fundamentals. WP SSRN.2349370 (2015)
16. Yordanov, V.: Risky Sovereign Capital Structure: Macrofinancial Diagnostics. WP SSRN.2600238 (2015)
17. Yordanov, V.: Multi-currency Risky Sovereign Bonds Arbitrage. WP SSRN.2349324 (2015)

7

The Impact of Cointegration on Commodity Spread Options

Walter Farkas, Elise Gourier, Robert Huitema and Ciprian Necula

Abstract In this work we explore the implications of cointegration in a system of commodity prices on the premiums of options written on various spreads on the futures prices of these commodities. We employ a parsimonious, yet comprehensive model for cointegration in a system of commodity prices. The model has an exponential affine structure and is flexible enough to allow for an arbitrary number of cointegration relationships. We conduct an extensive simulation study on pricing spread options. We argue that cointegration creates an upward sloping term structure of correlation, that in turn lowers the volatility of spreads and consequently the price of options on them.

Keywords Cointegration · Futures prices · Commodities · Spread options · Simulation

1 Introduction

A distinctive feature of commodity markets is the existence of long-run equilibrium relationships that exist between the levels of various commodity prices, such as the one between the price of crude oil and the price of heating oil. These long-run

W. Farkas (✉) · R. Huitema · C. Necula
Department of Banking and Finance, University of Zurich,
Plattenstrasse 14, 8032 Zurich, Switzerland
e-mail: walter.farkas@bf.uzh.ch

W. Farkas
Department of Mathematics, ETH Zurich, Rämistrasse 101, 8092 Zurich, Switzerland

W. Farkas
Swiss Finance Institute, Zurich, Switzerland

E. Gourier
School of Economics and Finance, Queen Mary, University of London, London, UK

C. Necula
Department of Money and Banking, Bucharest University of Economic Studies,
Bucharest, Romania

equilibrium relations can be captured in economic models by so-called *cointegration* relations.

In this work we employ the continuous time model of cointegrated commodity prices developed by the authors in Farkas et al. [6] in order to conduct a simulation study for assessing the impact of cointegration on spread options. In our model, commodity prices are non-stationary and several cointegration relations are allowed amongst them, capturing long-run equilibrium relationships. Cointegration (Engle and Granger [5]) is the property of two or more non-stationary time series of having at least one linear combination that is stationary.

There is a vast literature on modeling the price of a single commodity as a non-stationary process (see Back and Prokopczuk [1] for a comprehensive recent review). For example, Schwartz and Smith [13] assume the log price of a commodity to be the sum of two latent factors: the long-term equilibrium level, modeled as a geometric Brownian motion, and a short-term deviation from the equilibrium, modeled as a zero mean Ornstein–Uhlenbeck (OU) process. More recently, Paschke and Prokopczuk [11] propose to model these deviations as a more general CARMA process and Cortazar and Naranjo [3] generalize the Schwartz and Smith [13] model in a multi-factor framework.

However, the literature on modeling a system of commodity prices is still quite scarce. Two fairly recent models are proposed in Cortazar et al. [4] and Paschke and Prokopczuk [10], both of which account for cointegration by incorporating common and commodity-specific factors into their modeling framework. Amongst the common factors, only one is assumed non-stationary. Although they explicitly take into account cointegration between prices, the cointegrated systems generated by these two models are not covering the whole range of possible number of cointegration relations, but allow for none or for exactly $n-1$ relations to exist between the n prices. In Farkas et al. [6] we propose an easy-to-use, yet comprehensive, model for a system of cointegrated commodity prices that retains the exponential affine structure of previous approaches and allows, in the same time, for an arbitrary number of cointegration relationships.

The rest of the work is organized as follows. In Sect. 2 we briefly describe the model proposed in Farkas et al. [6] and point out some qualitative aspects regarding the dynamics of the system. Section 3 is devoted to an extensive simulation study focused on computing spread options prices and on assessing the impact of cointegration on pricing spread options. Section 4 is reserved for concluding remarks.

2 Outline of the Model

Before proceeding to the simulation study, in this section we present for the sake of completeness, a short description of the model developed in Farkas et al. [6].

Consider n commodities with spot prices $\mathbf{S}(t) = (S_1(t), \ldots, S_n(t))^\top$.

First it is assumed that the spot log-prices $\mathbf{X}(t) = \log \mathbf{S}(t)$ can be decomposed into three components:

$$\mathbf{X}(t) = \mathbf{Y}(t) + \boldsymbol{\varepsilon}(t) + \boldsymbol{\phi}(t), \tag{1}$$

where $\mathbf{Y}$(t) signifies the long-run levels, $\boldsymbol{\varepsilon}(t)$ is an n-dimensional stationary process capturing short-term deviations, and $\boldsymbol{\phi}(t) = \boldsymbol{\chi}_1 \cos(2\pi t) + \boldsymbol{\chi}_2 \sin(2\pi t)$ controls for seasonal effects with $\boldsymbol{\chi}_1$ and $\boldsymbol{\chi}_2$ being n-dimensional vectors of constants.

The notion of cointegration (Engle and Granger [5], Johansen [7], Phillips [12]) refers to the property of two or more non-stationary time series of having a linear combination that is stationary. For example, if $X_1(t)$ and $X_2(t)$ are two non-stationary processes, one says that they are cointegrated if there is a linear combination of them, $X_1(t) - \alpha X_2(t)$, that is stationary for some positive real α. Intuitively, cointegration occurs when two or more non-stationary variables are linked in a long-run equilibrium relationship from which they might depart only temporarily.

Regarding cointegration in the model, we stress that n cointegration relationships are implicitly assumed by (1): the n seasonally adjusted spot log-prices $\mathbf{X}(t) - \boldsymbol{\phi}(t)$ are cointegrated with their corresponding long-run levels, $\mathbf{Y}(t)$, since the linear combination $\mathbf{X}(t) - \boldsymbol{\phi}(t) - \mathbf{Y}(t)$ is stationary.

Secondly, cointegration is allowed to exist between the variables in $\mathbf{Y}(t)$ as well. We denote the number of cointegration relationships between them by h, where $h \geq 0$ and $h < n$. The corresponding cointegration matrix is symbolized by Θ, an $n \times n$ matrix with the last $n - h$ rows equal to zero vectors. Each of the h non-zero rows of Θ encodes a stationary (i.e., cointegrating) combination of the variables in $\mathbf{Y}(t)$, normalized such that $\Theta_{ii} = 1,\ i \leq h$. The total $n + h$ cointegration relationships between the variables in the vector $\mathbf{Z}(t) := (\mathbf{X}(t) - \boldsymbol{\phi}(t), \mathbf{Y}(t))^\top$ can be characterized by the $(2n \times 2n)$-matrix $\begin{bmatrix} \mathbf{I}_n & -\mathbf{I}_n \\ \mathbf{O}_n & \Theta \end{bmatrix}$ where $\mathbf{O}_n$ denotes the zero-matrix with dimension $n \times n$.

The dynamics of $\mathbf{X}(t)$ and $\mathbf{Y}(t)$ under the real-world probability measure is assumed to be given by:

$$d\begin{bmatrix} \mathbf{X}(t) - \phi(t) \\ \mathbf{Y}(t) \end{bmatrix} = \begin{bmatrix} \mathbf{0}_n \\ \mu_y \end{bmatrix} dt + \begin{bmatrix} -K_x & \mathbf{O}_n \\ \mathbf{O}_n & -K_y \end{bmatrix} \begin{bmatrix} \mathbf{I}_n & -\mathbf{I}_n \\ \mathbf{O}_n & \Theta \end{bmatrix} \begin{bmatrix} \mathbf{X}(t) - \phi(t) \\ \mathbf{Y}(t) \end{bmatrix} dt$$
$$+ \begin{bmatrix} \Sigma_x^{\frac{1}{2}} & \mathbf{O}_n \\ \Sigma_{xy}^{\frac{1}{2}} & \Sigma_y^{\frac{1}{2}} \end{bmatrix} d\begin{bmatrix} \mathbf{W}_x(t) \\ \mathbf{W}_y(t) \end{bmatrix}, \tag{2}$$

where $\mathbf{0}_n$ is an n-dimensional vector of zeros, and $\mathbf{W} := (\mathbf{W}_x, \mathbf{W}_y)^\top$ is a $2n$-dimensional standard Brownian motion. Furthermore, the matrix $\begin{bmatrix} -K_x & \mathbf{O}_n \\ \mathbf{O}_n & -K_y \end{bmatrix}$ measures the speed by which $\mathbf{Z}(t)$ reverts to its long-run (cointegration) equilibrium level. More specifically, K_x quantifies the speed of mean reversion of the elements in $\mathbf{X}$ around the long term levels in $\mathbf{Y}$. The matrix K_y is an $n \times n$ matrix with the last $n - h$ columns equal to zero vector, such that $K_y\Theta$ is an $n \times n$ matrix of rank h. Each of the h non-zero columns in K_y quantifies the speed of adjustment of each element in $\mathbf{Y}$ to the corresponding cointegration relation. The dynamics given by Eq. (2) is "error-correcting" in that a deviation from a given cointegration relation induces an appropriate change in variables in the direction of correcting the deviation.

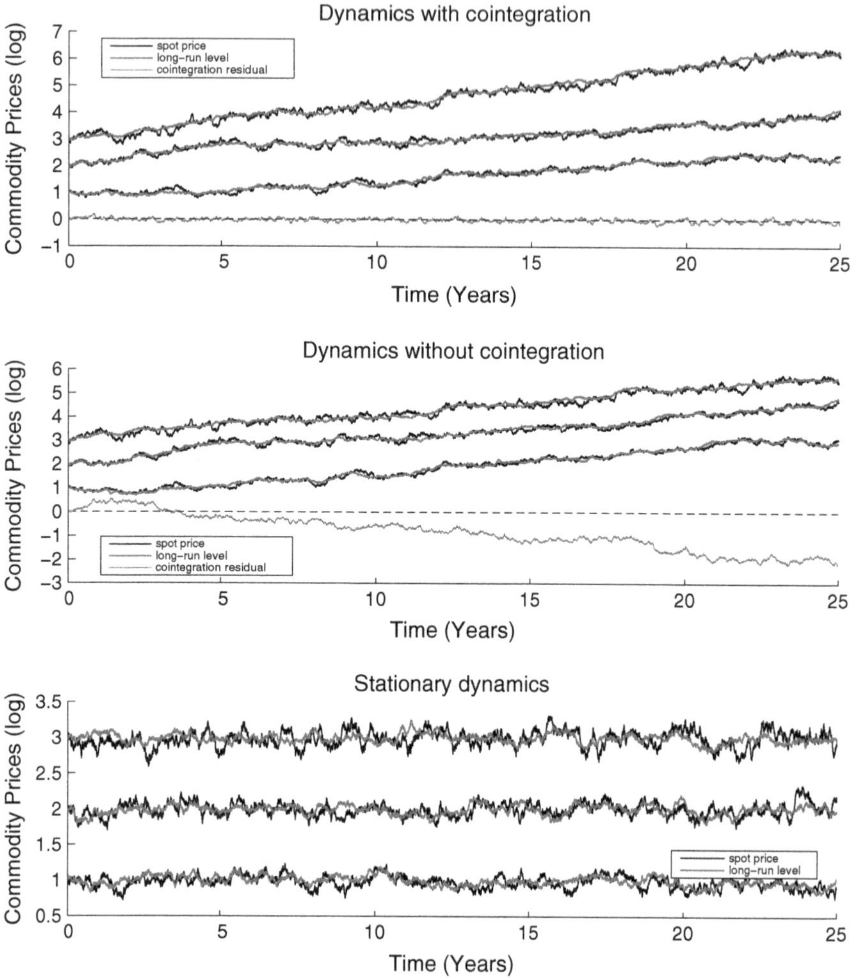

Fig. 1 Simulated price paths for various choices of the Θ matrix. *Top panel* prices are non-stationary and there is one cointegration relation. *Middle panel* prices are non-stationary and there is no cointegration. *Bottom panel* prices are stationary

In order to assess qualitatively the role of the cointegration matrix Θ on the properties of the dynamics of the system, Fig. 1 depicts the results of a simulation of a system of three variables for various choices of the Θ matrix.

In the top panel of Fig. 1 we assume that there is a cointegration relation and the first line of the Θ matrix is $\begin{bmatrix}1 & 1 & -1\end{bmatrix}$ and, therefore, the residual of the cointegration relation, $Y_1(t) + Y_2(t) - Y_3(t)$, is stationary. On the other hand, in the middle panel, depicts the case when Θ is the null matrix and, therefore, the prices are non-stationary and not cointegrated. For example, the residual of the cointegration relation from the previous case, $Y_1(t) + Y_2(t) - Y_3(t)$, is no longer stationary. In fact, there is no stationary linear combination of the long run levels in this case. Moreover, as depicted in the bottom panel, the model also allows for stationary prices, if the Θ matrix is of full rank.

The characteristic functions of $\mathbf{X}$ and $\mathbf{Y}$ can be readily computed analytically given they are normally distributed since the dynamics of $\mathbf{Z}(t) = (\mathbf{X}(t) - \boldsymbol{\phi}(t), \mathbf{Y}(t))^\top$ is in fact given by a multivariate Ornstein–Uhlenbeck (OU) process:

$$d\mathbf{Z}(t) = [\boldsymbol{\mu} - K\mathbf{Z}(t)]\,dt + \Sigma^{\frac{1}{2}} d\mathbf{W}(t), \tag{3}$$

with $\boldsymbol{\mu} := \begin{bmatrix} \mathbf{0}_n \\ \boldsymbol{\mu}_y \end{bmatrix}$, $K := \begin{bmatrix} K_x & -K_x \\ \mathbf{O}_n & K_y\Theta \end{bmatrix}$, $\Sigma^{\frac{1}{2}} := \begin{bmatrix} \Sigma_x^{\frac{1}{2}} & \mathbf{O}_n \\ \Sigma_{xy}^{\frac{1}{2}} & \Sigma_y^{\frac{1}{2}} \end{bmatrix}$, $\mathbf{W}(t) := \begin{bmatrix} \mathbf{W}_x(t) \\ \mathbf{W}_y(t) \end{bmatrix}$.

At the same time, the vector of spot prices $\mathbf{S}(T)$ can be written as an exponential function of $\mathbf{X}(t)$ and $\mathbf{Y}(t)$:

$$\begin{aligned} \mathbf{S}(T) = \exp\Big\{ & e^{-K_x(T-t)}\mathbf{X}(t) + \psi(T-t)\mathbf{Y}(t) + \left[\phi(T) - e^{-K_x(T-t)}\phi(t)\right] \\ & + \left[\int_t^T \psi(T-u)du\right]\mu_y + \int_t^T \left[e^{-K_x(T-u)}\Sigma_x^{\frac{1}{2}} + \psi(T-u)\Sigma_{xy}^{\frac{1}{2}}\right] d\mathbf{W}_x(u) \\ & + \int_t^T \psi(T-u)\Sigma_y^{\frac{1}{2}} d\mathbf{W}_y(u)\Big\}. \end{aligned} \tag{4}$$

where

$$\psi(\tau) := K_x\left[\int_0^\tau e^{-K_x(\tau-u)}e^{-K_y\Theta u}du\right].$$

Given the affine structure of the model, futures prices can also be obtained in closed form. Under the simplifying assumption of constant market prices of risk, one has that $d\begin{bmatrix} \mathbf{W}_x^*(t) \\ \mathbf{W}_y^*(t) \end{bmatrix} = d\begin{bmatrix} \mathbf{W}_x(t) \\ \mathbf{W}_y(t) \end{bmatrix} + \begin{bmatrix} \boldsymbol{\lambda}_x \\ \boldsymbol{\lambda}_y \end{bmatrix} dt$ where $\mathbf{W}_x^*(t)$ and $\mathbf{W}_y^*(t)$ are standard Brownian motions under the risk-neutral measure, and $\boldsymbol{\lambda}_x, \boldsymbol{\lambda}_y$ are the market prices of $\mathbf{W}_x(t)$ and $\mathbf{W}_y(t)$ risks, respectively.

Under these circumstances it can be shown that at time t the vector of futures prices for the contracts with maturity T is given by

$$\mathbf{F}(t,T) = \exp\{\alpha(t,T) + \beta(T-t)\mathbf{X}(t) + \psi(T-t)\mathbf{Y}(t)\}, \tag{5}$$

with $\beta(\tau) := e^{-K_x\tau}$ and with $\alpha(t,T)$ defined by

$$\begin{aligned} \alpha(t, t+\tau) := & \left[\phi(t+\tau) - e^{-K_x\tau}\phi(t)\right] - \left(\mathbf{I}_n - e^{-K_x\tau}\right)K_x^{-1}\boldsymbol{\mu}_x^* + \left(\int_0^\tau \psi(\tau-u)du\right)\boldsymbol{\mu}_y^* \\ & + \operatorname{diag}\left\{\frac{1}{2}\left[\mathbf{I}_n\ \mathbf{O}_n\right]\left[e^{-K\tau}\left(\int_0^\tau e^{Ku}\Sigma e^{Ku}du\right)e^{-K\tau}\right]\begin{bmatrix}\mathbf{I}_n \\ \mathbf{O}_n\end{bmatrix}\right\}, \end{aligned} \tag{6}$$

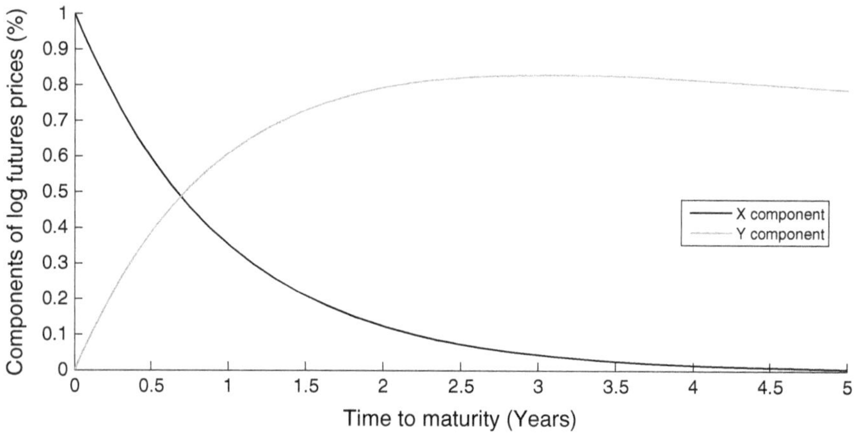

Fig. 2 The relative contribution of various components to log futures prices

where diag(A) returns the vector with diagonal elements of A, and where

$$\boldsymbol{\mu}^* = \begin{bmatrix} \boldsymbol{\mu}_x^* \\ \boldsymbol{\mu}_y^* \end{bmatrix} = \boldsymbol{\mu} + \Sigma^{\frac{1}{2}} \begin{bmatrix} \boldsymbol{\lambda}_x \\ \boldsymbol{\lambda}_y \end{bmatrix}.$$

To better assess qualitatively the impact of the two factors, $\mathbf{X}(t)$ and $\mathbf{Y}(t)$, on the term structure of futures prices, we depict in Fig. 2 the relative contribution of the corresponding two terms in Eq. (5) to the logarithm of the futures prices on one of the commodities in a cointegrated system.

The contribution of the $\mathbf{X}(t)$ component decreases exponentially as a function of time to maturity. On the other hand, the $\mathbf{Y}(t)$ component contributes significantly for higher maturities. Therefore, the two factors capture the short-end and, respectively, the long-end of the term-structure of futures prices.

By Itô's lemma, the risk-neutral dynamics of $\mathbf{F}(t, T)$ is given by

$$\frac{d\mathbf{F}(t,T)}{\mathbf{F}(t,T)} = \left[e^{-K_x(T-t)} \Sigma_x^{\frac{1}{2}} + \psi(T-t) \Sigma_{xy}^{\frac{1}{2}} \right] d\mathbf{W}_x^*(t) + \psi(T-t) \Sigma_y^{\frac{1}{2}} d\mathbf{W}_y^*(t), \tag{7}$$

and it follows immediately that the variance–covariance matrix of returns on futures prices is given by:

$$\begin{aligned} \Xi(\tau) = {} & e^{-K_x \tau} \Sigma_x e^{-K_x^\top \tau} + \psi(\tau) \Sigma_{xy}^{\frac{1}{2}} (\Sigma_x^{\frac{1}{2}})^\top e^{-K_x^\top \tau} + e^{-K_x \tau} \Sigma_x^{\frac{1}{2}} (\Sigma_{xy}^{\frac{1}{2}})^\top \psi^\top(\tau) \\ & + \psi(\tau) \Sigma_{xy} \psi^\top(\tau) + \psi(\tau) \Sigma_y \psi^\top(\tau) \end{aligned} \tag{8}$$

where $\tau = T - t$.

Since the term structure of correlation of futures prices returns plays an important role in the results of the simulations performed in the following section, it is worthwhile to point out some qualitative results about this term structure.

First, Eq. (8) shows that unless $K_x = \mathbf{O}_n$, the variance–covariance matrix $\Xi(\tau)$ depends on τ.

Second, let us consider the case that there is no instantaneous correlation between the shocks driving the dynamics, meaning that Σ_x and Σ_y are diagonal matrices and Σ_{xy} is the null matrix. Moreover, let us assume that K_x is diagonal, meaning that the spot price of a commodity reacts only to its deviation from the long run level and not to deviations of the other commodities. It follows that the first term in Eq. (8) is a diagonal matrix and the next three terms are null matrices. If, in addition, there is no cointegration in the system, meaning that Θ is the null matrix, then the last term in Eq. (8) is a diagonal matrix since $\psi(\tau)$ is also a diagonal matrix. So, in this case, the variance–covariance matrix $\Xi(\tau)$ is diagonal and, therefore, there is no correlation at any maturity. However, if there is at least one cointegration relation in the system, then the last term in Eq. (8) is no longer a diagonal matrix since $\psi(\tau)$ is not diagonal. Therefore, cointegration induces correlation at various maturities although it was assumed there is no instantaneous correlation between the Brownian motions in the model.

3 Spread Option Prices

In this section, we focus on futures prices and prices of European-style options written on the *spread* between two or more commodities, such as the difference between the price of electric power and the cost of the natural gas needed to produce it, or the price difference between crude oil and a basket of various refined products, known as the crack spread. The crack spread is in fact related to the profit margin that an oil refiner realizes when "cracking" crude oil while simultaneously selling the refined products in the wholesale market. The oil refiner can hedge the risk of losing profits by buying an appropriate number of futures contract on the crack spread or, alternatively, by buying call options of the crack spread. Since spread options have become regularly and widely used instruments in financial markets for hedging purposes, there is a growing need for a better understanding of the effects of cointegration on their prices.

There is extensive literature on approximation methods for spread and basket options on two (e.g. Kirk [8]) or more than two commodities, with recent contributions from Li et al. [9] and Caldana and Fusai [2]. However, mostly for simplicity, we relay in this chapter on the Monte-Carlo simulation method for pricing spread options written on two or more than two commodities.

From Eq. (7), it follows that $\mathbf{F}(t, T)$ (conditional on information available up to time $s \leq t \leq T$) is distributed as follows:

$$\mathbf{F}(t,T) \sim \log \mathcal{N}\left(\log \mathbf{F}(s,T) - \frac{1}{2}\int_s^t \operatorname{diag}(\Xi(T-u))du, \int_s^t \Xi(T-u)du\right), \tag{9}$$

where $\operatorname{diag}(X)$ denotes the vector containing the diagonal elements of the matrix X. Note that $\mathbf{F}(s,T)$ can be either computed from (5) or observed from data.

The fact that the distribution function of $\mathbf{F}(t,T)$ is known in an easy-to-use and analytic form is one of the key features of the model we employ. It allows us to simulate futures price curves at any time t in the future based on today's curves (time s) almost effortlessly. Hence, the price of a call option on the time-T value of a certain spread can be simply obtained by carrying out the following steps:

(i) compute or observe today's futures price curves $\mathbf{F}(s,T)$;

(ii) compute M realizations $\mathbf{F}^{(m)}$ $(m = 1,\ldots,M)$ of $\mathbf{F}(T,T)$ by sampling from (9) as follows:

$$\mathbf{F}^{(m)} = \mathbf{F}(s,T)\exp\left\{\boldsymbol{\varepsilon}^{(m)}\right\},$$

where $\boldsymbol{\varepsilon}^{(m)}$ is generated from a multivariate normal distribution with mean $-\frac{1}{2}\int_s^T \operatorname{diag}(\Xi(T-u))du$ and variance–covariance matrix $\int_s^T \Xi(T-u)du$[1];

(iii) compute the Monte-Carlo estimate of a call with strike k on the spread

$$\sum_{n=1}^{N} \omega_n S_n(T) \quad \left(= \sum_{n=1}^{N} \omega_n F_n(T,T)\right),$$

with $\omega_n, n = 1,\ldots,N$ the weights of each component in the spread, as follows:

$$\frac{1}{M}\sum_{m=1}^{M} \max\left\{\left[\sum_{n=1}^{N} \omega_n F_n^{(m)}\right] - k, 0\right\}. \tag{10}$$

For the sake of clarity we have set the risk-free rate curve equal to zero. We note that the random variables $\boldsymbol{\varepsilon}^{(m)}$ can be simply re-used for pricing spread options with different maturity dates.

In the following we consider a system of three commodities[2] characterized by one cointegration relation with $\Theta = \begin{bmatrix} 1 & -0.4 & -0.6 \\ 0 & 0 & 0 \\ 0 & 0 & 0 \end{bmatrix}$. The rest of the parameters describing the dynamics are $K_x = \begin{bmatrix} 1.5 & 0 & 0 \\ 0 & 1 & 0 \\ 0 & 0 & 0.5 \end{bmatrix}$, $\Sigma_x = \begin{bmatrix} 0.0625 & 0.0562 & 0.0437 \\ 0.0562 & 0.0900 & 0.0262 \\ 0.0437 & 0.0262 & 0.1225 \end{bmatrix}$, $\mu_y =$

[1]Here the technique of antithetic variables is used to reduce the number of random samples needed for a given level of accuracy.

[2]The structure of the parameters is chosen, in a parsimonious manner, taking into consideration the key facts of the empirical study conducted in Farkas et al. [6], where the results provide compelling evidence of cointegration between various commodities.

$\begin{bmatrix} 0.025 \\ 0.025 \\ 0.025 \end{bmatrix}$, $K_y = \begin{bmatrix} 1.5 & 0 & 0 \\ 0 & 0 & 0 \\ 0 & 0 & 0 \end{bmatrix}$, $\Sigma_y = \begin{bmatrix} 0.0225 & 0 & 0 \\ 0 & 0.0225 & 0 \\ 0 & 0 & 0.0225 \end{bmatrix}$, $\Sigma_{xy} = \mathbf{O}_3$. Since K_x is diagonal, each spot price is error-corrected only with respect to deviations from its own long-run level. Moreover, given the specific form of the K_y matrix, deviations from the cointegration relationships between the long-run levels influence only the dynamics of the first spot price. In this respect, the second and third commodities are "exogenous" in that their dynamics is not influenced by the variables characterizing the other commodities. Regarding instantaneous dependence, the shocks driving the dynamics of the long-run factors are not correlated, whereas we imposed positive correlations between the shocks driving the dynamics of the $\mathbf{X}(t)$. More specifically, the instantaneous variance–covariance matrix Σ_y for long-run shocks corresponds to an annual volatility of 0.15 for all three commodities. At the same time, the instantaneous variance–covariance matrix Σ_x for short-run shocks corresponds to an annual volatility of 0.25 for the first commodity, of 0.30 for the second and of 0.35 for the third and to a correlation coefficient of 0.75 between the first and the second commodities, of 0.50 between the first and the last and of 0.25 between the second and the third. For simplicity, we also assume there is no correlation between the two categories of shocks. Since we focus on the impact of cointegration on spread options, in the following simulations we have set, for illustration purposes, the vector of risk premiums $\boldsymbol{\lambda}_x$ and $\boldsymbol{\lambda}_y$ and the risk-free rate curve equal to zero.[3]

Figure 3 depicts the term structure of correlation, over a period of 5 years, between the returns of futures prices of the three commodities in the system in two cases: the one when the cointegration relation is taken into account and, respectively, the one where the cointegration relation is abstracted from (i.e. $\Theta = \mathbf{O}_3$).

One can observe that, regarding the correlation term structure between commodities 2 and 3, the two curves are identical (Fig. 3, bottom panel). This is not surprising since these two commodities are "exogenous" as explained above and their dynamics is not influenced by the cointegration relation. However, cointegration induces additional correlation when it comes to the commodities 1 and 2 and commodities 1 and 3, as also pointed out at the end of the previous section. In the absence of cointegration, the correlation vanishes after 2–3 years, whereas when the cointegration relation is taken into account the correlation exists also in the long run.

Next, we consider three spreads on two commodities, respectively $S_1(t) - S_2(t)$, $S_1(t) - S_3(t)$, $S_2(t) - S_3(t)$, and one spread on all the three commodities in the system $S_1(t) - 0.5(S_2(t) + S_3(t))$. We assume that at time 0, the two factors are such that $\mathbf{X}(0) = \mathbf{Y}(0) = \begin{bmatrix} 2 \\ 2 \\ 2 \end{bmatrix}$ and, therefore, the current spot prices of all four spreads equal 0. We focus on studying the prices of the at-the-money (ATM) European-style call spread options with up to 5 years to maturity. Figure 4 shows the term structure of

[3] In a real-world application the parameters of the model can be estimated using futures prices data for the corresponding commodities. Given the features of the model one can implement an estimation procedure based on the Kalman filter.

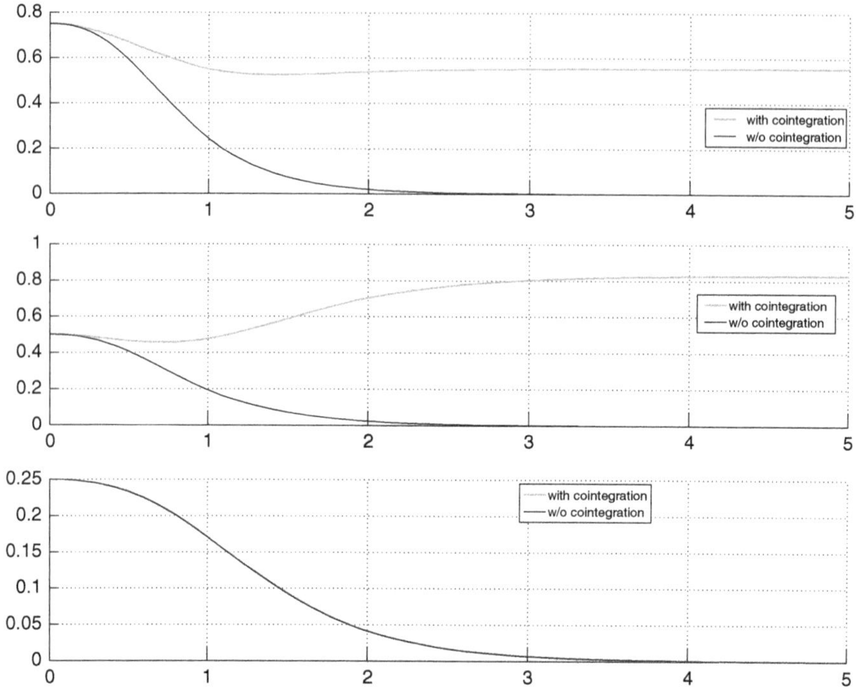

Fig. 3 Term structure of correlation, over a period of 5 years, between the futures log-returns of three commodities (from *top* to *bottom*: between 1 and 2, between 1 and 3, between 2 and 3)

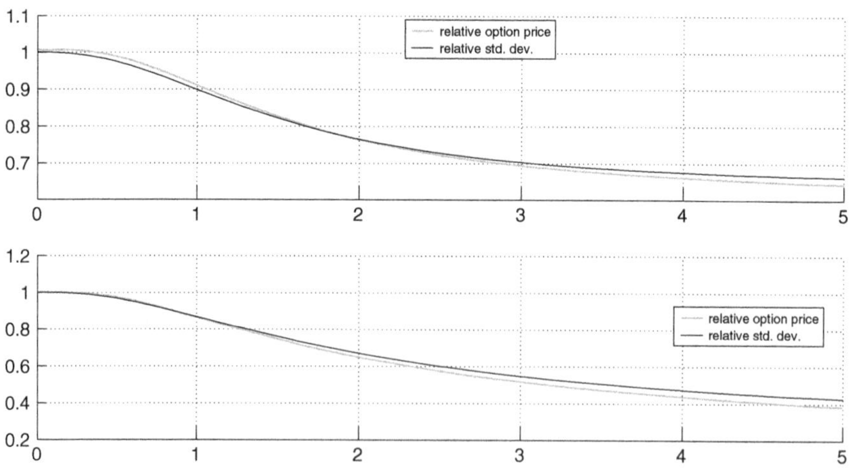

Fig. 4 Relative ATM call spread option prices with up to 5 years to maturity, and relative standard deviations of the spread distribution at maturities up to 5 years. *Top panel* for the spread $S_1(t) - S_2(t)$. *Bottom panel* for the spread $S_1(t) - 0.5(S_2(t) + S_3(t))$

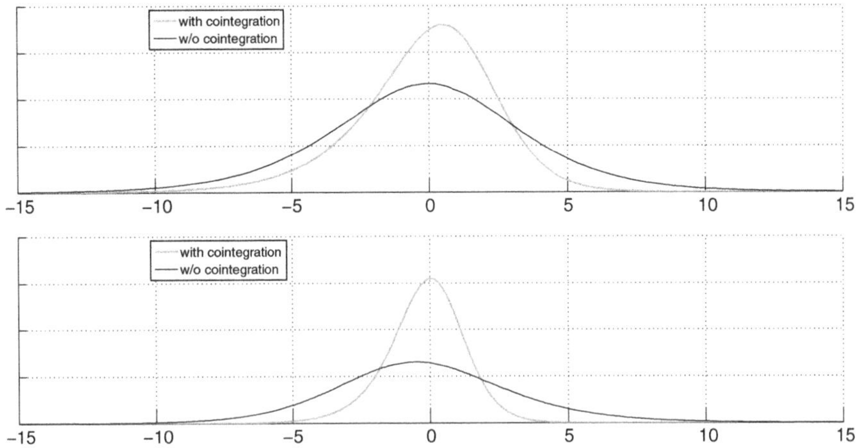

Fig. 5 The distribution of the spread at maturity (5 years). *Top panel* for the spread $S_1(t) - S_2(t)$. *Bottom panel* for the spread $S_1(t) - 0.5(S_2(t) + S_3(t))$

prices in the case with cointegration relative to the prices in the case the cointegration is not accounted for.[4]

Cointegration has a significant impact on spread option prices, with the price for the call with 5 years to maturity on the $S_1(t) - S_2(t)$ spread being almost 30 % lower in the case with cointegration and for the call on the $S_1(t) - 0.5(S_2(t) + S_3(t))$ spread being almost 60 % lower. This can be explained by the fact that cointegration induces additional correlation that acts to lower the standard deviation of the distribution of the spread at maturity. To give a better grasp of this fact, Fig. 5 depicts the distribution of the spread at maturity in the two cases. We omitted from the figures the other two spreads, because the results for the $S_1(t) - S_3(t)$ spread are similar to those for the $S_1(t) - S_2(t)$ spread, and for the $S_2(t) - S_3(t)$ spread there is, as expected given the "exogenous" nature of these two prices, no difference between the cases with and without cointegration.

If one were to add another cointegration relation to the system, linking the second and the third commodities in a long-run relationship, then the new cointegration relation would affect the prices of the options written on the $S_2(t) - S_3(t)$ spread. Moreover, the new cointegration relation might also affect the option prices written on the other three spreads, the magnitude of this influence depending on the structure of the K_y matrix that captures the strength of responses in various spot prices to deviations in the new long-run relationship.

To have a better grasp of the influence of cointegration, next we run a series of sensitivity analyses concerning the existence of a second cointegration relationship in the system. To account for the new cointegration relation, we assume a new structure

[4]Relative quantities in Fig. 4 are determined as the ratio between the quantity computed with the model accounting for cointegration and the corresponding quantity computed with the model without cointegration.

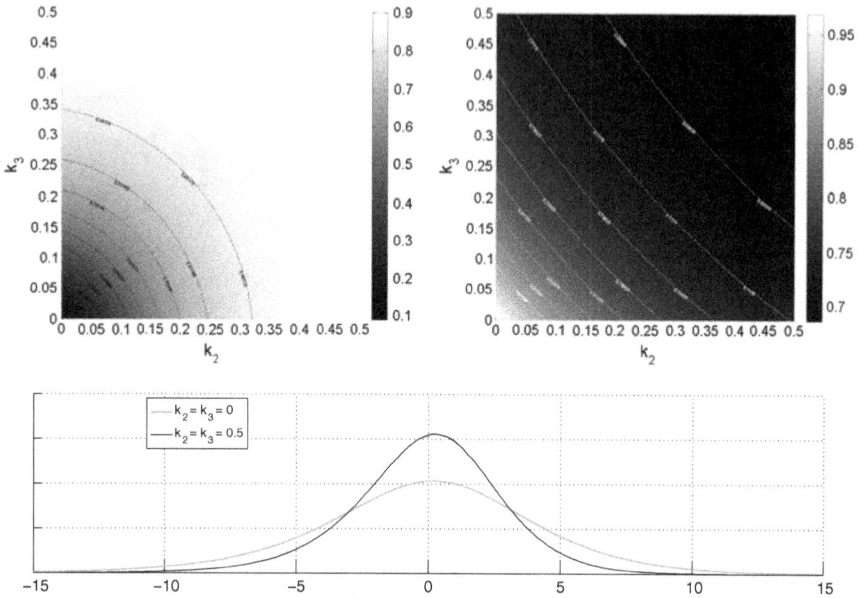

Fig. 6 The impact of k_2 and k_3 on the distribution of the spread $S_2(t) - S_3(t)$ at maturity (5 years). *Top left panel* correlation between the futures log-returns of the two commodities in the basket. *Top right panel* relative standard deviations of the spread distribution (the values are normalized by division with the standard deviation in the case $k_2 = k_3 = 0$). *Bottom panel* the distribution for the two extreme cases in the analysis

for $\Theta = \begin{bmatrix} 1 & -0.4 & -0.6 \\ -\theta & 1 & -0.8 \\ 0 & 0 & 0 \end{bmatrix}$ and $K_y = \begin{bmatrix} 1.5 & k_1 & 0 \\ 0 & k_2 & 0 \\ 0 & -k_3 & 0 \end{bmatrix}$, where $\theta, k_1, k_2, k_3 > 0$. The other parameters have the same values as before. We first focus on the impact of the parameters k_2 and k_3 on the $S_2(t) - S_3(t)$ spread. These two parameters quantify the strength that the second and, respectively, the third commodity reacts to deviations in the newly added cointegration relation. In the extreme case when both k_2 and k_3 are zero, we are in the same situation as before since the two commodities do not react to deviations. However, with the increase of these parameters the new cointegration relation will start to matter for the dynamics of the two commodities, and will have an impact on the distribution of the spread at maturity. Figure 6 presents the results of the sensitivity analysis when k_2 and k_3 are varied between 0 and 0.5, with the other parameters kept fixed at a level $\theta = 0.2$ and $k_1 = 0$.

A higher value for the two reaction parameters produces a higher extra correlation induced by the second cointegration relation, which, in turn, is reflected in a lower standard deviation of the distribution of the spread at maturity. Over a 5-years horizon, the standard deviation for the case $k_2 = k_3 = 0.5$ is 32 % lower than in the case the two parameters are equal to zero, and the ATM call price is 35 % lower.

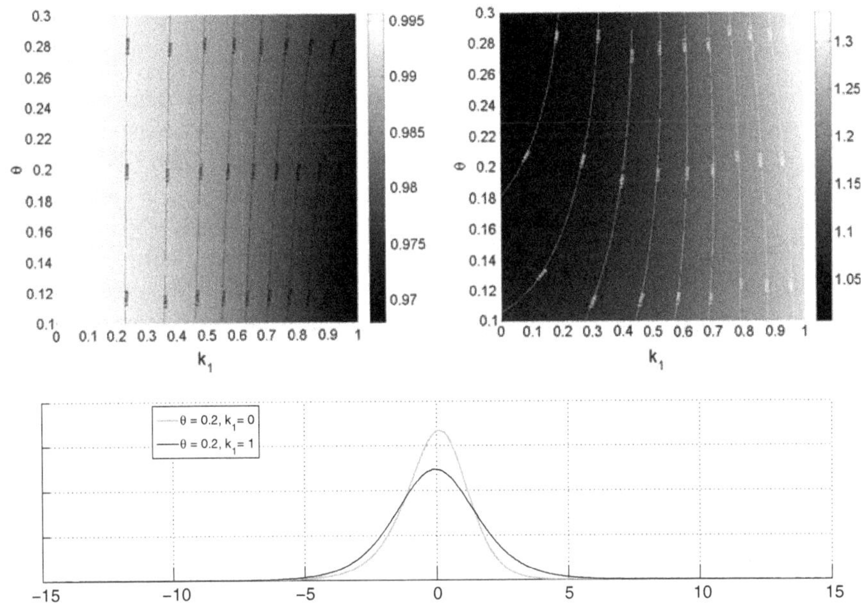

Fig. 7 The impact of k_1 and θ on the distribution of the spread $S_1(t) - 0.5(S_2(t) + S_3(t))$ at maturity (5 years). *Top left panel* correlation between the futures log-returns of the first commodity and the sum of the other two. *Top right panel* relative standard deviations of the spread distribution (the values are normalized by division with the standard deviation in the case $k_1 = 0, \theta = 0.2$). *Bottom panel* the distribution for two specific cases in the analysis

Next, we focus on the impact of θ and k_1 on the $S_1(t) - 0.5(S_2(t) + S_3(t))$ spread. The parameter θ is a free variable that determines the second cointegration relationship and the parameter k_1 measures the magnitude of the response of the first commodity to deviations from the second cointegration relation. Figure 7 presents the results of the sensitivity analysis when k_1 and θ are varied between 0 and 1 and, respectively, between 0.1 and 0.3, with the other parameters kept fixed at a level $k_2 = 0.25$ and $k_3 = 0.25$. An increase of k_1 generates a reduction in the correlation between the components of the spread, showing that the second cointegration relationship has the effect of pulling the components of the spread away from each other. This effect is marginally stronger for the smaller θ. The result of the reduction in correlation is a higher standard deviation of the distribution of the spread at maturity.

For a maturity of 5 years, the standard deviation for the case $k_1 = 1$ is around 33 % higher than in the case the parameter equals zero, and the ATM call price is about 40 % higher. Therefore, the two cointegration relations influence the distribution of the $S_1(t) - 0.5(S_2(t) + S_3(t))$ spread in different directions, the first one generating a reduction, and the second one an increase in the standard deviation. The overall impact depends on the magnitude of the parameters quantifying the responses of the commodities to deviations in the two cointegration relations.

4 Concluding Remarks

In this work, we explored the implications of cointegration between commodity prices on the premiums of options written on various spreads between these commodities. We employed the continuous time model of cointegrated commodity prices developed in Farkas et al. [6] and conducted a simulation study for a cointegrated system of three commodities. We calculated the prices of several spread options and found that cointegration significantly influences these prices. Furthermore, we pointed out that cointegration leads to an upward sloping correlation term-structure which lowers the volatility of spreads and therefore it also lowers the value of options on spreads. Although we restricted in this chapter to a simulation study, it is worthwhile to mention that the model can also be estimated using futures prices on various commodities, as shown in Farkas et al. [6].

Acknowledgements The KPMG Center of Excellence in Risk Management is acknowledged for organizing the conference “Challenges in Derivatives Markets - Fixed Income Modeling, Valuation Adjustments, Risk Management, and Regulation”.

References

1. Back, J., Prokopczuk, M.: Commodity price dynamics and derivative valuation: a review. Int. J. Theor. Appl. Financ. **16**(6), 1350032 (2013)
2. Caldana, R., Fusai, G.: A general closed-form spread option pricing formula. J. Bank. Financ. **37**, 48934906 (2013)
3. Cortazar, G., Naranjo, L.: An N-factor Gaussian model of oil futures prices. J. Futur. Mark. **26**(3), 243268 (2006)
4. Cortazar, G., Milla, C., Severino, F.: A multicommodity model of futures prices: using futures prices of one commodity to estimate the stochastic process of another. J. Futur. Mark. **28**(6), 537–560 (2008)
5. Engle, R.F., Granger, C.W.: Co-integration and error correction: representation, estimation, and testing. Econometrica **55**(2), 251–276 (1987)
6. Farkas, W., Gourie, E., Huitema, R., Necula, C.: A two-factor cointegrated commodity price model with an application to spread option pricing. Available at SSRN http://dx.doi.org/10.2139/ssrn.2679218 (2015)
7. Johansen, S.: Estimation and hypothesis testing of cointegration vectors in Gaussian vector autoregressive models. Econometrica **59**, 1551–1580 (1991)
8. Kirk, E.: Correlation in the energy markets. In: Managing Energy Price Risk, pp. 71–78. Risk Publications and Enron, London (1995)
9. Li, M., Zhou, J., Deng, S.-J.: Multi-asset spread option pricing and hedging. Quant. Financ. **10**(3), 305324 (2010)
10. Paschke, R., Prokopczuk, M.: Integrating multiple commodities in a model of stochastic price dynamics. J. Energy Mark. **2**(3), 4782 (2009)
11. Paschke, R., Prokopczuk, M.: Commodity derivatives valuation with autoregressive and moving average components in the price dynamics. J. Bank. Financ. **34**, 2742–2752 (2010)
12. Phillips, P.: Error correction and long-run equilibrium in continuous time. Econometrica **59**(4), 967–980 (1991)
13. Schwartz, E., Smith, J.E.: Short-term variations and long-term dynamics in commodity prices. Manag. Sci. **46**(7), 893–911 (2000)

8

The Dynamic Correlation Model and its Application to the Heston Model

L. Teng, M. Ehrhardt and M. Günther

Abstract Correlation plays an essential role in many problems of finance and economics, such as pricing financial products and hedging strategies, since it models the degree of relationship between, e.g., financial products and financial institutions. However, usually for simplicity the correlation coefficient is assumed to be a constant in many models, although financial quantities are correlated in a strongly nonlinear way in the real market. This work provides a new time-dependent correlation function, which can be easily used to construct dynamically (time-dependent) correlated Brownian motions and flexibly incorporated in many financial models. The aim of using our time-dependent correlation function is to reasonably choose additional parameters to increase the fitting quality on the one hand, but also add an economic concept on the other hand. As examples, we illustrate the applications of dynamic correlation in the Heston model. From our numerical results we conclude that the Heston model extended by incorporating time-dependent correlations can provide a better volatility smile than the pure Heston model.

Keywords Time-dependent correlations · Heston model · Implied volatility · Nonlinear dependence

1 Introduction

Correlation is a well-established concept for quantifying interdependence. It plays an essential role in several problems of finance and economics, such as pricing financial

---

L. Teng (✉) · M. Ehrhardt · M. Günther
Lehrstuhl für Angewandte Mathematik und Numerische Analysis,
Fakultät Mathematik und Naturwissenschaften, Bergische Universität
Wuppertal, Gaußstr. 20, 42119 Wuppertal, Germany
e-mail: teng@math.uni-wuppertal.de

M. Ehrhardt
e-mail: ehrhardt@math.uni-wuppertal.de

M. Günther
e-mail: guenther@math.uni-wuppertal.de

products and hedging strategies. For example, in [3] the arbitrage pricing model is based on that correlation as a measure for the dependence among the assets, and in portfolio credit models the default correlation is one fundamental factor of risk evaluation, see [1, 2, 12].

In most of the financial models, the correlation has been considered as a constant. However, this is not a realistic assumption due to the well-known fact that the correlation is hardly a fixed constant, see e.g. [7, 13]. For example, in many situations the pure Heston model [9] cannot provide enough skews or smiles in the implied volatility surface as market requires, especially for a short maturity. A reason for this might be that deterministically correlated Brownian motions (BMs) of the price process and the variance process are used, as the correlation mainly affects the slope of implied volatility smile. If the correlation is modeled as a time-dependent dynamic function, better skews or smiles will be provided in the implied volatility surface by reasonably choosing additional parameters. Furthermore, compared with the way to extend a model by using time-dependent parameter, e.g., [6, 10] for the Heston model, a time-dependent correlation function adds an economic concept (nonlinear relationship) and its application will be considerably simpler.

The key of modeling correlation as a time-dependent function is being able to ensure that the boundaries -1 and 1 of the correlation function are not attractive and unattainable for any time. In this work, we build up a appropriate time-dependent correlation function, so that one can reasonably choose additional parameters to increase the fitting quality on the one hand but also add an economic concept on the other hand.

The outline of the remaining part is as follows. Section 2 is devoted to a specific dynamic correlation function and its (analytical) computation. In Sect. 3, we present the concept of dynamically (time-dependent) correlated Brownian motions and the corresponding construction. The incorporation of our new dynamic correlation model in the Heston model is illustrated in Sect. 4. Finally, in Sect. 5 we conclude.

2 The Dynamic Correlation Function

In this section we introduce a dynamic correlation function. Actually, it is in high demand to find such a correlation function which must satisfy the correlation properties: it provides only the values in the interval $(-1, 1)$ for any time; it converges for increasing time. We find the following simple idea: we denote the dynamic correlation by $\bar{\rho}$ and propose simply using

$$\bar{\rho}_t := E\left[\tanh(X_t)\right], \quad t > 0 \tag{1}$$

for the *dynamic correlation function,* where X_t is any mean-reverting process with positive and negative values. For the known parameters of X_t, the correlation function $\bar{\rho}_t : [0, t] \to (-1, 1)$ depends only on t. We observe that the dynamic correlation model (1) satisfies the desired properties: first, it is obvious that $\bar{\rho}_t$ takes values only in $(-1, 1)$ for all t. Besides, it converges for increasing time due to the mean reversion of the used process X_t.

Although we could intuitively observe that the function tanh is eminently suitable for transforming value to the interval $(-1, 1)$, one might still ask whether other functions can also be applied for this purpose, like trigonometric functions or $\frac{2}{\pi}\arctan(\frac{\pi}{2}x)$. In theory, such functions could be used for this purpose. However, the problem is whether one can obtain the expectation of the transformed mean-reverting process by such functions in a closed-form expression. Furthermore, our experiments show that the tendency of the function tanh is more suitable for modeling correlations, see [13].

X_t in (1) could be any mean-reverting process which allows positive and negative outcomes. As an example, let X_t be the *Ornstein–Uhlenbeck process* [14]

$$dX_t = \kappa(\mu - X_t)dt + \sigma dW_t, \quad t \geq 0. \tag{2}$$

We are interested in computing $E[\bar{\rho}_t]$ as a function of the given parameters in (2). We compute $\bar{\rho}_t = E[\tanh(X_t)]$ as

$$\bar{\rho}_t = E[\tanh(X_t)] = E\left[1 - \mathrm{e}^{-X_t} \cdot \frac{2}{\mathrm{e}^{-X_t} + \mathrm{e}^{X_t}}\right] = 1 - E\left[\mathrm{e}^{-X_t} \cdot \frac{1}{\cosh(X_t)}\right]. \tag{3}$$

We set $g(X_t) = 1/\cosh(X_t)$. Applying the results by Chen and Joslin [4], the expectation in (3) can be found in closed-form expression (up to an integral) as

$$\frac{1}{2\pi}\int_{-\infty}^{\infty} \hat{g}(u) \cdot E[\mathrm{e}^{-X_t}\mathrm{e}^{iuX_t}]\,du, \tag{4}$$

where $i = \sqrt{-1}$ denotes the imaginary unit and $\hat{g}$ is the Fourier transform of g, in this case is known analytically by $\hat{g}(u) = \pi/\cosh(\frac{\pi u}{2})$. Denoting $CF(t, u|X_0, \kappa, \mu, \sigma)$ as the characteristic function of X_t, the expectation in (4) can be presented by $CF(t, i + u|X_0, \kappa, \mu, \sigma)$. Thus, we obtain the closed-form expression for $\bar{\rho}_t$:

$$\bar{\rho}_t = 1 - \frac{1}{2}\int_{-\infty}^{\infty} \frac{1}{\cosh(\frac{\pi u}{2})} \cdot CF(t, i + u|X_0, \kappa, \mu, \sigma)du. \tag{5}$$

The next step is to calculate $CF(t, i + u|X_0, \kappa, \mu, \sigma)$. The process X_t is an Ornstein–Uhlenbeck process and its characteristic function $CF(t, u|X_0, \kappa, \mu, \sigma)$ can be obtained analytically, e.g. using the framework of the affine process, see [5]. Then, we only need to substitute $u + i$ for u in the characteristic function of X_t to calculate $CF(t, i + u|X_0, \kappa, \mu, \sigma)$ which is given by

$$CF(t, i + u|X_0, \kappa, \mu, \sigma) = \mathrm{e}^{-A(t) - \frac{B(t)}{2} + iu(A(t)+B(t)) + u^2\frac{B(t)}{2}}, \tag{6}$$

with

$$A(t) = \mathrm{e}^{-\kappa t} X_0 + \mu(1 - \mathrm{e}^{-\kappa t}), \quad B(t) = -\frac{\sigma^2}{2\kappa}(1 - \mathrm{e}^{-2\kappa t}) \tag{7}$$

Finally, the dynamic correlation function $\bar{\rho}_t$ can be computed by

$$\bar{\rho}_t = 1 - \frac{\mathrm{e}^{-A(t)-\frac{B(t)}{2}}}{2} \int_{-\infty}^{\infty} \frac{1}{\cosh(\frac{\pi u}{2})} \cdot \mathrm{e}^{iu(A(t)+B(t))+u^2\frac{B(t)}{2}} du, \tag{8}$$

where $A(t)$ and $B(t)$ are defined in (7). In fact, X_0 in $A(t)$ is equal to $\operatorname{artanh}(\bar{\rho}_0)$.

To illustrate the role of each parameter in (8), we plot $\bar{\rho}_t$ for several values of the parameters. First in Fig. 1, we let $\kappa = 2$ and $\sigma = 0.5$ and display $\bar{\rho}_t$ with different values of μ, which is set to be $0.5,\ 0$, and -0.5, respectively. Obviously, μ determines the long term mean of $\bar{\rho}_t$. However, μ is not the exact limiting value. Considering Fig. 1a where the initial value of the correlation function is 0, we see that $\bar{\rho}_t$ is increasing to a value around $\mu = 0.5$ and decreasing to a value around $\mu = -0.5$ as t become larger, when $\mu = 0.5$ and -0.5, respectively. Besides, for $\mu = \bar{\rho}_0 = 0$ we observe that the correlation function $\bar{\rho}_t$ yields always 0 which is the same as constant correlation $\rho = 0$. Now, we set $\bar{\rho}_0 = 0.3$ and keep the value of all other parameters unchanged, then display the curves of $\bar{\rho}_t$ in Fig. 1b.

Next, we fix $\kappa = 2$ and $\mu = 0.5$ and then display $\bar{\rho}_t$ for the varying $\sigma = 0.5,\ 1$ and 2 in Fig. 2. Obviously, σ shows the magnitude of variation from the transformed mean value of X_t ($\mu = 0.5$). In Fig. 2a we see, the larger the value of σ is, the stronger the deviations of $\bar{\rho}_t$ is from the transformed mean value of X_t. More interesting is that $\bar{\rho}_t$ first decreases until $t \approx 0.25$, then increases and converges to a value, see Fig. 2b where $\bar{\rho}_0 = 0.3$ and $\sigma = 2$.

Again, in order to illustrate the role of κ, we set $\mu = 0.5,\ \sigma = 2$ and vary the value of κ, see Fig. 3. From Fig. 3a it is easy to observe that κ represents the speed of $\bar{\rho}_t$ tending to its limit. Especially, as we have seen in Fig. 2b, the curve is more

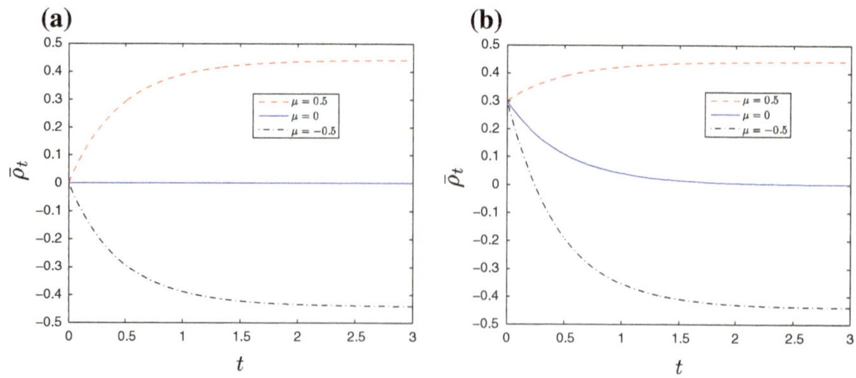

Fig. 1 Dynamic correlation $\bar{\rho}_t$ for varying μ ($\kappa = 2$ and $\sigma = 0.5$). **a** $\bar{\rho}_0 = 0$. **b** $\bar{\rho}_0 = 0.3$

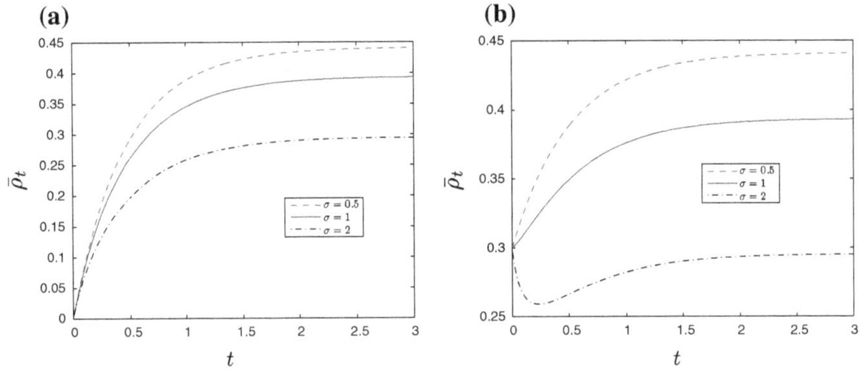

Fig. 2 Dynamic correlation $\bar{\rho}_t$ for varying σ ($\kappa = 2$ and $\mu = 0.5$). **a** $\bar{\rho}_0 = 0$. **b** $\bar{\rho}_0 = 0.3$

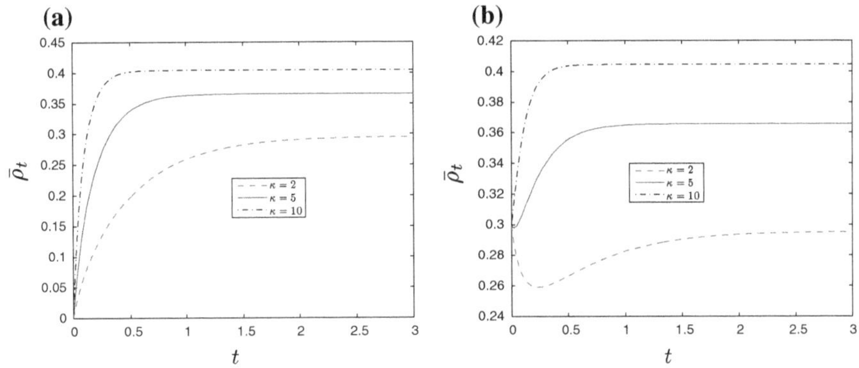

Fig. 3 Dynamic correlation $\bar{\rho}_t$ for varying κ ($\mu = 0.5$ and $\sigma = 2$). **a** $\bar{\rho}_0 = 0$. **b** $\bar{\rho}_0 = 0.3$

unstable for $\kappa = 2$ and $\sigma = 2$ in Fig. 3b. However, if σ remains constant while the value of κ is increased, we can see that curves of $\bar{\rho}_t$ become more stable and tend straightly to its limit. If one incorporates the dynamic correlation function (8) to a financial model, the parameter $\bar{\rho}_0$, κ, μ, and σ could be estimated by fitting the model to market data.

3 Dynamically Correlated BMs and Their Construction

We fix a probability space $(\Omega, \mathscr{F}, \mathbb{P})$ and an information filtration $(\mathscr{F}_t)_{t\in\mathbb{R}^+}$, satisfying the usual conditions, see e.g. [11]. At a time $t > 0$, the correlation coefficient of two Brownian motions (BMs) W_t^1 and W_t^2 is defined as

$$\rho_t^{1,2} = \frac{E\left[W_t^1 W_t^2\right]}{t}. \tag{9}$$

If we assume that $\rho_t^{1,2}$ is constant, $\rho_t^{1,2} = \rho^{1,2}$ for all $t > 0$, say W_t^1 and W_t^2 are correlated with the constant $\rho^{1,2}$.

Therefore, we give the definition of dynamically correlated BMs.

Definition 1 Two Brownian motions W_t^1 and W_t^2 are called *dynamically correlated* with correlation function ρ_t, if they satisfy

$$E\left[W_t^1 W_t^2\right] = \int_0^t \rho_s ds, \tag{10}$$

where $\rho_t : [0, t] \to [-1, 1]$. The *average correlation* of W_t^1 and W_t^2, ρ_{Av}, is given by $\rho_{Av} := \frac{1}{t}\int_0^t \rho_s ds$.

We consider first the two-dimensional case and let ρ_t be a correlation function. For two independent BMs W_t^1 and W_t^3 we define

$$W_t^2 = \int_0^t \rho_s dW_s^1 + \int_0^t \sqrt{1-\rho_s^2}\, dW_s^3, \tag{11}$$

with the symbolic expression

$$dW_t^2 = \rho_t dW_t^1 + \sqrt{1-\rho_t^2}\, dW_t^3. \tag{12}$$

It can be easily verified that W_t^2 is a BM and correlated with W_t^1 dynamically by ρ_t. Besides, the covariance matrix and the average correlation matrix of $\mathbb{W}_t = (W_t^1, W_t^2)$ can be determined, given by

$$\begin{pmatrix} t & \int_0^t \rho_s ds \\ \int_0^t \rho_s ds & t \end{pmatrix} \quad \text{and} \quad \begin{pmatrix} 1 & \frac{1}{t}\int_0^t \rho_s ds \\ \frac{1}{t}\int_0^t \rho_s ds & 1 \end{pmatrix},$$

respectively.

The construction above could be also generalized to n-dimensions. We denote a standard n-dimensional BM by $\mathbb{Z}_t = (Z_{1,t}, \ldots, Z_{n,t})$ and the matrix of dynamic correlations $\mathscr{R}_t = (\rho_t^{i,j})_{1<i,j<n}$ which has the Cholesky decomposition for each time t, $\mathscr{R}_t = \mathbb{A}_t \mathbb{A}_t^\top$ with $\mathbb{A}_t = (a_t^{i,j})_{1<i,j<n}$. We define a new n-dimensional process $\mathbb{W}_t = (W_{1,t}, \ldots, W_{n,t})$ by

$$W_{i,t} = \sum_{j=1}^{n} a_t^{ij}\, dZ_{j,t}, \quad i = 1, \ldots, n. \tag{13}$$

We can easily verify that $\mathbb{W}_t$ satisfies the following properties:

- $\mathbb{W}_0 = \mathbf{0}$ and the paths are continuous with probability 1.
- The increments $\mathbb{W}_{t_1} - \mathbb{W}_{t_0}$ and $\mathbb{W}_{t_2} - \mathbb{W}_{t_1}$ are independent for $0 \le t_0 < t_1 < t_2 < t$.
- For $0 \le s < t$, the increment $\mathbb{W}_t - \mathbb{W}_s$ is multivariate normally distributed with mean zero and covariance matrix $\Sigma : \mathbb{W}_t - \mathbb{W}_s \sim N(0, \Sigma)$ with

$$\Sigma = \begin{pmatrix} t-s & \int_s^t \rho_u^{1,2} du & \dots & \int_s^t \rho_u^{1,n} du \\ \int_s^t \rho_u^{2,1} du & t-s & \dots & \int_s^t \rho_u^{2,n} du \\ \vdots & \vdots & \ddots & \vdots \\ \int_s^t \rho_u^{n,1} du & \int_s^t \rho_u^{n,2} du & \dots & t-s \end{pmatrix}.$$

We call the process $(\mathbb{W}_t)_{t \ge 0}$ *an n-dimensional dynamically correlated Brownian motion,* with the correlation matrix $\mathscr{R}_t$.

4 Dynamic Correlation in the Heston Model

As mentioned before, in many situations the pure Heston model has a limitation on reproducing properly a volatility smile. For this problem, several time-dependent Heston models have been proposed for good fitting to implied volatilities, e.g. [6] and [10]. In this section, we show how to incorporate our time-dependent correlation function into the Heston model.

4.1 Incorporating Dynamic Correlations

Heston's stochastic volatility model is specified as

$$dS_t = \mu_S S_t dt + \sqrt{v_t}\, S_t\, dW_t^S, \tag{14}$$

$$dv_t = \kappa_v(\mu_v - v_t)dt + \sigma_v \sqrt{v_t}\, dW_t^v, \tag{15}$$

where (14) is the price of the spot asset, (15) is the volatility (variance) and W_t^S and W_t^v are correlated with a constant correlation ρ_{Sv}. To incorporate the time-dependent correlations, we assume that dS_t and dv_t are correlated by a time-dependent correlation function $\bar{\rho}_t$ instead of the constant correlation ρ_{Sv}. The extended Heston model with dynamic correlation $\bar{\rho}$ is specified as

$$dS_t = \mu_S S_t dt + \sqrt{v_t}\, S_t\, dW_t^1, \tag{16}$$

$$dv_t = \kappa_v(\mu_v - v_t)dt + \sigma_v \sqrt{v_t} \left(\bar{\rho}_t\, dW_t^1 + \sqrt{1 - \bar{\rho}_t^2}\, dW_t^2 \right), \tag{17}$$

where W_t^1 and W_t^2 are independent. Applying Itô's lemma and no-arbitrage arguments yields [9]

$$\frac{1}{2}\nu S^2\frac{\partial^2 U}{\partial S^2} + \bar{\rho}_t\sigma_\nu\nu S\frac{\partial^2 U}{\partial S\partial\nu} + \frac{1}{2}\sigma_\nu^2\nu\frac{\partial^2 U}{\partial\nu^2} + rS\frac{\partial U}{\partial S} + [\kappa_\nu(\mu_\nu - \nu) - \tilde{\lambda}(S, \nu, \bar{\rho}, t)\nu]\frac{\partial U}{\partial\nu} - rU + \frac{\partial U}{\partial t} = 0, \quad (18)$$

where $\bar{\rho}_t$ is defined in (8) but with the parameter $\bar{\rho}_0$, κ_ρ, μ_ρ, and ν_ρ. It is worth mentioning that the market price of volatility risk depends also on the dynamic correlation, which could be written as $\tilde{\lambda}(S, \nu, \bar{\rho}_t, t)$. This means, the price of correlation risk embedding in the price of volatility risk has been considered.

We consider, e.g. a European call option with strike price K and maturity T in the Heston model

$$C(S, \nu, t, \bar{\rho}_t) = SP_1 - KP(t, T)P_2, \quad \tau = T - t, \quad (19)$$

where $P(t, T)$ is the discount factor and both in-the-money probabilities P_1, P_2 must satisfy the PDE (18) as well as their characteristic functions, $f_1(S_t, \nu_t, \bar{\rho}_t, \phi, t)$ and $f_2(S_t, \nu_t, \bar{\rho}_t, \phi, t)$

$$f_j(S_t, \nu_t, \bar{\rho}_t, \phi, t) = E[\mathrm{e}^{i\phi\ln S_T}|S_t, \nu_t, \bar{\rho}_t] = \mathrm{e}^{C_j(\tau,\phi)+D_j(\tau,\phi)\nu+i\phi\ln S_t}, \quad j = 1, 2, \quad (20)$$

where $C_j(0, \phi) = 0$ and $D_j(0, \phi) = 0$. By substituting this functional form (20) into the PDE (18) we can obtain the following ordinary differential equations (ODEs) for the unknown functions C and D:

$$-\frac{1}{2}\phi^2 + \bar{\rho}_t\sigma_\nu\phi iD_j + \frac{1}{2}\sigma_\nu^2D_j^2 + u_j\phi i - b_jD_j + \frac{\partial D_j}{\partial t} = 0, \quad (21)$$

$$r\phi i + \kappa_\nu\mu_\nu D_j + \frac{\partial C_j}{\partial t} = 0, \quad (22)$$

with the initial conditions $C_j(0, \phi) = D_j(0, \phi) = 0$

$$u_1 = 0.5, \quad u_2 = -0.5, \quad b_1 = \kappa_\nu + \lambda - \bar{\rho}_t\sigma_\nu \quad \text{and} \quad b_2 = \kappa_\nu + \lambda, \quad (23)$$

where

$$\bar{\rho}_t = 1 - \frac{\mathrm{e}^{-A(t)-\frac{B(t)}{2}}}{2}\int_{-\infty}^{\infty}\underbrace{\frac{1}{\cosh(\frac{\pi u}{2})}\cdot\mathrm{e}^{iu(A(t)+B(t))+u^2\frac{B(t)}{2}}}_{:=g(u)}du, \quad (24)$$

with $A(t) = \mathrm{e}^{-\kappa_\rho t}\mathrm{artanh}(\bar{\rho}_0) + \mu_\rho(1 - \mathrm{e}^{-\kappa_\rho t})$, $B(t) = -\frac{\sigma_\rho^2}{2\kappa_\rho}(1 - \mathrm{e}^{-2\kappa_\rho t})$.

Obviously, (21) and (22) cannot be solved analytically. Therefore, we need to find an efficient way to compute the option price numerically. We firstly generate the

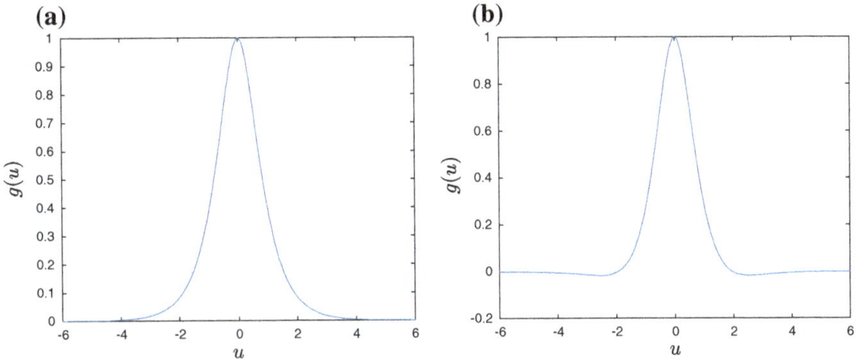

Fig. 4 $g(u)$ under $\rho_0 = 0.3, \kappa_\rho = 2, \mu_\rho = -0.8, \sigma_\rho = 0.1$. **a** $t = 0.1$. **b** $t = 10$

dynamic correlations using (24). We observe that $g(u)$ is a symmetric function about $u = 0$ and vanishes (approaches zero) for a sufficiently large absolute value of u, see Fig. 4. For these two reasons, the numerical integration in (24) is computationally fast. Next we use an explicit Runge–Kutta method, the matlab routine `ode45`, to obtain C and D in (21) and (22) and thus also the characteristic functions (20). Finally, we employ the COS method [8] to obtain the option price $C(S, \nu, t, \bar{\rho})$ in (19). Thanks to the COS method, although we solved that ODE system numerically, the time for obtaining European option prices is less than 0.1 s so that a calibration can be performed. Obviously, the error consists of the error using `ode45` for (21) and (22) and the error using COS method. The detailed analysis of error using COS method has been provided in [8].

4.2 *Calibration of the Heston Model Under Dynamic Correlation*

In this section we calibrate the Heston model extended by our time-dependent correlation function to the real market data (Nikk300 index call options on July 16, 2012) and compare these to the pure Heston model [9] and the time-dependent Heston model [10].

We consider a set of N maturities $T_i,\ i = 1, \ldots, N$ and a set of M strikes $K_j,\ j = 1, \ldots, M$. Then for each combination of maturity and strike we have a market price $V^M(T_i, K_j) = V_{ij}^M$ and a corresponding model price $V(T_i, K_j; \Theta) = V_{ij}^\Theta$ generated by using (19). We choose the relative mean error sum of squares (RMSE) for the loss function $\frac{1}{M \times N} \sum_{i,j} \frac{(V_{ij}^M - V_{ij}^\Theta)^2}{V_{ij}^M}$, which can be minimized to obtain the parameter estimates

$$\hat{\Theta} = \arg\min \frac{1}{M \times N} \sum_{i,j} \frac{(V_{ij}^M - V_{ij}^\Theta)^2}{V_{ij}^M}. \tag{25}$$

For the optimization we restrict $\bar{\rho}_0$ to the interval $(-1, 1)$ but not the value of μ_ρ. Since it is not the direct limit of the correlation function but the mean reversion of the Ornstein–Uhlenbeck process, thus, it could take any value in $\mathbb{R}$. Our experiments showed, that it is sufficient and appropriate to restrict μ_ρ to the interval $[-4, 4]$.

We state our estimated parameters and the estimation error for the pure Heston model (abbr. PH), the Heston model under our time-dependent correlations (CH), the time-dependent Heston model by Mikhailov and Ngel [10] (MN) in Tables 1, 2 and 3, respectively. We see that the estimation error using the CH model is significantly less than the error using the PH model and almost the same to the error (sum of errors for each maturity) under the MN model. To illustrate more clearly, for each maturity we compare the implied volatilities for all the models to the market volatilities in Fig. 5. We can observe that the implied volatilities for the CH model are much closer to the market volatilities than the implied volatilities for the PH model, especially the CH model has better volatility smile for the short maturity $T = 1/12$. Compared to the MN model, the implied volatilities for our model are almost the same. However, our CH model has an economic interpretation, namely the correlation is nonlinear

Table 1 The estimated parameters for the pure Heston model using call options on the Nikk300 index on July 16, 2012 for the maturities 1/12, 1/4, 1/2, 1

The pure heston model

$\hat{\nu}_0$	$\hat{\kappa}_\nu$	$\hat{\mu}_\nu$	$\hat{\sigma}_\nu$	$\hat{\rho}$	Estimation error
0.029	4.746	0.053	1.108	−0.355	1.10×10^{-3}

Table 2 The estimated parameters for the Heston model under time-dependent correlations using call options on the Nikk300 index on July 16, 2012 for the maturities 1/12, 1/4, 1/2, 1

The extended Heston model by using our time-dependent correlation function

$\hat{\nu}_0$	$\hat{\kappa}_\nu$	$\hat{\mu}_\nu$	$\hat{\sigma}_\nu$	$\hat{\bar{\rho}}_0$	$\hat{\kappa}_\rho$	$\hat{\mu}_\rho$	$\hat{\sigma}_\rho$	Estimation error
0.027	5.542	0.055	1.224	−0.165	5.333	−0.752	0.434	2.38×10^{-4}

Table 3 The estimated parameters for the time-dependent Heston model by Mikhailov and Ngel using call options on the Nikk300 index on July 16, 2012

The time-dependent Heston model by Mikhailov and Ngel

Maturity	$\hat{\nu}_0$	$\hat{\kappa}_\nu$	$\hat{\mu}_\nu$	$\hat{\sigma}_\nu$	$\hat{\rho}$	Estimation error
1/12	0.025	2.749	0.095	1.172	−0.201	1.78×10^{-4}
1/4	0.012	2.936	0.076	0.524	−0.411	2.45×10^{-5}
1/2	0.011	2.890	0.058	0.592	−0.430	1.14×10^{-5}
1	0.001	2.911	0.051	0.558	−0.389	4.28×10^{-6}

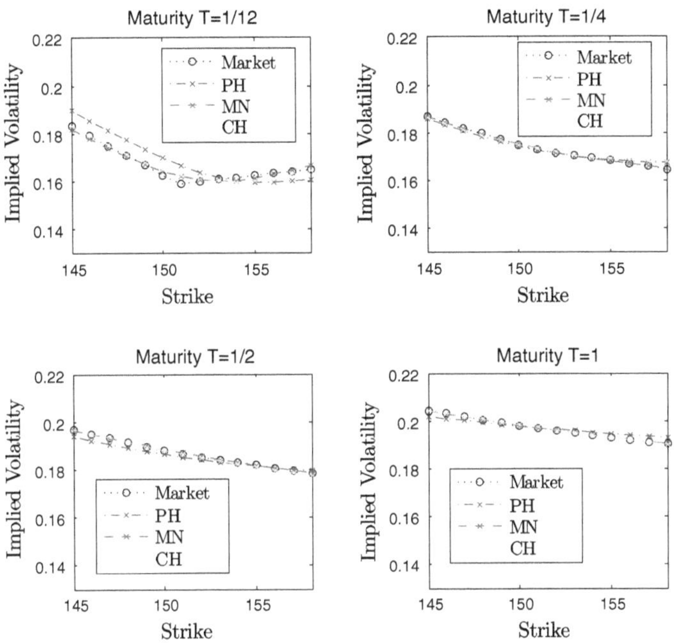

Fig. 5 The comparison of implied volatilities for all the models to the market volatilities of the call options on the Nikk300 index on July 16, 2012, where the spot price is 150.9

and time-dependent as market requires. We conclude that the Heston model extended by incorporating our time-dependent correlations can provide better volatility smiles compared to the pure Heston model. The time-dependent correlation function can be easily and directly introduced into the financial models.

5 Conclusion

In this work, we first investigated the dynamically (time-dependent) correlated Brownian motions and their construction. Furthermore, we proposed a new dynamic correlation function which can be easily incorporated into another financial model. The aim of using our dynamic correlation function is to reasonably choose additional parameters to increase the fitting quality on the one-hand side, but also add an economically meaningful perspective.

As an application, we incorporated our time-dependent correlation function into the Heston model. An experiment on estimation of the models using real market data has been provided. The numerical calibration results show that the Heston model extended by using our time-dependent correlation function provides better volatility smiles compared to the pure Heston model. Besides, this time-dependent correlation function could be easily and directly imposed to the financial models and thus it is preferred to use instead of a constant correlation.

Acknowledgements The authors acknowledge the much appreciated inspiration and in-depth discussions with Dr. Jörg Kienitz from Deloitte Düsseldorf, Germany.

The work was partially supported by the European Union in the FP7-PEOPLE-2012-ITN Program under Grant Agreement Number 304617 (FP7 Marie Curie Action, Project Multi-ITN STRIKE—Novel Methods in Computational Finance).

The KPMG Center of Excellence in Risk Management is acknowledged for organizing the conference "Challenges in Derivatives Markets—Fixed Income Modeling, Valuation Adjustments, Risk Management, and Regulation".

References

1. Brigo, D., Capponi, A.: Bilateral counterparty risk with application to CDSs. Risk Mag. **23**(3), 85–90 (2010)
2. Brigo, D., Chourdakis, K.: Counterparty risk for credit default swaps: impact of spread volatility and default correlation. Int. J. Theoret. Appl. Financ. **12**, 1007–1026 (2009)
3. Campbell, J., Lo, A., MacKinlay, A.: The Econometrics of Financial Markets. Princeton University Press, Princeton (1997)
4. Chen, H., Joslin, S.: Generalized transform analysis of affine processes and applications in finance. Rev. Fin. Stud. **25**(7), 2225–2256 (2012)
5. Duffie, D., Filipović, D., Schachermayer, W.: Affine processes and applications in finance. Ann. Appl. Probab. **13**(3), 984–1053 (2003)
6. Elices, A.: Affine concatenation. Wilmott J. **1**(3), 155–162 (2009)
7. Escobar, M., Götz, B., Neykova, D., Zagst, R.: Stochastic correlation and volatility mean-reversion - empirical motivation and derivatives pricing via perturbation theory. Appl. Math. Fin. **21**(6), 555–594 (2014)
8. Fang, F., Oosterlee, C.W.: A novel pricing method for European options based on Fourier-cosine series expansions. SIAM J. Sci. Comput. **31**, 826–848 (2008)
9. Heston, S.L.: A closed-form solution for options with stochastic volatility with applications to bond and currency options. Rev. Fin. Stud. **6**(2), 327–343 (1993)
10. Mikhailov, S., Nögel, U.: Heston's stochastic volatility model: implementation, calibration and some extensions. Wilmott Mag. 74–79 (2003)
11. Øksendal, B.: Stochastic Differential Equations. Springer, Berlin (2002)
12. Teng, L., Ehrhardt, M., Günther, M.: Bilateral counterparty risk valuation of CDS contracts with simultaneous defaults. Int. J. Theoret. Appl. Financ. **16**(7), 1350040 (2013)
13. Teng, L., van Emmerich, C., Ehrhardt, M., Günther, M.: A versatile approach for stochastic correlation using hyperbolic functions. Int. J. Comput. Math. **93**(3), 524–539 (2016)
14. Uhlenbeck, G.E., Ornstein, L.S.: On the theory of Brownian motion. Phys. Rev. **36**, 823–841 (1930)

9

Pricing Shared-Loss Hedge Fund Fee Structures

Ben Djerroud, David Saunders, Luis Seco and Mohammad Shakourifar

Abstract The asset management business is driven by fee structures. In the context of hedge funds, fees have usually been a hybrid combination of two different types, which has coined a well-known business term of "2 and 20". As an attempt to provide better alignment with their investors, in a new context of low interest rates and lukewarm performance, a new type of fund fees has been introduced in the last few years that offers a more symmetric payment structure, which we will refer to as *shared loss*. In this framework, in return for receiving performance fees, the fund manager provides some downside protection against losses to the investors. We show that the position values of the investor and the hedge fund manager can be formulated as portfolios of options, and discuss issues regarding pricing and fairness of the fee rates, and incentives for both investors and hedge fund managers. In particular, we will be able to show that, from a present value perspective, these fee structures can be set up as being favorable either to the hedge fund manager or to the investor. The paper is based on an arbitrage-free pricing framework. However, if one is to take

This research was supported in part by the Natural Sciences and Engineering Research Council of Canada.

B. Djerroud · M. Shakourifar (✉)
Sigma Analysis & Management, Toronto, ON, Canada
e-mail: mohammad@sigmanalysis.com

B. Djerroud
e-mail: ben_d@sigmanalysis.com

D. Saunders
Department of Statistics and Actuarial Science, University of Waterloo, Waterloo, Canada
e-mail: dsaunders@uwaterloo.ca

L. Seco
Department of Mathematics, University of Toronto, Toronto, Canada
e-mail: seco@math.utoronto.ca

into account the value to the business that investor capital brings to a fund, which is not part of our framework, it is possible to create a situation where both investors as well as asset managers win.

Keywords Hedge funds · Fee structures · First-loss · Shared-loss · Black-Scholes option pricing

1 Introduction

Hedge Funds are pooled investment vehicles overseen by a management company. They generally aim at absolute return portfolios and their success is usually linked to market inefficiencies, such as instrument mispricing, misguided market consensus or, in general terms, the manager's intelligence to anticipate market moves. The nature of these investments is that they exploit investment opportunities that are rare. This is a characteristic that they share with private equity investments, but they share with the mutual fund industry the fact that they often trade in liquid, marketable securities. Fund sizes are more in line with private equity investing than with the mammoth mutual fund industry. Their compensation structure, because of their limited access to opportunity, is also more in line with the private equity universe, and usually consists in a fixed, asset-based fee, and a variable, performance fee base. Because of market conditions that have been in place over the last several years, in particular the low interest rate environment, coupled with the lukewarm performance of the hedge fund sector in the recent years, investors have become increasingly more sensitive to fee structures. The traditional 2&20 fee structure, consisting of a flat fee of 2 % of assets under management together with a performance fee of 20 % of net profits is considered unfair on the basis of the asymmetry: the management company will always earn a fee, whereas the investor is only guaranteed to pay that fee. The advent of the 40-ACT funds[1] has, in particular, dispensed with the performance fee base in favor of a fixed management fee, which is more in line with the mutual fund industry than with the hedge fund industry. This compensation model essentially rewards funds for becoming asset gatherers instead of the alpha-seeking business the hedge fund was set out to be. In this paper we will examine, from a quantitative perspective, a suite of symmetric performance fee structures which are gaining traction with more sophisticated investors, known as first-loss (or shared-loss) fee structures. In this new framework, in return for receiving performance fees, the fund manager provides some downside protection against losses to the investors.

The issue of the incentives created by hedge fund fees bears much similarity to issues surrounding the structure of executive compensation. At first glance, the optionality inherent in both would seem to incentivize greater risk taking. However, the reality is more subtle. Carpenter [2] studies the case of executive compensation,

[1] Pooled investment vehicles, enforced and regulated by the Securities and Exchange Commission, that are packaged and sold to retail and institutional investors in the public markets.

when the manager cannot hedge options provided as compensation by trading the underlying. In certain conditions, a utility-maximizing manager may choose to reduce rather than increase the volatility of the underlying firm. Ross [9] gives necessary and sufficient conditions for a fee schedule to make a utility-maximizing manager more or less risk-averse. Hodder and Jackwerth [6] consider the effects of hedge fund fee incentives on a risk manager with power utility, and also in the presence of a liquidation barrier. They find that over a one-year horizon, risk-taking varies dramatically with fund value, but that this effect is moderated over longer time horizons. Kouwenberg and Ziemba [7] consider loss-averse hedge fund managers and find that higher incentive fees lead to riskier fund management strategies. However, this effect is reduced if a significant portion of the manager's own money is invested in the fund. They further provide empirical evidence showing that hedge funds with incentive fees have significantly lower mean returns (net of fees), and find a positive correlation between fee levels and downside risk. They find that risk is increasing with respect to the performance fee if the manager's objective function is based on cumulative prospect theory, rather than utility, and provide empirical evidence. Recent work on the analysis of hedge fund fee structures includes that of Goetzmann et al. [3], who value a fee structure with a highwater mark provision, using a PDE approach with a fixed investment portfolio, Panageas and Westerfield [8], who consider the portfolio selection decision of maximizing the present value of fees for a risk-neutral manager over an infinite horizon, and Guasoni and Obłój [4], who extend this work to managers with risk-averse power utility. Closest to the current work is He and Kou [5], who analyze shared-loss fee structures for hedge funds by looking at the portfolio selection decision of a hedge fund manager whose preferences are modeled using cumulative prospect theory. The problem is considered in the presence of a manager investing in the fund, and with a predetermined liquidation barrier. Analytical solutions of the portfolio selection problem are provided, and the result (cumulative prospect theory) for both the investor and the manager is examined. It is found that depending on the parameter values, either a traditional fee structure or a first-loss fee structure may result in a riskier investment strategy. While for some parameter values, the first-loss structure improves the utility of both the investor and the hedge fund manager, they find that for typical values, the manager is better off, while the investor is worse off. In this paper, we investigate the shared-loss fee structures from the perspective of risk-neutral valuation, with no further assumptions about investor preferences, while He and Kou [5] solve the stochastic control problem (under the real-world measure) corresponding to the manager maximizing the utility function from cumulative prospect theory, and also evaluate the investor's payoff using the same type of criterion.

The paper is organized as follows. First, we will review the traditional fee structures in some detail. Next, we will introduce the notion and mechanics of the first-loss structures, and a framework for a fee pricing based on the theory of option price valuation. After that, we will introduce the concept of net fee, a number that will allow us to determine whether the investor or the management company is the net winner in a given fee agreement. Finally, we will present a set of computational examples that will display the net fee as a function of the agreement and market variables.

2 Hedge Fund Fees

The hedge fund manager charges two types of fees to the fund investors:

- A fixed management fee, usually ranging from 1 % to 2 % of net asset values.
- A performance fee, most commonly equal to 20 % of net profits obtained by the fund.

In this paper we assume a single investor and a single share issued by the fund. The extension to the case of multiple investors and multiple shares is straightforward. Although fees are paid according to a determined schedule (usually monthly or quarterly for management fees and annual for performance fees), we will assume a single payment at the end of a fixed term T.

The fund value evolution and fee payment mechanics are denoted as follows: the initial fund supplied by the investor is X_0. The hedge fund manager then invests fund assets to create future gross values X_t, for $t > 0$. The gross fund value X_t is split between the investor's worth I_t (the net asset value) and the manager's fee M_t:

$$X_t = I_t + M_t .$$

At time 0, $X_0 = I_0$ and $M_0 = 0$.

There are countless variations to this basic framework, including hurdles, claw-backs, etc. (for more details on first-loss arrangements see Banzaca [1]). We will ignore those and assume the commonly used version of a management fee equal to $m \cdot X_0$ (m represents a fixed percentage of the initial investment by the investor), and a performance fee of

$$\alpha \cdot (X_T - (1+m)X_0))_+ ,$$

payable only when it is positive, and equal to zero when it is negative. Hence,

$$M_T = m \cdot X_0 + \alpha \cdot (X_T - (1+m)X_0)_+) \tag{1}$$

In other words, while the management fee is a fixed future liability to the investor, the performance fee is a contingent claim on the part of the manager. As a consequence, we will be pricing the management fee simply as a fixed guaranteed fee with a predetermined future cash value, and we will be valuing the performance fee as the value of a certain call option. In our setting, we will assume normally distributed log-returns for the invested assets X_t, which allows us to value the performance fee in the Black–Scholes framework. It is worth mentioning that hedge funds managers can speculate on volatility, credit risks, etc. and in contrast to the traditional money managers, they can go long and short. The diversity in investment styles and the different levels of gross and net exposure that they can employ could result in leptokurtic (non-normal) properties in their returns, which is revealed through frequent large negative returns to the left of the return distribution. Generalization of the current framework to models that account for non-normality of the hedge fund returns, for example by employing generalized autoregressive conditional heteroskedasticity (GARCH) models, could be a subject for future research.

3 The First-Loss Model

Calpers announced in 2014 that they were exiting hedge fund investments WSJ [10]. While not the main stated reason for their decision, one they mentioned was high fees payable to their hedge fund managers, something that has caught the attention of investors worldwide in the contemporary context of a widely accepted notion that hedge fund fees nowadays are too high. Certain hedge funds are reacting to this shifting balance of power between the sell-side and the buy-side of the investment business with the creation of innovative fee structures which still reward the intellectual capital of the hedge fund manager and allow for business growth but at the same time offer the investor a more symmetric compensation structure.

An example of a first-loss structure is the following:

- The investor provides an investment of \$100M to a fund.
- The fund manager will absorb the first-loss up to 10 % of the initial investment.
- The investor pays a management fee of 1 % to the manager, and performance fee of 50 %.

In our paper we will present a quantitative comparison of the fees payable to the manager and the risk-neutral valuation of the guarantee offered to the investor. We want to note, for the sake of completeness, that there are many other qualitative considerations which are relevant when analyzing both the fee structure as well as the business value offered to a management company by the investor, which are not the objective of this paper. In fact, hedge fund start-ups have become more difficult in recent times, increasing value to any investor action that allows a hedge fund business to succeed. That value is linked to a wide variety of fund characteristics, including the size of assets under management (AUM), the track record, or historical performance, and the reputation of its investor base, among others.

In addition to the initial investment X_0, the management fee m and the performance fee α, payable at a fixed time horizon T, we will now also consider a deposit amount c, as a percentage of the initial investment X_0, which the manager will provide as a guarantee for losses. Our objective is to analyze the relationship between all four variables to determine whether the investor, or the manager, is the net winner of value-add from a risk-neutral valuation perspective.

4 An Option Pricing Framework

The fund value X_t is split between the investors I_t and the manager M_t, where, $X_t = I_t + M_t$. In the following sub-sections we derive the payoff function of each player separately, and then price the positions accordingly.

4.1 *Payoff to the Investor*

The payoff to the investor at the terminal time T is:

$$I_T = \begin{cases} X_T - mX_0 - \alpha(X_T - mX_0 - X_0) & \text{when } X_T - mX_0 \geq X_0 \\ X_0 & \text{when } (1-c)X_0 \leq X_T - mX_0 \leq X_0 \\ X_T + (c-m)X_0 & \text{when } X_T - mX_0 \leq (1-c)X_0 \end{cases}$$

or, writing the payoff in a more compact form:

$$\begin{aligned} I_T = \quad & X_T - mX_0 && \text{(pays a management fee)} \\ & -\alpha(X_T - mX_0 - X_0)_+ && \text{(pays a performance fee)} \\ & +(X_0 - X_T + mX_0)_+ - ((1-c)X_0 - X_T + mX_0)_+ && \text{(receives a guarantee)} \end{aligned}$$

Thus, we see that the position of the investor is equivalent to the following portfolio:

- A position in the hedge fund assets, with initial investment X_0, less management fee, that is, $X_0 - mX_0$.
- A short position in α call options on the hedge fund assets, with strike price $X_0 + mX_0$ (the performance fee, or performance call option, given to the hedge fund manager).
- A long position in a put option on the fund assets, with the strike price $X_0 + mX_0$ (the insurance put option).
- A short position in a put option on the fund assets, with strike price $(1-c)X_0 + mX_0$ (yielding a cap on the insurance payment).

4.2 *Payoff to the Manager*

The payoff to the manager is $M_T = X_T - I_T$. In other words, the payoff to the hedge fund manager results from the manager having the opposite position in all of the options of the investor. More explicitly,

$$
\begin{aligned}
M_T = \quad & mX_0 && \text{(receives a management fee)}\\
& +\alpha(X_T - mX_0 - X_0)_+ && \text{(receives a performance fee)}\\
-(X_0 - X_T + mX_0)_+ + & ((1-c)X_0 - X_T + mX_0)_+ && \text{(provides a guarantee)}
\end{aligned}
$$

which implies that the hedge fund manager has a portfolio of options consisting of:

- A constant position in the fixed management fee of mX_0.
- A long position in α call options on the hedge fund assets, with strike price $X_0 + mX_0$.
- A short position in a put option on the fund assets, with the strike price $X_0 + mX_0$.
- A long position in a put option on the fund assets, with strike price $(1-c)X_0 + mX_0$.

Note that net income to the management company is now no longer guaranteed to be positive. In addition, since the options trades constitute a zero-sum game (the positions of the manager and the investor are opposite each other), the sum of the investor payoff and the manager payoff is equal to X_T.

4.3 Valuation: Pricing Fees as Derivatives

In this section, we will value the positions of the investor and the hedge fund manager using a simple Black–Scholes model for the underlying fund value process. In particular, we employ risk-neutral valuation, and assume that under the risk-neutral probabilities, the fund value process satisfies the stochastic differential equation:

$$dX_t = rX_t\,dt \;+\; \sigma\, X_t\, dW_t, \tag{2}$$

with solution:

$$X_t = X_0 \exp\left((r - \tfrac{\sigma^2}{2})t + \sigma W_t\right) \tag{3}$$

where W_t is a standard Brownian motion, and r and σ are positive constants, giving the continuously compounded risk-free interest rate and the volatility of the hedge fund assets respectively. It should be noted that the Black–Scholes framework is applicable to our context as the underlying, that is the fund value, can be dynamically traded. Moreover, in a managed account context, even the liquidity of the fund can be made to match the liquidity of the underlying traded securities.

The Black–Scholes formula can be used to derive the price of the investor's position under the Black–Scholes model:

$$
\begin{aligned}
V_I(0) = X_0 - e^{-rT}mX_0 - \alpha C(X_0, T, X_0 + mX_0, r, \sigma)&\\
+P(X_0, T, X_0 + mX_0, r, \sigma) - P(X_0, T, (1-c)X_0 + mX_0, r, \sigma)& \quad (4)
\end{aligned}
$$

where $C(X, T, K, r, \sigma)$ is the Black–Scholes price of a call option on a non-dividend paying asset with current value of the underlying X, time to expiration T, strike price

K, risk-free interest rate r and volatility σ, and $P(X, T, K, r, \sigma)$ is the Black–Scholes put option price with the same parameters as arguments.

5 Consequences of the Derivative Pricing Framework

5.1 *Graphical Analysis*

To compare and contrast the traditional and shared-loss fee structures, in our base case we take the investment horizon to be one month, that is $T = 1/12$, the performance fee $\alpha = 50\,\%$, the manager deposit $c = 10\,\%$, the risk-free interest rate $r = 2\,\%$, the volatility $\sigma = 15\,\%$, and the initial investment $X_0 = \$1$. For simplicity and without loss of generality we assume a *zero management fee* for our base case.

With our base case parameters, the total value of the investor's payoff is 1.0073, and the value of the manager's payoff is −0.0073. Notice that the value of the investor's payoff is greater than the initial investment of 1. In contrast, the price of the traditional investor payoff (without the insurance part of the payoff—i.e. removing both put options) is 0.9909, and the value of the manager's payoff in this instance is 0.0091.

5.1.1 Payoff Functions of the Investor and the Manager

The payoff functions of the investor under the shared-loss and the traditional fee structures are given in Fig. 1. The payoff to the hedge fund manager using the aforementioned benchmark values and under the shared-loss fee structure is also depicted in Fig. 2 along with the traditional payoff structure with only the performance fee $\alpha(X_T - X_0)_+$. Observe that since the options trades constitute a zero-sum game (the positions of the manager and the investor are opposite each other), the sum of the investor payoff and the manager payoff is equal to X_T.

Figure 3 illustrates the 'fair performance fee', where investor gets a payoff with present value equal to his initial cash injection, X_0, given volatility and manager's deposit levels, i.e. we set $V_I(0) = X_0$. The fair performance fee can be easily obtained from Eq. (4) as,

$$\alpha_{\text{fair}} = \frac{-e^{-rT} m X_0 + P(X_0, T, X_0 + mX_0, r, \sigma) - P(X_0, T, (1-c)X_0 + mX_0, r, \sigma)}{C(X_0, T, X_0 + mX_0, r, \sigma)}$$

Interested reader can derive explicit, well-known expressions for the sensitivities of the α_{fair} relative to different parameters in terms of the Greeks and Vega of the involving options. As can be seen from the figure, for small values of volatility, the fair performance fee is indifferent to the levels of manager's deposit; however, as volatility increases, a higher level of deposit by the manager translates into a higher

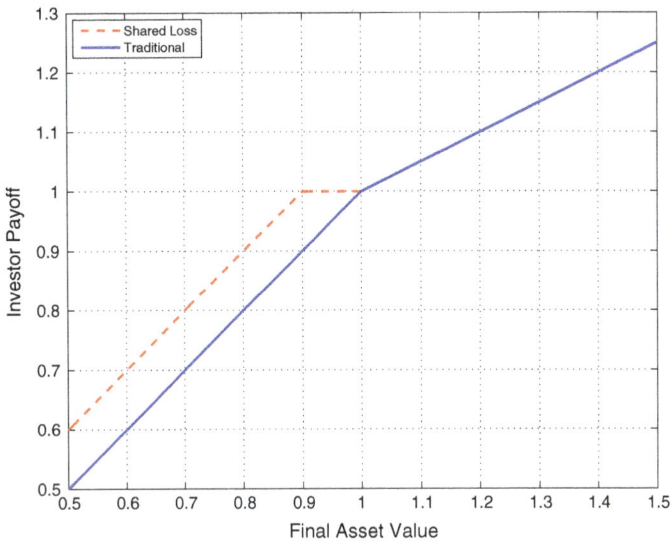

Fig. 1 Payoff for the hedge fund investor

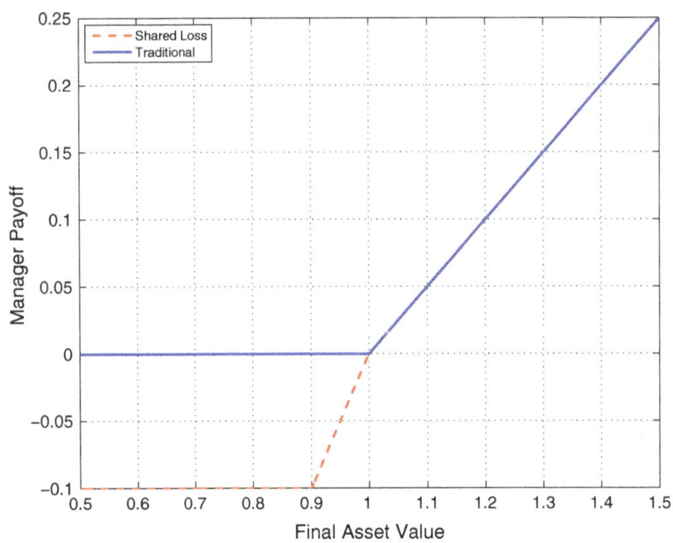

Fig. 2 Payoff for the hedge fund manager

performance fee paid by the investor to make the deal a fair one. In Fig. 4, we normalize the volatility on the horizontal axis by the manager's deposit defined *as a percentage of the initial investment* X_0. For a given level of deposit, the higher the volatility of the underlying investment, the higher the probability that the loss incurred by the manager exceeds the deposit. In other words, the probability that the manager

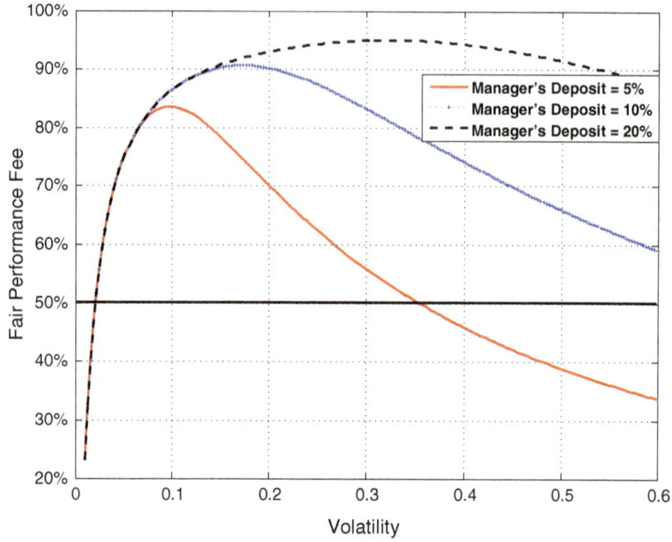

Fig. 3 Fair performance fee versus volatility

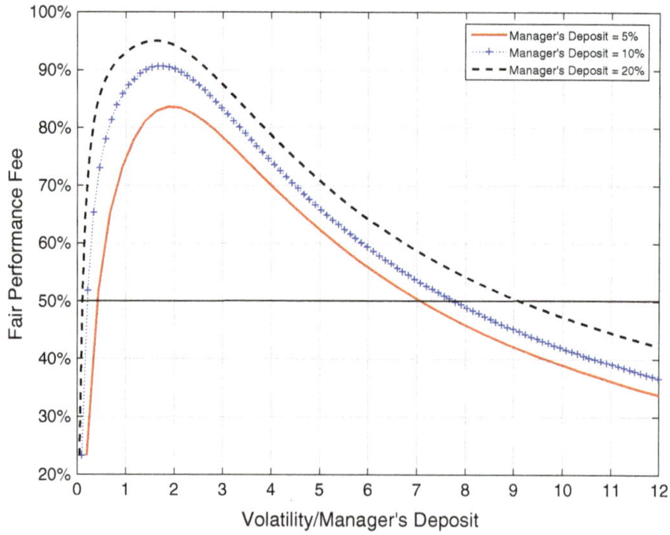

Fig. 4 Fair performance fee versus normalized (by deposit) volatility

exercises the put option offered by the investor increases, which results in a reversal in the fair performance fee for higher levels of volatility. This is clearly illustrated in Fig. 4 where volatility and deposit are combined in a single scaling variable, that is, volatility/deposit, *where the deposit is expressed as a percentage of the initial investment* X_0. The corresponding maximum value for the fair performance fee increases with the size of the deposit; that's because for higher deposits, the manager will have to lose more and more before the investor starts bearing the residual loss, therefore his compensation should be higher accordingly. Note that the x-axis in Figs. 3 and 4 is incorporating the annual volatility of the fund assets; however, the performance fee is crystallized on a monthly basis which suggests a comparison between the deposit level and *monthly* volatility, as opposed to annual volatility. Since returns are assumed to follow a normal distribution in our Black–Scholes framework, one can explicitly calculate the probability of the returns falling into a certain interval, in particular, with about 68 % probability, the return falls within 1 standard deviation of the mean. This explains why the curves for various deposits reach a maximum roughly around the same level of (annual) volatility/deposit ratio, in the $[1, 2]$ interval.

5.2 *Sensitivity Analysis*

In this section, we perform a sensitivity analysis of the prices of the investor's and manager's payouts, as a function of the different model parameters.

5.2.1 Volatility (σ)

Figure 5 shows the value of the investor's position as a function of the volatility parameter σ, as σ ranges from 5 % to 60 %.

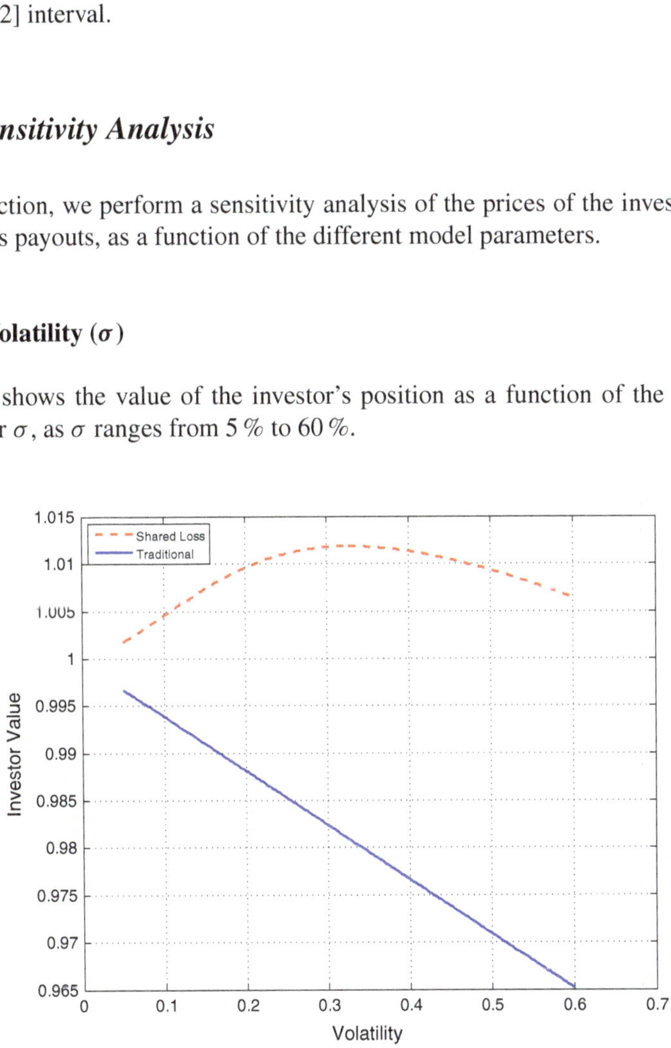

Fig. 5 Value of the investor's position versus volatility σ

We see that the position is initially an increasing function of the volatility, owing to the increasing value of the investor's put option as a function of σ. However, as the volatility becomes very large, the value of the investor's position starts to decline as the hedge fund's call option, as well as its put option, become more valuable. The maximum value for the investor occurs at a volatility around $\sigma = 32.5\,\%$. Observe however, that the value is relatively insensitive to the level of σ, with a minimum value of 1.0016, and a maximum value of 1.0118.

5.2.2 Manager Deposit (c)

We varied the manager deposit between 1 % and 25 %, while holding all other parameters at their base case values. The results of the sensitivity analysis are shown in Fig. 6.

As would be expected, the value of the investor's position is an increasing function of the manager's deposit. The value of the position is equal to one (break-even point, or 'fair fee point') at around $c = 0.0233$. Any deposit level less than $c = 0.0233$ puts the investor at a disadvantage, and the investor is indifferent to deposit levels higher than 10 %.

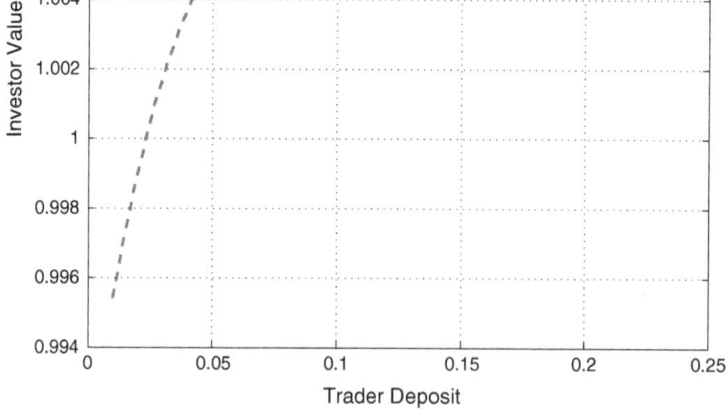

Fig. 6 Value of the investor's position versus manager's deposit c

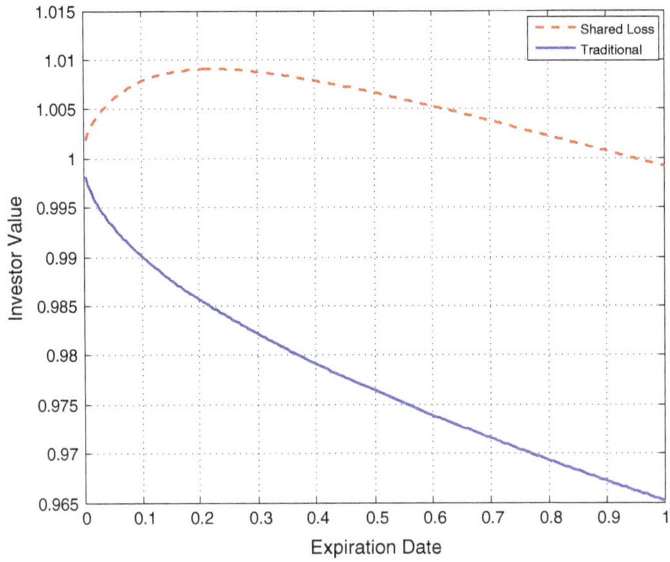

Fig. 7 Value of the investor's position versus the expiration date T

5.2.3 Maturity Date (T)

The dependence on the time to maturity is of interest specially when adapting the results of this paper to realistic situations. As we mentioned earlier, our mathematical assumption is that fees will be paid at a fixed time in the future. In practice, fees are payable according to calendars agreed between the investors and the manager. In the graphs that follow, we address this by varying the expiration date T from 1 day to 1 year. The results are shown in Fig. 7.

Initially, the value of the position is increasing in T, but eventually, it begins to decrease in T, as the options given to the hedge fund manager become more valuable. The maximum value of the investor's position occurs at T around one quarter of a year ($T \sim 0.22$).

6 Conclusion

The exchange of business value between the manager and the investor is always a complex one: beyond fees paid, there are intangibles the investor gives the manager. An asset management business is valued taking into account many factors, such as track records, years in business, assets under management, the reputation of its investors, and of course fees. In this paper we focus on first-loss fee structures, which are bringing novel points of attention between investors and hedge fund managers in the historical discussions on fair compensation. We focus only on the fee payable by the investor and the guarantee offered by the manager, which is the main novelty in this set up. The main challenge in this new paradigm is to evaluate the value of the guarantee offered by the hedge fund manager in relation to the fee paid by the investor. In this paper, we developed a mathematical approach to compare the two features of guarantee and performance fee from an option pricing perspective. The framework is flexible and can be used for different specific investment settings and can account for slight variations from one fund to another. Our salient leitmotif is: fee agreements must be structured to be attractive to managers so they are willing to participate, and at the same time provide a cushion against losses to the investor. A significant contribution, that sheds light on the road-map and paves the way for deeper investigations, is to see, and more importantly formulate, the underlying fee structure from the lens of option valuation. By employing a risk-neutral framework and options pricing theory, one is able to not only price, but also analyze the sensitivity of the value of the investor's and manager's positions in reference to a set of influential parameters.

Acknowledgements We wish to express our gratitude to Sigma Analysis & Management Ltd., and especially to Dr. Ranjan Bhaduri and Mr. Kurt Henry for many endless valuable discussions.

The KPMG Center of Excellence in Risk Management is acknowledged for organizing the conference "Challenges in Derivatives Markets - Fixed Income Modeling, Valuation Adjustments, Risk Management, and Regulation".

References

1. Banzaca, J.: First loss capital arrangements for hedge fund managers: Structures, risks and the market for key terms. The Hedge Fund Law Report **5**(37), (2012)
2. Carpenter, J.: Does option compensation increase managerial risk appetite? J. Financ. **55**(5), 2311–2331 (2000)
3. Goetzmann, W., Ingersoll, J., Ross, S.: High-water marks and hedge fund management contracts. J. Financ. **58**(4), 1685–1717 (2003)
4. Guasoni, P., Obłój, J.: The incentives of hedge fund fees and high-water marks, forthcoming. Mathematical Finance (2013)
5. He, X., Kou, S.: Profit sharing in hedge funds. www.ssrn.com (2013)
6. Hodder, J., Jackwerth, J.: Incentive contracts and hedge fund management. J. Financ. Quant. Anal. **42**(4), 811–826 (2007)
7. Kouwenberg, R., Ziemba, W.: Incentives and risk taking in hedge funds. J. Bank Financ. **31**, 3291–3310 (2007)
8. Panageas, S., Westerfield, M.: High-water marks: high risk appetites? Convex compensation, long horizons, and portfolio choice. J. Financ. **64**(1), 1–36 (2009)
9. Ross, S.: Compensation, incentives, and the duality of risk aversion and riskiness. J. Financ. **59**(1), 207–225 (2004)
10. WSJ: Calpers to Exit Hedge Funds. http://www.wsj.com/articles/calpers-to-exit-hedge-funds-1410821083?alg=y (2014)

10

Negative Basis Measurement: Finding the Holy Scale

German Bernhart and Jan-Frederik Mai

Abstract Investing into a bond and at the same time buying CDS protection on the same bond is known as buying a basis package. Loosely speaking, if the bond pays more than the CDS protection costs, the position has an allegedly risk-free positive payoff known as "negative basis". However, several different mathematical definitions of the negative basis are present in the literature. The present article introduces an innovative measurement, which is demonstrated to fit better into arbitrage pricing theory than existing approaches. This topic is not only interesting for negative basis investors. It also affects derivative pricing in general, since the negative basis might act as a liquidity spread that contributes as a net funding cost to the value of a transaction; see Morini and Parampolini (Risk, 58–63, 2011, [23]).

Keywords Negative basis measurement · Bond-CDS basis · Hidden yield

1 Introduction

On first glimpse, it is surprising that investing into a bond and buying CDS protection on that underlying bond, henceforth called a basis package, can earn an attractive spread on top of the risk-free rate of return, as it appears to be free of default risk. This excess return over the risk-free rate is informally called *negative basis*[1]; more formal definitions are given in the main body of this article. [8] has even devoted an entire book to the topic. If, conversely, the cost of CDS protection exceeds the bond earnings, one speaks of a positive basis. In this article, we only speak of negative bases, as fundamentally the concepts of positive and negative basis are simply inverse.

---

[1] Sometimes also called *bond-CDS basis*.;

G. Bernhart · J.-F. Mai (✉)
XAIA Investment, Sonnenstraße 19, 80331 München, Germany
e-mail: jan-frederik.mai@xaia.com

G. Bernhart
e-mail: german.bernhart@xaia.com

The appropriate measurement of negative basis plays an important role with regard to the cost of funding literature, which has become of paramount interest in the financial industry since the recent liquidity crisis. Generally speaking, this stream of literature reconsiders the pricing of derivatives under the new post-crisis fundamentals regarding funding, liquidity, and credit risk issues. Substantial contributions have been made, among others, by [5, 7, 12, 13, 23, 27, 29]. Loosely speaking, most references agree upon the fact that, at least under certain simplifying assumptions (full, bilateral, and continuous collateralization), derivative contracts can be evaluated in the traditional way, only the involved discount factors have to be adjusted by means of a spread accounting for funding and liquidity charges. In particular, [23] show in a simple, theoretical framework that the negative basis is a spread which plays an essential role in this regard. In order to set these theoretical findings into action in the industry's pricing machinery, it is therefore an essential task to establish viable and reasonable measurements for the negative basis. The present article shows that this topic is not only important but also challenging, and contributes a careful comparison of three different measurement methods. In particular, we point out why the most common measurement approaches (denoted by (Z) and (PE) below) are not recommended, and propose a decent alternative.

In the present article, we take the point of view of a negative basis investor whose goal is to detect interesting negative basis positions and to monitor the evolution of such investments over time. Alternatively, consider a bank which has to evaluate its derivative book. As the aforementioned references show that the required discount factors for the pricing algorithms might have to be adjusted by means of the negative basis, one faces the task of measuring this negative basis appropriately. For the effective implementation of these tasks, it is crucial to come up with a reliable and viable, yet reasonable mathematical definition of what the negative basis actually is. Specific focus is put on simple-to-implement approaches that rely on commonly applied pricing methodologies for bonds and CDS, described in, e.g., [18, 25]. In total, we discuss three different measurements (two traditional and one innovative):

- Difference between Z-spread of the bond and CDS running spread, as presented, e.g., in [8], and defined by Bloomberg on the screen YAS.
- Par-equivalent CDS-methodology, as described in the Appendix of [2], who apply this definition for an empirical study, see also [3].
- A hidden yield approach that assumes the risk-free discounting curve to be a reference interest rate curve shifted by the (initially unknown) negative basis.

Important to note is that, according to all these definitions, a negative basis is assigned to a bond, not to an issuer. This means that two different bonds issued by the same company are allowed to have two different negative bases. This viewpoint stands in glaring contrast to some of the more macro-economic considerations carried out in references cited in the next section. CDS protection typically refers to a whole battery of eligible bonds by a reference issuer, and normally the major driver for CDS spreads is considered to be the issuer's default risk. However, some of the deliverable bonds might trade at diverse yields for reasons other than the issuer's default risk—for instance legal issues, liquidity issues, or funding issues, cf. [21] and Sect. 2.

The rest of this article is organized as follows. Section 2 recalls reasons for the existence of negative basis. Section 3 introduces general notations, which are used throughout the remaining sections. Section 4 reviews the traditional methods (Z) and (PE), Sect. 5 discusses the innovative method (HY), and Sect. 6 concludes.

2 Why Does Negative Basis Exist?

There are a couple of intuitive explanations for the existence of negative basis, see, e.g., [1, 2, 4, 6, 10, 19, 24, 26, 30]. For the convenience of the reader, we briefly recall some of them in the sequel.

- **Liquidity issues**: Some bond issues are distributed only among a few investors. If one of these investors has to sell her bonds, for instance due to regulatory requirements or demand for liquidity, supply may exceed demand and thus the price of the bond must drop significantly in order for the bond to be sold. At the same time the CDS price might remain unaffected.
- **Funding costs**: From a pure credit risk perspective, selling CDS protection economically is the same risk as buying the underlying bond. However, buying a bond requires an initial investment that must be funded, whereas selling CDS protection typically requires much less initial funding (unless the CDS upfront exceeds the bond price). Therefore, in times of high funding costs there is an incentive to sell CDS rather than to buy bonds, which might lead to an increase in supply of CDS protection, making it cheap relative to bond prices.
- **Market segmentation**: Empirical observations suggest that bond trades sometimes have larger volumes and might be motivated much less by quantitative aspects than CDS trades. Arguing similarly, [6, p. 5, l. 5–7] conjecture that *"market-implied [risk] measures have a stronger impact on the CDS market, while the more easily available rating information affects the bond market more strongly"*. Such instrument-specific differences might contribute to the existence of negative basis.
- **Legal risk**: The bond of the negative basis position might bear certain risks that cannot be protected against by means of a CDS. Examples are certain collective action clauses, debt restructuring events, or call rights for the bond issuer. Such "legal gaps" explain parts of the negative basis.
- **Counterparty credit risk**: A joint default of both the CDS counterparty and the issuer of the bond could lead to a loss for the basis position.[2] These potential losses imply that CDS protection is not 100 % and consequently might contribute to the negative basis, see, e.g., [5, 22].
- **Mark-to-market risk**: The negative basis might further increase after one has entered into the position, due to one of the aforementioned reasons. In this case, one

[2]However, counterparty credit risk can be reduced significantly by a negative basis investor when the CDS is collateralized, which is the usual case.

loses money due to mark-to-market balancing. In theory, one gets this money back eventually, but it might occur that mark-to-market losses exceed one's personal tolerance level during the bond's lifetime. In this case, one has to exit the position and realize the loss. This risk is especially significant if the negative basis position is levered (which has happened heavily during the financial crisis). Part of the negative basis might be viewed as a risk premium for taking this mark-to-market-risk.

Basis "arbitrageurs" are investors that try to earn the negative basis by investing into basis packages. This means that they consider the negative basis an adequate compensation for taking the aforementioned risks. In classical arbitrage theory, their appearance improves trading liquidity. Counterintuitively, however, [9] argue that the advent of CDS was detrimental to bond markets and [20] find some evidence that basis arbitrageurs bring new risks into the corporate bond markets.

3 General Notations

All definitions to follow rely on the pricing of CDS and a plain vanilla coupon bond according to the most simple mathematical setup we can think of. This is in order to make the article as reader-friendly as possible; furthermore, we think the setup is already rich enough in order to convey the main ideas. The only randomness considered in the present article is the default time of the bond issuer, which is formally defined on a probability space $(\Omega, \mathscr{F}, \mathbb{Q})$, with state space Ω, σ-algebra $\mathscr{F}$, and probability measure $\mathbb{Q}$. Expected values with respect to the pricing measure $\mathbb{Q}$ are denoted by $\mathbb{E}$. The default intensity $\lambda(.)$ of the issuer's default time τ is assumed to be deterministic, i.e. $\mathbb{Q}(\tau > t) = \exp(-\int_0^t \lambda(s)\,\mathrm{d}s)$. Sometimes the function $\lambda(.)$ is constant, sometimes piecewise constant, depending on our application. For example, the computation of a so-called Z-spread requires $\lambda(.)$ to be constant,[3] whereas the joint consistent pricing of several CDS quotes with different maturities requires $\lambda(.)$ to be piecewise constant.

Generally speaking, it is our understanding that a negative basis is a measure for the mispricing between CDS and bonds with respect to default risk alone. This explains why considering the default time as the sole stochastic object corresponds to the most minimal modeling approach possible. Besides the non-randomness of the default intensity, the following further simplifying assumptions are taken for granted throughout:

- We ignore recovery risk: Upon default, the bond holder receives the constant proportion $R \in [0, 1]$ of her nominal. Default is assumed to instantaneously trigger a credit event of the CDS. The bond is assumed to be a deliverable security in the auction following the CDS trigger event, and the auction process is assumed to yield the same recovery rate R. Although this is an unrealistic assumption in

[3] See below in Step 3 of Definition 1.

principle (see, e.g., [17]), a negative basis investor can always eliminate recovery risk by delivering his bonds into the auction (physical settlement), in which case he gets compensated by the (nominal-matched) CDS for the nominal loss of the bond.[4] Consequently, our assumption is not severe for the present purpose.

- We ignore interest rate risk: The discounting curve is deterministic and the discount factors are denoted by $DF(t) := \exp(-\int_0^t r(s)\,\mathrm{d}s)$ with some given deterministic short rate function $r(.)$. All presented negative basis figures are measurements relative to the applied short rate function $r(.)$.

Under these assumptions we introduce the following notations:

- $t_j^{(B)}$ denotes the coupon payment dates of the bond.
- The bond's lifetime is denoted by T, i.e. T denotes the last coupon payment date, which at the same time is the redemption date. Moreover, the bond is assumed to pay a constant coupon rate C at each coupon payment date.
- $t_i^{(C)}$ denotes the payment dates of the considered CDS contracts, which typically are quarterly on the 20th of March, June, September, and December, respectively, according to the terms and conditions of ISDA standard contracts.[5]
- For a CDS with maturity T, the (usually standardized) running coupon is denoted by $s(T)$ and the upfront payment to be made at CDS settlement by $\text{upf}(T)$.
- The expected discounted value of the sum of all premium payments to be made by the CDS protection buyer (the premium leg) is denoted by[6]

$$\begin{aligned}
&EDPL(\lambda(.), r(.), s(T), \text{upf}(T), T)\\
&\quad := \text{upf}(T) + s(T) \sum_{0<t_i^{(C)}\le T} \left(t_i^{(C)} - t_{i-1}^{(C)}\right) DF\left(t_i^{(C)}\right) \mathbb{Q}\left(\tau > t_i^{(C)}\right)\\
&\quad = \text{upf}(T) + s(T) \sum_{0<t_i^{(C)}\le T} \left(t_i^{(C)} - t_{i-1}^{(C)}\right) DF\left(t_i^{(C)}\right) e^{-\int_0^{t_i^{(C)}} \lambda(s)\,\mathrm{d}s}.
\end{aligned}$$

- The expected discounted value of the sum of all default compensation payments to be made by the CDS protection seller (the default/protection leg) is denoted by

$$\begin{aligned}
EDDL(\lambda(.), r(.), R, T) :&= (1-R)\,\mathbb{E}[1_{\{\tau\le T\}}\,DF(\tau)]\\
&= (1-R) \int_0^T DF(y)\,\lambda(y)\,e^{-\int_0^y \lambda(s)\,\mathrm{d}s}\,\mathrm{d}y.
\end{aligned}$$

---

[4] Interestingly, a mismatch between bond and CDS recovery is often favorable for the negative basis investor, since the CDS recovery rate tends to be lower than the bond recovery, see, e.g., [14]. Thus, it might make sense for a negative basis investor to opt for cash settlement of the CDS and sell his bonds in the marketplace, speculating on a favorable recovery mismatch.

[5] See http://www2.isda.org/asset-classes/credit-derivatives/.

[6] For the sake of notational convenience we ignore accrued interest upon default, which can, of course, be incorporated easily.

- The model price of the bond is given by

$$\begin{aligned}\text{Bond}(\lambda(.), r(.), R, C, T) &:= C \sum_{0<t_j^{(B)}\leq T} \big(t_j^{(B)} - t_{j-1}^{(B)}\big)\, DF\big(t_j^{(B)}\big)\, \mathbb{Q}\big(\tau > t_j^{(B)}\big) \\ &\quad + DF(T)\, \mathbb{Q}(\tau > T) + R\, \mathbb{E}[1_{\{\tau\leq T\}}\, DF(\tau)] \\ &= C \sum_{0<t_j^{(B)}\leq T} \big(t_j^{(B)} - t_{j-1}^{(B)}\big)\, DF\big(t_j^{(B)}\big)\, e^{-\int_0^{t_j^{(B)}} \lambda(s)\,ds} \\ &\quad + DF(T)\, e^{-\int_0^T \lambda(s)\,ds} + R \int_0^T DF(y)\, \lambda(y)\, e^{-\int_0^y \lambda(s)\,ds}\, dy.\end{aligned}$$

4 Traditional Measurements

4.1 *The Z-Spread Methodology*

The main idea of the *Z-spread methodology* is to define the negative basis as the difference between (expected) annualized bond earnings and annualized protection costs. This method is described, e.g., in [8]. The negative basis $NB^{(Z)}$ is computed by the following algorithm.

Definition 1 (*Negative Basis (Z)*)

1. A reference discounting curve, resp. the associated short rate $r(.)$, is chosen and used in all subsequent steps, e.g. bootstrapped from quoted prices for interest rate derivatives according to one of the methods described in [15, 16].
2. From a term structure of quoted CDS with different maturities, piecewise constant intensities $\lambda(.)$ are bootstrapped, as described, e.g., in [25]. For this, a recovery assumption is made, i.e. R is model input.[7]
3. Denoting by B the quoted market price of the bond, the bond's **Z-spread** z is defined as the root of the function[8]

$$x \mapsto \text{Bond}(x, r(.), 0, C, T) - B, \tag{1}$$

[7]If CDS prices are quoted in running spreads with zero upfronts, then these quotes typically come naturally equipped with a recovery assumption that is required in order to convert the running spreads into actually tradable standardized coupon and upfront payments. However, after this conversion the recovery rate is a free model parameter.

[8]For a reader-friendly explanation of the Z-spread see [28]. In particular, it is useful to observe that $\text{Bond}(x, r(.), R, C, T) = \text{Bond}(0, r(.) + x, R, C, T)$ for $R = 0$, implying that the Z-spread equals a constant default intensity under a zero recovery assumption.

if existent. In words, the Z-spread is the amount by which the reference short rate $r(.)$ needs to be shifted parallelly in order for the discounted bond cash flows to match the market quote. The root, whenever existing at all, is unique.

4. The (zero-upfront) running CDS spread $s(T)$ for a CDS contract, whose maturity matches the bond's maturity, is defined as

$$s(T) := \frac{EDDL(\lambda(.), r(.), R, T)}{EDPL(\lambda(.), r(.), 1, 0, T)},$$

i.e. the fair running spread when no upfront payment is present.

5. $NB^{(Z)} := z - s(T)$.

Intuitively, the Z-spread z is a measure of the annualized excess return of the bond on top of the "risk-free" rate $r(.)$, whereas $s(T)$ is the annualized CDS protection cost. Hence, $NB^{(Z)}$ equals the difference between earnings and costs (expected in case of survival). If the function (1) does not have a root in $(0, \infty)$, this means that the bond is less risky than the default risk intrinsic in the chosen discounting curve $r(.)$. Especially since the liquidity crisis, when the interbank money transfer ran dry, significant spreads between discounting curves obtained from overnight rates and LIBOR-based swap rates are observed. Consequently, one could recognize, e.g., German government bonds with a "negative Z-spread" with respect to the interest rate curve $r(.)$, which was obtained from 6-month EURIBOR swap rates. For such reasons it has become market standard to extract the "risk-free" discounting curve from overnight rates rather than from LIBOR-based swap rates. Moreover, [19] point out that the difference between bond yields and CDS spreads can depend on whether treasury rates or swap rates are used for discounting. Since negative basis investors are typically trading in the high yield sector, the function (1) normally does have a root in $(0, \infty)$ for several canonical choices of $r(.)$, be it extracted from swap rates with overnight tenor, 3-month tenor, or 6-month tenor. But it is important to stress that all presented negative basis measurements are always relative measures depending on the applied interest rate curve $r(.)$.

The Z-spread methodology has some drawbacks:

- **Imprecision:** Earnings and costs are not measured accurately, but only approximately. The Z-spread is only a rough estimate for the expected annualized earnings, and the zero-upfront running CDS spread is also not really tradable, but only a fictitious quantity. Furthermore, the Z-spread is earned on the bond value, whereas the CDS spread is paid on the (bond and) CDS nominal, which may result in a nonsense measurement for bonds trading away from par, see Example 1 below. To this end, [10] proposes to replace the Z-spread by an asset swap spread. It is possible to define more accurate measurements of earnings and costs taking into account actual cash flows. However, in the present article we do not elaborate on these fine-tunings, since the "earnings and costs"-perspective in general suffers from the following second difficulty.
- **Inaccurate hedge:** The measurement assumes that bond and CDS have the same maturity and nominals and furthermore implicitly assumes a survival

until maturity. Upon a default event the PnL of the position might be considerably different, depending on the timing of the default, see Fig. 1 in Example 1 below. Hence, the assumed CDS hedge cannot really be considered to be default-risk eliminating (it might either profit from or lose on a default event), and consequently the number $NB^{(Z)}$ does not deserve to be called a return figure after elimination of default risk, which the negative basis should be in our opinion.

4.2 The Par-Equivalent CDS Methodology

The *par-equivalent CDS methodology* is described in the Appendix of [2]. A similar idea is also outlined in [8, p. 101 ff] and [3]. The negative basis $NB^{(PE)}$ is computed along the steps of the following algorithm.

Definition 2 (*Negative Basis (PE)*)

1. A reference discounting curve, resp. the associated short rate $r(.)$, is chosen and used in all subsequent steps, e.g. bootstrapped from quoted prices for interest rate derivatives according to one of the methods described in [15, 16].
2. From a term structure of CDS contracts on the reference entity, piecewise constant intensities $\lambda(.)$ are bootstrapped, as described, e.g., in [25]. For this a recovery assumption is made, i.e. R is model input.
3. The (zero-upfront) running CDS spread $s(T)$ for a CDS contract, whose maturity matches the bond's maturity, is defined as

$$s(T) := \frac{EDDL(\lambda(.), r(.), R, T)}{EDPL(\lambda(.), r(.), 1, 0, T)},$$

   i.e. the fair running spread when no upfront payment is present.
4. Denoting by B the quoted market price of the bond, a shift $\tilde{z}$ is defined as the root of the function

$$x \mapsto \text{Bond}(\lambda(.) + x, r(.), R, C, T) - B,$$

   if existent. In words, the bond is priced with the default intensities $\lambda(.)$ that are consistent with CDS quotes, which are then shifted parallelly until the bond's market quote is matched.
5. A second (zero-upfront) running CDS spread $\tilde{s}(T)$ for a CDS contract, whose maturity matches the bond's maturity, is defined as

$$\tilde{s}(T) := \frac{EDDL(\lambda(.) + \tilde{z}, r(.), R, T)}{EDPL(\lambda(.) + \tilde{z}, r(.), 1, 0, T)},$$

   i.e. the fair spread when no upfront payment is present, but now with the shifted intensity rates $\lambda(.) + \tilde{z}$, which are required in order to price the bond correctly.
6. $NB^{(PE)} := \tilde{s}(T) - s(T)$.

The main idea of (PE) is to question the default probabilities bootstrapped from the given CDS quotes, and to adjust them in order to match the bond quote. On a high level, this negative basis measurement is based on the difference between default probabilities that are required in order to match the bond price and default probabilities that are required in order to fit the CDS quotes.

The methodology (PE) has some drawbacks:

- **No link to arbitrage pricing theory:** In our view, there is no convincing economic argument as to why two different survival functions for the same default time should be used. In particular, the method provides no joint pricing model for bond and CDS that explains the negative basis as one of its parameters. The method is "decoupled" from arbitrage pricing theory.
- **No link to "earnings and costs"-perspective:** Unlike the method (Z), the method (PE) does not have a clear link to an earnings measure above a reference rate, which is what the negative basis is informally thought of.

5 An Innovative Methodology

In our opinion, the negative basis should be a spread on top of a reference discounting curve which can be earned without exposure to default risk. This means we question the usual assumption that the applied discounting curve $r(.)$ is the appropriate risk-free rate to be used, because there is actually a higher rate that can be earned "risk-free" (recalling that default risk is the only risk within our tiny model). This motivates what we call the *hidden yield approach*. The negative basis $NB^{(HY)}$ is computed along the steps of the following algorithm.

Definition 3 (*Negative Basis (HY)*)

1. A reference discounting curve, resp. the associated short rate $r(.)$, is chosen and used in all subsequent steps, e.g. bootstrapped from quoted prices for interest rate derivatives according to one of the methods described in [15, 16].
2. Denote by $\lambda_x(.)$ the piecewise constant intensity rates that are bootstrapped from CDS market quotes, when the assumed discounting curve is $r(.) + x$, as described, e.g., in [25]. The recovery rate R is fixed and chosen as model input.
3. The negative basis $NB^{(HY)}$ is defined as the root[9] of the function

$$x \mapsto \text{Bond}(\lambda_x(.), r(.) + x, R, C, T) - B.$$

In words, $NB^{(HY)}$ is precisely the parallel shift of the reference short rate $r(.)$ which allows for a calibration such that the model prices of bond and CDS match the observed market quotes for bond and CDS.

[9] Lemma A.1 in the Appendix guarantees that this root typically exists and is unique.

The idea of method (HY) can also be summarized as follows: If the risk-free interest rate curve is assumed to be $r(.) + NB^{(HY)}$, then the market quotes for bond and CDS are arbitrage-free (as we have found a corresponding pricing measure). It allows for the intuitive interpretation of the negative basis as a spread earned on top of a reference discounting rate after elimination of default risk. Abstractly speaking, assuming no transaction costs and availability of CDS protection at all maturities $T > 0$ (= perfect market conditions), arbitrage pricing theory suggests the existence of a trading strategy which buys the bond and hedges it via CDS, and which earns[10] precisely the rate $r(.) + NB^{(HY)}$ until the minimum of default time τ and bond maturity T. Since this way of thinking about $NB^{(HY)}$ is its distinctive property and highlights its intrinsic coherence with arbitrage pricing theory, the following lemma demonstrates by a heuristic argument how the rate $r(.) + NB^{(HY)}$ can be earned in a risk-free way.

Lemma 1 (The rate $r(.) + NB^{(HY)}$ can be earned without default risk) *Assuming perfect market conditions, there exists a (static) portfolio, which is long the bond and invested in several CDS, which earns the rate* $r(.) + NB^{(HY)}$ *until* $\min\{\tau, T\}$.

Proof (heuristic) We denote by $\mathbb{Q}$ the probability measure under which τ has piecewise constant default intensity $\lambda_{NB^{(HY)}}(.)$. We discretize the time interval $[0, T]$ into m buckets $0 =: t_0 < t_1 < \ldots < t_m := T$, but m may be chosen arbitrarily large such that the mesh of the discrete-time grid tends to zero as m tends to infinity. We introduce the following $m + 1$ probabilities:

$$w_j^{(m)} := \mathbb{Q}\big(\tau \in (t_{j-1}, t_j]\big), \quad j = 1, \ldots, m, \quad w_{m+1}^{(m)} := \mathbb{Q}(\tau > t_m).$$

Now let $\tau^{(m)}$ denote a random variable with distribution

$$\mathbb{Q}\Big(\tau^{(m)} = \bar{t}_j\Big) = w_j^{(m)}, \quad \bar{t}_j := \frac{t_{j-1} + t_j}{2}, \quad j = 1, \ldots, m,$$
$$\mathbb{Q}\Big(\tau^{(m)} > t\Big) = \mathbb{Q}(\tau > t), \quad t \geq t_m, \Big(\text{in particular, } \mathbb{Q}(\tau^{(m)} > t_m) = w_{m+1}^{(m)}\Big).$$

Notice that $\tau^{(m)} \approx \tau$ in distribution, with the approximation improving with increasing m. In the sequel, we work with $\tau^{(m)}$, assuming that default during $[0, T]$ can only take place at the possible realizations $\bar{t}_1, \ldots, \bar{t}_m$ of $\tau^{(m)}$ in $[0, T]$. We now consider a portfolio of $m + 1$ instruments, namely the bond and one CDS for each maturity $t_1, \ldots, t_m$. We assume that the bond nominal is given by N_0. Furthermore, $N_i \in \mathbb{R}$ denotes the nominal of the CDS with maturity t_i. Negative nominal means that we sell the bond or sell CDS protection. Let's have a look at the following random variables, which are functions of $\tau^{(m)}$:

[10]By "earning" $r(.) + NB^{(HY)}$ we mean that the internal rate of return of the position is the reference rate $r(.)$ plus a spread $NB^{(HY)}$.

$$V^{(0)}\left(\tau^{(m)}\right) := \left(r(.) + NB^{(HY)}\right)\text{-discounted value of all cash flows from the bond,}$$
$$\text{when default takes place at } \tau^{(m)},$$
$$V^{(i)}\left(\tau^{(m)}\right) := \left(r(.) + NB^{(HY)}\right)\text{-discounted value of all cash flows from the CDS with}$$
$$\text{maturity } t_i\text{, when default takes place at } \tau^{(m)}, \quad i = 1, \ldots, m.$$

All random variables $V^{(i)}\left(\tau^{(m)}\right)$ take on only $m+1$ possible values, since their value on the event $\{\tau^{(m)} > t_m\}$ does not depend on $\tau^{(m)}$ (as there are no cash flows after t_m). So without loss of generality we may write $V^{(i)}\left(\tau^{(m)}\right) = V^{(i)}\left(\bar{t}_{m+1}\right)$ for some arbitrary $\bar{t}_{m+1} > t_m$ on the event $\{\tau^{(m)} > t_m\}$. Our goal is to show that it is possible to find a non-zero vector $(N_0, \ldots, N_m) \in \mathbb{R}^{m+1}$ such that

$$\underbrace{N_0\, V^{(0)}\left(\tau^{(m)}\right) + \sum_{i=1}^{m} N_i\, V^{(i)}\left(\tau^{(m)}\right)}_{\left(r(.)+NB^{(HY)}\right)\text{-discounted value of outcome}} \equiv \underbrace{N_0\, B + \sum_{i=1}^{m} N_i \operatorname{upf}(t_i)}_{\text{initial investment amount}}, \tag{2}$$

where B denotes the market bond price and $\operatorname{upf}(t_i)$ the market upfront of the CDS with maturity t_i. This mathematical statement intuitively means that the considered portfolio of bond and CDS earns the rate $r(.) + NB^{(HY)}$ until $\min\{\tau^{(m)}, T\}$ in a risk-free manner, regardless of the actual timing of the default. Now why is this possible? Considering the randomness on the left-hand side of Eq. (2), we actually have $m+1$ equations for the $m+1$ unknowns $N_0, N_1, \ldots, N_m$. Rewriting Eq. (2) in terms of linear algebra, we obtain

$$\begin{pmatrix} V^{(0)}\left(\bar{t}_1\right) - B & V^{(1)}\left(\bar{t}_1\right) - \operatorname{upf}(t_1) & \ldots & V^{(m)}\left(\bar{t}_1\right) - \operatorname{upf}(t_m) \\ \vdots & \ddots & & \vdots \\ \vdots & & \ddots & \vdots \\ V^{(0)}\left(\bar{t}_{m+1}\right) - B & V^{(1)}\left(\bar{t}_{m+1}\right) - \operatorname{upf}(t_1) & \ldots & V^{(m)}\left(\bar{t}_{m+1}\right) - \operatorname{upf}(t_m) \end{pmatrix} \begin{pmatrix} N_0 \\ N_1 \\ \vdots \\ N_m \end{pmatrix} = \begin{pmatrix} 0 \\ 0 \\ \vdots \\ 0 \end{pmatrix}. \tag{3}$$

In order to prove the existence of a non-trivial solution $(N_0, \ldots, N_m)$ to Eq. (3), it suffices to verify that the associated $(m+1) \times (m+1)$-matrix does not have full rank. Now here enters the essential heuristic argument: it follows from the definition of $NB^{(HY)}$ that

$$\sum_{j=1}^{m+1} w_j^{(m)}\, V^{(0)}\left(\bar{t}_j\right) \approx B = \sum_{j=1}^{m+1} w_j^{(m)}\, B,$$
$$\sum_{j=1}^{m+1} w_j^{(m)}\, V^{(i)}\left(\bar{t}_j\right) \approx \operatorname{upf}(t_i) = \sum_{j=1}^{m+1} w_j^{(m)} \operatorname{upf}(t_i), \quad i = 1, \ldots, m,$$

with the approximations becoming equalities as $m \to \infty$. In other words, this means that the rows of the equation system (3) are linearly dependent. Consequently, the associated matrix cannot have full rank and the columns must also be linearly dependent, i.e. there exists a non-zero solution $(N_0, \ldots, N_m)$ of Eq. (3), and hence (2), as desired. Finally, taking a close look at the structure of the involved cash flows, it is obvious that a solution must satisfy $N_0 \neq 0$. Without loss of generality we may hence set $N_0 = 1$ (because if $(N_0, \ldots, N_m)$ is a solution, so is $\alpha\,(N_0, \ldots, N_m)$ for arbitrary $\alpha \in \mathbb{R}$). Concluding, the portfolio we have found is long the bond. □

We present an example that demonstrates how different the three presented measurements of negative basis can be in practice. The specifications are inspired by a real-world case.

Example 1 We consider a bond with maturity $T = 3.5$ years paying a semi-annual coupon rate of $C = 8.25\,\%$. It trades far below par value, namely at $B = 46.5\,\%$. An almost maturity-matched CDS contract is available at an upfront value of $\text{upf}(T) = 53\,\%$ with a running coupon of $s(T) = 5\,\%$, payed quarterly. This means a nominal-matched negative basis investment comes at a package price of $46.5 + 53 = 99.5\,\%$, and pays a coupon rate of $8.25 - 5 = 3.25\,\%$ until default (however, the bond and CDS coupon payments have different frequencies and payment dates). In the sequel we assume a recovery rate of $R = 20\,\%$, and the reference rate $r(.)$ is bootstrapped from 3-month tenor-based interest rate swaps according to the raw interpolation method described in [15, 16]. Because the bond trades far below par, the measurement (Z) is highly questionable and returns $NB^{(Z)} = -0.42\,\%$, which is clearly not an appropriate measurement. As indicated earlier, improved versions of earnings and costs-measurements must be used in order to deal with such extreme situations of highly distressed bonds, but this lies outside the scope of the present article. The par-equivalent CDS methodology returns the measurement $NB^{(PE)} = 2.29\,\%$, whereas the hidden yield methodology returns the significantly lower number $NB^{(HY)} = 1.18\,\%$. While the authors are not aware of a strategy how to monetize the (PE)-measurement 2.29 %, Lemma 1 provides a clear interpretation for the (HY)-measurement 1.18 % in terms of an internal rate of return that can be earned on top of the risk-free rate, when the negative basis investment is structured as indicated in the proof of Lemma 1.

Now if the described nominal-matched investment seems to earn a rate of 3.25 %, which equals a spread of around 1.75 % above the chosen reference rate $r(.)$ in the present example, why is the measurement $NB^{(HY)}$ so low? Fig. 1 visualizes the discounted value of the sum over all cash flows from the nominal-matched investment in dependence of the default time. For instance, in case of survival until maturity, this value equals approximately 104 %, yielding a return (after discounting) of 5.61 % on the initial investment of 98.39 % (which equals the package price minus accrued CDS coupon, the bond accrued equals zero). Distributed on the 3.5-year investment horizon, this corresponds to a rate of approximately 1.6 % per annum. However, in case of a default just before the first or second bond coupon payment date the

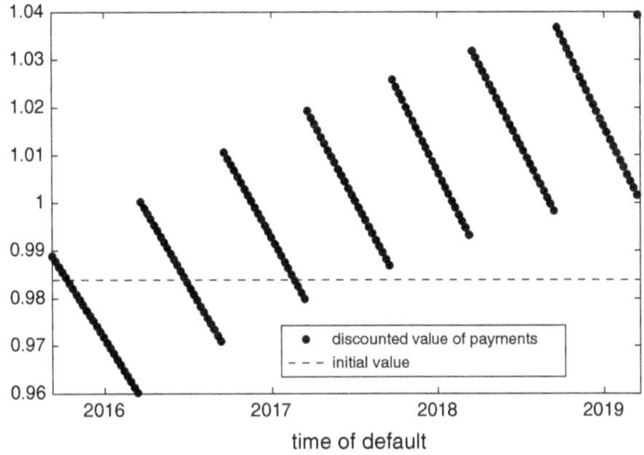

Fig. 1 Sum over all discounted cash flows arising from the described nominal-matched negative basis investment are depicted, in dependence on the time of default

described negative basis investment faces a loss. The additional short-dated CDS-protection required in order to hedge these potential losses decreases the earnings potential of the investment, which is accounted for in the (HY)-methodology, as explained in the proof of Lemma 1.

6 Conclusion

We proposed an innovative measurement for the negative basis, denoted $NB^{(HY)}$. Compared to traditional approaches, it is based on an arbitrage-free pricing model for the simultaneous pricing of the bond and the CDS, which provides a sound economic interpretation. Within a simple model with only default risk being present, the negative basis is perfectly explained as the spread on top of a reference interest rate curve $r(.)$. It was pointed out how the rate $r(.) + NB^{(HY)}$ can be earned without exposure to default risk.

Acknowledgements The KPMG Center of Excellence in Risk Management is acknowledged for organizing the conference "Challenges in Derivatives Markets - Fixed Income Modeling, Valuation Adjustments, Risk Management, and Regulation".

Appendix: The algorithm in Definition 3 is well-defined

The following technical lemma guarantees that Step 3 in Definition 3 admits a unique solution that can be found efficiently by means of a bisection routine.

Lemma A.1 (Method (HY) is well-defined)

(a) *The function* $x \mapsto Bond(\lambda_x(.), r(.) + x, R, C, T)$ *is continuous.*

(b) The function $x \mapsto$ *Bond*$(\lambda_x(.), r(.) + x, R, C, T)$ *is decreasing on the interval* $[-\inf\{r(t) \,:\, t \geq 0\}, \infty)$.

(c) We have the lower bound Bond$(\lambda_x(.), r(.) + x, R, C, T) \geq \frac{R}{1-R}$ *upf*(T).

Proof We prove parts (a), (b), and (c) separately.

(a) For fixed x, the function $\lambda_x(.)$ is piecewise constant, so actually we only deal with a finite vector of values of the default intensity, depending on x. For the remainder of the proof we denote these values by $(y_1(x), \ldots, y_m(x))$. In other words, we observe m CDS maturities $T_1, \ldots, T_m$ and the value $y_k(x)$ is the level of the default intensity on the piece $(T_{k-1}, T_k]$, for $k = 1, \ldots, m$, with $T_0 := 0$. Obviously, the bond price then equals a concatenation of continuous functions if each $y_k(x)$ is continuous in x. However, this is guaranteed by the implicit function theorem since $y_k(x)$ is defined as the implicit function yielding the root of a smooth function. Concluding, continuity of the bond price is clear.

(b) In order to see that the bond price is decreasing in x, we first re-write it as

$$\begin{aligned}\text{Bond}(\lambda_x(.), r(.) + x, R, C, T) &= e^{-\int_0^T \lambda_x(s)+r(s)+x\,\mathrm{d}s} \\ &\quad + C \sum_{0<t_j^{(B)}\leq T} \left(t_j^{(B)} - t_{j-1}^{(B)}\right) e^{-\int_0^{t_j^{(B)}} \lambda_x(s)+r(s)+x\,\mathrm{d}s} \\ &\quad + \frac{R}{1-R} EDPL(\lambda_x(.), r(.) + x, \text{upf}(T), T),\end{aligned}$$

where we have used $EDPL = EDDL$ from the CDS boostrap. This shows that it suffices to check that the function

$$x \mapsto \lambda_x(t) + x$$

is increasing for each fixed t, because all summands in the above bond formula are then obviously decreasing.

We proceed with an auxiliary observation. If τ_1 and τ_2 are two positive random variables with distribution functions F_1 and F_2, satisfying $F_1 \geq F_2$ pointwise on an interval (T, ∞) and $F_1 \equiv F_2$ on $[0, T]$, then $\mathbb{E}[g(\tau_1)] \geq \mathbb{E}[g(\tau_2)]$ for any bounded function $g : (0, \infty) \to [0, K]$, which is non-increasing on (T, ∞). To verify this,[11] define the non-decreasing function $h := -g$ and use integration by parts:

[11]One says that τ_1 is less than τ_2 in the usual stochastic order, and the following computation is standard in the respective theory.

$$\begin{aligned}\mathbb{E}[g(\tau_1)] &= -\int h\,\mathrm{d}F_1 = -\int_{(0,T]} h\,\mathrm{d}F_1 - \int_{(T,\infty)} h\,\mathrm{d}F_1\\ &= -\int_{(0,T]} h\,\mathrm{d}F_2 - \Big(h(\infty)\underbrace{F_1(\infty)}_{=1=F_2(\infty)} - h(T)\underbrace{F_1(T)}_{=F_2(T)} - \int_{(T,\infty)} F_1\,\mathrm{d}h\Big)\\ &\geq -\int_{(0,T]} h\,\mathrm{d}F_2 - \Big(h(\infty)\,F_2(\infty) - h(T)\,F_2(T) - \int_{(T,\infty)} F_2\,\mathrm{d}h\Big)\\ &= -\int_{(0,T]} h\,\mathrm{d}F_2 - \int_{(T,\infty)} h\,\mathrm{d}F_2 = -\int h\,\mathrm{d}F_2 = \mathbb{E}[g(\tau_2)].\end{aligned}$$

Now we proceed inductively over $k = 1, \ldots, m$ by showing that $x \mapsto \lambda_x(t) + x$ is non-decreasing for all fixed $t \in (T_{k-1}, T_k]$, i.e. that $x \mapsto y_k(x) + x$ is non-decreasing. We start the induction for $k = 1$. To this end, recall that $y_1(x)$ is the unique root of the equation

$$EDPL(y_1(x), r(.) + x, s(T_1), \mathrm{upf}(T_1), T_1) = EDDL(y_1(x), r(.) + x, R, T_1).$$

For the sake of a more compact notation we denote the left-hand side of the last equation by $LHS(x, y_1(x))$ and the right-hand side by $RHS(x, y_1(x))$. Furthermore, we denote the value of both sides by $V(x) := LHS(x, y_1(x)) = RHS(x, y_1(x))$. Since all the summands of LHS depend on the function $x \mapsto x + y_1(x)$ in a monotonic way, it is obvious that $V(x)$ is non-increasing in x if and only if the function $x \mapsto x + y_1(x)$ is non-decreasing. Hence, it suffices to prove that $V(x)$ is non-increasing in x. To this end, we (obviously) observe with $\varepsilon > 0$ that

$$LHS(x + \varepsilon, y_1(x)) \leq LHS(x, y_1(x)) = V(x), \tag{4}$$

$$RHS(x + \varepsilon, y_1(x)) \leq RHS(x, y_1(x)) = V(x). \tag{5}$$

Furthermore, the function $y \mapsto LHS(x + \varepsilon, y)$ is obviously strictly decreasing. Concerning the right-hand side, we denote by $\mathbb{E}_y[f(\tau)]$ the expectation over $f(\tau)$ when the default time τ has an exponential distribution with parameter y. The function

$$y \mapsto RHS(x + \varepsilon, y) = (1 - R)\,\mathbb{E}_y\Big[e^{-\int_0^\tau r(s)+x+\varepsilon\,\mathrm{d}s}\,1_{\{\tau \leq T_1\}}\Big]$$

is non-decreasing on the claimed interval by the auxiliary observation we have derived above (increasing y corresponds to increasing the distribution function of the default time τ pointwise[12]). We now distinguish two cases:

[12] Here, we have used that the function $\tau \mapsto \exp(-\int_0^\tau r(s) + x + \varepsilon\,\mathrm{d}s)\,1_{\{\tau \leq T_1\}}$ is non-increasing if $x \geq -\inf\{r(t) : t \geq 0\}$.

(i) $LHS(x+\varepsilon, y_1(x)) \leq RHS(x+\varepsilon, y_1(x))$:
In this case $y_1(x+\varepsilon) \leq y_1(x)$, because otherwise we would observe the following contradiction:

$$\begin{aligned} LHS(x+\varepsilon, y_1(x+\varepsilon)) &< LHS(x+\varepsilon, y_1(x)) \leq RHS(x+\varepsilon, y_1(x)) \\ &\leq RHS(x+\varepsilon, y_1(x+\varepsilon)). \end{aligned}$$

This implies that

$$V(x+\varepsilon) = RHS(x+\varepsilon, y_1(x+\varepsilon)) \leq RHS(x+\varepsilon, y_1(x)) \overset{(5)}{\leq} V(x).$$

(ii) $LHS(x+\varepsilon, y_1(x)) > RHS(x+\varepsilon, y_1(x))$:
In this case $y_1(x+\varepsilon) \geq y_1(x)$, because otherwise we would observe the following contradiction:

$$\begin{aligned} RHS(x+\varepsilon, y_1(x+\varepsilon)) &\leq RHS(x+\varepsilon, y_1(x)) < LHS(x+\varepsilon, y_1(x)) \\ &\leq LHS(x+\varepsilon, y_1(x+\varepsilon)). \end{aligned}$$

This implies that

$$V(x+\varepsilon) = LHS(x+\varepsilon, y_1(x+\varepsilon)) \leq LHS(x+\varepsilon, y_1(x)) \overset{(4)}{\leq} V(x).$$

Concluding, $V(x)$ is non-increasing in x and the induction start is finished. We proceed with the induction step, assuming that we already know that $x + \lambda_x(t)$ is non-decreasing in x for each fixed $t \leq T_{k-1}$. To this end, recall that $y_k(x)$ is the unique root of the equation

$$EDPL(\lambda_x(.), r(.)+x, s(T_k), \text{upf}(T_k), T_k) = EDDL(\lambda_x(.), r(.)+x, R, T_k),$$

where $y_k(x)$ enters the equation as the function value of $\lambda_x(.)$ on the interval $(T_{k-1}, T_k]$. The left-hand side of the last equation can be rewritten as follows, using the standard market convention of standardized CDS strike rates $s(T_{k-1}) = s(T_k) =: s$:

$$\begin{aligned} &EDPL(\lambda_x(.), r(.)+x, s, \text{upf}(T_k), T_k) \\ &\quad = EDPL(\lambda_x(.), r(.)+x, s, upf(T_{k-1}), T_{k-1}) + \text{upf}(T_k) - \text{upf}(T_{k-1}) \\ &\quad + s \sum_{T_{k-1} < t_i^{(C)} \leq T_k} \left(t_i^{(C)} - t_{i-1}^{(C)}\right) e^{-\int_0^{t_i^{(C)}} \lambda_x(s)+r(s)+x \, ds}. \end{aligned}$$

Similarly, the right-hand side can be rewritten as follows:

$$\begin{aligned} EDDL(\lambda_x(.), r(.)+x, R, T_k) &= EDDL(\lambda_x(.), r(.)+x, R, T_{k-1}) \\ &\quad + (1-R)\, y_k(x) \int_{T_{k-1}}^{T_k} e^{-\int_0^t r(s)+x+\lambda_x(s) \, ds} \, dt. \end{aligned}$$

Since the values $(y_1(x), \ldots, y_{k-1}(x))$ have been determined before, we may subtract the *EDDL* and *EDPL* with maturity T_{k-1} on both sides of the defining equation for $y_k(x)$, simplifying the latter to

$$\operatorname{upf}(T_k) - \operatorname{upf}(T_{k-1}) + s \sum_{T_{k-1} < t_i^{(C)} \le T_k} \left(t_i^{(C)} - t_{i-1}^{(C)}\right) e^{-\int_0^{t_i^{(C)}} \lambda_x(s) + r(s) + x \, \mathrm{d}s}$$
$$= (1 - R)\, y_k(x) \int_{T_{k-1}}^{T_k} e^{-\int_0^t r(s) + x + \lambda_x(s) \, \mathrm{d}s} \, \mathrm{d}t.$$

Again, we denote the left-hand side of the last equation by $LHS(x, y_1(x), \ldots, y_k(x))$, and the right-hand side is denoted $RHS(x, y_1(x), \ldots, y_k(x))$. Furthermore, we denote the value of both sides by

$$V(x) := LHS(x, y_1(x), \ldots, y_k(x)) = RHS(x, y_1(x), \ldots, y_k(x)).$$

By induction hypothesis, the function $x \mapsto x + \lambda_x(t)$ is non-decreasing for each $t \le T_{k-1}$. With $\varepsilon > 0$ this obviously implies that

$$\begin{aligned} &LHS(x+\varepsilon, y_1(x+\varepsilon), \ldots, y_{k-1}(x+\varepsilon), y_k(x)) \\ &\quad \le LHS(x, y_1(x), \ldots, y_k(x)) = V(x), \end{aligned} \tag{6}$$

$$\begin{aligned} &RHS(x+\varepsilon, y_1(x+\varepsilon), \ldots, y_{k-1}(x+\varepsilon), y_k(x)) \\ &\quad \le RHS(x, y_1(x), \ldots, y_k(x)) = V(x). \end{aligned} \tag{7}$$

Also, the function $y \mapsto LHS(x+\varepsilon, y_1(x+\varepsilon), \ldots, y_{k-1}(x+\varepsilon), y)$ is obviously non-increasing, whereas the function $y \mapsto RHS(x+\varepsilon, y_1(x+\varepsilon), \ldots, y_{k-1}(x+\varepsilon), y)$ is non-decreasing by a similar argument as in the induction start, namely: the right-hand side has the form[13]

$$\begin{aligned} &RHS(x+\varepsilon, y_1(x+\varepsilon), \ldots, y_{k-1}(x+\varepsilon), y) \\ &\quad = (1-R)\, \mathbb{E}_y\left[e^{-\int_0^\tau r(s)+x+\varepsilon \, \mathrm{d}s} \, 1_{\{\tau \in (T_{k-1}, T_k]\}}\right], \end{aligned}$$

which is non-decreasing in y. Why? Because an increase of y increases the distribution function of τ pointwise on $[T_{k-1}, \infty)$ but leaves it unchanged on $[0, T_{k-1}]$, and the function $\tau \mapsto \exp(-\int_0^\tau r(s) + x \, \mathrm{d}s)\, 1_{\{\tau \in (T_{k-1}, T_k]\}}$ is clearly non-increasing on (T_{k-1}, ∞) (so that our auxiliary observation above applies). Like in the induction start, showing that $x \mapsto x + y_k(x)$ is non-decreasing in x is equivalent to showing that $V(x)$ is non-increasing in x. The remaining proof is now completely analogous to the induction start (this is an exercise we leave to the reader).

[13] Similar as in the induction start, we denote by $\mathbb{E}_y[f(\tau)]$ the expectation over $f(\tau)$ when the default time has piecewise constant intensity with the level y on the piece $(T_{k-1}, T_k]$.

(c) Denoting by $\mathbb{Q}_x$ the probability measure in dependence of the default intensities $\lambda_x(.)$, we have

$$\text{Bond}(\lambda_x(.), r(.)+x, R, C, T) := C \sum_{0<t_j^{(B)}\leq T} DF\left(t_j^{(B)}\right)\left(t_j^{(B)} - t_{j-1}^{(B)}\right)\mathbb{Q}_x\left(\tau > t_j^{(B)}\right)$$
$$+ DF(T)\,\mathbb{Q}_x(\tau > T) + R\,\mathbb{E}_x[1_{\{\tau\leq T\}}\,DF(\tau)].$$

We know from the consistent CDS pricing that the appearing expectation can be replaced by the premium leg of the CDS, which allows to be estimated by the upfront, i.e.

$$\mathbb{E}_x[1_{\{\tau\leq T\}}\,DF(\tau)] = \frac{R}{1-R}\,EDPL(\lambda_x(.), r(.)+x, s(T), \text{upf}(T), T)$$
$$\geq \frac{R}{1-R}\,\text{upf}(T),$$

which in turn implies the claim.

References

1. Andritzky, J., Singh, M.: The pricing of credit default swaps during distress. IMF Working Paper 06/254 (2006)
2. Bai, J., Collin-Dufresne, P.: The determinants of the CDS-Bond basis during the financial crises of 2007–2009. Working Paper (2011)
3. Beinstein, E., Scott, A., Graves, B., Sbityakov, A., Le, K., Goulden, J., Muench, D., Doctor, S., Granger, A., Saltuk, Y., Allen, P.: Credit Derivatives Handbook. J.P. Morgan Corporate Quantitative Research (2006)
4. Blanco, R., Brennan, S., Marsh, I.W.: An empirical analysis of the dynamic relation between investment-grade bonds and credit default swaps. J. Financ. **60**(5), 2255–2281 (2005)
5. Brigo, D., Capponi, A., Pallavicini, A.: Arbitrage-free bilateral counterparty risk valuation under collateralization and application to Credit Default Swaps. Math. Financ. **24**(1), 125–146 (2014)
6. Bühler, W., Trapp, M.: Explaining the bond-CDS basis-the role of credit risk and liquidity. In: Risikomanagement und kapitalmarktorientierte Finanzierung: Festschrift für Bernd Rudolph zum 65. Geburtstag, Knapp-Verlag, Frankfurt a. Main, pp. 375–397 (2009)
7. Burgard, C., Kjaer, M.: In the balance. Risk pp. 72–75 (2011)
8. Choudhry, M.: The Credit Default Swap Basis. Bloomberg Press, New York (2006)
9. Das, S., Kalimipalli, M.: Did CDS trading improve the market for corporate bonds? J. Financ. Econ. **111**(2), 495–525 (2014)
10. De Wit, J.: Exploring the CDS-Bond basis. National Bank of Belgium working paper No. 104 (2006)
11. Doctor, S., White, D., Elizalde, A., Goulden, J., Toublan, D.D.: Differential discounting for CDS: J.P. Morgan Europe Credit Research (2012)
12. Fries, C.: Discounting Revisited: Valuation Under Funding, Counterparty Risk and Collateralization. Working paper (2010), available at SSRN: http://ssrn.com/abstract=1609587
13. Fujii, M., Shimada, Y., Takahashi, A.: Collateral Posting and Choice of Collateral Currency. CIRJE Discussion Papers (2010)
14. Gupta, S., Sundaram, R.K.: Mispricing and arbitrage in CDS auctions. J. Deriv. **22**(4), 79–91 (2015)

15. Hagan, P.S., West, G.: Interpolation methods for curve construction. Appl. Math. Financ. **13**(2), 89–129 (2006)
16. Hagan, P.S., West, G.: Methods for constructing a yield curve. Wilmott magazine pp.70–81 (2008)
17. Höcht, S., Kunze, M., Scherer, M.: Implied recovery rates-auction and models. In: Innovations in Quantitative Risk Management. Springer, Berlin pp. 147–162 (2015)
18. Hull, J., White, A.: Valuing credit default swaps I: no counterparty default risk. J. Deriv. **8**(1), 29–40 (2000)
19. Hull, J., Predescu, M., White, A.: The relationship between credit default swap spreads, bond yields, and credit rating announcements. J. Bank. Financ. **28**, 2789–2811 (2004)
20. Li, H., Zhang, W., Kim, G.H.: The CDS-Bond basis and the cross section of corporate bond returns. Working paper (2011)
21. Longstaff, F.A., Neis, E., Mithal, S.: Corporate yield spreads: default risk or liquidity? New evidence from the credit-default swap market. J. Financ. **60**(5), 2213–2253 (2005)
22. Mai, J.-F., Scherer, M.: Simulating from the copula that generates the maximal probability for a joint default under given (inhomogeneous) marginals. In: Melas, V.B. et al.: Topics in Statistical Simulation: Springer Proceedings in Mathematics and Statistics, vol. 114, pp. 333–341, Springer, Heidelberg (2014)
23. Morini, M., Prampolini, A.: Risky funding with counterparty and liquidity charges. Risk pp. 58–63 (2011)
24. O'Kane, D.: The link between Eurozone sovereign debt and CDS prices. EDHEC-Risk Institute Working Paper (2012)
25. O'Kane, D., Turnbull, S.: Valuation of credit default swaps. Fixed Income Quantitative Research Lehman Brothers (2003)
26. Palladini, G., Portes, R.: Sovereign CDS and bond pricing dynamics in the Euro-area. Centre for Economic Policy Research Discussion Paper No. 8651 (2011)
27. Pallavicini, A., Perini, D., Brigo, D.: Funding Valuation Adjustment: A Consistent Framework Including CVA, DVA, Collateral, Netting Rules and Re-Hypothecation. Working paper (2011), available at SSRN: http://ssrn.com/abstract=1969114
28. Pedersen, C.M.: Explaining the Lehman Brothers option adjusted spread of a corporate bond. Fixed Income Quantitative Credit Research, Lehman Brothers (2006)
29. Piterbarg, V.: Funding beyond discounting: collateral agreements and derivatives pricing. Risk, pp. 97–102 (2010)
30. Zhu, H.: An empirical comparison of credit spreads between the bond market and the credit default swap market. BIS Working Paper No. 160 (2004)

11

The Impact of a New CoCo Issuance on the Price Performance of Outstanding CoCos

Jan De Spiegeleer, Stephan Höcht, Ine Marquet and Wim Schoutens

Abstract Contingent convertible bonds (CoCos) are new hybrid capital instruments that have a loss absorbing capacity which is enforced either automatically via the breaching of a particular CET1 level or via a regulatory trigger. The price performance of outstanding CoCos, after a new CoCo issue is announced by the same issuer, is investigated in this paper via two methods. The first method compares the returns of the outstanding CoCos after an announcement of a new issue with some overall CoCo indices. This method does not take into account idiosyncratic movements and basically compares with the general trend. A second model-based method compares the actual market performance of the outstanding CoCos with a theoretical model. The main conclusion of the investigation of 24 cases of new CoCo bond issues is a moderated negative effect on the outstanding CoCos.

Keywords Contingent convertibles · CoCo bonds · New issuance

1 Introduction

Contingent convertible bonds or CoCo bonds are new hybrid capital instruments that have a loss absorbing capacity which is enforced either automatically via the breaching of a particular CET1 level or via a regulatory trigger. CoCos either convert

J. De Spiegeleer (✉) · I. Marquet · W. Schoutens
Department of Mathematics, KU Leuven, Celestijnenlaan 200B, Box 2400, 3001 Leuven, Belgium
e-mail: Jan.Spiegeleer@mac.com

I. Marquet
e-mail: Ine.Marquet@wis.kuleuven.be

W. Schoutens
e-mail: wim@schoutens.be

S. Höcht
Assenagon GmbH, Prannerstraße 8, 80333 München, Germany
e-mail: Stephan.Hoecht@assenagon.com

into equity or suffer a write-down of the face value upon the appearance of such a trigger event.

The financial crisis of 2007–2008 triggered an avalanche of financial worries for financial institutions around the globe. After the collapse of Lehman Brothers, governments intervened and bailed out banks using tax-payers money. Preventing such bail-outs in the future, and designing a more stable banking sector in general, requires both higher capital levels and regulatory capital of a higher quality. The implementation under the new regulatory frameworks like Basel III and Capital Requirement Directive IV (CRD IV) tries to achieve this in various ways, i.e. with the use of CoCo bonds (Basel Committee on Banking Supervision [1], European Commision [2]). CoCo bonds are allowed as new capital instruments by the Basel III guidelines. The Swiss regulators have forced their systemic important banks to issue large amounts of these instruments. Further, the European CRD IV which entered into force on 17 July 2013 enforces all new additional Tier 1 instruments to have CoCo features.

The specific design of a CoCo bond enhances the capital of a bank when it is in trouble in an automatic way. Hence, a loss-absorbing cushion is created with the aim to avoid or at least to reduce potential interventions using tax-payers' money.

The first CoCos have been issued in the aftermath of the credit crisis. In December 2009 Lloyds exchanged some of their old hybrid instruments into this new type of bonds in order to strengthen their capital position after the bank had been hit very hard due to the financial crisis of 2008. Since then a lot of other banks have been issuing CoCos and one is expecting that many will follow in the next years. The market of CoCos is currently above USD 100 bn and is expanding very rapidly.[1]

When an issuer has already some CoCos outstanding and is announcing the issuance of a new CoCo bond, there are at least two opposite forces at work. On one hand, a new issue means that the capital of the issuing institute is strengthened (at the additional Tier 1 or Tier 2 level). Due to the new issue, the losses in case of a future trigger event will be shared over a larger bucket and hence recovery rates are expected to be higher. On the other hand, there are the market dynamics and investors who often prefer to invest rather in the new CoCo than in the older ones. This can be just due to the fact that one prefers new things above old stuff, but also because one believes there is a basis spread to be earned on a new issuance. Some believe a new issuance is brought to the market with a certain discount, to attract investors and to make the whole capital raising exercise a success. Investors then will move out of the old bonds and ask for allocation in the new issue.

In this paper, we estimate the price impact on the outstanding CoCos via two methods. The first method compares the returns of the outstanding CoCo bonds after an announcement of a new issue with some overall CoCo indices. More precisely, we compare the performance with CS Contingent Convertible Euro Total Return index and the BofA Merrill Lynch Contingent Capital index. Here we basically compare the performance of the outstanding CoCos with the general market performance. However such a comparison does not take into account idiosyncratic movements; it

[1] Source: Bloomberg.

basically compares with the general market trend. The issuing company is nevertheless exposed to market dynamics. Its stock price, its credit worthiness etc. can exhibit different timely evolutions compared with the respective quantities of their competitors. This can be especially the case around capital raising announcements since then financial details of the company are published and discussed at, for example roadshows around the new issuance. Therefore, we also deploy a second methodology taking into account idiosyncratic movements. Using an equity derivatives model, we compare the actual market performance of the outstanding CoCo bonds, with a theoretical model performance taking into account idiosyncratic effects, like movements in the underlying stock, credit default spreads or volatilities. The model is derivatives based and is taking as such forward-looking expectations into account.

In total, we investigate 24 cases of new CoCo bond issues. The main conclusion of the investigation is that there is a moderated negative effect on outstanding CoCo bonds. This is confirmed by both methodologies and the impact is an underperformance of about 25–50 bps on average in between the announcement date and the issue date. An extra negative impact of 40 bps was observed in the 10 trading days after the issue.

The analysis in this paper is constrained to CoCo bonds only, but a similar study could be done for other types of bonds as well. A comparative study for corporate bonds was, e.g. done in Akigbe et al. [3], where the authors investigate the impact of 574 outstanding debt issues. The investigation was divided by different reasons of a new debt issue. A significant negative impact on the price of the outstanding debt and equity was observed in case the public debt securities were issued to finance unexpected cash flow shortfalls. No significant reaction was observed when the new debt issues were motivated by unexpected increase in capital expenditures, unexpected increase in leverage or expected refinancing of outstanding debt.

This paper is organized as follows. We first provide in the next section the details of the equity derivatives model. In Sect. 3, we provide details on the data set used and in particular overview the new issuances of a whole battery of issuers that are part of our study. Next, we report on the exact methodology and results of our comparison with other CoCo indices. The final part of that section reports and discusses the results of the Equity Derivatives model. The final section concludes.

2 The Equity Derivatives Model

CoCos are hybrid instruments, with characteristics of both debt and equity. This gives rise to different approaches for pricing CoCos. Without considering the heuristic models, two main schools of thoughts exist, namely the structural models and market-implied models. Structural models are based on the theory of Merton and can be found in Pennacchi [4] and Pennacchi et al. [5]. We will apply a market-implied model where the derivation is based on market data such as share prices, credit default spreads and volatilities. The models were introduced in a Black–Scholes framework in De Spiegeleer and Schoutens [6] and De Spiegeleer et al. [7]. Pricing CoCos under smile conform models can be found in Corcuera et al. [8]. Based on the Heston model, the impact of skew is discussed in De Spiegeleer et al. [9]. In De Spiegeleer et al. [10] the implied CET1 volatility is derived from the market price of a CoCo bond. Further extensions and variations can be found in De Spiegeleer and Schoutens [11, 12], Corcuera et al. [13], De Spiegeleer and Schoutens [14], Cheridito and Zhikai [15], Madan and Schoutens [16].

The actual valuation of a CoCo incorporates the modelling of both the trigger probability and the expected loss for the investor. Notice that the trigger is defined by a particular CET1 level or decided upon a regulator's decision. Since these trigger mechanisms are hard to model or even quantify, we project the trigger into the stock price framework as considered in the equity derivatives model of De Spiegeleer and Schoutens [6]. This means that the CoCo will be triggered under the model once the share price drops below a specified barrier level, denoted by $S^\star$. We infer from existing CoCo market data the share price at the moment the CoCo bond gets triggered and we will call this the (implied) trigger level. As a result the valuation of a CoCo bond is transformed into a barrier-pricing exercise in an equity setting.

Under such a framework the CoCo bond can be broken down to several different derivative instruments. In first place, the CoCo behaves like a standard (non-defaultable) corporate bond where the holder will receive coupons c_i on regular time points t_i together with the principal N at maturity T. However, in case the share price drops below the trigger level $S^\star$, the investor will lose his initial investment and all future coupons. This will be modelled by short positions in binary down-and-in (BIDINO) options with maturities t_i for each coupon c_i and a BIDINO with maturity T to model the cancelling of the initial value. After the trigger event has occurred, the investor of a conversion CoCo will receive C_r shares. We can model this with C_r down-and-in asset-(at hit)-or-nothing options on the stock. For a write-down CoCo, the investor does not receive any shares and we can just set C_r equal to zero in this case. Therefore, the price of a CoCo can be calculated with the following formula:

$$\begin{aligned} P = &\text{ Corporate bond} \\ &-N \times \text{binary down-and-in option} \\ &-\sum_i c_i \times \text{binary down-and-in option} \\ &+C_r \times \text{down-and-in asset-(at hit)-or-nothing option on the stock} \end{aligned}$$

Under the Black–Scholes model, we can find an explicit formula for the price of the CoCo at time t:

$$\begin{aligned} P = &\, N \exp(-r(T-t)) + \sum_{i=1}^{k} c_i \exp(-r(t_i - t)) \\ &-N \times \exp(-r(T-t))[\Phi(-x_1 + \sigma\sqrt{T-t}) + (S^\star/S)^{2\lambda-2}\Phi(y_1 - \sigma\sqrt{T-t})] \\ &-\sum_i c_i \times \exp(-r(t_i-t))[\Phi(-x_{1i} + \sigma\sqrt{t_i-t}) + (S^\star/S)^{2\lambda-2}\Phi(y_{1i} - \sigma\sqrt{t_i-t})] \\ &+C_r \times S^\star \left[\left(\frac{S^\star}{S}\right)^{a+b} \Phi(z) + \left(\frac{S^\star}{S}\right)^{a-b} \Phi(z - 2b\sigma\sqrt{T-t}) \right] \end{aligned} \tag{1}$$

with

$$z = \frac{\log(S^\star/S)}{\sigma\sqrt{T-t}} + b\sigma\sqrt{T-t} \qquad x_1 = \frac{\log(S/S^\star)}{\sigma\sqrt{T-t}} + \lambda\sigma\sqrt{T-t}$$

$$a = \frac{r-q-\frac{1}{2}\sigma^2}{\sigma^2} \qquad y_1 = \frac{\log(S^\star/S)}{\sigma\sqrt{T-t}} + \lambda\sigma\sqrt{T-t}$$

$$b = \frac{\sqrt{(r-q-\frac{1}{2}\sigma^2)^2 + 2r\sigma^2}}{\sigma^2} \qquad x_{1i} = \frac{\log(S/S^\star)}{\sigma\sqrt{t_i-t}} + \lambda\sigma\sqrt{t_i-t}$$

$$\lambda = \frac{r-q+\sigma^2/2}{\sigma^2} \qquad y_{1i} = \frac{\log(S^\star/S)}{\sigma\sqrt{t_i-t}} + \lambda\sigma\sqrt{t_i-t}$$

where Φ is the cdf of a standard normal distribution, r is the risk free rate, q the dividend yield and σ the volatility.

Applying this equity derivatives pricing model, a CoCo price can be found for a trigger level $S^\star$. However, the other way around is often more interesting. Knowing the market CoCo price, we can filter out an implied trigger $\widehat{S^\star}$ in such a way that market and model price match. Since CoCos of one financial institution with the same contractual trigger should trigger at the same time, their implied trigger levels should theoretically also be the same. Hence the implied barriers give us a way to compare different CoCos in order to detect over- or undervaluation, irrespectively of different currencies and maturities.

Our goal is to compare the actual market performance of the outstanding CoCo bonds with the theoretical model performance. This theoretical price takes idiosyncratic effects into account. Any changes in the actual market performance compared to the theoretical model performance will be described to the effect of the announcement of a new CoCo issuance. The research can also be translated in terms of implied trigger levels. In case the new CoCo does not influence the outstanding CoCo, the implied barrier of the outstanding CoCo should remain constant. Whereas if its implied barrier derived from the market will change, this change will be caused by the new CoCo issuance.

3 Measuring the Price Performance of the Outstanding CoCos

3.1 New Issuances

The impact of a new CoCo issuance is investigated on the outstanding CoCos of the same issuing company. The issuers in our study contain UBS, Barclays, Crédit Agricole, Sociéty Généràl, Deutsche Bank, UniCredit, Credit Suisse, Santander, Rabobank, Danske and BBVA. The effect on the outstanding CoCos is investigated in the period between announcement and issuance of the new CoCo, which are summarised in Table 1. Notice that UBS, Barclays and Crédit Agricole all have

Table 1 Announcement date, issue date and issue size (in bn) of the new CoCos

Name	ISIN	Announc.	Issue	Size	Curr.
ACAFP 6 5/8 09/29/49	USF22797YK86	11/09/2014	18/09/2014	1,250	USD
ACAFP 6 1/2 04/29/49	XS1055037177[a]	01/04/2014	08/04/2014	1,000	EUR
ACAFP 7 7/8 01/29/49	USF22797RT78	15/01/2014	23/01/2014	1,750	USD
BACR 7 06/15/49	XS1068561098[b]	13/06/2014	17/06/2014	697.60	GBP
BACR 8 12/15/49	XS1002801758	03/12/2013	10/12/2013	1,000	EUR
BACR 8 1/4 12/29/49	US06738EAA38	13/11/2013	20/11/2013	2,000	USD
BBVASM 6 3/4 12/29/49	XS1190663952	10/02/2015	18/02/2015	1,500	EUR
CS 6 1/4 12/29/49	XS1076957700	10/06/2014	18/06/2014	2,500	USD
CS 7 1/2 12/29/49	XS0989394589	04/12/2013	11/12/2013	2,250	USD
CS 5 3/4 09/18/25	XS0972523947	11/09/2013	18/09/2013	1,250	EUR
CS 6 09/29/49	CH0221803791	20/08/2013	04/09/2013	290	CHF
DANBNK 5 7/8 04/29/49	XS1190987427	11/02/2015	18/02/2015	750	EUR
DB 7 1/2 12/29/49	US251525AN16	18/11/2014	21/11/2014	1,500	USD
RABOBK 5 1/2 01/22/49	XS1171914515	15/01/2015	22/01/2015	1,500	EUR
SANTAN 6 1/4 09/11/49	XS1107291541	02/09/2014	11/09/2014	1,500	EUR
SANTAN 6 3/8 05/29/49	XS1066553329	08/05/2014	19/05/2014	1,500	USD
SOCGEN 6 10/27/49	USF8586CXG25	19/06/2014	25/06/2014	1,500	USD
SOCGEN 6 3/4 04/07/49	XS0867620725	28/03/2014	07/04/2014	1,000	EUR
SOCGEN 7 7/8 12/29/49	USF8586CRW49	11/12/2013	18/12/2013	1,750	USD
UBS 7 1/8 12/29/49	CH0271428317[c]	13/02/2015	19/02/2015	1,250	USD

(continued)

Table 1 (continued)

Name	ISIN	Announc.	Issue	Size	Curr.
UBS 5 1/8 05/15/24	CH0244100266	08/05/2014	15/05/2014	2,500	USD
UBS 4 3/4 02/12/26	CH0236733827	06/02/2014	13/02/2014	2,000	EUR
UBS 4 3/4 05/22/23	CH0214139930	15/05/2013	22/05/2013	1,500	USD
UCGIM 6 3/4 09/29/49	XS1107890847	03/09/2014	10/09/2014	1,000	EUR

[a]Incl. XS1055037920
[b]Incl. US06738EAB11 and XS1068574828
[c]Incl. CH0271428333 and CH0271428309
Source Bloomberg/own calculations

issued different CoCos on the same day. Since it is not possible to distinguish their influence from each other, these new CoCos are assumed to have one general impact on all the outstanding CoCos of the same issuing company.

3.2 CoCo Index Comparison

The first analysis is based on indices as a benchmark to observe a certain impact. It basically compares the returns of the outstanding CoCo bonds after an announcement of a new issue with some overall CoCo indices. More precisely, we compare the performance with the CS Contingent Convertible Euro Total Return index and the BofA Merrill Lynch Contingent Capital Index (whenever the data is available). The methods are explained for one particular new CoCo issuance, namely the USF22797YK86 CoCo of Crédit Agricole. In the end, the overall results and conclusions are shown.

3.2.1 Method

In a first step, we analyse the impact of each new CoCo separately on all the outstanding CoCos of the same issuer. The simple returns are derived for the outstanding CoCos during the period between the announcement date and the issue date of the new CoCo. In a second step, we accumulate these simple returns and obtain the returns between announcement and issue date. As an example, the first steps are shown for two outstanding CoCos of Crédit Agricole in Fig. 1.

On each day, we calculate the (equally weighted) average of the cumulative simple returns of all outstanding CoCos. In a last step, we take the difference between these averages and the cumulative returns of the CoCo index on each day between the announcement date and issue date of the new CoCo.

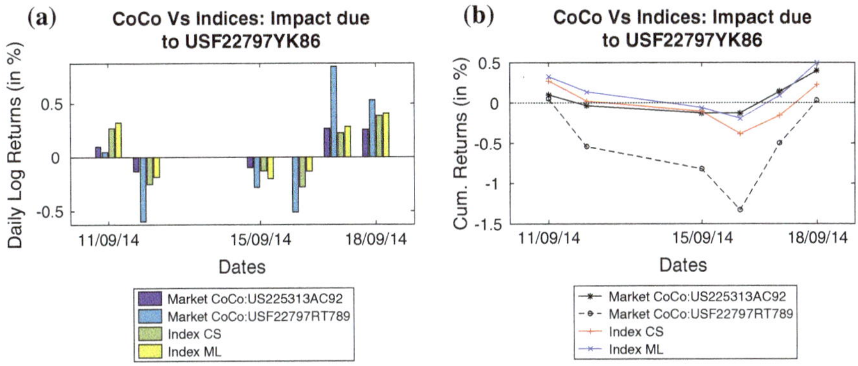

Fig. 1 Impact of USF22797YK86. **a** Daily returns. **b** Cumulative returns

3.2.2 Results

In Table 2, the difference in cumulative returns over the observation period, meaning the period between announcement and issuance, is shown. For some observation periods, the Merrill Lynch index did not yet exist. When the CoCo does show a significant change compared to the global index, we can assume that this change is due to the new CoCo issuance. The averaged difference over all new CoCos analysed is shown in Fig. 2. These averaged differences in cumulative returns are shown for one day until five days after the announcement of the new CoCo and also over the full period as was given in Table 2. As a conclusion, we see that on average the outstanding CoCos get a negative impact of around 25 bps on their return between announcement and issuance due to a new CoCo.

Multiple CoCo indices can be used for this analysis but CoCo indices are relatively new on the market. As such we are obliged to restrict our analysis to indices already available during the period of each analysis. Remark also that we need to handle these indices with care, in the sense that the indices are applied to give a global market view on the CoCos. A point of criticism to this approach can be that the indices are not that representative for the true market. There is also high concentration on some issuers in the indices, e.g. for the ML index the top 5 issuers almost make 50 % of the index (as of December 2014).

Furthermore, this comparison with the general market performance does not take into account idiosyncratic movements but compares with the general market trend. The issuing company is nevertheless exposed to individual dynamics. Its stock price, its credit worthiness, etc. can change differently from their competitors. This can be especially the case around capital raising announcements since then financial details of the company are published and discussed at, for example road-shows around the new issuance. Therefore, we move on to a second methodology taking into account idiosyncratic movements.

Table 2 Averaged difference in cumulative returns (in %) between the outstanding CoCos and the Credit Suisse CoCo index (left column) and Merrill Lynch CoCo index (right column) over the observation period of the new CoCo

Issuer	ISIN	CS index	ML index
ACAFP	USF22797YK86	0.06	−0.21
	XS1055037177	−0.06	0.07
	USF22797RT78	−0.21	−0.47
BACR	XS1068561098	−0.25	−0.12
	XS1002801758	0.08	/
	US06738EAA38	0.56	/
BBVA	XS1190663952	−0.51	−1.18
CS	XS1076957700	0.31	0.60
	XS0989394589	−0.28	/
	XS0972523947	−0.50	/
	CH0221803791	1.09	/
DANBNK	XS1190987427	−1.32	−2.27
DB	US251525AN16	−0.13	−0.29
RABOBK	XS1171914515	−0.36	−0.41
SANTAN	XS1107291541	−1.38	−1.19
	XS1066553329	−0.49	−0.06
SOCGEN	USF8586CXG25	0.23	0.17
	XS0867620725	−0.27	−0.02
	USF8586CRW49	1.24	/
UBS	CH0271428317	−0.46	−1.01
	CH0244100266	−0.12	0.42
	CH0236733827	0.37	0.31
	CH0214139930	−1.15	/
UCGIM	XS1107890847	−1.75	−1.48
Mean		**−0.22**	**−0.42**
Std Dev		**0.71**	**0.77**

Source Bloomberg/own calculations

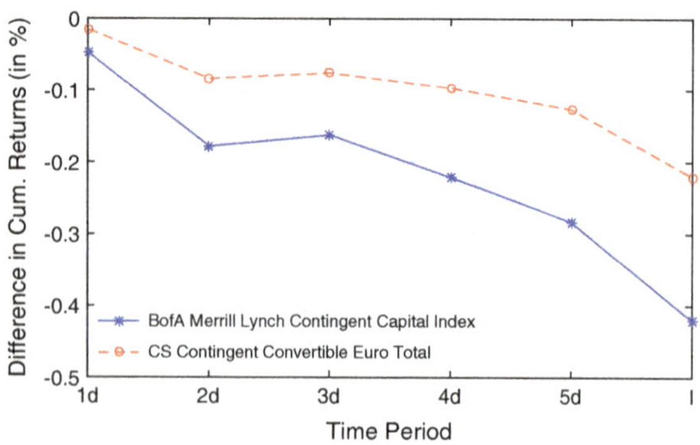

Fig. 2 Averaged difference in cumulative returns between the outstanding CoCos and the Credit Suisse and Merrill Lynch CoCo index

3.3 *Model-Based Performance*

As experienced by all CoCo investors, the difficulty in these financial products lies in their different characteristics which are hard to compare like the trigger type, conversion type, maturity, coupon cancellation, and so on. However, the implied barrier methodology can be used as a tool to compare CoCos with different characteristics. In this second approach, we will use the implied barrier to derive theoretical values for the outstanding CoCos under the assumption of no impact by the new CoCo issuance and compare them with the actual market values.

3.3.1 Method

The implied barrier can be interpreted as the stock price level (assumed by the market) that is hit (for the first time) when the CoCo gets converted or written down. If nothing changes, the market will keep the same idea about the implied barrier level and hence result in a constant implied barrier over time. In other words, when there is no impact due to this new CoCo, no change could theoretically be observed in

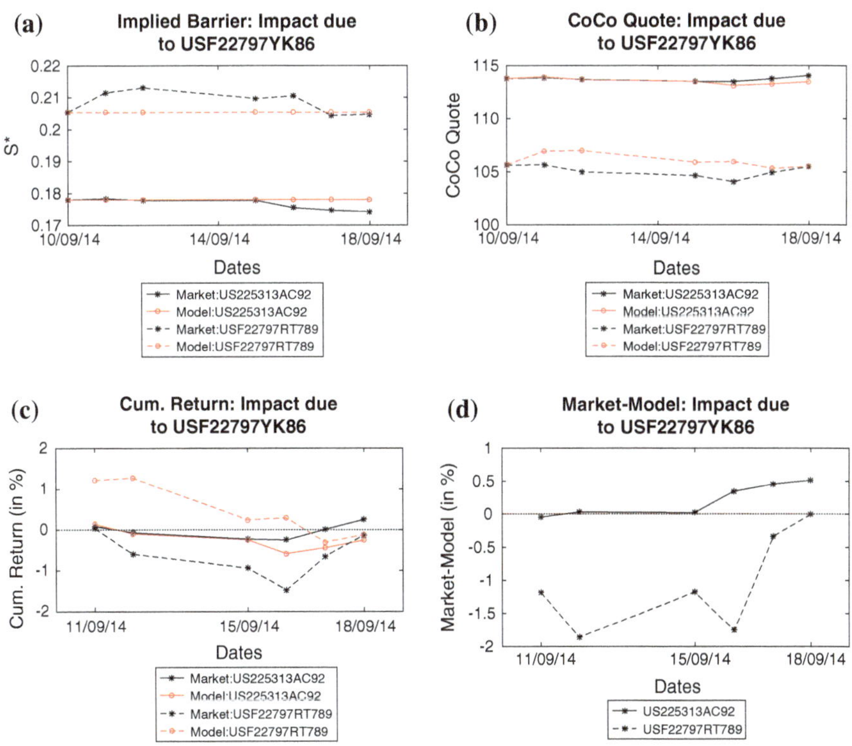

Fig. 3 Impact of USF22797YK86. **a** Implied barriers. **b** CoCo quotes. **c** Returns compared with announcement. **d** Difference in returns

the implied barrier. As such we can see in the levels of the implied barrier if there is an impact due to the announced new CoCo. This leads us easily to the second approach of our impact analysis. As an example, we show the implied barriers of the two outstanding CoCos of ACAFP from the previous section in Fig. 3a.

As from the previous section, the implied barriers can be translated into CoCo quotes. The theoretical CoCo price does not take any information of a new CoCo issuance into account by assuming a constant implied barrier. These values can be used as our reference. Any change in the market compared with this reference, is then due to the impact of the announcement of a new CoCo issuance. As such we can calculate the theoretical CoCo prices from a constant implied barrier and compare them with the market values. The results of our CoCo examples are shown in Fig. 3b. As a last step, we define cheapness as the difference between the market CoCo return and the theoretical CoCo return until the announcement date. In Fig. 3, the cheapness of the two outstanding CoCos of Crédit Agricole is shown.

Table 3 Averaged difference between the market and model CoCo cumulative returns (in %)

Issuer	ISIN	Cheapness
ACAFP	USF22797YK86	0.14
	XS1055037177	−1.45
	USF22797RT78	−0.19
BACR	XS1068561098	0.17
	XS1002801758	−0.05
	US06738EAA38	−0.38
BBVA	XS1190663952	−1.91
CS	XS1076957700	0.12
	XS0989394589	0.53
	XS0972523947	−2.63
	CH0221803791	1.44
DANBNK	XS1190987427	−3.25
DB	US251525AN16	0.65
RABOBK	XS1171914515	0.31
SANTAN	XS1107291541	−2.24
	XS1066553329	0.07
SOCGEN	USF8586CXG25	1.26
	XS0867620725	−2.31
	USF8586CRW49	1.67
UBS	CH0271428317	0.71
	CH0244100266	−1.23
	CH0236733827	1.03
	CH0214139930	−0.89
UCGIM	XS1107890847	−1.60
Mean		**−0.42**
Std Dev		**1.37**

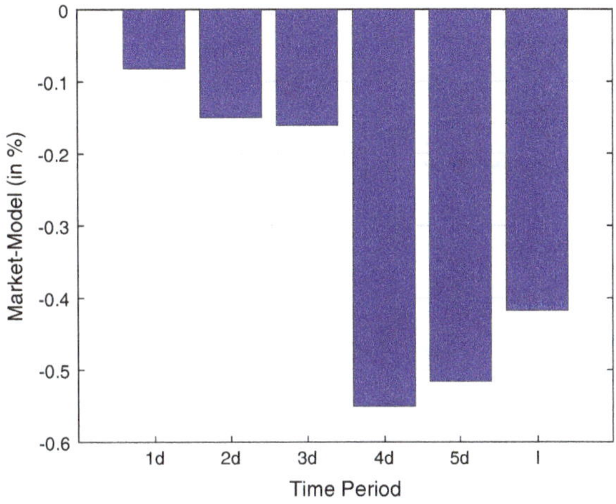

Fig. 4 Overall difference between the market and model CoCo cumulative returns

3.3.2 Results

An overall view is derived for the cheapness by averaging the differences in theoretical and market CoCo prices for each outstanding CoCo during the observation period of the new CoCo. We averaged the differences of all the CoCos on one day until five days after the announcement and also on the issue date of the new CoCo (Table 3).

Clearly, from Fig. 4, on average the cheapness on each day of our observation period is negative, meaning that market price is below the theoretical price assuming no impact. As such we conclude also from this approach that there is a negative impact of about 42 bps on average on the outstanding CoCos when a new CoCo issuance is announced.

4 Impact After Issue Date

At this point, we investigated the impact of a new CoCo issuance between the announcement and issue date. In this section, we show the results for a longer observation period. More concrete, both analyses are extended to 10 trading days after the issue date.

From our first analysis, where we compare the outstanding CoCos with the CoCo indices, a downward trending impact is observed in Fig. 5a. The second analysis which compares the market and model prices of the outstanding CoCos is shown in Fig. 5b. In both analyses, the negative impact gets more significant after the issue dates. Hence until 10 trading days after the issue date, there is still a negative impact observable.

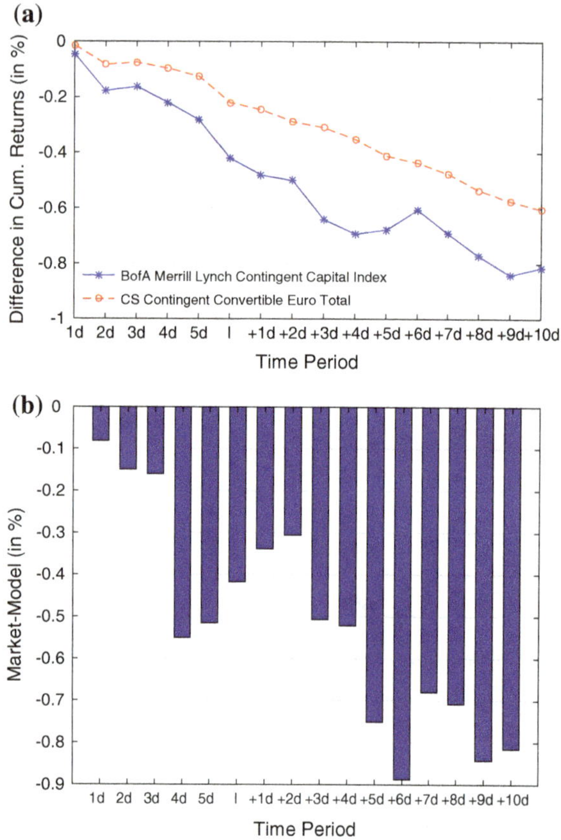

Fig. 5 Impact from the announcement date until 10 days after the issue date. **a** Method 1. **b** Method 2

5 Conclusion

The price performance of outstanding CoCos was investigated after a new CoCo issue is announced by the same issuer. Based on two approaches, we estimated the price impact on the outstanding CoCos. The first method compared returns of the outstanding CoCos with some overall CoCo indices. As a conclusion, we found that the return of the outstanding CoCos, during the period between announcement and issuance, was slightly lower than the returns of the CoCo indices. There was an underperformance of about 22 bps compared with the Credit Suisse index and about 42 bps with the Merrill Lynch index (although with relative high standard deviations). Since this first study did not take idiosyncratic movements into account, we used also a second method based on the equity derivatives model for CoCos. In this method we compared the actual market performance of the outstanding CoCo bonds with a theoretical model performance taking into account idiosyncratic effects, like movements in the underlying stock, credit default spreads and volatilities. This second approach also concludes that the averaged market returns of the outstanding CoCos were about 42 bps lower than one would expect in case of no influence.

In total, we investigate 24 cases of new CoCo bond issues. The main conclusion of the investigation is that there is a moderated negative effect on outstanding CoCo bonds. This is confirmed by both methodologies and the impact is an underperformance of about 20–40 bps on average in between the announcement date and the issue date. During the period of 10 trading days after the issue date, an extra decrease of 40 bps was observed.

Acknowledgements The authors would like to thank Robert Van Kleeck and Michael Hünseler for useful discussions on the topic.

The KPMG Center of Excellence in Risk Management is acknowledged for organizing the conference "Challenges in Derivatives Markets - Fixed Income Modeling, Valuation Adjustments, Risk Management, and Regulation".

References

1. Basel Committee on Banking Supervision: Basel III: A global regulatory framework for more resilient banks and banking systems. Bank for International Settlements, Dec. 2010
2. European Commision: Possible Further Changes to the Capital Requirements Directive. Working Document. Commission Services Staff (2010)
3. Akigbe, A., Easterwood, J.C., Pettit, R.R.: Wealth effects of corporate debt issues: the impact of issuer motivations. Financ. Manag. **26**(1), 32–47 (1997)
4. Pennacchi, G.: A Structural Model of Contingent Bank Capital (2010)
5. Pennacchi, G., Vermaelen, T., Wolff, C.: Contingent capital: the case for COERCs. INSEAD. Working paper (2010)
6. De Spiegeleer, J., Schoutens, W.: Contingent convertible contingent convertibles: a derivative approach. J. Deriv. (2012)
7. De Spiegeleer, J., Schoutens, W., Van Hulle, C.: The Handbook of Hybrid Securities: Convertible Bonds, CoCo Bonds and Bail-in. Wiley, New York (2014), Chap. 3
8. Corcuera, J.M., De Spiegeleer, J., Ferreiro-Castilla, A., Kyprianou, A.E., Madan, D.B., Schoutens, W.: Pricing of contingent convertibles under smile conform models. J. Credit Risk **9**(3), 121–140 (2013)
9. De Spiegeleer, J., Forys, M., Marquet, I., Schoutens, W.: The Impact of Skew on the Pricing of CoCo Bonds. Available on SSRN: http://ssrn.com/abstract=2418150 (2014)
10. De Spiegeleer, J., Marquet, I., Schoutens, W.: CoCo Bonds and Implied CET1 Volatility. Available on SSRN: http://ssrn.com/abstract=2575558 (2015)
11. De Spiegeleer, J., Schoutens, W.: Steering a bank around a death spiral: multiple Trigger CoCos. Wilmott Mag. **2012**(59), 62–69 (2012)
12. De Spiegeleer, J., Schoutens, W.: CoCo Bonds with Extension Risk (2014)
13. Corcuera, J.M., De Spiegeleer, J., Fajardo, J., Jönsson, H., Schoutens, W., Valdivia, A.: Close form pricing formulas for CoCa CoCos. J. Bank. Financ. (2014)
14. De Spiegeleer, J., Schoutens, W.: Multiple Trigger CoCos: contingent debt without death spiral risk. Financ. Mark. Inst. Instr. **22**(2) (2013)
15. Cheridito, P., Zhikai, X.: A reduced form CoCo model with deterministic conversion intensity. Available on SSRN: http://ssrn.com/abstract=2254403 (2013)
16. Madan, D.B., Schoutens, W.: Conic coconuts: the pricing of contingent capital notes using conic finance. Math. Financ. Econ. **4**(2), 87–106 (2011)

Permissions

All chapters in this book were first published by Springer; hereby published with permission under the Creative Commons Attribution License or equivalent. Every chapter published in this book has been scrutinized by our experts. Their significance has been extensively debated. The topics covered herein carry significant findings which will fuel the growth of the discipline. They may even be implemented as practical applications or may be referred to as a beginning point for another development.

The contributors of this book come from diverse backgrounds, making this book a truly international effort. This book will bring forth new frontiers with its revolutionizing research information and detailed analysis of the nascent developments around the world.

We would like to thank all the contributing authors for lending their expertise to make the book truly unique. They have played a crucial role in the development of this book. Without their invaluable contributions this book wouldn't have been possible. They have made vital efforts to compile up to date information on the varied aspects of this subject to make this book a valuable addition to the collection of many professionals and students.

This book was conceptualized with the vision of imparting up-to-date information and advanced data in this field. To ensure the same, a matchless editorial board was set up. Every individual on the board went through rigorous rounds of assessment to prove their worth. After which they invested a large part of their time researching and compiling the most relevant data for our readers.

The editorial board has been involved in producing this book since its inception. They have spent rigorous hours researching and exploring the diverse topics which have resulted in the successful publishing of this book. They have passed on their knowledge of decades through this book. To expedite this challenging task, the publisher supported the team at every step. A small team of assistant editors was also appointed to further simplify the editing procedure and attain best results for the readers.

Apart from the editorial board, the designing team has also invested a significant amount of their time in understanding the subject and creating the most relevant covers. They scrutinized every image to scout for the most suitable representation of the subject and create an appropriate cover for the book.

The publishing team has been an ardent support to the editorial, designing and production team. Their endless efforts to recruit the best for this project, has resulted in the accomplishment of this book. They are a veteran in the field of academics and their pool of knowledge is as vast as their experience in printing. Their expertise and guidance has proved useful at every step. Their uncompromising quality standards have made this book an exceptional effort. Their encouragement from time to time has been an inspiration for everyone.

The publisher and the editorial board hope that this book will prove to be a valuable piece of knowledge for researchers, students, practitioners and scholars across the globe.

List of Contributors

Zorana Grbac
Laboratoire de Probabilités et Modèles Aléatoires, Université Paris Diderot - Paris 7, Case 7012, 75205 Paris Cedex 13, France

Laura Meneghello and Wolfgang J. Runggaldier
Dipartimento di Matematica Pura ed Applicata, Università di Padova, Via Trieste 63, 35121 Padova, Italy

Christian P. Fries
DZ BANK AG, Frankfurt, Germany
Department of Mathematics, LMU Munich, Munich, Germany

Christoph Berns
KPMG AG, Am Flughafen, 60549 Frankfurt am Main, Germany

Michael Hünseler
Credit Portfolio Management, Assenagon Asset Management S.A., Zweigniederlassung München, Prannerstrae 8, 80333 Munich, Germany

Dirk Schubert
Financial Services KPMG AG Wirtschaftsprüfungsgesellschaft, The Squaire, Am Flughafen, 60549 Frankfurt am Main, Germany

Ernst Eberlein
Department of Mathematical Stochastics, University of Freiburg, Eckerstr. 1, 79104 Freiburg im Breisgau, Germany

M'hamed Eddahbi
Faculty of Sciences and Techniques, Department of Mathematics, Cadi Ayyad University, B.P. 549, Marrakech, Morocco

Sidi Mohamed Lalaoui Ben Cherif
Faculty of Sciences Semlalia, Department of Mathematics, Cadi Ayyad University, B.P. 2390, Marrakech, Morocco

Vilimir Yordanov
Vienna Graduate School of Finance, Vienna, Austria
Karlsruhe Institute of Technology, Karlsruhe, Germany

Walter Farkas
Department of Banking and Finance, University of Zurich, Plattenstrasse 14, 8032 Zurich, Switzerland
Department of Mathematics, ETH Zurich, Rämistrasse 101, 8092 Zurich, Switzerland
Swiss Finance Institute, Zurich, Switzerland

Robert Huitema
Department of Banking and Finance, University of Zurich, Plattenstrasse 14, 8032 Zurich, Switzerland

Elise Gourier
School of Economics and Finance, Queen Mary, University of London, London, UK

Ciprian Necula
Department of Banking and Finance, University of Zurich, Plattenstrasse 14, 8032 Zurich, Switzerland
Department of Money and Banking, Bucharest University of Economic Studies, Bucharest, Romania

L. Teng, M. Ehrhardt and M. Günther
Lehrstuhl für Angewandte Mathematik und Numerische Analysis, Fakultät Mathematik und Naturwissenschaften, Bergische Universität Wuppertal, Gaußstr. 20, 42119 Wuppertal, Germany

Ben Djerroud and Mohammad Shakourifar
Sigma Analysis & Management, Toronto, ON, Canada

David Saunders
Department of Statistics and Actuarial Science, University of Waterloo, Waterloo, Canada

Luis Seco
Department of Mathematics, University of Toronto, Toronto, Canada

German Bernhart and Jan-Frederik Mai
XAIA Investment, Sonnenstraße 19, 80331 München, Germany

Jan De Spiegeleer, Ine Marquet and Wim Schoutens
Department of Mathematics, KU Leuven, Celestijnenlaan 200B, 3001 Leuven, Belgium

Stephan Höcht
Assenagon GmbH, Prannerstraße 8, 80333 München, Germany

Index

www.ingramcontent.com/pod-product-compliance
Lightning Source LLC
LaVergne TN
LVHW051045220926
848485LV00001BA/12
* 9 7 8 1 6 4 7 2 8 5 1 5 9 *